To Janice and our children

Amanda, Sara Marie, Lowell, Christopher, and Catherine

and to persons everywhere who dream about producing a movie.

ACKNOWLEDGMENTS

I want to thank the following persons, in the politically correct alphabetical order, for their inspiration and help in my legal career and the preparation of this book:

Wilford Brimley for telling me, "you gave me the best . . . ones!"

Johnny & June Cash for showing me the best side of talent.

Sheri Dew for her knowledge of the publishing world.

Professor Paul Goldstein for his sound words of wisdom.

Xiang Ji for his comments on the manuscript.

Michael Edmunds and Steve Ramirez for moving me in the direction of the movie business.

Jane Kagon, the guru of entertainment and media education, for her inspiration and unwaivering support.

Gabrielle Kelly for her conceptual analysis of the manuscript.

Alex Kochan whose creativity and ethics have always inspired me.

Gary Lewis for his friendship and support and without whom "Cowboys" would have never happened.

Matt Mazer for his view of the movie business as a "noble profession."

Thomas McCarthy for his assistance on publicity rights.

Waddie Mitchell and Lisa Hackett for helping me to stay in touch with my roots.

Jerry Molen for being the perfect Hollywood mentor and example of what a producer should be.

Jennifer Ortega for being a great sounding board and consigliri.

Cindy Radtke for her help with styles.

Judge William Scheffield for his interest and comments on the manuscript.

Sheryl Shade who is in a talent-agent league of her own.

Ike Shapiro for being my legal mentor.

Stuart Snyder for being a great example of an entertainment exec.

Donald Stirling for our long philosophical conversations about the entertainment industry.

Ken Suddleson for being the best example of an entertainment lawyer.

Michiko Tachikawa for being my right hand for over ten years.

Kerry Tucker for her skill and patience in editing the first draft.

Dana Walden for his belief in the cowboy songs.

Walter Weintz, my first editor, for taking my pitch about a movie
book.

Michael Williams for his life-long support and creativity.

(Cowboy) Bob Williams for showing me the ropes on the movie set.

Michael Young for giving me direction in the law and in life.

And for my students at UCLA Extension for their probing questions
and comments about an early draft and for making the discussion
about law and the movie business fun.

In addition to Jack Sallay, my diligent and competent editor, I'd
also like to thank the following people from Simon & Schuster for
their tireless efforts on the book: Carolyn Reidy, President; David
Rosenthal, Publisher; Aileen Boyle and Deb Darrock, Associate Publishers; Irene Kheradi, Managing Editor; Victoria Meyer, Vice President of Publicity; Alexis Welby, Publicist; Gypsy da Silva, Associate
Director of Copyediting; Estelle Laurence, Copy Editor; Kathleen
Rizzo, Assistant Production Editor; John Wahler, Production Manager; Karolina Harris, in-house Designer; Michael Accordino, Cover
Art Director.

I'd like to also list the following people in the business who have
encouraged my career in law and entertainment: Adam Anderegg,
Yoko Asakura, Rod Boaz, John Bell, Matt Berger, Ivy Bierman,
George Caplan, Brett Chapman, Chunghwan Choi, James Cochran,
Jerry Cohen, Bob Cooper, Barry Cooper, Nick Crincoli, Mike De-
Stefano, Joe Diffie, Ed Duffy, Sally Edmunds, Don Edwards, Shinya
Egawa, Ty England, Bill Gable, John Garbett, John Gelwicks, Alan
Gershowitz, Laurie Hansen, Bill Hanson, Monte Hellman, Alex Ho,
Ayano Ichida, Takayuki Kataoka, Kimihito Kato, Art Klebanoff, Jon
Levin, Yanjun Li, Daniel McIntosh, Micah Merrill, Takahide Morita,

Toby Myerson, John Nee, Mace Neufeld, Rodney Omanoff, Dennis Packard, Greggory Peck, Monkey Punch, David Ranes, Richard Rich, Lyle Shamo, Michiya Sumitani, Allen Sussman, Chet Thomas, Tomo-hiro Tohyama, Steve Toronto, Shoji Udagawa, Bob Vermillion, Mark Westaway, Kyoshi Watanabe, Rusty Weiss, Lance Wickman, Bob Woll, Rob Word, and Chao Yijun.

Finally, I'd like to thank my immediate family for their love and support: My sisters, Bonnie and Renon (and their husbands, Rex and Gilbert), my children, Amanda, Sara, Lowell, Chris, and Catherine, and my wife, Janice, for patiently enduring the hours I spent typing on my computer.

CONTENTS

FOREWORD

BY GERALD R. MOLEN

My introduction to the glitter and glamour of the film industry came when I was twelve years old. In 1946, my family moved to Southern California from Montana. To make a living my father established and operated a small cafe directly across the street from the old Republic Studios (that stood where the current CBS Studio Center is located). My kid brother and I were mesmerized by the notion that some of our greatest heroes—John Wayne, Gene Autry, Roy Rogers, and Gabbie Hayes, to name a few—were making movies behind the gates right in front of our eyes.

The guards at the studio took a liking to us. Once in a while they allowed us on the lot and even on the various sets where movies were being filmed. They would show us a spot and tell us not to move during the filming. Even at that young age, we sat still. Sometimes, we could only hear what was going on. It was a great day when we were able to see our childhood heroes in action.

After my discharge from the Marine Corps in 1956, I was looking for an entry into the movie business. I had no particular goal in mind, but I knew I wanted to be part of this magical world. One day, I received a telephone call from Republic Studios offering me a job as a truck driver. That was good enough for me. It gave me a chance to get to know my way around the studio lot and was the start of my education about the movie production process.

In mid-1959, I moved over to Universal Studios, where I worked in the transportation department until the 1970s. In 1970, I left the movie industry to start my own business. It was a tough time and ultimately the business didn't work out, but I learned some valuable lessons about myself and about life. In 1972, I came back to the motion picture business. I became an independent transportation coordinator and worked on numerous independent films, such as *Being There, Ordinary People, Breakheart Pass, Breakout, Absence of Malice, The Godfather: Part II,* and four pictures for the Walt Disney Company.

In 1979, I took a significant step toward becoming a movie producer. I received two letters of recommendation and became a member of the Directors Guild of America, as a unit production manager (sometimes referred to as a UPM). I worked as a UPM on *The Postman Always Rings Twice, Tootsie, A Soldier's Story,* and *The Color Purple,* my first association with director, Steven Spielberg, and with Amblin Entertainment. As a UPM, I learned more about how a movie is made and more about the business of moviemaking.

In my next pictures, I progressed upward through the ranks of producer credits. I received an associate producer credit on Amblin Entertainment's *batteries not included,* an executive producer credit on the United Artists' release, *Bright Lights, Big City,* and a coproducer credit on the United Artists' Academy Award winning *Rain Man.* My experience with *Rain Man* was a special one. I had read the script at a very early stage in the development of that project. Something inside spoke to me that this movie was special. It was a great experience to be involved with the evolution and the production of this movie as it went on to enjoy the great success I first envisioned.

In 1991, for the first time, I received a "produced by" credit on the motion picture, *Hook,* directed by Steven Spielberg. During this time, I also became the Head of Physical Production of Amblin Entertainment, Mr. Spielberg's production company located on the lot of Universal Pictures. These were magical years for me, as I was privileged to be a producer on Amblin's *Jurassic Park, Schindler's List,* and *The Lost World.* I was an executive producer on Amblin's *Casper, The Flintstones,* and *Twister.* My last Amblin Entertainment film was *Minority Report,* directed by Steven Spielberg and starring Tom Cruise, where I acted as producer.

The art and magic of the movies is what drew me in, but I soon learned that the business of the industry is what keeps the mill moving. I didn't have a chance to take courses at film school or attend business or law school. I learned the business of moviemaking one movie at a time. Henry Ford was once quoted as saying that "whenever I need a lawyer, I push a button." I certainly did not command the empire that Henry Ford built, but I did have access to studio and production company lawyers to help me through the various business and legal necessitities of moviemaking. The movie business is bound up by agents and attorneys. Every established writer, actor, producer, cinematographer, and director has an agent or lawyer or both to represent them in connection with their service contracts. Every contract contains matters established by industry custom and shaped by existing laws. My experience taught me that producers cannot ignore these issues, because if problems are not resolved in a timely manner they become harder and harder to overcome.

I recently participated as a producer in a wonderful, but smaller independent motion picture entitled *The Other Side Of Heaven*. I found myself interfacing with a young lawyer who had been hired to assist with the legal aspects of the production. At least two or three times a week, from our location in the South Pacific, I would talk by telephone to this young man in Los Angeles who helped me resolve questions having to do with the rules of the Screen Actors Guild, contractual obligations, and other minutia that is part and parcel of making a movie. It was a healthy reminder of the producer's need to attend to business details.

From the age of twelve, with only a brief detour, I have labored in the magical world of movies. As a child, I remember sitting in the theater where the images on the screen allowed me to travel around the world, ride with the cowboys, and be with warriors in the heat of battle. After each journey to the theater, I would think and relive the adventure I had just experienced. Even to this day, when I see a scary movie, I get scared. When I see something touching, I'm moved. After all these years working on a movie set, with its literal jungle of wires and equipment in plain view, movies have the ability to suck me in.

I am often asked about my personal favorite among the movies that I have worked on. Each of these movies has a magical quality, of course, and this is a difficult question, but I have to say that *Schindler's List* represents a crowning moment in my long career. Occasionally, a story comes along with the power to change a person's perspective of life. *Schindler's List* was such a project. I saw the change this story worked on Mr. Spielberg and the many others of us who worked to portray in film the story of redemption of the urbane and materialistic Oscar Schindler, who, in a world gone mad, found within himself the humanity and courage to save the lives of persons who were less than human in the eyes of the Nazi state. This was a movie based in truth. We walked together on the same ground tred by hundreds of thousands of others, many to their death. This emotional experience was capped by being awarded, along with Mr. Spielberg and Branko Lustig, an Academy Award for Best Picture.

I cherish my experience with some of Hollywood's greatest creative minds. I had the privilege of working with Steven Spielberg on seventeen films, in one capacity or another. I know that he, like others who have come and gone in this industry, shares my love of the magic of the motion picture.

I certainly have no regrets. A motion picture can be magic. No two days of a movie set are ever the same. You move from one location to the next. You move from one story to the next, each with its own cast of characters and costumes. It is never boring and always magical. The call of the next project will reach out for you.

For all of you who have felt this call, I recommend Kelly Crabb's book, *The Movie Business: The Definitive Guide to the Legal and Financial Secrets of Getting Your Movie Made.* I have worked with Mr. Crabb and have benefited from his counsel. His book is a brilliant discourse on the subject of entertainment law. Every chapter methodically and intelligently details the proper application of the legal principles involved with every step of the production process and every aspect of the entertainment industry. This book is a necessary tool for every individual engaged in the pursuit of "making the deal," whether in film production, television, music, video, casting, insurance, distribution, royalties, licensing rights, or any other part of the business requiring legal advice, application, or execution. Mr. Crabb has captured the art of law in entertainment in a no-nonsense, easily understood collection of legalisms that will serve the novice as well as the professional. It's an outstanding book. I only wish I would have had this book thirty years ago.

JERRY MOLEN

THE
MOVIE
BUSINESS

PREFACE

My goal in writing this book is to give a fairly simple and straight-forward overview of how the law and the movie industry work to-gether in practice.

I wrote it pretty much, at least in the beginning, off the top of my head. I figured that after twenty years of practicing law and after pro-ducing a (very small) movie myself that if I needed to do a lot of li-brary research I would probably be delving deeper into the subject than necessary. I wanted to stick to the basics.

In writing the book, I found myself "speaking," as it were, to the would-be movie producer, and those who aspire to assist and work with and for the producer, about why legal matters shouldn't be ig-nored or left to the last minute. I believe that all producers are better off if they have at least a glib understanding of the basic legal notions of why things happen the way they do in making a movie. Lawyers can give advice and counsel (we call lawyers "counselors" for sure), but any producer leaves the decisions to another person, lawyer or not, at his own peril.

In this "chat," I want to explain in an easy-to-understand way why it is important to own or control the rights to the story upon which the movie will be based—why this task is not always intuitive and why, if certain things are not handled in a timely manner, nasty problems can arise down the road.

The book starts with an "idea" that springs into a "story" and moves through the three basic stages of a movie's life: development, production, and distribution. I try to give the big picture of moviemaking—from concept to raking in the last dollar after the movie is made.

Along the way, I offer illustrations from actual movie contracts to show how the basic deals for each of these three stages are put together. And I explain in plain and simple terms what the contracts are trying to say and why.

The book won't offer any easy formulas on how to strike it rich—there aren't any. It won't make you a lawyer or an industry accountant—that's not what you want to be. But it will take you through the basic business and legal principles you need to know to be a professional producer.

In the United States alone, there are over eighty film schools or programs and over thirty law schools that either offer an entertainment law course of study or have entertainment law societies that support students who want to pursue a career in entertainment. In the working world, moreover, there are hundreds of apprentice producers trying to take that first step toward being Jerry Bruckheimer or Kathleen Kennedy.

The movie business remains one of the strongest pillars of American industry: In 2003, for example, theaters in the United States alone took in $9.3 billion, while the home video market for the same year was $23.8 billion; add another $12 billion for pay and premium television and still more for free television and movie-related merchandise. Internationally, in 2003, the success of movies rose to over $20 billion in theatrical box office alone.

And every day, thousands of people—and you may be one of them—say "I have a great idea for a movie." For those who want to make a serious run at it, I wrote this book.

KELLY CHARLES CRABB

BOOK ONE

I HAVE A GREAT IDEA FOR A MOVIE

With the invention of motion photography in the early part of the twentieth century and the rise of the motion picture industry in Hollywood came a new vision of art, glamour, and wealth in America. The drama on the screen often gives way to drama off the screen as each new generation of young treasure seekers try to follow that dream of "lights, action, camera." And every day in America, someone says silently or to others, "I have a great idea for a movie."

Your Quest and Help Along the Way

ABOUT THIS BOOK AND HOW TO MAKE THE MOST OF IT

Since there are always persons (and you may be one of them) for whom the word "hobby" holds no meaning, I decided to write this book. It is for the would-be movie producer (the person who gets the vision, develops the blueprint, assembles the players and crew to make the dream a reality, and then—if all goes well—finds the treasure at the end of the rainbow), as told from my perspective—an entertainment industry lawyer.

What this book is.
This book will take you through the basic transactional steps of movie production—development, production, and distribution—and answer many of your questions. It will also introduce you to some fundamental principles of intellectual property law. These are things that you will need to know to get your project off the ground, avoid some potential problems down the road, and give you a shot at realizing your dream.

What this book is not.
It might be helpful to say what this book is not: This book is *not* about how to come up with a commercial idea, script, or movie. If I could tell you that, I would be living on a ranch near Jackson,

Wyoming, writing movie scripts and collecting big gaudy writing fees and royalty checks.

Likewise, this book is not a technical manual about how to physically create a motion picture. It is not about camera angles, setups, or cinematography. Reading this book won't prepare you for being a "best boy," "grip," or "gaffer."

A word of caution about the contract illustrations.

From time to time in this book I will use more or less authentic contract language to illustrate how certain deal terms and legal principles might appear and are applied in real life. It would be a mistake, however, to assume that the contract language is complete, the best possible wording, or applicable for any and all circumstances. A given term may or may not be applicable to a certain situation, but you will need an experienced attorney to help you, one who fully understands the circumstances. Moreover, I have purposefully avoided talking about the so-called contract "boilerplate" (language that clarifies the choice of law and a number of other things that first-year law students learn in their contracts courses). The contracts are not complete and should not be used or relied on as forms or exemplars.

PASSWORDS AND TOKENS (LEARNING THE LINGO)

Pay attention to the terminology. You will learn, if you haven't already, that Kingdom Hollywood is like a mystical land with signs and tokens. "Will the studio put up P&A?" a producer might ask. "I'm going to use a negative-pickup deal to finance my movie," another might say.

Like many professions, Hollywood insiders seem to have a language of their own. You will need to learn this language. To help you bridge this gap, I have put certain standard terms and phrases in quotes and have listed them in the index in the back.

A LINEAR VIEW OF THE MAP: DEVELOPMENT, PRODUCTION, AND DISTRIBUTION

The basic steps of moviemaking are called development, production, and distribution.

Development.

The goal of this step is a "packaged script." The road to a packaged script is often referred to as "development hell," for reasons that are readily apparent to those who have experienced it. Nevertheless, all moviemaking starts with this unavoidable step. The best solution is to do it well and pray for good luck.

Idea. Since you have a "great idea for a movie," you already have accomplished the first development step. Most (note that we will seldom use the word "all" in this book) good movies start with a great idea. How to tell whether your idea is commercially viable is beyond the scope of this (or any) book. I will take it on faith that your idea is "great" (and it better be—if it is to propel you through the adventure that lies ahead).

Treatment. Once you have your idea, you will need to develop it into a story (usually reduced to writing in the form of a "treatment" or "synopsis"). Treatments can be as short as one paragraph or as long as a novel, with everything in between.[1] You will need a treatment for several important reasons. First, a well-developed treatment or synopsis can be an important tool for introducing your idea to others, such as the writer who will develop a screenplay based on your idea, possible development financiers, and others who might help you get your project off the ground. Second, a treatment is often the first step in obtaining copyright protection for your project. An accurate legal adage of copyright law is "you can't copyright an idea—only the tangible expression of an idea." Unless your project is based on an earlier copyrighted work, like a novel, comic book, or prior movie, the treatment is the most simple and earliest tangible expression of your idea.

Why all this sudden talk about protection? As you will see, the question "Who owns this story?" is one that should occupy an important place on your ever-increasing list of concerns.

Screenplay. From the treatment, you will develop the "script" or "screenplay"—a standardized art form. You should learn this form yourself (by taking classes, reading one of the several helpful books on the subject of writing screenplays, or by carefully following the form of an acceptable sample—successful screenplays are often published; there are also computer software screenwriting programs that guide the writer through the correct format). The screenplay, like the treatment, incorporates the story and is a copyrightable tangible form of expression. The screenplay, unlike the treatment (which is usually a narrative description of the story), is characterized by a series of scenes that form the structure of the story. The screenplay contains the dialogue and describes in order the actions of the characters.

Packaging. Once the script is finished, the ideal next step is to get a well-known actor and/or director "attached." An actor who has credibility at the "box office" or a director who has made successful movies in the past can, in theory, attract the attention of studios or independent financiers. Attaching "elements" (actors, directors, attractive locations, sponsors, etc.) is called "packaging." For reasons explained later, packaging—especially by an independent producer—is challenging and becoming more so.

Setup. The happy ending of the development stage is a "green light" for your screenplay (which is necessarily accompanied by lots of other green things—dollars). If your screenplay (packaged or not) is as great as your idea, someone may either buy it from you—in which case this book will end for you shortly—or back you by literally putting his or her money on the line to let you produce the movie. When the money is in place, your project is "set up."

Production.
Production is the process of putting on film (or some digital format that may emerge in the future) the idea expressed in the script. It takes a lot of work and if you are thinking that this is the "fun" part, think again (that's what directors are for—to have the fun you thought you were going to have). There are usually three phases within the production stage: preproduction, production, and postproduction.

Preproduction. By now, you have set your project up for production by obtaining a commitment for the production money and are ready to start. It's time to get serious about pulling your cast together; hiring a director (if you don't already have one attached) and a crew; finding and securing locations; designing sets; designing costumes; and in other ways getting ready for the hundreds of decisions and problems that are coming your way. You will also want to come up with a budget that will actually work, because along the way you will write a lot of checks. Did I mention the guilds (unions)? Many actors, directors, crew, and even musicians belong to collective bargaining units or unions and if you use guild members you will have to deal with these guilds. You'll need insurance. You'll need an accountant. And, yes, you'll need a lawyer. This is the job you are signing up for. The producer oversees all of this.

Production or principal photography. Then comes that magic day—the day that "principal photography" (or the "shooting") begins. The script is finished. The locations and sets are ready. The cast is there. The costumes are hanging on the rack. The hairdressers and makeup artists are at the ready. The cameras and crews are poised. The accountants have their checkbooks. The lawyers give a discreet nod. Everything is ready to go. Right?! If you did your job correctly during development and preproduction, you may make it through this.

Postproduction. The film is "in the can" (in other words all of the scenes have been filmed) and the crew and cast have gone their way. Now it's time to finish the job. The film has to be edited and the soundtrack finished. And all the relevant items have to be readied for delivery to the distributor—and that's when you get to find out if you have been keeping track of the process. Did you remember the legal things? If you start thinking about such things during postproduction, it is too late.

Distribution.

Ultimately, it will depend on the distributor to get this newly created masterpiece to the public and vindicate the hours of abuse you have taken from all those naysayers who said you couldn't do it. Theaters have to be persuaded to show it and the people have to be enticed to come. "Prints" of the now completed movie will be made and the "advertising" process will begin. All of this comes with a cost.

Theatrical distribution. The primary initial goal is to get the finished movie into the local movie theater. The big screen is still considered the best first step for getting the movie out there. The system is geared for this: The critics write their reviews, the ads come out (newspapers, television, posters, etc.), the word of mouth starts to spread, and the box office results are reported. All this publicity helps the launch of the movie along its destined path. A theatrical release can take different forms: A "general release" is designed to cover a wide, national audience; a "platform release" is targeted to a smaller demographic or geographic area at first in order to build toward a wider base. A movie can even be "four-walled" (played in a single theater). If the movie is a certain type, it may also find its way into a specialized distribution network—the "art" film is the prime example of this.

Video. With the advent of the video recorder (and the legal cases which allowed its use at home[2]), movies on videocassette and now DVD (and who can predict what the future holds) have become a common feature of our lives—and an important secondary source of revenue. You can rent or buy them.

Television. Eventually, the movie will find its way to the small screen. Television is also an important and long-term source of revenue.

Ancillary markets. Movies yield a surprising variety of money-making possibilities. Sound-track albums featuring the musical score and songs from the movie are one popular source of revenue. Certain movies spawn toys and other merchandise.

THERE'LL BE HELP ALONG THE WAY

And you will need help. Even a casual observation should teach you that the process of making a movie is one part art, one part science, and all business. Illusion on film is a product of technology, skill, and even daring. The legal and business challenges are no less complicated than in any walk of life. You won't be able to do it alone. Following is a sample of the people who will enter your life:

Lawyers.

Oh, I know, "let's kill all the lawyers."[3] But wait a minute. Years ago, there were a series of television commercials for Fram oil filters. A workaday mechanic appears in the ad making reference to a blown engine. "Too bad," says the mechanic about the unfortunate owner of the car, "if he would have come to me earlier I could have installed one of these"—he holds up (you guessed it) a Fram oil filter—"for six bucks, but now it's going to cost him big." Then our mechanic delivers the catch line: "You can pay me now or pay me later."

Unfortunately for you, and lucky for lawyers (like me), there are certain legal issues in the film business that are like the latent motor engine problems that the Fram oil filter was designed to prevent. Early consultation with a lawyer regarding these issues can help avoid costly patchwork—or worse, disaster—later on. It is critical to have some basic understanding of the key legal issues yourself. But your own knowledge should not be substituted for access to a lawyer who has an in-depth knowledge of and experience in the legal aspects of the movie industry—especially "intellectual property" (as it relates to the creation, ownership, and exploitation of stories, music, trademarks, and other so-called nontangible assets) and other issues related to film industry customs.

Lawyer types. In the industry, there are lawyers and there are lawyers. Some lawyers are specialists even within the entertainment industry—they cater to certain types of clients. The type of practice an entertainment lawyer has may also affect his fee arrangement—some lawyers may be willing to take you on a percentage-of-what-you-earn basis and some lawyers may not. Generally speaking, lawyers representing producers prefer hourly billing, with certain tasks related to the actual production process performed on a "flat fee" or "capped fee" basis. Lawyers representing "talent" (directors and actors, for the most part) will often work for a percentage of the talent's revenues. Most lawyers will insist that, regardless of the fee structure, you will have to pay your own disbursements (copying and telephone charges, for example).

Lawyer services. In a way, it is jumping the gun to try to summarize what film lawyers do for producers, as this is the subject matter of this book. But perhaps a quick overview will help put everything in perspective as we venture forth into the land of detail. As noted earlier, to reach the quest—get your movie out there—you will move through three stages: development, production, and distribution (or exploitation). Here's what lawyers will generally do in each stage:

A lawyer's services during development. A lawyer will help you establish a strong (hopefully unassailable) "chain of title" (a pedigree so to speak) related to the most important asset in this process—the story and all the permutations of the story: the treatment, the screenplay, and the movie itself. He or she will help you with contracts that clarify your position regarding the rights (optioning the film rights to a book, for example). Lawyers will help you hire a writer and, at the same time, help you maintain control and ownership of the writer's work product. If you are able to get a director or actor interested in your project, a lawyer will help you get that director or actor committed. Unless you are already well established (and if you are, I am flattered that you would consider reading this book), and even then, most lawyers will want to charge you an hourly fee for this type of work, as it is virtually impossible to predict how difficult/complicated or easy/simple it will be to accomplish.

A lawyer's services during production. You will need a lawyer's help in connection with the financing of your project, as any investor will likely insist on a contract clarifying the benefits of his or her bargain. You will need locations, costumes, designers, makeup artists, camera people, electricians, music composers, sound technicians, gaffers, grips, best boys, and, yes, of course, actors and actresses. You will need contracts, and hence lawyers, for each of these purposes and persons. Lawyers perform services related to the financing of a motion picture on an hourly basis. These transactions are generally complicated and involve a lot of paperwork. The other contracts related to the actual production of the movie are sometimes performed on a "flat fee" basis or "capped fee" basis. In this event, the lawyer and you will decide what services are included in the flat or capped fee and what services are not. For example, litigation or resolving disputes that may arise will normally not be covered under flat fee or fee cap.

A lawyer's services during distribution. In order to make money, the movie must be exploited—play at theaters, be sold in the form of DVDs and/or videocassettes, and later broadcast on television. Merchandise and soundtrack albums, related to or based on the movie, might also be sold or licensed. These transactions too require contracts and lawyers to do them.

In sum, you will need lawyers to help you on your adventure. You will need lawyers who are competent in basic intellectual property law, film financing and entertainment transactions, licensing, and other related areas, such as trademarks.

Professional writers and others who may own your idea.

It is virtually impossible today in the United States to get a movie made without a screenplay. For now, you will have to trust me on this. You have two choices: You can write it yourself or, if you don't have the experience or the skill, you can hire (or, if you have no money, persuade) someone else to write it for you. Most producers hire writers to get the screenplay finished.

If you write the screenplay exclusively by yourself, on your own time (meaning that you are not writing it within the scope of your day job—if you have any question about this, you had better see a lawyer), without taking money from others and without signing a piece of paper to the contrary, then you will *probably* be the owner (unless of course you copied or based your script on someone else's work).

If someone else writes the script, even if it is your brother, best friend, or spouse, that person may own it as a matter of law. Or, if you write it together with someone else, you may own it together as a matter of law. And please note that this "writing something together" thing can sneak up on you. Suppose you borrow your aunt Lucy's formulation of dialogue or insert an anecdote told you by your cousin Lenny in the screenplay, the use of someone else's contribution, however small, can raise questions related to copyright law. For the most part, unless you get that other person to sign a piece of paper with certain magic language and perhaps do other things consistent with that piece of paper, these problems will persist and—like the problems facing the imprudent motorist who failed to use the Fram oil filter—will loom larger than life later on.

Agents, managers, and their constituents.

Unless you intend to use your local high school drama program students to do the acting, you are destined to interface with the world of professional "talent"—a term which often refers to actors or actresses, but can also mean directors and other "artists" whose skills are relied on to enhance the quality of the movie. The professional talent world, like any system, has its own structure, culture, and traditions. An established actor, for example, will have a "manager," an "agent," a "publicist," and a lawyer, each with a specific role to play.

Managers. The manager is generally responsible for running the "business" that is embodied in the artist's career. The manager may help the artist invest the income, file taxes, and make important business decisions whether related to the artist's entertainment career or not. Some managers are professional accountants (or CPAs) and a few come from the legal profession, but there is no general rule. Unlike agents, managers do not have to "register," but technically they are restricted from doing what agents do—find work for their clients.[4] Managers can work with one or many clients and there are solo managers as well as large talent management companies. The manager will likely be in proximity to the artist and so he or she may be a great way to make the "pitch."

Agents. In essence, an "agent" is responsible for bringing work to the artist he or she represents. Depending on the current stature of the talent, the agent is the artist's sword or shield. For example, an agent who represents a promising, but not-yet-established performer will spend a good deal of time calling producers, or more particularly "casting agents," who represent producers, on a particular movie project, pitching the artist's promising future and trying to secure work. But if the performer is well established, the agent may spend some or all of each day screening the many offers that come in the door without solicitation; the rest of the day may be spent calling well-established producers who have a "hot" property that is attractive to the client.

Some agents may read screenplays (or read the "coverage" by professional readers) and play an active role in helping the client decide whether or not to accept the project; other agents may simply pass the opportunity on to the artist (or the artist's manager). The corollary wisdom bears noting—some performers read screenplays and make their own decision and others (at their own peril, I believe) rely on advice. Agents, usually well versed in the art of the transaction, may also play a highly active role in the basic negotiations of a deal. Agents work on a commission basis (usually 10 percent of the client's compensation) and can, therefore, be relied on to aggressively pursue the highest compensation possible. They will also demand creature comforts (first-class hotels and travel and private dressing rooms, for example) for artists as well—agents know that an unhappy client is not good for business.

The talent agent world is dominated by large agencies with formidable staying power: William Morris Agency (the granddaddy of talent agencies whose history reaches back to the early 1900s), Creative Artists Agency or CAA (started by former William Morris agents in 1975), and International Creative Management or ICM are traditionally known as the "big three," but upstarts such as United Talent Agency or UTA and Endeavor are also forces to be reckoned with. There are many smaller agencies as well, some with specialities (such as the Gorfaine/Schwartz Agency, which represents songwriters, composers, and music supervisors).

Talent agencies are regulated in the state of California and a person must qualify to become an agent there under the Talent Agency Act[5] which also limits the scope of the agent's business. Agents who represent professional actors must also qualify under the rules of the Screen Actors Guild (SAG) and must sign an agreement that prohibits them from being producers of projects featuring their own client's services, as this is seen by SAG as a "conflict of interest"—a situation where the agent is tempted to put his or her own interests ahead of the client's. Agents well understand the clout that actors have in getting projects made and attracting people to the theaters. If the agents were the producers, they might lose their objectivity and "sell" their clients on an inferior project just to line their own pockets (or so goes the reasoning behind SAG's position). Agents on the other hand wonder why managers, who are not restricted by the Talent Agency Act or any agreement with SAG, escape the conflict-of-interest trap. This requirement on the part of agents to comply with the Talent Agency Act is a major source of friction between agents, who are bound by the act and must register, and managers, who are not bound by legal restrictions of the act or the requirement to register.[6]

Other professionals in your future.

A producer also needs access to a good film accountant, in the event that he or she actually finds someone to back the project financially. A producer should make lists of qualified unit production managers (or UPMs), who can help locate a crew and handle the technicalities of an ever-increasing technology-laden business. You will need help preparing an accurate and industry-acceptable budget. Accountants and "line producers" can help with this process. Eventually, you will need a director (who is the captain of your ship), a casting agent, a cinematographer, costume designers, set designers, location managers, and builders, electricians, grips, best boys, editors, sound engineers, drivers, caterers, and so on. If you are lucky (or unlucky, as the case may be), you will meet them all. Some, but not all of these people are represented by agents.

From Idea to Treatment

SOME FUNDAMENTALS OF COPYRIGHT LAW

In order to encourage people to be creative, the framers of the United States Constitution decided that it would be a good thing to protect creators and owners of creative works.[1] Modern laws enacted under the Constitution extend copyright protection to movies and all of their component parts.[2] It is necessary for the would-be movie producer to understand the basic principles of these laws.

Protection.

The owner of a copyright of a movie, for example, has certain exclusive rights. Only the copyright owner can make or allow others to make copies of the movie, naturally, and only the owner can make works (like a novel, a television series, toys, and merchandise) based on the movie. This protection doesn't last forever; it is for a limited time.[3]

The treatment—fixation.

The treatment is a written summary of the story (usually in the actual sequence of scenes or events) of the motion picture. It is an important document in many ways. It is the embodiment of your "great idea" for creative purposes and, usually, it is the first copyrightable expression of the story. The story is copyrightable in treatment form, because it has been "fixed" in a tangible mode of expression. "Fixation" is a requirement of copyright protection. Even stories that are long and detailed are not protectable unless and until they are recorded by some means. Usually, the form of "fixation" is the printed word, but stories spoken into a tape recorder will also pass the test—assuming that the story is more than an "idea."

Ideas are not protected.

A fundamental axiom of copyright law is that "ideas" are not protected. You can protect the tangible expression of an idea, but not the idea itself. For example, Shakespeare wrote *Romeo and Juliet,* the story of two young people from warring families who fall in love with tragic results. Even if *Romeo and Juliet* were under copyright protection today (which it isn't[4]), that protection would probably not prevent you from doing a story of two young lovers caught in the tragic enmity between their respective families. I say "probably," because if you use the same specific scenes, characters, and story elements (even if you change them to another setting) so that it is "substantially similar" to *Romeo and Juliet,* it might be possible for the writer to bring an action for infringement against you. Nevertheless, the mere fact that the story plot has two lovers, involves their families, who hate each other, and has an unhappy ending, is not enough to stop you.

So how does this affect you? Well, suppose you tell a friend that you have a great idea for a movie and she says that her uncle is in the "biz." You go over to her uncle's house and after chit chat you tell (the word is "pitch") him your idea. And let's suppose he yawns and says, "It's a nice idea, but not a great one," and you shake his hand and leave. And then let's suppose about two years later you go to the movies and see your idea on the screen and, sure enough, there on the credits you see the name of the uncle. You're angry, right? You can sue him and win on theory of copyright infringement, right? Well, maybe not. Did you reduce your idea to a tangible form of expression (by writing it down or recording it on an audiotape, for example)? Is his movie based on just the idea of your pitch? For instance, suppose you say, "I've got this great idea to take a Shakespeare play and update it." Or: "I read in the newspaper about this murder mystery and I'd like to make a movie about that." In either of these situations, you may not be in such good shape.

Protection automatic.

Another fundamental but often misunderstood aspect of copyright law is that in the United States (as well as in other nations that ad-

here to the same principles contained in the Berne Convention[5])
copyright protection attaches to the work at the very moment it is reduced to a tangible form of expression—when your story is written
down or recorded by some other means. You don't need to register
the work with the United States Copyright Office (USCO), affix the
famous "©" mark, or do anything else—copyright protection is automatic. I know that makes you feel good, but I can guess that you are
wondering why people nevertheless go to the trouble of registering
works with the USCO and affixing the "©" mark. Good questions—
and there are answers to these questions.

Why register? Even though copyright protection is automatic, registration of a treatment is important in at least two ways:[6]

Evidence. First, in an infringement action the plaintiff has to present evidence of when the work was created, because he needs to
show that his work predates the infringing work. When you file your
work with the USCO (we talk more about this later), the USCO
stamps the accompanying application form to certify that the work
was filed and on a certain date. You can present the USCO certificate as evidence that your work existed at least as early as the date
on it.

Jurisdiction. Another main reason to file for copyright protection
for your treatment with the USCO is that in order to bring an action for infringement under the United States Copyright Act (the
Copyright Act),[7] you must first register. One can register after the
infringement arises, but all claims (and damages) related to the work
prior to registration may be lost under the Copyright Act, which gives
you immediate access to the federal courts and also allows you to
seek substantial remedies, such as injunctions, attorneys' fees, destruction of illegal copies, and special damages (referred to appropriately as "statutory damages"), readily available under the act. The
statutory damages, of course, are not available outside the Copyright Act.

A possible problem with registration. There is one possible reason *not* to register a work with the USCO (at least not at the treatment stage), notwithstanding the compelling reasons *to* register.
The USCO registration is public. This means that after you register
your glorious work, some vile person can come along and pull your
treatment and read it for its idea content. Let's suppose that you write
a treatment entitled *The Quest,* about a young prince who inherits a

strange talisman on the day his father, the king, dies. Mr. Nogood can pull your treatment and, as long as he doesn't copy the story expression for expression, he may be able to write a treatment of his own based on the same story idea.

REGISTRATION

Filing with the USCO. The registration process is straightforward and simple. You must fill out a two-page form (Form PA, at this time, which you can obtain from the USCO's Web site) listing the name of the work, the author, how to contact the author and other information. You enclose your treatment (or other original work) and send the form and the fee ($20 at this time) to the USCO. The USCO processes your application to make sure it is complete and that you haven't submitted anything inconsistent with the information on the form. (For example, if you write a musical play—play and music—and try to register only the script without a recording or written musical score, the USCO will reject the application on the basis that the music for which protection is being sought has not been submitted.) If everything is okay, about the time you are wondering whether or not the USCO has lost your treatment and application form, you will receive it back stamped with an official-looking seal confirming that your treatment has been registered.

Registered mail.
Because of the risk that some snoopy person might go through the public files and come across your idea, producers and their attorneys have devised other ways to establish a certain date on which your work was created for copyright purposes: One way, believe it or not, is the old chestnut of putting your treatment in an envelope and sending it to yourself by registered mail. In theory, this method should work well enough, but note the following cautions:

- Don't open the letter. Leave it sealed and, when the time comes, open it before the judge in your infringement action or at another appropriate time and place at the advice of your attorney.
- Therefore, you should make a note on the *outside* of the envelope containing the work: "Treatment—*The Quest.*" If you forget to do this—well, you can figure out what the problem is.
- Keep the unopened envelope in a safe place.

WGA registration.

Perhaps a better alternative is to register your work with the Writers Guild of America (WGA), which allows its members (and others for a fee) to register scripts and—from time to time—treatments. The WGA registration system is closed; persons other than the person who registered the material cannot gain access to it. Since the WGA does not always accept treatments, WGA registration may not be available for this stage of the project, but should be considered for the script.

"Chain of title" and security interests—eventual registration.

You will eventually have to register the script with the USCO because along the way you will have to prove your "chain of title" to others. Most distribution companies, for example, will not distribute the movie, most financiers will not finance the movie, and SAG will not allow its members to act in the movie, unless and until there is a clear chain of title. The crown jewel in the "chain of title" process is the USCO registration. Moreover, SAG and other guilds and investors who might finance your movie will require registration of the screenplay and then the movie at the USCO to allow for the recordation of a "security interest" against these assets. A security interest puts the "secured party" (or party who holds the interest) in a more favorable position than a general creditor in case the copyright owner declares bankruptcy.

Copyright notice.

The form of the copyright notice is: First, the word "copyright" or the symbol "©" (or both), then the year of creation and last the name of the author or authors: For example: "© 2005 Kelly Crabb." If you don't have a word processing program or typewriter (for those of you old enough to remember what that is) that will make the symbol, you can type the notice as follows: "Copyright (c) 2005 Kelly Crabb." (You can even use my name, if you want—just kidding.)

Why affix the notice? The big question, I know, is what terrible thing happens if you don't affix the notice. Well, the result may not be earth shattering. Remember, copyright protection is automatic at the moment you "fix" your work in a tangible form of expression. Thus, even if you do not affix the notice, you still have protection.[8] Then why do it? Okay, if you really must know, in practice, the purpose may be international protection. In theory, looking back at the development of copyright law principles, the notice was designed to give *all* people (even the innocent ones) notice that the work is claimed by you. The principle is that even if some bad guy takes your work and sells it to an innocent third party, since the notice is affixed, even the innocent guy will know that you are the copyright claimant. That theory, especially in the United States, where substance has largely won out over form, doesn't work so well with draft manuscripts. With the reproduction capabilities available today, removing the copyright notice is simple. However, outside the United States, in some nations, form still matters and so it is a good idea to affix the copyright line, even on manuscripts. For published works publicly distributed, mass produced, and packaged, it is important to get the copyright notice printed on the work.

IMPLIED CONTRACT

Under certain circumstances, copyright law will not be applicable. But there are other legal theories that might apply.

Desney v. Wilder.

Let's go back to the rule that ideas are not copyrightable. Remember your "pitch" meeting with your friend's uncle? He took your idea, made a movie, and there's nothing you can do, right? Well, maybe there is something you can do. If your idea is truly an "idea" or based on a story that is readily available to the public, it is true that you may not win on a theory of copyright infringement. But you may be able to claim that you and your friend's uncle had a "contract" pursuant to which he was obligated to pay you.

In the main case, *Desney v. Wilder*,[9] Mr. Desney called Paramount Pictures at the office of the famous movie director Billy Wilder, with a "great idea" for a movie, based on the true-life experience of a young boy named Floyd Collins, who attracted a news media circus when he became trapped in a cave in the 1920s. Desney told Wilder's secretary that he had a sixty-five-page treatment and wanted Wilder to read it. Wilder's secretary, knowing that her boss would not read sixty-five pages, helpfully offered to have Desney's treatment summarized in a shorter document. Desney declined, saying that he would condense the treatment himself. Two days later, after reducing his story to a three-page outline, Desney called back. Wilder's secretary asked Desney to read the outline over the telephone so she could take it down in shorthand, which he did and she did. The secretary then told Desney that she would show the outline to Wilder. In parting, Desney told the secretary that, if the story was used, he expected to be paid.

You can imagine the reaction of our hero, Desney, when he learned that Paramount Pictures had made a feature film about the Floyd Collins story. Of course, he didn't learn this from Paramount or Mr. Wilder; he didn't get any money from them either. He sued. Desney's lawyers, however, were faced with a dilemma—even though the movie contained a fictionalized incident, created by Desney and included in the three-page outline, Desney's story was an "idea" based on an actual event. The facts of Floyd Collins's ordeal were well documented in contemporary news sources and available to the public at large— they were in the "public domain" [10]—and Mr. Desney actually could claim no special right in these facts. These legal realities forced Desney's lawyers to base Desney's claim on a theory other than copyright and, so, they claimed on the facts stated above that an "implied contract" was created between Desney and Wilder. Happily, for Mr. Desney, the court bought this argument and held that under the circumstances Wilder had agreed to pay Desney for the use of his outline in developing the movie.

Making submissions.

The *Desney v. Wilder* case, along with similar cases which followed,[11] have perked up the attention of the legal departments of motion picture studios, major producers and directors, actors, and others to whom submissions are made on a regular basis. In most cases, a policy of refusing to accept any unsolicited submission is in effect. If you send your "pitch," without permission, the studio, for example, will send it back to you unopened. Sometimes the studio will accept submissions from established agents and entertainment attorneys whom they know (the theory, I guess, is that such persons are not out there making a living from suing distributors and major talent). In some cases, studios will accept submissions *if* the person submitting the material signs a submission agreement. The form of agreement may differ, but the substance is the same—the person making the submission acknowledges and agrees that the studio (or other entity) is working on a lot of projects and may have something similar to the one being submitted and, therefore, such person waives any right to sue the studio (etc.) for infringement and, of course, implied contract.[12]

If you are presented with a submission form, you should read it carefully and consult an attorney before signing it. Be warned, however, that there won't be a lot of negotiation on the form. History shows that studios have indeed been targets for litigation based on unsolicited submissions. Moreover, as you can imagine, most unsolicited material comes from first-time writers, producers, or other amateurs hoping to strike it rich in Hollywood. Finally, the sheer volume of submissions would undoubtedly be staggering—anyone living in L.A. for any length of time can vouch that virtually everyone here is writing a screenplay or teleplay; to sift through this mountain of material would take time and money. With these three strikes against submissions, the studios have adopted the policy and are not likely to change it.

Please note, notwithstanding the above discussion, there are still pressures on the studios to (1) take submissions (there will always be the need to find great stories and creative people who come up with them) and (2) reward even first-time submitters for good stories (if they can come up with one winner, they might be able to do it again). I am confident that a major studio would rarely knowingly base a motion picture on a script for which clear chain of title had not been firmly established. If nothing else, however, *Desney v. Wilder* and the cases that followed pointed out the circumstances in which both the submitter and the recipient of material may be especially at risk.

Receiving submissions.

Before leaving the subject of submissions, it is important to note that this is one of those coins that has two sides. Producers, like yourself, will often be in the position of receiving material. As noted above, there are good reasons that the studios don't have free submissions policies—and when you are on the receiving end of a submission you should follow the studios' lead. Imagine that someone sends you a treatment of a story about the Revolutionary War. Well, that might be okay unless you or your company also has a development project on the same topic. Or suppose that someone sends you a letter attaching a newspaper article or enclosing a public domain story or book. Before the submission, you had just as much right as every other person in the world to stories about the Revolutionary War, the story in the newspaper article or book. But now, because you are on the receiving end, and because of the holding in *Desney v. Wilder,* you could be in a worse position than even the public at large. Thus, it is wise to establish policies for and documentation with respect to receiving material. Either (1) take submissions only from persons you know or whose reputations are verifiable or (2) cause the submitter to sign a submission agreement, sometimes referred to as a "literary release." Again, the submissions agreement will cover the basic studio concerns. For example, consider the following sample provisions from a typical literary release:

Representations and warranties. First, since we will encounter representations and warranties in almost every contract we discuss, I need to help you understand why they are so important. This requires a very brief understanding of the history of the legal system we use in America, which we borrow from Merry Old England. From very early times, judges in England were fond of reducing legal principles to axioms. One of these axioms, still relevant today, is caveat emptor, or "let the buyer beware." In England, the legal rule was that someone bought a piece of merchandise at the buyer's risk. If there was a latent defect in the merchandise, too bad—unless, there was fraud (for example, if you bought an apple that didn't look rotten from the outside, but was rotten in the middle—too bad, unless the seller told you that the apple wasn't rotten, knowing that it was). So, how did buyers' lawyers create a scenario where their client would be protected? Easy; they asked the seller questions about the merchandise. If the seller told a lie (i.e., made a "misrepresentation"), that's fraud. Thus, making a representation about the product you are selling is tantamount to warranting the product—hence the phrase "representations and warranties."

> I hereby represent and warrant that: (a) the Material was created by and is wholly original with me; (b) I have the exclusive right to grant all rights in the Material; (c) I have exclusive rights in the title, with regard to its use in any connection with the Material; and (d) I have the full right and authority to submit the Material to you upon all of the terms and conditions herein stated and to enter into this Literary Release. I agree to indemnify you and hold you harmless from and against any claim, loss, obligation, liability, cost or expense, including attorneys' fees and costs, which may be asserted against you or incurred by you, that arise out of or in connection with the Material or any use thereof.

The party submitting the treatment (or screenplay or any other type of intellectual property) "represents and warrants" (i.e., says, "I guarantee that I am telling you the truth") that the material being submitted is original or, if not original, is based on material the rights to which have been obtained from relevant third parties by the submitting party. In other words, the submissions form must clarify that there is an unbroken chain of title and that, if the material is used, you, the producer, will receive all the rights necessary to make and freely exploit a movie based on such material. The representations and warranties are accompanied by a promise to indemnify you if you incur any loss (including attorneys' fees and costs) should such representations and warranties turn out to be untrue.

This pattern—representations and warranties followed by a promise to make it right if the representations are not true—will be repeated many times in movie business contracts.

Making disclosures. What happens if the submission form contains a statement that is not true? Let's suppose, for example, that, since you used Aunt Lucy's story in your treatment, the statement, "the Material was created by and is wholly original with me . . ." is not true. Go ahead and sign it any way? No! Don't tell a lie—that's fraud. Rather, tell the truth. You can say, for example, "Except for the material that I disclosed to you in writing, the Material was created by and is wholly original with me." What happens here? Well, if you took steps to own or at least control Aunt Lucy's story for use in your treatment, everything will be cool, because your chain of title will be intact and you will be able to make the other representations and warranties. If you didn't take these steps . . . well, remember the story about Fram Oil Filters?

To pay or not to pay. The submitting party will wish to clarify that the material can't be used unless you, the producer, negotiate a deal providing compensation to the submitting party.

> You agree that you will not use the Material as the basis for a motion picture or television program unless you first negotiate with me compensation for such use; but I understand and agree that your use of material containing features or elements similar to or identical with those contained in the Material shall not obligate you to negotiate with me or entitle me to any compensation, if you determine that you have an independent legal right to use such other material, which is not derived from me (either because such features or elements were not new or novel, or were not originated by me, or because another person, including your employees, has submitted or

may hereafter submit material containing similar or identical features or elements). Without limiting the foregoing, it is understood that you may use any part of the Material, which could be freely used by a member of the public, without liability to me.

The form simply states what the *Desney v. Wilder* decision holds as a matter of law. However, this obligation to negotiate with and pay the submitter will be subject to several important considerations: The producer will be able to freely use material that is deemed—by the producer (since this is, after all, the producer's form)—to be available to the producer from an independent source. For example, if the producer receives material from another person that is similar or identical to the material being submitted, the producer can use that other material without negotiating with or paying this submitter. Alternatively, the producer may determine that the material submitted is not new or novel or original with the submitter—for example, a treatment for a movie about the signing of the Declaration of Independence. Similarly, the form will clarify that the producer will not be in a worse position than the general public related to the submitted material—if the material is in the public domain, for example, the producer will have the right to use it, notwithstanding *Desney v. Wilder* and the implied contract theory.

No agreement. And speaking of *Desney v. Wilder,* the producer's form will always clarify that no agreement is created by the submission alone; there must be a future negotiation and a written agreement. Otherwise, the producer has no obligation toward the submitter.

There is no agreement between us, express or implied, relative to your use of the Material. I agree that any discussion we may have with respect to the Material shall not constitute any agreement, express or implied, as to the purchase or use of the Material, or any portion thereof, which I am hereby disclosing to you either orally or in writing. Should you decide to acquire the Material, I agree to negotiate with you in good faith with respect thereto. I agree that you shall have no obligation to me in any respect whatsoever with regard to the Material unless or until we have executed a written agreement, which, by its terms and provisions, will be the only contract between us.

Limited right to complain. The form gives the submitting party a limited time (in this case, ninety days after notice—unless the legal "statute of limitations" cuts it off sooner) to register a complaint.

If, notwithstanding my release set forth above, I should hereafter claim that you have used the Material, or any portion thereof, without my consent or authorization, I specifically agree that I must give you written notice by certified or registered mail, at your address set forth above, of any claim arising in connection with any alleged use by you of the Material or arising in connection with the terms of this Literary Release, within the period of time prescribed by the applicable statute of limitations, but in no event more than ninety (90) calendar days after I acquire knowledge of such Claim, or if it be sooner, within ninety (90) calendar days after I acquire knowledge of facts sufficient to put me on notice of any such Claim, as an express condition precedent to the initiation of any action hereunder. My failure to give you written notice will be deemed an irrevocable waiver of any rights I might otherwise have with respect to such Claim. I shall further withhold commencing the arbitration proceeding, as specified below, for a period of thirty (30) days after said written notice to allow you time to investigate any Claim.

As the form provides, the complaint must be made in a formal way (here by certified or registered mail). The submitter's failure to raise the claim, according to the form, will act as a legal waiver of the claim (in other words, the submitter gives up the claim). Finally, the producer gets another period of time, according to the form, to investigate the claim.

Arbitration. Many submission agreements require the matter to be arbitrated, as opposed to litigated in a court. I have chosen not to go into all the procedural detail related to arbitration here, but it may be helpful to understand why the producer might choose arbitration in the form. First, arbitration is handled by an expert (usually an entertainment lawyer or a retired judge, who is familiar with entertainment issues) and not by a jury. Producer defendants generally like to avoid juries because they are unpredictable and, in the United States, sometimes award very high damages to the plaintiff. Second, generally speaking, arbitration is less time consuming—and, therefore, cheaper.

No responsibility for loss. The form clarifies that the submission does not involve the only copy of the material and the submitting party has retained a copy—thereby eliminating the added claim that the producer lost the only manuscript or other valuable material.

I have retained a copy of said Material, and I release you from any liability for loss or other damage to the copy or copies submitted by me.

Release. Now we come to the actual release language. The submitter formally declares in the form that he or she releases the producer from liability, unless a claim is brought in accordance with the form.

Except as otherwise provided in this Literary Release, I hereby release you of and from any and all claims, demands and liabilities of every kind whatsoever, known or unknown, that may arise in relation to the Material or by reason of any claim now or hereafter made that you have used or appropriated the Material.

Consideration. Under basic contract law, all contracting parties must give something of value—known to first-year law students as "consideration." What is the producer giving? He is giving his time to consider the submission. If he accepts the material, there is an implied promise that he will give something of value to the submitter—as in the Desney case. The details are left to another day. What is the submitter giving? The obvious answer is a chance for the producer to obtain the material. The not so obvious answer is the release of the producer from liability. The producer is saying, in essence, "Okay, I'll take a look, but not unless you release me from the risks that are incurred by accepting material."

I acknowledge that but for my agreement to the above terms and conditions, you would not accept my request to receive and consider the Material, which I am hereby submitting to you.

WHO IS THE AUTHOR OF THE TREATMENT?

"Who wrote this?" is a simple enough question. But as you will see, the answer is complicated.

Who is the author?
One of the questions on the USCO copyright form asks, Who is the author? Under normal circumstances, if you write the treatment yourself, with no contribution from any third party and not as part of your

job or because someone paid you to do it under contract, you can put your own name as the author. You can list yourself as author in other situations too, but careful housekeeping is required. I am not saying that you must write the treatment by yourself. But it is important that you fully understand the implications of joint authorship or having third parties write it on their own. Don't go to sleep here!

Joint authors and third-party authors.

Remember that copyright protection is automatic. No registration is required. So, when you sit down with your friends and relatives to brainstorm the story, the moment you put their ideas into your treatment they (not you) are automatically copyright owners of that part which was "created" by them. The same principles apply to other persons who are asked (or hired) to write the treatment with or for you. When another person creates the treatment, even if it is your idea, that other person is the "author" and under the copyright statute enjoys copyright protection. And you thought this automatic protection was great stuff, didn't you? Well, here is the dark side of the coin.

Chain of title again (and not the last time either).

Why is all this jabbering on about copyright law so important? Because, at several points along the way, you will be required to prove your chain of title. That means that you must demonstrate that you (or your production company) have a clear and unbroken chain of title to the treatment and—later on—the screenplay that may be based upon such treatment. Of course, Aunt Lucy would never sue you for infringement (and maybe that is right). But if she does (and she would only do so after you sell the screenplay and it starts to do mega business), there could be trouble. Buyers of screenplays, like investors and distributors, do not like this kind of trouble—so, they will get angry at you and they will call their lawyers and their lawyers will do nasty things. It's too horrible to describe.

The certificate of authorship—"belt and suspenders."

There are two major ways for you, the producer, to own the copyright in the treatment (the same applies to the screenplay), even if you collaborate (on a formal or informal basis) with another person or have another person write the treatment in total. First, if the person writing or collaborating with you on the treatment is your "employee" and writes the treatment within the scope of his or her duties as your employee, the "work-made-for-hire" doctrine may make the treatment yours. Second, even if the writer or collaborator is not your employee, he or she can still make an assignment to you of all that individual's rights in and to the treatment. Both ways will require the help of an experienced lawyer. The bottom line—as a producer, you want to have anyone who touches your treatment or screenplay sign a piece of paper, referred to as a "certificate of authorship" or "waiver," acknowledging that (1) the writer's contribution to the treatment was done as a work-made-for-hire and/or (2) the writer assigns to you his or her right, title, and interest in and to the treatment. Many certificates of authorship state that the writer acknowledges the legal theory in clause (1), but in case some subsequent court doesn't agree with that theory, then the theory described in clause (2) is applicable. Thus, the conventional wisdom for the prudent producer is to use both the "belt" and the "suspenders" to secure claim to the work.

Work-made-for-hire doctrine. From your (the producer's) point of view, the beauty of the work-made-for-hire doctrine is that you are the author/owner from the very beginning. In fact, the USCO registration form requires that, in a work-made-for-hire situation, the employer be listed as the author. The producer owns the treatment from the beginning. There is no need for a contract transferring ownership that could be found to have a defect; thus, the work-made-for-hire doctrine is favored by producers.

The reasoning underlying the common view that producers need the certificate of authorship to say that the work is both a work made for hire and an assignment of rights, however, is because the work-made-for-hire doctrine has some twists and turns. If you are a producer, for example, and hire writers to do screenplays for you full time, and pay Social Security, withholding tax, and benefits and in other ways act like a true employer, then it should be relatively simple to take the position, under the work-made-for-hire doctrine, that you own the material the writers write for you. Under the Copyright Act, in order for the doctrine to apply, the work must be "specially commissioned" pursuant to a "written contract" and fall into one or more of the following categories:

- Contribution to a collective work
- Part of a motion picture or other audiovisual work
- A translation

- Supplementary work
- Compilation
- Instructional text
- Test or answer material for a test
- Atlas

Obviously, "part of a motion picture or other audiovisual work" is most relevant for our discussion here. A screenplay or treatment would easily fit this definition, as both contain scenes, characters, plots, and so forth, that are "part of a motion picture." Still, you need a written document and have to have the other evidence that the writer is your employee.

Another issue related to the work-made-for-hire doctrine is timing. The question is whether the doctrine applies when the writer (or creator) starts work before the contract is signed. Suppose that you want to hire a writer to write your treatment. You meet the writer at the local café to discuss the terms over a milkshake. Eventually, you reach an agreement; you will pay $2,000 and the first draft treatment will be delivered in four weeks. And you will own the copyright. Then you call your lawyer and four weeks later, about the time the writer brings you the first draft, the lawyer delivers a contract and the writer signs it. Everything is cool, right? Well, maybe not. In 1995, in *Playboy v. Duma*,[13] a federal court found that even though the parties didn't sign their contract until after the work was done, the work-made-for-hire doctrine nevertheless applied to make the employer the "author" for the purpose of the Copyright Act. Like the example above, the court felt that, as long as the two parties had an agreement that the doctrine would apply, it didn't matter that they signed the written document after the work was done. However, in 2002, the same federal court ruled that the doctrine may not apply. In *Marvel Characters, Inc. v. Joseph H. Simon*,[14] the Second Circuit found that the work-made-for-hire doctrine did not apply to work done by Mr. Simon even though he had signed a settlement agreement in 1969 acknowledging that he had done the work many years before, for the predecessor of Marvel. This case seems to say that there wasn't really an agreement between the parties before he started the work. The moral of this story is to get the paperwork done before the work starts.

Independent contractors. A problem arises when the person you hire is not an employee, but an "independent contractor." This term has a special meaning under the law, because tax-withholding obligations and certain other employment-related issues turn on whether a person is an employee or an independent contractor. If the writer is a true independent contractor for tax purposes, then the producer will not have to (1) withhold taxes and issue a Form W2 (although he will have to issue a Form 1099) to the writer, (2) pay benefits (unless, of course, the writer is a member of the WGA in which case the payment of benefits is part of the producer's contractual obligation), or (3) (in most states) pay workers' compensation. Thus, the producer's desire to avoid certain tax-related reporting and withholding burdens may be at odds with the work-made-for-hire doctrine[15] and the producer should weigh the importance of maintaining the independent contractor argument against the advantages obtained through the doctrine.

Assignments. An assignment of rights is based on a different legal theory than work made for hire. In a work-made-for-hire situation, the assumption is that, since the writer is an employee, any work produced by that person belongs from the beginning to the employer. An assignment, on the other hand, is based on the assumption that the copyright was originally owned by the writer and, therefore, to get the copyright into the hands of the producer the writer must transfer or assign ownership to the producer. In the first situation, the writer never owned the work and the employer is the "author" for copyright purposes; in the other situation, the writer is the author and owner, but then assigns ownership in and to the copyright to the producer. With regard to the USCO copyright registration form, the major practical effect of this difference is in the way the copyright form is filled in. As we discussed, if the work being registered is a work made for hire, the producer's name will go under author. If the work-made-for-hire doctrine is not going to be used, the writer's name will be listed as author and a notation will have to be made that the rights have been assigned to the person or entity submitting the application.

There are more differences, however, than mere form. As noted above, an assignment requires a contract—which is subject to termination for breach. If an assignment agreement is in fact terminated, the rights go back to the assignor. In a work-made-for-hire situation, an unhappy employee might be able to bring some claim against the employer, but the rights would stay with the employer—the deemed author of the work. Thus, giving up on the work-made-for-hire doctrine, even at the expense of having to withhold taxes and provide other benefits, may not be worthwhile.

Sample certificate of authorship. Today, the usual practice is to recite both theories in the certificate of authorship. In this section, we will look at a standard and relatively complete certificate of authorship employing both theories, among other things. Note that the version discussed below contains a complete set of representations and warranties, an indemnity, authorization to use the name and likeness of the author for publicity and other standard purposes, a waiver of moral rights and other provisions that give third parties comfort on the major rights related issues respecting the author's contribution. Don't be concerned about the detailed language of the certificate right now—we will cover all these issues later in greater detail in the context of the writer's agreement.

The preamble of the certificate of authorship clarifies who the parties are and what the project is. If the certificate is related to a formal writer's agreement that agreement is referenced. One may ask why, if there is a separate writer's agreement, a separate certificate of authorship is necessary. In large measure, the reason is for convenience in proving the chain of title to third parties, if the need arises. The certificate of authorship does not contain the financial and other proprietary terms of the agreement and is focused on the matter of rights. It can be given to third parties (for example distributors and financiers) without disclosing proprietary information.

> I, Robert J. Writealot, hereby certify that I am engaged to render writing services in connection with that feature-length theatrical motion picture tentatively entitled "The Quest" (the "Picture") within the scope of my engagement pursuant to and subject to all of the terms and conditions of that certain writer's agreement (the "Agreement"), dated as of April 6, 2005, between me and Quest Productions, LLC ("Producer").

The certificate of authorship clarifies that the producer, who pays for the author's services or for the material itself, will receive the rights exclusively. Note that the certificate contains the magic language related to the work-made-for-hire doctrine (that the material is "specially ordered or commissioned by Producer for use as part of a motion picture or other audiovisual work") and contains the backup theory of assignment (that the author grants, assigns and sets over the rights).

> I hereby represent, warrant and agree that: (a) all of my services in connection with the Picture will be rendered for good and valuable consideration, the receipt and sufficiency of which are hereby acknowledged; (b) all of the results and proceeds of my services and all material of whatever kind or nature created, written or furnished by me in connection with the Picture (all such results and proceeds and all such material being collectively referred to herein as the "Material") shall be considered "works made for hire" specially ordered or commissioned by Producer for use as part of a motion picture or other audiovisual work, with Producer being deemed the sole author thereof forever and throughout the universe; and (c) Producer shall solely and exclusively own, and I hereby grant, assign and set over (and, to the extent that the same shall be impermissible or ineffective in any jurisdiction, hereby exclusively license) to Producer, forever and throughout the universe, all right, title and interest now known or hereafter created that I may have in and to the Material and each and every part thereof (including all incidents, plots, dialogue, characters, action and titles forming a part thereof), including all copyrights therein, all renewals and extensions of such copyrights and all other proprietary rights of any kind, nature or description (including all motion picture, television and allied and incidental rights), that may be secured under the laws now or hereafter in effect in the United States of America or any other jurisdiction, and all proceeds derived therefrom and in connection therewith, with the right to make such changes therein and such uses and dispositions thereof, in whole or in part, as Producer may from time to time determine.

The certificate also requires the author to waive "moral rights," a set of rights that are relevant in nations that have adopted the civil law system, such as France, Germany, and Japan. This is important and we will discuss this in greater detail later on.

> I hereby irrevocably waive all "moral rights of authors" and all similar rights which I may now or hereafter have in or to the Material or any part thereof.

The certificate of authorship, like the writer's agreement itself, requires that the author make certain representations and warranties related to the material submitted to the producer. As we have discussed, and as we will see later on, a writer's representations and warranties relate to the originality of the work and the absence of claims against the rights. I'll explain later about the absence of claims under the laws of "publicity" and "defamation," which are included in the author's representations and warranties here. Also, note the author's clarification that the author's representations and warranties do not relate to any material added by the producer or other third parties.

> I hereby represent, warrant and agree that all of the Material is and will be written solely by and is wholly original with me, does not and will not infringe any copyright of any person, is not the subject of any actual or threatened litigation or claim and does not and will not constitute a libel or slander of any person or infringe upon or violate the right of privacy or any other right of any person; provided, however, that the preceding representations, warranties and agreements in this sentence shall not be applicable to any specific material taken directly by me from material supplied by Producer for incorporation into the Material or to any specific material incorporated into the Material by employees or officers of Producer other than me.

As we discussed above, the result of breaching a representation and warranty is the obligation to indemnify—or to make whole—the producer who pays for the services or material.

> I hereby agree to indemnify and hold harmless Producer and Producer's successors, assigns, licensees, directors, officers, employees and agents from and against any and all liabilities, losses, damages, costs and expenses (including reasonable attorneys' fees) in connection with any claim or action arising out of any breach of any of my representations, warranties or agreements hereunder; provided, however, that I shall not be required to indemnify and hold harmless with respect to third-party defamation, invasion of privacy or publicity claims where Producer requests me to prepare literary materials which are based in whole or in part on any actual individual, whether living or dead, provided that I accurately and timely provide all information reasonably requested by Producer for the purpose of permitting Producer to evaluate the risks involved in the utilization of such materials.

Perhaps an example will help. Suppose Robert Writealot submits a treatment to Peter Pro, a producer. In the certificate of authorship that Peter asks Robert to sign, Robert states that he is the sole author of the treatment and that the treatment is original with him. Peter Pro then hires a screenwriter to draft a screenplay based on Robert's treatment, assembles a cast and a lot of money and makes a movie. A week after the movie is released in theaters, Robert's Aunt Maggie hires a lawyer and sues Peter—Robert is family, after all—for money damages. As it turns out, Robert actually wrote the treatment based on Aunt Maggie's children's book without her permission. The suit begins and Peter hires a team of lawyers costing about $50,000. Nevertheless, Aunt Maggie wins $1 million and the judge orders Peter to pay up. However, Peter remembers Robert's representations and warranties. Unter the certificate of authorship, because the story in the treatment wasn't original with Robert, Robert must now "indemnify" Peter (make Peter whole) by paying him the $1 million Peter lost to Aunt Maggie and the $50,000 he paid to his lawyers (yes, that amount might be "reasonable" depending on the factors involved), even though Robert wasn't a party in the lawsuit.

The same indemnification obligation arises on the part of the producer to the author for breaches in the representations and warranties of the producer respecting material added by the producer.

> Producer hereby agrees to defend, indemnify and hold harmless me and my heirs, executors, administrators, successors and assigns from and against any and all liabilities, losses, damages, costs and expenses (including reasonable attorneys' fees) in connection with any claim or action (other than any claim or action arising out of a breach of any of my representations, warranties or agreements hereunder) respecting (i) material supplied by Producer for incorporation into my work, or incorporated into my work by employees or officers of Producer other than me, or (ii) Producer's production, distribution or exploitation of any motion picture or other production which incorporates the Material.

Let's change the example given above. Suppose that after Robert submits the treatment, Peter decides to add some different characters and plots. Peter gets someone to write the new screenplay, gathers the money, and produces and releases the movie. A week later, Aunt Maggie sues Robert, not Peter, because "Robert has always been a little brat." Robert hires a lawyer, who charges him $50,000, but he still loses $1 million in the end. Robert then goes to Peter and demands to be indemnified, because the basis of Aunt Maggie's claim was the characters and plots added at Peter's direction. To make Robert whole, Peter has to pay Robert $1 million and the legal costs.

The author also agrees to provide "further assurances" to the producer. This means that the author agrees to sign documents and do other things that might have been ignored or overlooked at the time the producer and author entered into their deal (when they were more worried about the screenplay than the legal stuff). Note that the producer often demands that the author grant a "power of attorney" so that the producer can sign the documents and do these other things on behalf of the author.

> I hereby agree to perform such further acts and to execute, acknowledge and deliver such further documents consistent herewith as Producer shall deem reasonably necessary or advisable to obtain, perfect, maintain, evidence or enforce Producer's rights hereunder, and if for any reason I fail to do any of the foregoing within ten (10) days after Producer's written request therefor, I hereby irrevocably appoint Producer as my attorney-in-fact (such appointment being coupled with an interest), with full power of substitution and delegation, with the right (but not the obligation) to perform any such acts and to execute, acknowledge and deliver any such documents on my behalf.

Related to the "publicity rights" referred to above, the producer wants to make sure that he has the right to use the name and likeness of the author in certain ways related to the picture.

> I hereby grant to Producer the right to issue and authorize publicity concerning me, and to use my names, voices, approved likenesses and approved biographical data in connection with the distribution, exhibition, advertising, marketing, promotion and exploitation of the Picture. I shall exercise approvals hereunder reasonably and within ten (10) days after request by Producer, or such approvals shall be deemed given.

The provision that follows means that if the author does have a valid claim against the producer, the author agrees to be satisfied with receiving money and that the author will not have the right to stop the project. In addition, the producer wants the author to know that

the producer has no obligation to actually use the material created
by the author.

> I hereby acknowledge and agree that in the event of any breach or
> alleged breach by Producer of any of its obligations to me, I shall be
> limited to my remedies at law for damages actually suffered (includ-
> ing reasonable attorneys' fees and costs), if any, and shall not be
> entitled to terminate or rescind either the Agreement or this certifi-
> cate, or to seek equitable or injunctive relief, or to enjoin, restrain or
> otherwise interfere with the development, production, distribution,
> exhibition, advertising, use or other exploitation of the Picture or
> any other production based on the Material.

And finally, the certificate of authorship clarifies that the referenced
agreement is a more authoritative document.

> This certificate is executed in accordance with and is subject to all of
> the terms, conditions and provisions contained in the Agreement,
> all of which terms, conditions and provisions are herein incorpo-
> rated by reference.

Derivative works.
Why worry so much about the copyright status of the lowly treatment? As you will see, nothing can happen until the screenplay is fully
developed. However, since your screenplay will be based on the treatment, the treatment forms the first important link in the chain of
title. If you forge that chain well, then each subsequent link will benefit from its strength. The reason is that an artistic work formed from
or based on a previous work is a "derivative work" of such previous
work.[16]

Under the copyright law, you as the owner of a work have the exclusive right to make derivative works based on it. If someone else,
without your permission, tries to make a screenplay based on your
treatment, that person will be guilty, under the law, of copyright infringement. Conversely, if you want to make a screenplay based on a
treatment or novel or some other printed work owned by another
person or entity, you will have to get permission from such person or
entity.

The term "chain of title" can be observed by an examination of
the concept of "derivative work" in action. Note the examples below:

In these four cases, each work is a derivative work of the one that

Case One (Story)
The Sting ➤ *The Sting* ➤ *The Sting*
(treatment)   (screenplay)   (movie)

Case Two (Novel)
The Firm ➤ *The Firm* ➤ The Firm
(novel)   (screenplay)   (movie)

Case Three (Movie)
The Seven Samurai ➤ *The Magnificent Seven* ➤ *The Magnificent Seven*
(Japanese movie)   (American screenplay)   (American movie)

Case Four (Stage Play)
Romeo and Juliet ➤ *West Side Story* ➤ *West Side Story* ➤ *West Side Story*
(stage play)   (treatment)   (musical play)   (movie)

proceeds it. Obviously, screenplays can be based on works other than treatments: *The Magnificent Seven,* a successful motion picture starring Yul Brynner, among others, was based on *The Seven Samurai,* a famous Japanese film written and directed by the legendary Japanese director Akira Kurosawa, and starring Toshiro Mifune. *The Firm* was based on the novel of the same name by John Grisham. The motion picture *West Side Story,* with Natalie Wood, George Chakiris, Rita Moreno, and others, was based on the musical play, of the same name, conceived by Jerome Robbins and written by Arthur Laurents, Leonard Bernstein, and Steven Sondheim. Robbins, who originally conceived the play, based his idea on William Shakespeare's *Romeo and Juliet.* The play was adapted to modern-day terms: Instead of two warring families in Italy (as in *Romeo and Juliet*), Robbins used two West Side New York gangs of different ethnic backgrounds.

In order, then, to establish your chain of title, you must obtain the right from the owner of the "underlying" or original work to make the derivative work. In the case of a treatment owned by you (which it will be if you were paying attention above), you can write or cause another person to write a screenplay based on that treatment with no problem. However, in the case of a treatment, book, or other motion picture owned by another, you must first obtain a grant of rights from the original owner. You can't pick up the newest John Grisham novel in your local bookstore and draft and exploit a screenplay based on that novel without Mr. Grisham's permission. Also, you can't develop a screenplay featuring Luke Skywalker, Han Solo, Princess Leia, Chewbacca, R2-D2, and C-3PO without obtaining the permission of Lucasfilm—even if your story is totally different from *Star Wars*. Please note that I am not saying that getting this permission from the owners of such valuable properties will be possible— indeed, of the few predictions that I am willing to make in this book, I can assure you that obtaining a license from John Grisham and Lucasfilm to make derivative works based on their property will be beyond the ability of any normal producer, even where money is not an issue. And, in the case of franchise properties, such as *Star Wars* or *Indiana Jones*, obtaining permission will be impossible (yes, I used that word intentionally).

A derivative work can also be something tangible or dramatic. A piece of merchandise derived from another work is still a derivative work. Imagine, for example, a Harry Potter board game, computer software game, figurine, etc.—it's not hard, because all these things are out there in the real world. Thus, without the permission of Ms. J. K. Rowling, these things cannot be produced by anyone but her.

Public domain.

It is important to note the one major exception in the chain of title discussion as it relates to derivative works. As a matter of public policy, lawmakers have chosen not to give copyright protection forever. Thus, at some point in time, copyright protection for a work ceases. And when the copyright term is finished, the work is said to have fallen or entered into the public domain. And when it does, any member of the public may use it freely for any purpose without permission from the original copyright holder. You will have to consult an attorney in the close cases, because the rules governing the period of protection are complex. However, I can tell you with confidence that Messrs. Robbins, Laurents, Bernstein, and Sondheim did not have to worry at all about finding the living descendants of William Shakespeare—all of his works are in the public domain. So long as they have not been recently modified or enhanced (with commentary or explanatory footnotes, for example), you can reprint them, make movies and novels and comic books based on them without any problem.[17] Generally speaking, this level of comfort exists for works created in or before 1900.[18]

Note that it is not possible to make general assumptions about works created after that date—unless they were created recently, in which case you can assume that copyright protection still exists. It is possible for works created in the 1950s, for example, to be in the public domain, but it is also possible for such works to be protected. Ascertaining whether such is the case, however, is the work of attorneys who specialize in this area and who can only do so after researching various factors—such as when the work was originally "published" (a legal term of art), whether or not a renewal was required and, if so, made. If you have any questions—meaning, if the work was created after 1900—call a lawyer.

Using Someone Else's Story

THE OPTION AGREEMENT AND THE ACQUISITION

It's not necessary to come up with your own idea. Producers often opt to use the ideas and works of others to propel them forward on their quest to make and exploit a commercial movie. This requires a different approach, and a further knowledge of how copyright law works.

As touched on in the discussion about derivative works above, you can always "buy" or "option" a story (usually in the form of a book or short story) from someone else. The option agreement is the most common way to obtain the right to make a derivative work. The agreement contains three basic parts: The option, the purchase, and a description of the rights being optioned.

The option.

Producers do not normally buy the rights to make a movie based on a work immediately. Instead they purchase an "option" to buy the rights at a later date. The essence of an option agreement is that the owner of the work is paid a fee (an "option fee") to keep a property "off the market" for a certain period of time (called the "option period"). This gives the producer who purchases the option the exclusive right during the option period to develop a screenplay based on the property. The option period is usually between six and eighteen months and is often renewable at the producer's discretion. The option fee can be modest or great ($1 to $5,000 to $100,000 and more) per "option term;" the renewal cost is usually the same as the original option fee.

The practical reason for using an option agreement for development is to keep the costs of development low. As we will discuss later, developing a screenplay in America is always a speculative proposition and is, thus, fraught with risk. If the producer can set the project up before the expiration of the option period, the exercise or purchase price (the ultimate purchase price of the movie rights) will be paid by the production financier along with the other costs associated with the budget of the picture. Let's take a look at some of the nuts and bolts of an option agreement.

Option. The paragraph below shows the typical option structure—an initial option with the right on the part of the producer to extend the option if needed or desired. During the option period, the owner of the property typically cannot do anything with it and the control of the property rests in the hands of the producer.

Owner hereby grants to Producer the sole, irrevocable and exclusive option (the "Option") to acquire from Owner, in perpetuity throughout the world and in any and all languages, the "Rights" (as defined below) in and to the Property. The Option shall commence as of the date of this agreement and shall continue through and until the date which is twelve (12) months after the date first above written (the "Initial Option Period"). Producer shall have the right, exercisable by written notice to Owner at any time prior to the expiration of the Initial Option Period, to extend the Option for an additional twelve (12) months (the "Second Option Period") commencing upon the expiration of the Initial Option Period. The Initial Option Period and the Second Option Period, together with any extensions thereof provided in this agreement, are sometimes collectively referred to herein as the "Option Period." Producer may exercise the Option by written notice to Owner at any time prior to the expiration of the Option Period.

Note that some properties have such great value that the owner is not likely to sit by while the producer takes his time. In these cases, the owner of the property may impose conditions or "benchmarks" that the producer must meet in order to keep the project going forward. For example, suppose that a certain comic book property (such as Spiderman) spawns a bidding war among the major studios. The owner of the property will not be satisfied simply to take an option fee—even if the fee is $1 million! The owner wants to see the property made into a movie. Thus, if the producer fails to get a writer or attach a director or actor within a certain amount of time, the option period might end. In other cases, the owners of these types of properties won't agree to any type of option.

A typical option fee formulation. The paragraph below is typical of the fee structure in a motion picture option agreement.

As full and complete consideration for the Rights and all representations, warranties, indemnities and agreements made or given by Owner in connection herewith, Producer shall pay to Owner the following:

The producer pays a certain sum for a certain period of time. Then, if the producer needs more time to develop the property, he or she will have the option to extend the option period by the payment of an additional fee.

(a) With respect to the Initial Option Period, the sum of $5,000 (the "First Option Payment"), payable immediately upon the execution of this Agreement. The First Option Payment shall be applicable against the Purchase Price (defined below).

Typically (but not always), the first option fee will be applicable against the purchase price and the second option payment will not be applicable. Thus, in this case, in accordance with the provision below, if the purchase price is $50,000, the producer would pay $45,000, whether or not the option period is extended.

(b) If Producer elects to extend the Option for the Second Option Period, the sum of $5,000, payable upon Producer's written notice to Author of such election.

The purchase.
Before the end of the option term (or, if it comes earlier, the start of production), the producer must exercise the option—in other words, he must purchase the rights under the terms of the agreement or let it go back to the owner. There is a wide range—from thousands to millions of dollars—in purchase prices. Once the option is exercised, the rights (as defined in the option agreement) will belong to

the producer under the terms of the option agreement. Some producers, if the project is going well and the opportunity to renew the option is not possible, will nevertheless purchase the rights to preserve their ability to continue with the project.

The exercise price. The provision below shows another way to say that the first option payment is applicable against the purchase price. Note that this contract provision applies only to the first option payment against the purchase price.

Note, also, that the parties agreed in this case that, if the budget of the picture goes over $30 million, the exercise price will also go up. The negotiation goes something like this: First, the producer says something like, "Come on, this will be a low-budget picture—cut me a break." Then, the owner says, "Well, okay, but what happens if you get a big star to play the role of the prince? The trip-wire formulation in the example above is a common way to meet this concern, but there are others. A more logical approach, perhaps, is to allow fee "bumps" to occur as similar bumps are made in the budget. For example, the owner and producer might agree to raise the exercise price for every $10 million or $15 million. At this point in the business, however, simplicity usually prevails—and in favor of the party with the greatest bargaining leverage.

> If Producer exercises the Option, then (i) upon such exercise, an amount equal to $50,000, less the First Option Payment, and (ii) in the event the final approved production budget of the first motion picture based on the Property produced by Producer (the "Picture") exceeds $30,000,000.00, an amount equal to $75,000.

Reversion. Although we will cover this point again later, owners of properties are usually not willing to sell the rights to their books, at any price, just to see them sit on the shelf forever. Thus, a common feature of option agreements and buyout or acquisition agreements (discussed later) is the "reversion" clause. In this case, even if the producer exercises the option (i.e., buys the property), he will have a set period of time (here, five years) to get the property ready to produce. The term "principal photography" has a particular meaning—the filming of the movie (also discussed later).

> Anything in this agreement to the contrary notwithstanding, in the event that principal photography of the Picture has not commenced within five (5) years after payment of the total amount of fixed com-

pensation specified above, then this agreement shall immediately terminate and shall thereafter be deemed null and void, and all rights granted to Purchaser hereunder shall automatically revert to Seller.

The acquisition (or "buyout").

Some novelists, John Grisham and Michael Crichton, for example, do not option their works. If you want to make a movie based on their novels, you must pony up with the exercise price at the outset. Obviously, novelists on this level can demand a heavy price. My guess is that you will not be in the market for an underlying work in this category. If you are (and you actually have the money to purchase the rights to one of these books), please call me. Again, even in this context, the author will insist on a reversion clause and may even require progress benchmarks (as discussed before). Authors want more than money—they want to see their work on the giant screen. If progress isn't being made or if the movie isn't being produced after a certain time, authors will want the rights to go back to the author.

RIGHTS GRANTED

A primary focus by lawyers in these agreements is the definition of the rights being granted. As you will soon discover, there is more than one way to slice up the rights.

Nature of intellectual property rights—split rights.

In the American film industry, the option agreement, in addition to the financial terms of the deal, provides a detailed description of the rights obtained by the producer upon the producer's exercise of the option. It is worth noting that an important feature of intellectual property rights is that the owner has the ability to separate the rights and exploit them one by one in various ways.

For example, the owner of a movie can divide up the movie rights along at least two dimensions. First, the rights themselves can be divided by *function*—for example, print publishing rights (books and comic books), theatrical distribution rights, television exhibition rights, and merchandise licensing rights. Second, the owner can exploit each of these functions *territory by territory*—for example, North America, Europe, Japan, and so on. The owner can also award one or all of the rights to a producer or distributor worldwide.

	Worldwide	North America	Japan	Europe	Rest of World
Print publishing	Company A				
Live-action movie	Company B				
Animation television		Company C	Company D	Company C	Company C
Toy merchandising		Company E	Company D	Company F	Company D

In this example, the owner has granted the print publishing rights and the live-action motion picture rights to Company A and Company B, respectively, on a worldwide basis. However, with respect to animation television rights, the owner has decided to split the rights up and award the North American, European, and Rest of the World rights to one company (Company C) and the Japanese rights to Company D. Company D also gets the toy merchandising rights for Japan and the Rest of the World, with those rights going to Company E, for North America, and Company F, for Europe.

The rights preamble.
With this feature lawyers take into account all the choices that the owner can make with respect to a given work and draft the language accordingly. The provision below, which introduces the rights portion of the agreement, takes into account the complexity of these possibilities.

Upon exercise of the Option, Producer automatically and irrevocably shall own and be vested in, and Owner automatically and irrevocably shall be deemed to have assigned, granted, conveyed, transferred and set over to Producer, solely and exclusively, throughout the world in perpetuity, in any and all languages, subject to Owner's reserved rights specified below, all motion picture, television and allied, ancillary and subsidiary rights (including all sequel, remake, merchandising, commercial tie-in, music, music publishing, soundtrack, videogram, interactive media, multimedia, virtual reality and theme park and attraction rights), under copyright, trademark and otherwise, in and to the Property, including the themes, stories, incidents, plots, dialogue, characters, settings, action and titles forming a part thereof (collectively, the "Rights"). Without limiting the generality of the foregoing, the Rights shall in any and all events include all of the following:

This provision is typical of the preamble to the list of rights. Note that the lawyer is careful to cover the following points: (1) granting language (legal language—mostly verbs—that clarifies that the owner is transferring his or her rights to the producer, (2) exclusivity (that only the producer will have the rights), (3) the territory (under principles of copyright law, it is possible to "split" the rights in a number of ways, including geographically; in this case, the rights are to be held exclusively by the producer "throughout the world"—you could, of course, say "universe" in order to cover those multiplexes on the moon and Mars and interstellar travel), (4) the duration (in this case "in perpetuity"—a lawyer's way of saying forever[1]) and (5) media (here, the standard "motion picture, television and allied, ancillary and subsidiary rights" is used, followed by an exhaustive list of examples). Notice that clause (5) is basically clarifying, once and for all, that the producer will be making derivative works based on the optioned property. This includes the right to use the story lines, plots, characters, themes, and other relevant elements of the property in question.

From time to time, the rights provision will necessarily clarify that the producer has the right to use the characters and themes of a work, but not certain stories. For example, suppose that the author of a famous comic book series agrees to grant you the right to make a network animated series for television broadcast. However, before entering into an agreement with you, the author granted the feature motion pictures rights to another producer, who developed a live-action theatrical motion picture based on the same characters and themes. Naturally (or at least I hope it is logical to you by now), the author of the comic book was probably not the author of the screenplay of the movie and, therefore, cannot grant you the story or story plot rights to the movie. The contract, in that case, would need to clarify that you do not have the right to copy the story of the live-action movie. You will have to invent your own story lines and be careful to use only characters (and the costumes and other design features) from the original comic book.

The last sentence of the introductory paragraph of the rights provision clarifies that the list to follow is not an exhaustive list. This, of course, favors the producer, who will want to argue that if he or she forgot to list something it is covered anyway.

Motion picture, remake, sequel, and similar rights.

In the list of rights that follows the preamble, the first relates to entertainment-oriented derivative works. The contract recites a long list.

The right to make, produce, adapt and copyright one or more motion picture adaptations or versions based in whole or in part on the Property, including sequels, remakes, prequels, spinoffs, musicals and serials, and for such purposes to record and reproduce and license others to record and reproduce in synchronization or timed relation with such motion pictures, spoken words taken from or based on the text or theme of the Property and any and all kinds of music, musical accompaniments and lyrics to be performed or sung by the performers in any such motion picture and any and all other kinds of sound and sound effects.

The list clarifies that the producer may make one or more movies based on the property or work. This is not automatic, however, and important issues arise from time to time related to the number of pictures. Take, for example, the author or owner of a property that exists successfully in another medium, such as a novel or comic book. From the author's perspective, the "franchise" (the ongoing business enterprise) to be created based on the property is the book, not the movie. If there is going to be any sequel or merchandising, it will belong to the author and not the film producer. To the author of the book, a motion picture is just another way to exploit the property. On the other hand, think of it from the movie producer's perspective. A movie may cost millions of dollars to produce and market. Moreover, it is often the movie that makes the property "famous" and turns it into a franchise. Which is the crucial element, the Ian Fleming novels about 007, alias James Bond, or the famous series of movies starring Sean Connery and a host of successors? Are all the movies based on Fleming's novels, or were the screenplays devices of the producer/ screenwriter? What about the Harry Potter series of books? Does Warner Bros., which acquired the movie rights, have the right to create sequels of its own making, or must Warner follow the sequence and plots of the books? This is the crux of the issue: Who controls the franchise? Should it be the film producer (your view, naturally)? Or should it be the original author? In this provision, the producer gets to make sequels at his or her discretion. But it might not always be the case. J. K. Rowling, for example, is not going to give up the Harry Potter franchise to a producer (and, given the popularity of her franchise, it is not likely that Warner would want to stray very far from the path Ms. Rowling has created). We'll talk more about this later, when we look at optioning the rights to a book.

There are various rights that are reserved under copyright law to the owner of a copyright, the primary right being the right to make a copy. This provision also makes sure that the producer has all those rights, especially the right to make a copy. The producer will need to make many copies in many ways. Thus, this provision clarifies the ways the producer can make copies; he can "record," "reproduce" (whether or not in "timed synchronization" or "timed relation" with the movies—which means the applicable material can be copied on to a soundtrack that runs alongside the moving pictures) and can speak or sing or make or copy sound effects from the work. The producer doesn't want to get a letter from the author's or owner's lawyer that says, "Look, it's okay to use words, but you can't use musical renditions of my work."

Media.
The copyright owner controls how the copyright can be used. Theoretically, the owner could say to one person, you can only copy my work on film. However, the world is constantly changing. The producer may need to copy the work or parts of it on tape or on a chip or hard drive or on some other device, so that he or she can create a derivative work that speaks to its medium. Note that the provision included the ability to use any medium, even one that is devised in the future (see the language "now known or hereafter devised"). Given the rapid developments in technology, this has become a standard and important concept.

> Such motion picture adaptations or versions may be fixed on film, tape, disc, wire, audiovisual cartridge, cassette or computer chip or by any other means or technical process now known or hereafter devised and may be in any and all sizes, gauges, colors and types.

The right to use and exploit the derivative work. Obviously, the producer wants to be able to do certain things with the work produced. The next cluster of rights are related to use and exploitation— what can the producer do?

> The right to fix, manufacture, reproduce, release, distribute, transmit, broadcast, display, vend, rent, lease, license, exhibit, perform, project, advertise, promote, publicize, publish, adapt, use, exploit and otherwise deal in or turn to account any motion picture or other adaptation or version produced hereunder in any and all media and by any and all means and technical processes, whether now known or hereafter devised, including film, tape, disc, wire, au-

diovisual cartridge, cassette, computer chip and any and all television (whether pay, free, cable, satellite, digital, pay-per-view or otherwise), theatrical, nontheatrical, fiber optic and other exhibition, broadcast and/or delivery systems, in any place whatsoever, including homes, theaters and elsewhere.

In the preamble discussed above, the producer was making sure the original work could be used in various ways in order to create his or her own masterpiece—namely, a derivative work. Here the producer is focused on the use of the derivative work itself.

The first half of this paragraph contains a rather exhaustive list of general uses—verbs—that describe what the producer can do with the movie or any other derivative work allowed under the agreement.

As I mentioned briefly above, it is possible for the owner of a copyrighted work to "split the rights." For example, the owner could license the television rights to one person and the stage rights to another and the animation rights to yet another, and so on. Because of this ability to split rights, lawyers for producers are always wanting to clarify that their client has the right to exploit the movie in "all media." Therefore, provisions like this drone on and on listing every example the lawyers can think of. Then he tops it off by saying that the producer gets to use a medium, even if it hasn't been invented yet. Before you scoff, think about the producers who took grants of rights before the invention of television. Can the studio owner of a movie created prior to that time now claim that it has the right to exploit it on television? What about the Internet? Can the producer of a movie now license it for distribution over the Internet? Currently, it is generally accepted that clauses giving the recipient of rights the ability to use the copyrighted work in any media, whether now in existence or hereafter developed, includes the Internet. This is a big point in contracts drafted even fifteen years ago, for example.

Ancillary rights. The producer also has the right to make other derivative works and exploit the movie in a variety of ancillary ways. Examples of other derivative works are printed works and films about the making of the movie. Making commercial tie-in deals (putting products in the movie in exchange for a fee) is another source of revenues. Merchandising (selling toys, T-shirts, and other merchandise trademarked by the movie) can also be a lucrative source of revenues.

Printed works. Producers can exploit the screenplay in various ways, including publishing it in printed form. As you may or may not know, people will buy screenplays of successful movies. Novels can also be written based on the screenplay—although novelization rights are almost always withheld by the author where the work being optioned is the author's novel. In addition, as is the case in this provision, the producer can create a book about making the movie and other such similar books.

> The rights will include the right to make and publish screenplays, teleplays and "making of" or similar books related to the production of any motion picture or other adaptation or version produced hereunder.

Recordings. The producer also has the right to make derivative works and exploit them on recorded media, such as records, tapes, and CDs.

> The rights will include the right to make, produce, reproduce, use, vend, distribute and otherwise exploit in any manner records, tapes (other than books-on-tape as set forth below), compact discs and other sound reproducing devices derived from or based on the Property or any motion picture or other adaptation or version produced hereunder.

Commercial tie-ins—product placements. A commercial tie-in is the promotion of a product in or in conjunction with a movie. A product placement is a form of commercial tie-in.[2]

Merchandise licensing. The sale of merchandise based on a motion picture has been a major consideration for producers since the advent of *Star Wars* (and even before, to a lesser extent—I admit that as a kid I begged for a set of Roy Rogers dishes). As the father of small children, I have invested vast sums in action figures of Luke Skywalker, Han Solo, Princess Leia, and Darth Vader, *Star Wars* bedsheets and pillowcases, *Star Wars* lunch boxes, pencils, and so on. Some major motion picture studios, most prominently Disney, have opened stores featuring loads and loads of movie- and television-themed merchandise in malls across the country.

> The right to exploit commercial tie-ins and merchandising (including board games, computer, video and electronic games, toys,

comic books, apparel, posters and other items) in connection with the Property or any motion picture or other adaptation or version produced hereunder.

Excerpts. Producers optioning novels and printed stories often request the right to use excerpts from the actual underlying work. Moreover, the producer will need for various reasons the right to make summaries of the story.

> The right to make and publish excerpts, synopses or summaries of the Property (not to exceed 7,500 words each and not to be serialized) for purposes of advertising, publicizing, promoting or exploiting the foregoing rights in and to the Property.

The author, of course, is not willing to allow the producer to reprint his entire novel. Thus, the provision above puts restrictions on how the producer can use the excerpts: The producer cannot use more than 7,500 words in any given summary or excerpt and cannot serialize these. Importantly, the provision clarifies that the printed derivative works may only be used for the purposes of promotion.

Title. Producers optioning novels will also want the right to use the title of the novel for the title of the movie. One of the obvious reasons producers option famous novels is to take advantage of the notoriety and popularity of the novel—known best by its title.[3]

> The right to use the title or subtitle by which the Property may be now or hereafter known, or any component of any such title or subtitle, (i) as the title or subtitle of any motion picture or other adaptation or version produced hereunder and/or in connection with the advertising, marketing, publicity, promotion and other exploitation thereof and (ii) in connection with songs, musical compositions, music and/or lyrics, whether or not included in any such motion picture or other adaptation or version.

This provision clarifies that the producer may use the title in a variety of ways: as the title or subtitle of the movie (think of two of John Grisham's novels—*The Firm* or *The Pelican Brief*). The producer will also want to use the title for the sound-track album featuring the music from the film or accompanying the marketing of the movie.

Adaptation and editing. The producer will also need the right to make changes to the novel or script or other original work. This common provision may lead to the oft heard complaint by authors that their work is being mutilated. Nevertheless, producers are not likely to compromise on the essential issue of creative control. Motion pictures are a unique art form, separate from books. Movies are a certain length, so it may be necessary to shorten the story *(Lord of the Rings)* or to lengthen it *(Minority Report)*. The original story may feature characters that are too old or too young for today's box office superstars. There are many reasons why a producer may wish or need to make changes to the original story. This right, by the way, is required by the issuer of E&O insurance, discussed later.

> In connection with the exercise of the rights granted herein, the right to edit, amend, adapt, translate, add to, subtract from, use, not use, alter, change, fictionalize or otherwise modify, and combine with any other material, the Property.

This short provision still seems to cover the breadth and depth of what is needed. The producer can add to the story or subtract from it. He can choose to use or not use. He can fictionalize a true story. He can combine the story with any other material. In essence, he can control the property creatively.

Cumulative rights; future versions. As discussed elsewhere, intellectual property has distinctive metaphysical characteristics. For instance, one possible way to interpret a rights agreement (especially one that reserves rights not granted to the producer) is that the person acquiring the rights obtains only the rights used. However, the producer wants to avoid this interpretation by clarifying that the rights can be used or not used and can be used together or separately. Moreover, the producer will want to clarify that his or her rights adhere to all permutations of the work being optioned and/or acquired. Suppose, for example, that you option the rights to a novel entitled *The Quest* and hire a screenwriter to draft a screenplay based on the novel. Then suppose that, two years later, the author of *The Quest* revises his novel to include a couple of new characters and a clever new plot line. As a producer you want to make sure that you have the right to use, without additional cost to you, this new material.

> All rights, licenses and privileges granted to Producer hereunder shall be cumulative, and Producer may exercise or use or not use any

or all of said rights, licenses and privileges together or separately. If Author hereafter makes, publishes or permits to be made or published any revision, adaptation, translation, dramatization, new issue or other version of or based on the Property, Producer shall have, and Author hereby grants to Producer, for no additional consideration, all of the same rights therein as are herein granted Producer with respect to the Property.

The first sentence of this provision clarifies that the producer may use or not use any or all of the rights enumerated in the agreement. For example, the producer may make a motion picture or a television series. (It isn't necessary that both be done and the producer doesn't have to give up the unused right.) The rights may also be used together. For example, the producer can make a screenplay, movie, merchandising and other properties, all based on the work. The rights can also be used separately—the producer can sublicense the live action motion picture rights to one company and the animation series rights to another company.

Let's revisit the notion, contained in this provision, that if the author creates new versions of the work that is optioned or acquired, the producer gets the new material with no additional cost. At first this may seem a bit aggressive on the part of the producer, but the fact of the matter is that without this right, the grantor could create competing works and even grant the rights to these works to another producer. One of the things that the purchaser of intellectual property rights purchases is the "good will" built up in the title of the property. This good will could be defeated if the producer did not have the rights to the new material.

The situation is a bit different in a series. Sue Grafton, famous detective novel writer, for example, has a series of novels based on the alphabet—*A Is for Alibi, B Is for Burglar,* and *C Is for Corpse,* to name the first three of the twenty-six novels Ms. Grafton intends to write. In a situation like this, although the producer who options the first novel would like to argue that the second novel is part of the first, the argument will not likely work. In a famous series like Ms. Grafton's, the producer will have to pay a hefty premium to buy the entire series; otherwise, the author will option or sell the novels off one at a time. Remember my comments about J. K. Rowling's *Harry Potter* series above. It would be extremely difficult to break the individual novels up, so the purchaser (in the case of the Harry Potter series of movies, Warner Bros.) must buy (there is no chance for an option with this famous property) the whole series.

Moral rights of authors.

Moral rights of authors, or *"droit moral"* in French, are recognized in those nations that have a civil law tradition.[4] This legal doctrine provides that creators of artistic works (including, for example, writers of books or screenplays) have certain rights (called "moral rights") related to the control of these works. Suppose that a painter in France does a beautiful portrait of a young prince. The painter then sells the work, including the right to make copies, to a wealthy buyer. Upon the sale of the painting, title (or legal ownership) is transferred to the buyer. So, at the end of the transaction, the buyer owns the painting outright and the exclusive right to make and sell copies of the painting. Let's suppose that a year after purchasing of the painting, the buyer decides that the young prince in the painting would look more princelike with a beard, so late at night he paints a beard on the prince's face. The next day, the buyer takes photographs of the painting and sends out new prints into the marketplace. Ah, but at this point the painter gets news of the altered painting and is—naturally—offended. The original painting is an extension of the painter's personality and the alteration makes the painting the work of another. Under the civil law, this philosophical argument is the basis of moral rights. Under that doctrine, a person can own a creative work (have legal title to it), but is restricted from making alterations.[5]

What does this have to do with making movies in the United States? First, movies produced in the United States may find audiences in France, Italy, or elsewhere in Europe, where civil law prevails. Further, these same rights are held by the writers of books and screenplays.[6] Thus, unless the writer of the book in this case cooperates, the producer's changes, edits, and so forth necessary to make a movie could be challenged.

The provision below, dealing with the issue of moral rights, is common to option and rights acquisition agreements.

Author hereby waives the exercise of any provision of law known as "droit moral" or any similar law which may now or hereafter be recognized in any jurisdiction and hereby agrees not to institute, support, maintain or permit any action, suit or proceeding on the ground that any motion picture or other adaptation or version produced hereunder, or any other exercise of any of the rights granted by Author hereunder, in any way constitutes an infringement or violation of any right of droit moral or any similar right, or is in any way a defamation or mutilation of the Property or any part thereof or of the reputation of Author, or in any way contains unauthorized variations, alterations, modifications, changes or translations.

This provision in its essence is a waiver of rights. The author agrees not to use the law of droit moral to counter any of the other provisions of the agreement. Legal scholars in some nations have stated that moral rights cannot be waived. As a practical matter, however, authors whose books form the basis of motion pictures do not ignore the waiver—a motion picture can be a great source of revenue and promotion of the book itself.

RESERVED RIGHTS

It is the common practice for the author, especially if the work is a novel or short story, to reserve print publishing and other rights related to the work being optioned or acquired. In some cases, these rights are gone before the producer becomes involved. For example, suppose that a producer wants to make a movie based on a successful play (think of *The Odd Couple* and other plays by Neil Simon) or musical (*The Sound of Music* by Rodgers and Hammerstein); naturally, the stage play rights will be reserved by the authors. Similarly, if the producer wants to base his movie on a published book (*Jurassic Park* or *To Kill a Mockingbird*, to name two of many possibilities), the author will not be in a position to grant any printing rights. Even where the work in question has not been published, if the writer has aspirations to be a successful novelist, the writer will not give this right up. Let's take a look at a typical reserved rights provision:

> Author hereby reserves the following rights, subject to the conditions and exceptions set forth in this agreement:

> **Print publishing rights.**
> The author of a novel or other printed work will invariably reserve to himself or herself (or, by contract, to the publisher of the work) the print publishing rights.

> The right to publish and distribute printed versions of the Book or any sequel thereto written solely by Author (each, an "Author Written Sequel") in book form (whether hardcover or softcover) and in magazines or other periodicals (whether in installments or other-

wise) and to record and distribute audio narrations (i.e., "books on tape") of the same.

Note the definition in this provision of "Author Written Sequel." Remember that a sequel of a book or movie is a book or movie that has the same characters, but a different and subsequent story line from such book or movie (a prequel is a book or movie that has the same characters, but a different and earlier story line). *The Empire Strikes Back* is a sequel to *Star Wars,* of course (*The Phantom Menace* is a prequel).

Therefore, in this case, the author retains the right to publish and distribute the book in question (including any other versions of the book) and any sequel that the author writes. Think about how this provision works with the grant of movie-sequel rights to the producer discussed above. There exists the chance, in this situation, that the movie sequel and book sequel could be entirely different. This, of course, could be fixed by various means, including giving the producer a first right of negotiation or similar right regarding author written sequels. The metaphysics of these types of approaches are complex and often restrictive on the author. Also, note here that the author reserves to himself or herself the right to record the book and distribute the recording in the form of audiotapes and CDs.

Electronic publishing rights.

Here is where the lawyers get hung up on word questions, like "What is a book?" or "What constitutes publishing?" It used to be easy to tell—books were made of paper. Ah, but now you can buy little hunks of plastic and/or metal, some of which sort of look like paper books and some of which do not, that have printed words. The author's lawyer wants to make sure that these little devices are retained by the writer and so adds a provision that reserves "electronic publishing" rights.

The right to exercise the electronic publishing rights in the Book or any Author Written Sequel. As used herein, "electronic publishing rights" shall mean and be limited to the right to nondramatic reproduction of the verbatim text of the Book or any Author Written Sequel in its entirety in an electronic form the result of which serves as a substitute for sales of the Book or any Author Written Sequel in book form, with the same content, form, organization, text and other material contained in the Book or any sequel thereto written by Author in its printed form, in the same order and without embellishment or abridgement or other additions, deletions or changes of any kind without Producer's prior written consent (not to be unreasonably withheld).

In this provision, electronic publishing rights are defined and limited: The rights encompass (1) nondramatic reproductions (2) the verbatim text of the work or "Author Written Sequel" and (3) the entirety of the work or "Author Written Sequel." Moreover, the end result must serve as a "substitute for sales of the Book or any Author Written Sequel in book form" and must have the same content and form, organization, text, order of material, without additions or deletions or changes. In other words, the producer is saying that the author can make electronic books, but that the electronic version must be just like the paper book—no more no less. Otherwise, says the producer, the author could conceivably create a work—complete with musical score and dramatic effects and pictures—that will compete with his movie.

Stage play rights.

Another common right reserved to the author is the right to produce and exploit a stage play based on the work. The stage rights to a work could be quite valuable, as is shown by the ever-increasing number of stage adaptations of motion pictures—*Footloose, The Producers, Hairspray,* and others.

The right to perform one or more dramatic and/or musical plays based on the Book or any Author Written Sequel on the speaking stage, in the immediate presence of a living audience; provided, however, that no broadcast, telecast, recording or other reproduction of such live stage performances shall be made without Producer's express written permission; and provided further, however, that Author shall not exercise, or permit any other person to exercise, any such reserved live stage rights until the earlier of five (5) years after the release of the Picture or seven (7) years after exercise of the Option in accordance with the provisions hereof.

The producer's lawyers will insist on certain limitations to the stage play rights, as this provision demonstrates. The stage play must be performed in front of a live audience on stage and may not be broadcast over television or otherwise and may not be made into a video. The obvious reason for this restriction is that a televised version or video of the stage play could directly compete with and impact the marketability of the movie.

In addition, note that the producer in this case is insisting on a "holdback" period in connection with the exercise of stage play rights. In this example, the author may not exercise this right (he must hold back) for a period of five years from the time the movie is released (or seven years from the exercise of the option). The rationale is that the producer will have time to complete the first cycle of life for the movie prior to the interference that the stage play could cause.

Radio plays.

The author will also wish to reserve the right to broadcast the work or any author written sequel over the radio (no moving pictures there).

> The right to broadcast by means of radio all or any part of the Book or any Author Written Sequel; provided, however, that the foregoing shall not be deemed to limit the radio rights granted to Producer above, including the right to promote a motion picture based on the Property by means of radio, the right to simulcast a motion picture based on the Property by means of radio and the right to transmit the soundtrack or any portion thereof by means of radio; and provided further, however, that Author shall not exercise, or permit any other person to exercise, any such reserved radio rights until the earlier of five (5) years after the release of the Picture or seven (7) years after exercise of the Option in accordance with the provisions hereof.

The producer is careful, in this provision, to clarify that the author's radio rights do not limit in any way the producer's right to promote the movie over the radio, simulcast the movie over the radio, or broadcast the soundtrack of the movie over the radio.

Again, the producer insists, in this case, that in any event the author may not exercise the radio broadcast right for a certain length of time—time enough to run the movie through its commercial life cycle.

Reserved "author written sequel" rights.

Consistent with the reserved rights related to author written sequels (discussed above), the author and his or her lawyer want to clarify that the author has the motion picture rights to author written sequels. Since this right goes to the heart of the benefit of producer's bargain, the producer and the lawyer representing the producer will carefully describe the limits of this right.

> The right to develop, produce, distribute and otherwise exploit one (1) or more motion pictures based on each Author Written Sequel (collectively, the "Reserved Author Written Sequel Picture Rights"); provided, however, that the foregoing shall not be deemed to limit the rights granted to Producer above, including the right to develop, produce, distribute and otherwise exploit one or more motion picture adaptations or versions based in whole or in part on the Property, including sequels, remakes, prequels, spinoffs, musicals and serials; and provided further, however, that Author shall not exercise, or permit any other person to exercise, any of the Reserved Author Written Sequel Picture Rights until the earlier of five (5) years after the release of the Picture or seven (7) years after exercise of the Option in accordance with the provisions hereof.

After the "proviso" (the part of this provision that starts with the words "provided, however," which means "but"), the producer has his or her say. First, the producer clarifies—in proper paranoid repetition of other sections of the agreement—that this language does not limit the producer's right to make a movie based on the work that is the subject of the option agreement.

Again, the producer says, "Okay, you can make movies based on your own sequels, but you can't do it until the commercial life cycle of my movie runs."

Right of first negotiation. I can predict (because I read ahead, naturally) that the producer wants some way to preserve the right to lay his or her hands on author written sequels. The rationale, stated above, is worth repeating. If the producer's movie under this agreement is successful, it will create a market for author written sequels, like the movie *Hunt for Red October* arguably created for *Patriot Games* and then *Clear and Present Danger* (although Mr. Clancy, the author of the books, might have a different view). One way to accomplish this goal is by means of the right of first negotiation, or one of its cousins, including a right of first refusal. A right of first negotiation, as the name implies, puts an obligation on the author to sit down and talk to the producer before talking to anyone else. The producer gets to be the first suitor at the table.

If, at any time subsequent to the holdback period set forth in the preceding sentence, Author intends to exercise, use or dispose of any of the Reserved Author Written Sequel Picture Rights, Author agrees that prior to making any such exercise, use or disposition, Author shall in each and every case first grant Producer a customary right of first negotiation for the acquisition of such rights for a period of thirty (30) days commencing upon Producer's receipt of written notice from Author.

Right of first refusal. A right of first refusal, as shown in the language below, requires the author to come back to Producer Number One with the terms offered by any third party who may be negotiating for the rights. From Producer Number One's perspective, this is better than a mere right of first negotiation, because the author has to do more than just talk—the author has to come back before making a deal with Producer Number Two and offer Producer Number One the opportunity to match or beat Producer Number Two's offer.

If Producer and Author fail to reach an agreement regarding such rights during the thirty (30) day period, Author shall be entitled to offer such rights to third parties; provided, however, that Author shall not enter into any agreement regarding the acquisition of such rights by any third party on material financial terms less favorable to Author than those last offered by Producer without first granting to Producer, for a period of fifteen (15) days after Producer's receipt of written notice from Author, the exclusive option to enter into an agreement with Author on the same less favorable material financial terms.

A right of first refusal will not be favored by the author's lawyer, so don't be surprised if this last refusal right is rejected. It is a true burden for the author. Think about it: The author has to complete his negotiations with Producer Number Two and then say, "Okay, I'm ready to sign your deal, but first I have to go talk to Producer Number One and see if he wants to match or beat your deal." Producer Number Two is likely to say something like, "Oh, great, I really enjoy paying legal fees to my lawyer so that Producer Number One can take the deal from me—not really!" More likely, Producer Number Two will just refuse to talk to the author.

REPRESENTATIONS, WARRANTIES, AND INDEMNITIES RESPECTING "CHAIN OF TITLE"

Representations and warranties.

We've talked about representations, warranties, and indemnities before; remember caveat emptor? It's worth talking about again, because as an attorney I can tell you that these three words, representations, warranties, and indemnities, get my attention. This is one of those pure legal parts of the option or buyout agreement (or any other agreement involving a license or sale of rights, for that matter). This is where the producer asks a number of questions to ferret out any problems in the chain of title and where the producer tries to shift liability to the author for things unknown.[7]

One of the biggest headaches that can confront a producer—as you know by now—is a problem with chain of title. A question here can lead to a lawsuit for infringement and/or other troubles. When movies cost millions of dollars to produce, infringement suits are not fun. When movies can generate millions, however, infringement suits are always possible. So, in the contract, the producer says to the author, in essence (lawyers have to use a lot more words, of course), "Since you wrote the book, if there are any chinks in the chain of title, it will be your responsibility if anybody makes a claim." Then the author says (of course his lawyer uses more words as well) to the producer, "Well, I wrote the book and I'll answer all your questions to the extent that I can, but I can't cover all the problems; you can't expect me to have all the facts . . ." The producer will say, "Well, you are in a better position than me to know . . ." And on they will go. Let's take a look at how this all works in an actual contract:

Author's legal competency. The author represents that he or she has the legal authority to enter into and perform this agreement. For example, a person who is a minor (under the age of eighteen in the state of California, for example) has no legal authority to enter into a contract.[8] Also, there could be other legal restrictions impairing the authority of the author—for example, the author might be a cowriter and may not alone have the authority to give the exclusive grant of rights described in the granting clause of the agreement.

> Author has the full right, power and authority to make and perform this agreement and to grant the rights granted or to be granted hereunder;

No third-party approval needed. Here, the author is required to say that he or she doesn't need to ask any other person for permission to grant the rights described above. If such permission is required (for example, from a joint author), of course, the author will say something like, "except for the consent of my coauthor, Mrs. Writealot, whose consent has been obtained . . ." at the beginning.

No other approval or consent is required with respect to this agreement or the transactions contemplated hereunder;

Author's sole work. This representation answers the question, "Who created the work?" The producer wants to know if there are other writers to worry about. If there are other writers, a new set of questions will arise: Did the other writer give the author his or her rights and if so how? Did the other writer do the work as a work made for hire? If the representations reveal these types of issues, the producer must work with the author to find a solution.

The Property was written and created solely by Author . . .

Publishing. This representation gives the producer an idea of how broadly the work has been disseminated and where it has been registered for copyright protection. This could be important in ascertaining the steps needed to further protect the work or secure the rights to the work.

Except as set forth in the initial paragraph of this agreement, the Property has not been published or registered for copyright in the United States of America or any other jurisdiction . . .

Public domain status. Since the copyright laws of every nation are different (even though many nations are signatories to the Berne Convention and/or the Universal Copyright Convention), the producer would like to understand if the work is still under protection— obviously, in nations where the work is in the public domain, anyone can create derivative works (including motion pictures). The producer wants this risk to fall on the author; the author doesn't want it.

To the best of Author's knowledge, the Property is not in the public domain in any jurisdiction of the world where copyright protection is available . . .

"Best-knowledge" qualifier. One way for the author to push the risk back toward the producer is by using the qualifier, "to the best of Author's knowledge." The author argues that it is impossible to know the copyright laws of Tonga and unfair to ask the author to bear that risk. The producer will argue that the author is in a better position to know than the producer. In reality, however, the proper question isn't, "Who is in the better position to know the fact"; rather, the proper question is, "Who is in the better position to bear the risk." Bargaining leverage, not logic, often supplies the answer.

Other previous dramatic works. The producer needs to know whether or not there are other movies, stage plays, television programs, or dramatic work out there that could pop up once the producer begins the time-consuming and costly process. Such other work could obviously interfere (because the quality is poor) or compete (because the quality is good or the ending is better or for many other reasons).

> The Property has not previously been exploited or authorized to be exploited, whether in whole or in part, as a motion picture, stage play or other dramatic adaptation or version;

Other persons. This is a similar question to the one previously discussed regarding other previous dramatic works. The producer wants to know if anyone else has been authorized to exercise the rights enumerated in the agreement. If there are disclosures here by the author, the producer is warned of possible trouble down the road. What were the terms of that previous arrangement? Is it possible that the person still thinks he or she has the right to make a movie? Will that person have a valid claim, if the producer moves forward on the project?

> None of the rights granted or to be granted to Producer hereunder has been exercised or authorized to be exercised by any person;

No derivative work. This harks back to the representation above where the author states that the work was "written and created solely by Author." Here, the author states that in addition to the work as a whole, "each and every element" of the work is original with the author or, if not, it is in the public domain (which means the author has the right to use it). Then, as a prime illustration of lawyers' tendency to make sure the entire waterfront has been covered, the provision

states that the author has not "adapted or copied" from other protected works. The end result is that the author, by consenting to this
wording, is taking the risk that some third party will make a claim that
the work infringes on such third party's work. Sometimes, authors will
request that "to the best of my knowledge" be used in this representation. However, producers should resist this, as this will substantially
weaken the legal effect of the representation.

> Except to the extent based on material in the public domain, the
> Property and each and every element thereof are wholly original
> with Author and have not been adapted or copied from any other
> literary, dramatic or other material . . .

No infringement, libel, or defamation or other violation. Now
that the producer has required the author's representations that indirectly go to the question of "Who bears the risk of infringement?"
it is time to go straight for the jugular vein. In this provision, the producer demands, "Tell me that there is no infringement." Again, producers will resist any attempt on the part of the author to limit this
representation by a best-of-knowledge qualifier.

> Neither the Property nor any element thereof in any way infringes
> upon any statutory, common law, literary, dramatic or other prop-
> erty, copyright, trademark or other rights of any person, or in any
> way constitutes a libel or defamation of any person, or in any way vi-
> olates any rights of any kind (including the right of privacy or pub-
> licity) of any person . . .

No violation of common law rights. One of the producer's other
legitimate concerns is that the producer's use of the rights will somehow result in the violation of some third party's rights under laws
other than the federal copyright statute. In the United States, notwithstanding the fact that copyright law has been enacted by Congress
on the national or federal level, there are certain state statutes and
cases that give the owner of a property added protection. Of course,
law students know that state laws that contradict federal laws may be
invalid.

> The production and exploitation of any motion picture or other
> adaptation or version based on the Property and the full use of the

rights granted or to be granted to Producer hereunder will not in any way infringe upon any statutory, common law, literary, dramatic or other property, copyright, trademark or other rights of any person, or in any way constitute a libel or defamation of any person, or in any way violate any rights of any kind (including the right of privacy or publicity) of any person . . .

Exclusive ownership. Here again is the relentless drive toward making sure that the producer will get the benefit of the exclusive nature of the author's grant. The rationale, of course, is that the author cannot give what the author doesn't have. Thus, the producer says, in yet another way, "Tell me that you are the exclusive owner of the right being granted." And the point is, as noted above, to shift the risk of problems to the author.

> Author is the sole and exclusive owner, throughout the universe in perpetuity, of all right, title and interest in and to the rights granted or to be granted to Producer hereunder . . .

No other grants. The producer wants to know that the author has not given these rights to any other person. If so, the producer will need to know the details of this prior transfer. (If there was a previous option to another party, for example, did the option expire?) The producer also wants to be assured that the work hasn't been "impaired" in any way. For example, suppose the author has written an article or given an interview to the effect that the work is not complete or is inferior to his other works.

> None of the rights granted or to be granted to Producer hereunder has in any way been granted, assigned, conveyed or otherwise transferred to any person or in any way prejudiced, limited, diminished or impaired . . .

No encumbrance. The producer has already asked questions to ensure that the rights haven't been granted to another person. A logical follow-up question concerns whether there are any encumbrances. Suppose the author offered the work as security for a loan from a bank. In such case, the bank might have a foreclosure right or the right to be paid prior to any transfer. Preexisting encumbrances may have a chilling effect on the producer's goals. Indeed, as we will discuss later, the producer will have to encumber the property when joining certain guilds or when securing bank financing. The presence of an encumbrance, therefore, raises problems.

> None of the rights granted or to be granted to Producer hereunder is subject to any liens, encumbrances, charges, claims or litigation, whether outstanding, pending or threatened . . .

No interference. This language speaks to past acts (a representation) and future acts (a covenant or promise). The author can give the rights exclusively and without encumbrance, but can then take devious actions to interfere with the producer's enjoyment of the rights. For example, suppose the author, after signing the option agreement, writes another almost identical work that is designed to compete with the producer or makes frivolous claims related to the work or purports to grant the rights to persons other than the producer. These acts would damage the value of the rights. This provision gives the producer a contractual claim for breach of contract in those events.

> Author has not done or omitted to do, and will not do or omit to do, any act or thing that will or may in any way prevent or interfere in any manner with the full and exclusive enjoyment by Producer of any and all of the rights granted or to be granted hereunder or that will or may in any way prejudice, limit, diminish, impair, impede, invalidate or encumber any or all such rights . . .

Protection. This is the positive counterpart to the previous provision. Here the author promises to take affirmative, positive steps to protect the producer and the benefit of producer's bargain. For example, in order to extend the life of the copyright, the author's signature on a piece of paper may be necessary. Or, if a third party makes a claim on the property, the author's participation in battling the third party might be necessary. This provision enlists that support.

> During the Option Period, Author will do all such acts and things as shall be necessary to preserve and protect all of the rights granted or to be granted to Producer hereunder and to prevent the Property or any portion thereof from falling into the public domain.

Indemnity.

If the representations and warranties and covenants are the shield, the indemnity provision is the sword. If the representations turn out to be untrue (even if the misrepresentation was an innocent mistake), the producer will turn to this provision for a remedy. It will be the author's duty, in this case, to "defend," "indemnify" and "hold harmless"—in other words, to make sure that the producer is not injured, to make sure the producer is made whole, and to make sure the producer is compensated for any losses arising out of such breach. (For the sake of brevity, I have left out the producer's representations and warranties in this discussion, but the same holds true in favor of the author, if any of the producer's representations, warranties, or agreements are breached. As you can imagine, the producer's representations and warranties are important, but not the central focus of the agreement, like those of the author.)

The scope of the indemnity. The language of the indemnity clause clarifies that the producer and his immediate circle—successors, assigns, licensees, officers, directors, etc.—are to be protected and made whole.

Author shall defend, indemnify and hold harmless Producer (and, if applicable, producer's successors, assigns, licensees, officers, directors, shareholders, partners, employees, agents, heirs, executors and administrators) from and against any claims, actions, demands, losses, penalties, liabilities, damages or expenses (including reasonable attorneys' fees) arising out of any breach or alleged breach of any representation, warranty or agreement made, or obligation assumed, by such party pursuant to this agreement.

Attorneys' fees. In most jurisdictions in the United States (remember that in the United States, each state has its own laws, and while these laws are similar from state to state, they are not always the same) the award of attorneys' fees is not automatic; it must be stated and agreed to by the parties.

The effectiveness of the indemnity. In the legal community, lawyers sometimes use the term "judgment proof" to describe people who are unable as a matter of fact to fully live up to a judgment against them. Suppose, for example, that after the motion picture is made and released a person comes forward with evidence that the author did not write the work, but that it was stolen from such person. The person demands millions of dollars in compensation for the infringement. If the author agreed to sign the representations and warranties as written above, the author would be liable for the millions. But more often than not, the author will not have several million dollars lying around. Even if the producer sues and wins, it won't solve all the producer's problems. Thus, the risk-shifting purpose of the representations and warranties provision might be limited or even defeated. Still, producers do not shy away from demanding the representations and warranties, because truthful answers will guide the producer toward solving any problems that arise. Moreover, a breach of the agreement by the author will, at least, give the producer the right to withhold and perhaps recoup from the author any payments made or owing under the agreement. In addition, producers secure insurance for this risk.[9]

PUBLICITY RIGHTS—NAME AND LIKENESS

The ability to use a person's name and likeness for commercial purposes is not a matter of copyright law; this right is grounded in the so-called right of publicity found by the United States Supreme Court in the Constitution. You won't find the words, "name and likeness," in the Constitution, but the concept that it is unlawful to use a person's name or likeness for commercial purposes without such person's consent is well established in case law. Virtually every services contract on a film—from the writer to the star—has a provision similar to the following:

> Author hereby grants to Producer the right, throughout the universe, in perpetuity, to use and reproduce and license others to use and reproduce the name, approved likeness and approved biographical data of Author in connection with (a) any motion picture or other adaptation or version produced hereunder, (b) the advertising, marketing, publicizing, promotion, exhibition, distribution or other exploitation of any such motion picture or other adaptation or version, and (c) any commercial tie-ins, merchandising and/or the advertising or publicizing of any commodities, products or services relating or referring to any such motion picture or other adaptation or version, provided that Author shall not be represented as using, consuming or endorsing any such commodity, product or service without Author's prior written consent. Author agrees to exercise any approvals of Author's likeness and/or biographical data reasonably and within five (5) days after Producer's or its licensee's request therefor or such approvals shall be deemed given.

Name and likeness and biographical data.

The producer here has bargained for the right to use (and allow others to use) the name and "approved" likeness and biographical data of the author. Note that here there is no mechanism prescribed for the approval process. Rather, it is left to the producer to make sure that the images and data chosen are okay with the author. The name, likeness, and biographical data can only be used in connection with the movies derived under this agreement, the advertising of such movies, and the products related to such movies. Some agreements will provide for an approval process. With regard to photographs, for example, the person granting the right simply preapproves a number of photographs from which the producer (or his designees) can choose.

Limitation on product tie-ins.

Notwithstanding the custom of authors allowing their name and likeness to be used in promoting and marketing the movie, authors (as with most celebrities) will want to avoid having their name used in endorsing products or services. There is a fine line between allowing your name to be used in connection with a commercial tie-in or merchandising and endorsing an article of merchandise. Perhaps the best way to think of it is that in the first instance, the author is promoting the movie and in the second instance the author is endorsing something else—a product. This is critical in the case of actors who have endorsement contracts with product manufacturers; to ignore the restrictive provisions in their endorsement contracts could lead to the actor being put in an untenable position regarding the actor's duties under this contract and that one. Moreover, some people, for health or religious or public relations reasons, refuse to endorse certain types of products—alcoholic beverages or cigarettes, for example.

Credit.

Another chapter in the book of publicity rights is the "credit." However, in this case, the impetus usually (although not always) comes from the author. Authors (and virtually everyone else who works on the movie) will demand a credit on the movie.

Based on ... Authors of novels, short stories, or other similar source materials (such as comic books and computer games), usually seek and are granted a credit that reads something like: "Based on the short story 'The Quest' by Kelly C. Crabb" (or if the movie bears the title of the work, "Based on the short story by Kelly C. Crabb").[10]

> With respect to any motion picture produced hereunder, Producer shall accord Author credit on all positive prints of the motion picture, in the main titles (or, if no individual credits are contained therein, then in the end titles), in a size of type not less than that of the credit accorded the screenwriter, substantially as follows: "Based on the Book 'The Quest' by Kelly C. Crabb" or, if the motion picture has the same title as the Property, "Based on the Book by Kelly C. Crabb."

Credit—position, size, and wording. Author's credit, in this agreement, goes on all "positive prints" (meaning the reels of films that are distributed to and run through the projectors in the theaters—as opposed to negative prints, which are used to make positive prints) of the movie. The credit also goes in the main titles (for the most part, these are the titles that run in the beginning of the movie—while everyone is watching—as opposed to those credits that roll at the end of the movie—while everyone is scurrying to the parking lot). In this case, the size of the credit must be the same size as the screenwriter's credit, which seems quite fair to me. There are other ways to describe the size: some contracts use point sizes (meaning type point) and some use percentages of the title as a guide (for example, the credit must be at least 50 percent of the size of the title of the movie).

Paid ads. The author here also gets to be in the "billing block" (the list of names that adorn the bottom portion of the official poster (or "one sheet," as it is called in the movie industry) of the movie. This billing block will almost always run on full-page newspaper ads and on television ads (for about a half second—but the author's mom almost always takes the author's word that his or her name was really there).

> With respect to any motion picture produced hereunder, Producer shall accord Author credit as specified above in the billing portion of all paid advertisements (subject to Producer's standard exclusions) issued by or under the control of Producer in connection with such motion picture, in a size of type not less than that of the credit accorded the screenwriter.

Standard exclusions. Note that this right to have a credit in all paid ads is subject to "producer's standard exclusions" (which turn out to be in most cases, coincidentally, the exclusions of the distributor who actually pays for the ads). Such exclusions might include smaller newspaper ads (where there is no room to put the author's credit) and radio ads, to name two. Notice again that in the example above that the author has linked his fortunes with the screenwriter for size.

No breach. The producer (having learned from the hard luck of some poor devil in the distant past) always hedges his bets by providing that there is no breach of contract for inadvertently leaving the author's credit out. Rather, the producer obligates himself to correct it the next time around. Think of the problems involved with failing to provide for this possible mistake: The author sues you for the value of the promotion to the writer's career. Or even worse, the author argues that the producer has to redo the credits on all the positive prints—an expensive proposition.

> No casual or inadvertent failure of Producer and no failure of any third party to comply with the provisions of this paragraph shall be deemed a breach of this agreement by Producer. Notwithstanding the foregoing, upon receipt by Producer of written notice from Author specifying such failure in reasonable detail, Producer shall use reasonable efforts prospectively to cure such failure for prints and advertisements prepared after Producer's receipt of such notice.

The guild rules win. The following provision often appears in book option deals, even though the author may not be a member of the Writers Guild of America (WGA). If the screenwriter (who will turn the book into a screenplay) is a member of the WGA and the author's credit is restricted under those rules, the producer will be bound by those rules because he must join the WGA in order to hire a WGA writer. On the other hand, the agreement will also provide that, if the guild rules restrict the producer from granting the author's desired credit, the producer has to do something affirmative to give credit to the author. They'll sit down and talk about what to do.

> The above credit shall be subject to any applicable guild restrictions and/or collective bargaining agreements; provided, however, that if the above credit is not permitted, the parties hereto shall negotiate

in good faith an alternative credit which complies with such restrictions and/or agreements.

MISCELLANEOUS PROVISIONS

Preproduction activities.

During the option period, the producer wants to get the screenplay done—because, as you will learn, nothing can happen without it. The producer wants to clarify that it is okay to make the screenplay (a derivative work) even before the producer officially takes the rights. A small point (which may be considered unnecessary because of well-established custom), but technically an important one. The most important activity is writing the screenplay—everything else is secondary. In addition, the producer will want to create treatments and summaries to use in pitches to talent.

> During the Option Period, Producer and its designees shall have the right to engage in all customary development and preproduction activities, including the preparation and/or submission of treatments and screenplays based upon the Property.

No obligation to proceed.

A prudent producer will want to come right out and say it—"As excited as you may be about the possibility of a movie being made based on your book, there is no guarantee that it will happen and, therefore, don't count your chickens before they hatch." The producer in this agreement is under no legal compulsion to exercise the option and make the movie. But remember our discussion about valuable properties. If a producer is fortunate enough to land a famous novel or other property, he will not be able to negotiate a provision like this one. Rather, the producer will be required to reach certain goals (hire a writer, produce a draft, etc.) along the way. If the producer doesn't achieve these benchmarks, he will not be able under the agreement to purchase the rights and the contract will terminate.

> Producer shall not be obligated to exercise the Option or to produce the Picture or any other adaptation or version hereunder or otherwise to exercise any of the rights granted or to be granted hereunder.

Copyright protection for future publications.
The maintenance of a copyright requires vigilance on the part of the original author and the assignee. Failure of the author to take certain steps, such as making applications for renewal in jurisdictions that require renewals, for example, could result in the work falling into the public domain. Thus, the producer will require the author to affirmatively take steps to ensure the continued validity of the protection. Since neither the producer nor the author can control what has happened in the past (and, besides, the representations and warranties section should have picked up most of the problems in past publications) the focus on this section is future publications.

> Author agrees that any future publication of the Property or any part thereof (including any revision, sequel, adaptation, translation, dramatization, new issue or other version of the Property or any part thereof) shall be with such notice of copyright and in such manner as shall afford to the Property (or part thereof) copyright protection in the United States of America and all jurisdictions adhering to the Berne Convention, the Pan American Copyright Convention and/or the Universal Copyright Convention.

Copyright notice on future publications. With regard to this provision, note (as we discussed above) that failure to affix the copyright notice is not fatal under the Copyright Act, which holds that substance is more important than form. Nevertheless, it is customary to put the notice on published works. Moreover, the copyright line may still be important under the laws of other jurisdictions; the information serves as a notice to others that the rights are being reserved and that the producer wants the copyright affixed to future publications.

Identical rights. The producer also wants to make sure that he gets the advantage under copyright law respecting future publications that he is granted under the agreement. Thus, the producer requires the author to make filings, sign applications, and do any procedure necessary to provide protection under copyright law and to prevent the future publication from falling into the public domain.

> Producer shall be deemed to have acquired, and is hereby granted and assigned for no additional consideration, all rights under any such copyright which are identical to Producer's rights hereunder with respect to the Property. If requested by Producer, Author

agrees to execute, acknowledge and deliver, or cause to be executed, acknowledged and delivered, to Producer any instruments that may be required by Producer to establish, vest and maintain in Producer such rights under such copyright. Author shall not cause, allow or sanction any future publication as aforesaid without reserving or securing for Producer, for no additional consideration, all of the aforesaid rights, and in any grants or agreements hereafter made or entered into by Author concerning the Property, Author shall expressly accept and reserve all of the rights herein granted or to be granted to Producer. Author shall do all acts necessary to prevent the Property and any portion thereof, now in existence or hereafter created, from falling into the public domain.

Enlarged rights. The producer also wants the benefit (but not the detriment) of any new or amended law. In this provision, the author is obligated to take advantage of any enlargement of rights under future law and the producer is allowed to benefit from the same.

Author agrees to secure or cause to be secured the renewal or extension of any copyright in the Property or any part thereof which may be renewed or extended under any present or future law relating thereto. Producer shall be deemed to have acquired, and is hereby granted and assigned for no additional consideration, all rights under any such renewed or extended copyright which are identical to Producer's rights hereunder with respect to the Property. If the present copyright law of the United States of America or any other jurisdiction where the Property is or may hereafter be protected shall be amended or changed, or a new copyright law enacted, so that the term of copyright is extended, enlarged or created, Producer shall be entitled to all of the rights herein granted to Author for such extended, enlarged or created term.

Author's cooperation. The producer also wants to make sure that if something goes wrong—for example, some third party infringes the copyright—the author is obligated to participate in any action against such third party, because the law of some jurisdictions might require the author's participation and because the author may have evidence.

Producer shall have the benefit of all copyrights in the Property and all remedies for enforcing such copyrights with respect to the

Rights. In Producer's sole judgment, Producer may join Author as a party plaintiff or defendant in any action, suit or proceeding relating to the Rights. All claims, causes of action, recoveries, damages, penalties, settlements and profits relating to or arising from any interference with or infringement of any of the Rights are hereby assigned to Producer. Author shall not compromise, settle or in any manner interfere with, and shall fully cooperate with Producer in connection with, any action, suit or proceeding threatened or instituted by or against Producer relating to any of the Rights.

No settlement. On the other hand, the producer wants to make sure that the author doesn't take charge of the dispute and make some settlement that might injure the producer's position. Imagine that you spent thousands of dollars developing a project and just prior to setting it up with a major studio, some third party writes the author to complain about a possible infringement. And then suppose that the author, in order to avoid a conflict, decides to settle the matter by making some concession—like conceding that the other work doesn't compete with the work he optioned to the producer. The producer is not going to like that.

Further assurances—short-form option and assignment of rights agreement. It becomes important to the producer, for a number of reasons, to have the public take notice of his or her claim of rights. Theoretically, the producer could file the entire option contract with the USCO as a basis for establishing the claim. However, remember that filings with the USCO are public and most producers are loath to disclose to the public the terms of a deal—if the producer pays the author too much, the former could be setting himself or herself up for catcalls from peers; if the producer pays too little, a phone call from the now unhappy author who heard from a friend that the deal was bad could be the result. Producers also don't want competitors' eyes scanning the limitations of the rights granted or any other substantive terms. Therefore, producers and authors sign short-form agreements that refer to, but don't disclose, the detailed terms of the main agreement. This short form is filed with the USCO (see below).

Further assurances. This provision is typical of the so-called "further assurances" provisions found in many business contracts. Basically, the producer (and the producer's lawyer) want to say, "Look, if we forgot anything or if something arises in the future that helps or is necessary to fulfill the promises you made under this agreement, you'd better do it." Hence, this catchall provision is called further assurances.

> Upon Producer's request, Author shall promptly perform (or cause to be performed) such further acts and promptly execute, acknowledge and deliver (or cause to be executed, acknowledged and delivered) to Producer such further documents as Producer shall deem necessary or advisable in order to carry out the intent and accomplish the purposes of this agreement and consummate the transactions contemplated hereby.

Power of attorney. Some producers like to add an extra tool (some might say "weapon"). In essence, if the author isn't around or refuses to cooperate for whatever reason, the producer marches down to the courthouse or the USCO or wherever the producer needs to and signs the document or takes the steps needed to be taken in the author's name as the author's attorney-in-fact under what is known in the law as a power of attorney. When you stop to think about it, this is a pretty onerous step. Suppose the producer and the author are having a little spat when some document needs to be filed (with "need" being defined by the producer). Well, under this provision, the producer simply pulls out the document and signs it for the author. And that is why producers insist on having a power of attorney in this situation—things are not so tense at the option stage of the game, but down the road, after thousands or millions have been spent on the project, producers do not want to hand the author a loaded gun.

> If for any reason Author shall fail to do any of the foregoing within five (5) days of Producer's written request therefor, Author hereby irrevocably appoints Producer as Author's true and lawful attorney-in-fact (such appointment being coupled with an interest), with full power of substitution and delegation, with the right but not the obligation to perform any such acts and to execute any such documents on Author's behalf.

Short-form agreements. This provision explains the uses of the short-form agreements. The "short-form option" agreement is filed with the USCO right after the option agreement is effective. The "short-form assignment agreement" or "grant of rights agreement" is filed when the option is exercised. If the producer doesn't exercise the option, the assignment agreement is void.

> Without limiting the generality of the foregoing, Author shall execute and deliver to Producer, simultaneously with the execution of this agreement, a short-form option in the form of Exhibit A attached hereto and incorporated herein by this reference (which instrument shall become effective immediately and may be recorded by Producer with the U.S. Copyright Office as evidence of the option herein granted to Producer) and a short form assignment in the form of Exhibit B attached hereto and incorporated herein by this reference. If such short form assignment is undated, Author hereby authorizes Producer to date such short form assignment and to record the same in the U.S. Copyright Office upon exercise of the Option in accordance with the provisions hereof. If Producer fails to exercise the Option prior to the expiration of the Option Period, then both the short form option and the short form assignment shall be void and Producer shall not be deemed to have acquired any rights in or to the Property.

Publisher's release. The producer may or may not be able to examine the deal between the author and the publisher of the book. Those contracts tend to be detailed and complex and give to the book publisher various rights and privileges, some of which could be read to overlap or interfere with the grant of rights the producer is taking under the option agreement. The publisher's waiver is designed to avoid any possibility that the publisher suddenly comes forward in the future and asserts some right in the movie.

> As soon as possible after execution of this agreement, Author shall provide Producer with an executed original publisher's release, in the form of Exhibit C attached hereto and incorporated herein by this reference, from the first publisher of the Book and (if different) each U.S. publisher of the Book. In addition, if Producer determines in its sole discretion that procuring the consent or release of any other person or persons may be necessary or advisable in connection with the exercise of any of the rights granted or to be granted to Producer hereunder, Author shall use best efforts to procure and deliver to Producer, as soon as possible after execution of this agreement, an executed original consent or release (in a form satisfactory to Producer) from each such person. In connec-

tion therewith, Author will provide Producer with executed original copies of any consents or releases previously obtained by Author in connection with the Property.

Other waivers. This is where the producer gets the author's cooperation and approval to go after other waivers from persons whose lives are implicated in the story (an issue of publicity rights) or who might have contributed to the story in a direct creative way (an issue of copyright law).

Turnaround and reversion.

The word "turnaround" is movie business jargon. I don't know where it came from, but here is what it means: The producer options or purchases the rights and starts down the development highway. It may be a good day and the condition of the road might be smooth and trouble free. Or it may be bad weather and a rocky road. In fact, after a couple of mediocre drafts of the screenplay or a couple of rejections by directors or stars or because some current event makes the project unpolitic or for about a hundred other reasons the producer might come to a place in the road where he or she can go no farther. The project is burdened with expense. It's going nowhere and it is here that the producer has to make a turn and go in a different direction. What happens to the rights? Well, that is the point of the turnaround provision. (Reversion is a different concept. It means that after a while, under certain circumstances, if nothing happens with the property, the author will get the rights back entirely—even if the producer has exercised the option.)

Author's turnaround right. In this provision, after the producer tries for seven years, it is the author's turn to try. He has one year, in this draft. If the author is successful in setting the project up (and keep in mind that the screenplay that didn't exist at the time the parties entered into the option agreement now exists at the expense of the producer), the producer agrees to deed the screenplay over to the author. The term here is "quit claim"—which means that the author gets whatever rights the producer has, no more no less, in the screenplay and there are no representations and warranties that go with it. The author has to pay for the screenplay, of course, and in this case the author is obliged to reimburse the producer for any out-of-pocket costs and expenses incurred in connection with the creation of the screenplay, plus interest. If the author is unsuccessful in setting up the project, then the author doesn't owe the producer anything.

If Producer exercises the Option but principal photography of the Picture does not commence within seven (7) years after such exercise, then as of the expiration of such seven (7) year period, Author shall have a one (1) year turnaround period within which to set up the Picture elsewhere. If during the turnaround period Author is able to set up the Picture elsewhere, Producer shall quitclaim all of Producer's rights in and to the Picture to Author or Author's designee provided that Producer is contemporaneously reimbursed for all out-of-pocket costs and expenses relating to the Picture (excluding any amounts previously paid to Author hereunder) plus accrued interest thereon at an annual rate equal to 125% of the prime rate announced from time to time by the Producer Friendly Bank in Bigville, California. If during the turnaround period Author is not able to set up the Picture elsewhere or Producer is not reimbursed for its out-of-pocket costs and expenses (plus interest thereon) as provided above, then Producer shall have no further obligations to Author under this paragraph.

Reversion. Most authors are not at all willing to accept a mere turnaround right; rather, they insist on a full reversion of rights. In a reversion, once the producer has had a chance to set up the project and failed, the agreement terminates and the rights (but usually not the right in the screenplay) revert to the author. Reversion is a harsh penalty for failing to set the project up. However, if the property is hot, it is onerous from the author's perspective for the property to be off the market for an inordinate amount of time. Something has to give. Producers who are fortunate enough to get a hot property, usually have about five years to make something happen—even after they exercise the option.

Anything in this agreement to the contrary notwithstanding, in the event that principal photography of the Picture has not commenced within five (5) years after the exercise of the Option pursuant to this agreement, then this agreement shall immediately terminate and shall thereafter be deemed null and void, and all rights licensed to Producer hereunder shall automatically revert to Author free and clear of any obligation to Producer.

Using Someone Else's Life—Publicity Rights

Many movie projects are not based on a novel or original story written by other persons or the producer; many stories are based on real events (for example, *Titanic* and *Pearl Harbor*) and real people (for example, *All the President's Men* and *Ali*). It is the real people aspect of this brand of movie project that raises some interesting legal questions. I think that it is always helpful to take a common sense view of legal situations and I think it is especially important in this area. Imagine that you become, without your permission, the subject of a movie. Thousands, maybe millions, of people will become familiar with the intimate—perhaps unflattering—details of your life. Imagine, moreover, that in this movie the producer gets some of these details wrong, giving the impression (or perhaps directly stating) that you have engaged in socially unacceptable or even reprehensible behavior.

Life story rights and consulting agreements.

The first question is this: Does the law afford a person "life story rights" that may be granted or withheld by such person? It may be surprising to you, but the short answer is no. The second question, therefore, is this: Then why do producers (and their attorneys) draft life story rights agreements? Indeed, it is customary in doing a "biopic" (a biographical picture) to negotiate a deal with and pay (in some cases a large amount of) money to people about whom a movie will be based.

It is easy to jump to the conclusion that an individual owns the exclusive right to his or her own life story. Lawyers talk about a "right of publicity" and a "right of privacy." But these two legal theories do not confer the exclusive right to anyone to control how his or her (or a deceased ancestor's) life story will be told. Therefore, a producer can make a movie based on true life events without paying the true life persons who participated in such events (or their living descendants).

Professor Thomas McCarthy, in his treatise *The Rights of Publicity and Privacy* explains why the law fails to grant life story rights exclusively to any person, including the person whose life it is:

A moment's thought about the relation between free speech, "news" and "history" reveals why this must be so. If the law mandated that the permission of every living person and the descendants of every deceased person must be obtained to include mention of them in the news and stories, both in documentary and docudrama telling, then they would have the right to refuse permission unless the story was told "their way." That would mean that those who are the participants in news and history could censor and write the story. And their descendants could do the same. This would be an anathema to the core concept of free speech and a free press. News should be written by free and independent reporters and history written by historians who tell the story the way they see it, not the way the participants and their heirs want it to be told.

The law does not give anyone the legal "right" to own history in this way. There is and should be no such thing as the "official news" or the "approved version of history." Thus, the law does not permit anyone to control who tells their story or how their story is told.[11]

Defamation and privacy.

Notwithstanding the fact that producers can legally base a movie on the life story or the life events of individuals, there are legal limits. The producer cannot tell injurious lies about a person, as this is defamation.[12] Likewise, producers cannot put someone in a false light.[13] Producers cannot disclose private and embarrassing facts about a person in violation of the privacy laws. Producers can pursue historical events and the persons who lived them, even if the portrayal of such is not flattering—but the producer must be careful.

The life story rights agreement.

Producers find two compelling reasons to pursue an agreement with the subjects of movies. First, the producer wants to avoid litigation. Thus, contracts with persons who are the subject of motion pictures usually require such persons to expressly waive their right to litigate. In addition, producers may find it to their advantage to have the cooperation of the subject (or the person's family) in providing story details and source material—diaries, photographs, personal artifacts, personal recollections, etc.—for the movie. Thus, the modern-day life story rights agreement is typically a combination waiver and consulting agreement.

Life story rights. The grant of life story rights resembles in form the grant of rights in any rights agreement. On closer examination, however, the rights referred to are not rooted in copyright law. Rather, the rights spoken of here are rooted in publicity rights (name and likeness) referred to in actors' agreements. The legal effect of this language is, in essence, a waiver by the person giving the grant of any claims that this person might otherwise have against the producer of the movie.

> For good and valuable consideration of $5,000, Johnny True Leif ("Leif") grants to Biopics R Us, LLC ("BRU") a two-year option to purchase the exclusive, unconditional, irrevocable and perpetual right to use, simulate and portray, and license to others to use, simulate and portray, the name, likeness, voice and biographical material of Leif, and to otherwise depict Leif in connection with one or more theatrical and/or television (including standard, cable, pay, syndicated or other) motion pictures, television programs (including, but not limited to, mini-series, specials, pilots and series), literary publications and/or other productions or works based upon the career and life events of Leif (individually and collectively referred to as the "Work"), and to advertise, publicize, promote and exploit the Work and all ancillary, subsidiary and related rights therein and thereto, throughout the universe in perpetuity, in any manner, by any means or methods and in any medium (whether now in existence or hereafter devised) which BRU may desire.

Portrayal. The producer wants to make sure that he has flexibility in using the life events of the person in question. The agreement should clarify, for example, that the producer can select any actor he or she wants to portray the person, without having to consult or give approval rights to the person (the person in question, of course, would love to have these rights—but the producer should resist). Moreover, the producer should clarify that he or she has the right to use the events in the person's name or not (as there may be reasons not to use real names—even in a story based on true events). An interesting problem is fictionalization. The producer will need some flexibility in using the life events for the sake of the story—producers need "dramatic license." The person granting the rights may wish to resist this type of flexibility for fear that the producer will take unwarranted liberties. If this issue arises, it will be important to negotiate for as much flexibility as possible. In the example below, the producer uses the words "in any manner which [producer] may deem appropriate," but this may not give producer the right to actually fictionalize.

Without limiting the generality of the foregoing, BRU will have the right to represent, depict and impersonate the life events and story of Leif, in whole or in part, under his own name or a fictitious name, in any manner which BRU may deem proper, and by any actor chosen by BRU to portray any incidents, episodes, exploits, characters, dialogues, scenes and situations of any nature whatsoever concerning Leif's life and career.

Agreement to consult. Another common (and often important) feature of a life story agreement is a promise on the part of the person granting the rights (or his or her family) to consult with the producer and supply personal materials, such as diaries and other personal effects.

The undersigned agrees to provide BRU access, on an exclusive basis, to all documentation in the possession or under the control of the undersigned relating to Leif (including, but not limited to, research material, memoirs, diaries, articles, notes whether written by Leif or by a third party or third parties, whether published or unpublished, whether or not in the public domain) and BRU shall have the right to make copies of all such documentation and use the same in connection with the development, production, distribution and/or exploitation of any Work hereunder. At mutually convenient times and places, Leif hereby agrees to meet with BRU and/or the writer(s) of any screenplay(s) or teleplay(s) for the Work and provide, as requested, information, on an exclusive basis, related to Leif's life story.

Representations and warranties. The representations and warranties of the subject reflect the different legal footing of the life story rights agreement. The producer wants to know that the person is who the person says he or she is, and is competent in a legal sense to enter into the agreement and there is no other person claiming anything inconsistent with the agreement.

The undersigned warrants and represents that he is Johnny True Leif and has the legal power and authority to execute this agreement and grant the rights herein granted; that the consent of no person or entity is required in order for Leif to enter into and perform this agreement; and that Leif is not aware of any person or entity claiming to have any interest in the life events or career of Leif or any of the rights granted to BRU by Leif.

Other provisions. The life story rights agreement, like the other rights agreements we have discussed, contains other provisions. Since this agreement is structured as a option agreement, the agreement must describe the mechanics of exercising the option and paying the purchase price. Other miscellaneous provisions (the right to assign the agreement, further assurances, and so forth) will also be added.

BOOK TWO

THE SCREENPLAY: NOTHING HAPPENS UNTIL IT'S FINISHED

Close your eyes and imagine the following scene. It's the first day of shooting for your great movie. Your star actor has just emerged from an expensive trailer. There are cameras everywhere. The quantity of the lighting and sound equipment boggle the mind. The crew is standing around. The catering truck is parked off to the side ready to serve the gaggle of cast and crew. The makeup trailer and costume trailer are there. The director is in his or her chair. And your accountant is there—keeping track of the thousands, perhaps millions, of dollars that are starting to slide into that huge sinkhole called a movie budget. Your idea is still great and your confidence is still strong, but wait. Where do we start? What are the actors suppose to say to the camera? What does the prince wear in this scene? Is this the castle scene or are they riding horses? Horses? Do we need horses? And meanwhile the money keeps sliding and sliding. What's happening here is that you are having a nightmare. There is no screenplay—no blueprint—from which to carefully plan every scene and detail that must be decided. And that's one of the reasons why, at least in America, nothing happens until the screenplay is finished.

Hiring a Writer

THE SCREENPLAY AS A BLUEPRINT

The screenplay (or script, as it is sometimes called) is the blueprint from which a motion picture is made. In America, a great deal of attention is paid to its creation. For high-profile projects, even the first draft of a screenplay can cost seven figures. Rewrites are virtually always required, often by various writers or teams of writers. All this attention exists because the general rule is that nothing happens until the screenplay is finished.

Exceptions do exist, but there are reasons for the rule. Go back to the beginning of book 2 and revisit the scene of chaos in your mind. The majority of movies in America are multimillion-dollar endeavors. Some movies cost as much as a medium-size corporation, an office tower in Century City, or a jet aircraft. No one in his or her right mind would try to build a business, erect a building, or create an airplane without a plan. And the same is true with a movie.

Until the screenplay is done, you are not ready to start. There are too many unanswered questions. How many scenes? How many and what type of special effects? The cast, the crew, and everything else is dependent on the screenplay. And the biggest question—"Is this story something that people will want to watch?"—hasn't been answered. The financial risk alone is too great. And, as we shall see, there are other reasons too why nothing really happens until the screenplay is finished.

Form.

The screenplay contains the scenes in chronological sequence (even though the director rarely shoots the motion picture in continuity—scene by scene in chronological order—anymore, the screenplay has to be read this way), gives the context and point of view of each scene, introduces the characters and sets forth the dialogue spoken by the characters and even describes the costumes, props, and other physical elements of each scene. There is a standard form used in writing a script. An explanation about this form is beyond the scope of this book. There are several books on screenwriting that will show the format and any class on screenwriting will cover that same ground. There are also several computer software programs that will help the writer generate the form. The first time I read a screenplay, the format was a distraction. But after reading several of them (especially ones that I thought were good), it became easy to project a mental image from the words on the page. Whether you like it not, you are not likely to make any inroads on changing the format. Learn it and love it.

Good, bad, and ugly.

As noted before, I do not know the formula for writing or identifying a script that will yield a "hit" movie. People will tell you that a good script has a beginning, a middle, and an end and is about 120 pages long (because a standard motion picture is around two hours and generally speaking, it is said, one page equals one minute of film time). All I know is that art is subjective and this leads to the following conclusion based in historical fact: Good ideas sometimes get made into bad scripts; bad ideas sometimes get made into good scripts; good scripts sometimes never get made (or take a long time to get made) into motion pictures; bad scripts sometimes get made into motion pictures; and so on. William Goldman, a famous Hollywood screenwriter, once wrote: *"Nobody knows anything."* [1]

Writers.

The pool of writers to draw from is large and diverse. The price ranges from dirt cheap to several million dollars. No easy rules here either—it is not always true (probably more true than not, however) that you will get what you pay for. However, the stature (and therefore the price) of the writer may be relevant to the "package" (discussed in detail later on). It is reasonable to expect a WGA writer to know the standard format and to be responsible for delivering the script within the schedule allotted. Most producers hiring a writer will call around about the writer's reliability and his price. Other producers will, as a matter of industry custom, generally disclose this information. They will expect you to return the favor someday.

Hiring a professional writer.

Of course, the world of writers can be divided into many categories (good and bad, for example), but the two categories that you should be concerned about, in a legal sense, are professional (in other words, a member of the WGA, or Writers Guild of America) and nonprofessional (or nonmember). The WGA rules demand that only a signatory of one of the applicable WGA agreements may hire a WGA member. Thus, a writer who is a WGA member cannot sign a contract with your production company, unless your production company is a WGA signatory. Moreover, a WGA signatory must hire only WGA writers.[2] Becoming a signatory is an involved process that will be discussed more specifically later on. Even so, you will need the advice of an attorney or more experienced producer in connection with the signatory process. The WGA agreement, as a collective bargaining agreement, gives WGA member writers certain rights, many of which will be discussed later. You will need an attorney to help you understand some of the nuances of this agreement.

PAPERING THE WRITER'S DEAL

The engagement.

The producer starts by engaging the writer to create a first draft and one set of revisions to that draft—the actual lingo is "a draft and a set." The producer specifically sets the parameters of the assignment by telling the writer on what material to base the screenplay. For example, the producer might tell the writer to base the screenplay on a treatment, a novel, a collection of news clippings, an old movie, a group of comic book characters, a magazine article, and so on. The producer clarifies that the producer has the right to shape the resulting screenplay by mandating the incorporation of the producer's ideas, concepts, changes, and/or suggestions.

Draft means the first draft of the script. The writer is required to deliver a draft of the script in standard format. The draft should be somewhere around 120 pages long. The draft, of course, can be based on another work (such as a treatment, book, or story pitch), historical event (which still means it can be based on a treatment or book, but can also involve newsprint and other research sources), a personal event (from your own life or someone else's); another motion picture (in which case the resulting motion picture is called a prequel, sequel, or a remake); a combination of some or all of the above, etc. The producer usually guides the story and other parameters of the assignment.

"Set of revisions" means a revision of a draft. The revisions are usually based on notes from the producer (you) and other creative persons attached to the project. A set of revisions is usually considered a bigger job than a "polish" (see below). Once the revisions are done, the resulting work, of course, is called a draft (in other words, the first set of revisions leads to the second draft). A revision usually incorporates significant changes in or elaborations of character development and story, or might even amount to a complete rewrite.

> Producer hereby engages Writer, and Writer hereby accepts such engagement, to write a first draft screenplay (the "First Draft") and a set of revisions thereto (the "First Revisions"). The First Draft and the First Revisions shall be based on the novel entitled *The Quest* written by Kelly C. Crabb and such other material as Producer may supply or assign to Writer (collectively, the "Property") and shall be written in accordance with and incorporate such materials, ideas, concepts, changes and/or suggestions as may be presented to Writer by Producer.

Additional set and polish.
The writing process rarely ends with a single set of revisions. Thus, the producer anticipates the need for more revisions and, in the end, the producer will want a polish. It is important to the producer, however, to have the ability to control whether this writer continues or not. The producer may determine after the first draft that a fresh writer is needed—or not. This is how the producer makes it his or her option.

"Optional set." This means a second set of revisions at the option of the producer. The option must be exercised within a certain time frame; after that, if the producer wants this writer to do the revision, he must wait for the writer's convenience. The option is sometimes

not the producer's. For example, if the writer's bargaining power is sufficient, the writer may insist that he or she get the assignment to do the revision. Alternatively, the writer may at least have the right to be offered the chance to do the revision. From the author's point of view, there may be more than vanity involved; as I will point out later, the author's bonus and participation, if any, could be affected by the involvement of other writers.

Polish. A final visit to the script to clean up all the formatting, spelling, numbering, and other problems is the polish. It will not usually incorporate major story changes or elaborations. Often, but not always, the polish is included within the fee for the first draft.

> Writer hereby grants to Producer the irrevocable option (the "First Option") to engage Writer to write a second set of revisions to the screenplay (the "Second Revisions") suitable for use in the production of the Picture. Producer may exercise the First Option by written notice to Writer at any time prior to eighteen (18) months after the expiration of the First Option Period (as defined below); provided, however, that if Producer exercises the First Option after the expiration of the First Option Period, Writer's obligation to write the Second Revisions shall be subject to Writer's then-prior conflicting professional writing obligations (determined at the time of such exercise). In addition, Writer hereby grants to Producer the irrevocable option (the "Second Option") to engage Writer to write a complete polish of the screenplay (the "Polish"). Producer may exercise the Second Option by written notice to Writer at any time prior to eighteen (18) months after the expiration of the Second Option Period (as defined below); provided, however, that if Producer exercises the Second Option after the expiration of the Second Option Period, Writer's obligation to write the Second Revisions shall be subject to Writer's then-prior conflicting professional writing obligations (determined at the time of such exercise). The Second Revisions and the Polish (if any) also shall be based on the Property and shall be written in accordance with and incorporate such materials, ideas, concepts, changes and/or suggestions as may be reasonably presented to Writer by Producer.

Writing period.

Producers are always in a hurry. Remember the time limits imposed by the option agreement for the underlying rights? Even if the movie is to be based on the producer's own treatment, once the producer starts laying out money for the screenplay, he will be in a hurry to get the money back. The only way he can do that is to finish the screenplay and get the movie made. Therefore, the producer will impose time limits on the writing. Here's how it works in the contract:

Start date. The writer usually starts immediately after the agreement is signed, but sometimes the writer and producer must negotiate the date. The writer may be finishing up another project or certain conditions to the effectiveness of the agreement may not have been fulfilled.

> Writer shall commence services in writing the First Draft on a date to be designated by Producer (but not later than ten (10) days after execution of this agreement).

Delivery date. A normal writing period is twelve weeks, but it is negotiable. The delivery date is important because it triggers the payment of the second half of the writing fee for the draft and starts the "first reading period" (see below).

> Not later than twelve (12) weeks after the date designated by Producer for the commencement of Writer's services hereunder, Writer shall deliver the First Draft to Producer.

Reading period and delivery of first set of revisions. After the first draft is submitted, there is a defined "reading period," during which the producer and the other creative consultants on the project (the director, for example) read the script and make their notes or comments. These notes are given to the writer and then the writer turns to the task of incorporating the notes into the screenplay. The writer is given a certain time, here six weeks, to deliver the first set of revisions.

> After such delivery, Producer may advise Writer of its requested additions to and deletions from and changes to be made in the First Draft and Writer shall write and deliver to Producer the First Revisions in accordance with such instructions not later than six (6) weeks after Producer shall have given such instructions to Writer; provided, however, that if Producer does not give such instructions

within six (6) weeks, Writer's obligation to write and deliver the First Revisions shall be subject to Writer's then-prior conflicting professional writing obligations (determined at the time such instructions are given).

Second set of revisions. As discussed above, if the screenplay still needs more work, the producer can either search for new blood or exercise his option to have the original writer do it. If the original writer is to perform the revision, the producer gives the screenplay and the notes from the first set of revisions to that person. After the notes are presented, the writer has another period, here six weeks, to finish and deliver the second set of revisions.

If Producer exercises the First Option, Producer may advise Writer of its requested additions to and deletions from and changes to be made in the material theretofore delivered and Writer shall write and deliver to Producer the Second Revisions in accordance with such instructions not later than six (6) weeks after Producer gives such instructions to Writer; provided, however, that if Producer does not give such instructions within four (4) weeks, Writer's obligation to write and deliver the Second Revisions shall be subject to Writer's then-prior conflicting professional writing obligations (determined at the time such instructions are given).

The polish. If the second set produces a screenplay that is almost finished, the producer may exercise his or her option to have the original writer do a polish. The producer can still ask for additions, deletions, and other changes in the polish, but the extent of these changes is limited. Here, the writer has four weeks to get the polish finished.

If Producer exercises the Second Option, Producer may advise Writer of its requested additions to and deletions from and changes to be made in the material theretofore delivered and Writer shall write and deliver to Producer the Polish in accordance with such instructions not later than four (4) weeks after Producer gives such instructions to Writer; provided, however, that if Producer does not give such instructions within four (4) weeks, Writer's obligation to write and deliver the Polish shall be subject to Writer's then-prior conflicting professional writing obligations (determined at the time such instructions are given).

Writer's compensation.

There are three common forms of compensation for the writer: (1) an "up-front fee" or "fixed compensation," (2) a "production bonus," and (3) a "back-end" participation. We'll discuss all three in the context of the writer's deal.

Up-front fee. The up-front fee (or fixed compensation) is the writer's guarantee. If he finishes the screenplay and lives up to the terms of the agreement, the writer will get the up-front fee. The other forms of compensation are contingent on the movie actually getting made. The amount of the fee is a matter of negotiation. The WGA minimum is often used as a gauge. The writer's previous fee quote (the writer can tell you the name of the producer who paid the last fee and you can call to confirm the quote) is another possible index. The success of the writer's last project might also be a factor. Awards (such as recognition by the WGA or the receipt of an Academy Award) will also be relevant.

> Provided that Writer is not in material default hereunder, as full and complete compensation for all of Writer's services hereunder, all of the results and proceeds of Writer's services, all rights granted or to be granted to Producer hereunder and all representations, warranties, indemnities and agreements made or given by Writer in connection herewith, Producer shall pay to Writer the sum of Ninety Thousand Dollars ($90,000) (the "Fee"). The Fee shall accrue upon completion and delivery of all forms of work required by Producer hereunder (including all optional forms of work) but shall be payable to Writer as follows: (i) Forty-five Thousand Dollars ($45,000) upon the full execution of this agreement and the commencement of Writer's services hereunder; and (ii) Forty-five Thousand Dollars ($45,000) upon completion and delivery of the First Draft.

It is customary to pay the writer one half of the up-front fee at the time the writer commences writing and the other half when the writer delivers the first draft of the screenplay.

Production bonus. Notice that in the provision below the writer receives a bonus only *if* the motion picture gets made. That's why it is called a "production bonus." The bonus, therefore, is contingent and not guaranteed. In addition, the writer doesn't get the bonus if he or she is in material breach of the agreement. The amount of the bonus is affected by other factors.

> If Producer produces the Picture based on the Material (as defined below) and Writer is not in material default hereunder, Producer shall pay to Writer . . .

"Sole writing credit." The writer gets 100 percent of the stated bonus (here, $50,000) if he or she gets sole writing credit. Some explanation is required here. If the producer hires only one writer (or one writer team) to write the screenplay (and no one else works on the screenplay) that writer or team is a lock to get sole or exclusive writing credit. However, usually, things are more complicated. The producer may hire a writer to write a draft and a set and then decide to bring in a second writer to write a second set and perhaps a third to do a polish. In such a case, who gets credit? If the writers are members of the WGA, the producer will be obliged to let the WGA sort out the credit situation.[3] Even where the writers are not members of the WGA, the producer and the writers often agree by contract to use the WGA guidelines in determining writer credit.

> If, in connection with the Picture, Writer receives sole "screenplay by" or sole "written by" credit, Producer will pay writer (i) an amount equal to the excess (if any) of the sum of Fifty Thousand Dollars ($50,000) (the "Bonus Amount"), payable within ten (10) days after final determination of the writing credits of the Picture, and (ii) an amount equal to two and one-half percent ($2\frac{1}{2}\%$) of 100% of the Net Proceeds (as defined below) derived from the Picture.

I should mention that some writers write as a team and sign contracts as a team. If that is the case, the sole writing credit provisions will apply to the team.

Two types of production bonuses. In the above example, there are two types of production bonuses: First, there is usually a stated fixed amount—here, $50,000 (but there is a wide range of amounts). This amount is paid out of the production budget of the picture and is paid within a short period of time (here, ten days) within the date that the sole credit status is determined. Second, the writer is entitled to a participation in "net profits" of a certain percentage (here, 2.5 percent, a common figure).

Shared credit. If a writer has to share writing credit with another writer (who is not a writing partner) for whatever reason, the writer will receive less than 100 percent of the production bonus. In this case, which is the most common, the formula allows the original writer (assuming that the writer gets any credit at all), to get one half of both the fixed bonus amount and the participation percentage. The basic theory, of course, is to allow the writers who share writing credit to share the bonus. Please note, however, that it is possible that more than two persons will get shared writing credit. The draft below, therefore, favors the original writer, because the second two writers—if your lawyer is doing his job when you sign on the next writers—will have to share what is left over.[4]

> If, in connection with the Picture, Writer receives shared "screenplay by" or shared "written by" credit with any other writer or writers, Producer will pay writer an amount equal to one-half of the Bonus Amount, payable within ten (10) days after final determination of the writing credits of the Picture.

Back-end participation. The third type of compensation to the writer is called a participation, because here the writer is participating in the profits of the movie—or the "back end" of the movie. We'll talk more about the concept of "profits" later on, but in general when the word is used in a movie context it means the revenue that is left over after the deduction of various costs. Simply put, profits can be stated in the following formula: "Gross revenues minus costs equals profits." In reality, of course, calculating profits can be very difficult. In the illustration below, assuming that the writer gets a *shared* credit, the writer gets 1¼ percent of 100 percent of the net proceeds (another way of saying net profits). Let's assume that the writer has to share the written by credit with another person. Let's also assume the producer is able to make the movie for $20 million and that 20 million people buy a ticket to the movie at $10 apiece. The gross (or total) revenue is $200 million—not bad. Roughly speaking, the theater owners will take about 50 percent of that amount (probably more) and certain charges and fees will be applied to the balance, in addition to the cost of the movie itself. If we assume that the various charges equal $60 million, theoretically there is a pool of $20 million of net profits from which the writer gets to take his 1.25 percent (or $250,000). That's the main idea—if only it always worked out this way. The actual formulas for net profits or net proceeds seldom yield any money at all, because the certain charges concept that I use so casually throughout above is often very large.

> If, in connection with the Picture, Writer receives sole "screenplay by" or sole "written by" credit, Writer will receive an amount equal to two and one-half percent (2½%) of 100% of the Net Proceeds derived from the Picture. If Writer receives shared "screenplay by" or shared "written by" credit with any other writer or writers, Producer will pay Writer an amount equal to one and one-quarter percent (1¼%) of 100% of the Net Proceeds derived from the Picture.

Future writing projects (sequels and remakes).
The original writer will take the opportunity as the first writer to the table, to try to lock in future writing assignments. From the producer's point of view, there are too many variables to promise the original writer an exclusive on future projects. For example, the original writer might not receive sole (or even any) writing credit on the project, the writer might not even be a professional writer at the time any sequel or remake of the movie is made. The writer's attorney will nevertheless seek ways to keep his writer in the game.

Conditions to future writing assignments. Notice that in the provision below the writer's right of first refusal is subject to several conditions: (1) The movie has to have been produced. Given the definition of remake and sequel, this condition is more or less obvious. Still lawyers want to avoid any doubt. Maybe a future project of the producer might look a lot like this project, but is based on other rights. Thus, the lawyer makes it clear that this movie is the base project. (2) The writer cannot be in material breach of the original writer's contract. The producer would hate to have to hire a writer who had failed to deliver a draft or set or polish on time the first time around, for example. (3) This writer has to receive sole writing credit in the original project. The producer wants to make sure that it is this writer's talents that got the picture made. (4) The writer has to be actively involved in the writing business. There is no way to predict when a sequel will be made. Remakes are presumed to be a ways off. The writer may be in retirement or on to different things. The producer doesn't want to be obligated to hire a has-been. (5) The writer must be available. The producer doesn't want to be in a position of having to wait to produce the movie. (6) The whole deal is subject to studio or network approval. The producer doesn't want to be obligated to hire a writer the studio or network will reject (right along with the project).

> Provided that the Picture is produced, Writer is not in material default hereunder, Writer receives sole "screenplay by" or sole "written by" credit upon final determination of the writing credits of the Picture, and Writer is then actively engaged as a writer in the motion picture or television industry (as applicable) and is available to render writing services as and when reasonably required by Producer, then if Producer intends to engage a writer to perform writing services in connection with a theatrical sequel or remake or (subject to approval by the applicable network or other licensor) a television sequel or remake (including a series pilot or an initial episode if there is no pilot, an episodic series or a mini-series) within seven (7) years after the initial release of the Picture . . .

Right of first negotiation. If all these conditions are met, the producer will give the writer the first chance to negotiate a deal for writing services with respect to the sequel or remake. This provision is written as a first right of negotiation, but there are other ways to state this right.[5] It is stipulated here that the future deal must be no less favorable to the writer than this deal. From the producer's point of view, this can be justified on the assumption that there will be inflation in the marketplace as time goes by and, thus, future deals will probably cost more than this deal. This logic is a bit tortured, however, because there are a lot of factors involved—the writer's future track record, for one. The producer protects himself a bit by saying that the deal will be in accordance with "industry standards," but who knows what that is and, even if it can be deciphered now, what it will be in the future.

> [P]rior to engaging any other writer(s) to render writing services in connection with such sequel or remake, Producer will negotiate in good faith with Writer with respect to such sequel or remake on terms no less favorable than those hereunder for a theatrical sequel or remake or on terms to be negotiated in good faith in accordance with industry standards for a television sequel or remake.

Additional payments (bonuses) related to sequels and remakes.
Although not listed in this illustration, if the writer is successful in negotiating a right of first refusal, etc., with respect to sequels and remakes, the writer will also want to negotiate the same type of structure with respect to compensation: a fixed fee (which is given no matter what), a production bonus (which is received if the picture is produced), and a participation (or piece of the net). The general compensation formula for such services is one half of the original writer's fee for sequels and one third for remakes—this normally applies to the production bonus and the participation only (the writer still wants the fee for writing). In addition, the writer's bonus and participation are normally subject to dilution for shared credit. Thus, if there are three writers who get credit, the writer will get one third of what he would have received for sole credit.

Expenses.
The writer will want to have his job-related expenses covered. For example, there are possible travel, accommodations, ground transportation, and per diem (meals and incidentals).

Long distances. When is it reasonable for writers to require travel expenses? Because hours can be spent arguing this point, a customary solution is to provide for expenses when the writer has to work at a location more than a hundred miles from home.

> In the event that Producer requires Writer to render services at a location more than 100 miles from Writer's principal residence (which Writer represents is and will be in the Los Angeles, California, metropolitan area) . . .

Class distinctions. Writers and producers will argue over class distinctions when it comes to air travel and hotel accommodations. This, of course, is a money issue for the producer and a convenience issue for the writer. How big is your bargaining power?

> Producer shall furnish Writer with one (1) round trip transportation (by air, if available) between such residence (or wherever Writer may be at the time, if closer) and such location. In addition, during the continuance of such services required by Producer at such location, Producer shall provide Writer with reasonable hotel accommoda-

tions, reasonable ground transportation and a reasonable per diem in light of the location.

Credit.

Given that the bonus and the participation are based on sole or shared credits and that future employment depends on establishing a track record, it will not surprise you to learn that credits are a big deal in the writer's agreement. First, there is the issue of whether or not the writer gets a credit at all. Second, the producer and writer will discuss the size and use of the credit.

Writer shall be accorded credit for Writer's writing services hereunder in accordance with the following guidelines:

Wording of credit. The accepted forms of credit are "Screenplay by Kelly Crabb," "Screenplay Kelly Crabb" and "Written by Kelly Crabb," with the third formulation meaning that the writer has written the screenplay and has developed the original story on which it is based. The following illustration is taken from a standard attachment to a writer's agreement with the title "Credit Policies and Procedures." It is is more or less reflective of the custom in the industry.[6]

Screen credit for the screenplay authorship of a feature-length picture will be worded "Screenplay by Kelly C. Crabb" (or "Screenplay Kelly C. Crabb").

Limitation of credits. The producer and writer can agree that there will be a limit on the number of persons getting credit. Here the limit is three individual writers or two teams of writers. This could be a problem later on for reasons that are obvious. If the first three writers fail to get the job done, your options related to the other writers you bring in are limited. However, "script doctors" (writers hired at the last stages to fix problems in an existing screenplay) often work without a credit—you may have to pay them accordingly.

Except in unusual cases, screen credit for the screenplay will not be shared by more than two (2) writers and in no case will the names of more than three (3) writers be used; provided, however, that two (2) established writing teams recognized and employed as such and of not more than two (2) members each may share screen credit for screenplay.

Standard. In the illustration below, the standard is "chiefly responsible." I don't know exactly what this standard means, but I can say that it is subjective. One person could write a hundred words and another a thousand words and it would still be possible, I suppose, to say that the first person was chiefly responsible.

> The intention and spirit of the award of credits being to emphasize the prestige and importance of the screenplay achievement, the one (1), two (2) or at most three (3) writers, or two (2) teams, chiefly responsible for the completed work will be the only screen writers to receive screenplay credit. The only exception to the foregoing shall be a picture on which one (1) writer (or a team) writes both the original story and screenplay. In this case the credit may be worded "Written by."

Writer's input. If there is more than one writer and all agree which two or three (remember that three is the maximum number in this illustration) will be given a credit, that decision will stand. However, note that the producer normally is the one who gets to decide who has substantially contributed.

> When more than one (1) writer has substantially contributed to the screenplay authorship of a picture, then all such writers will have the right to agree unanimously among themselves as to which one (1) or two (2) or in exceptional cases three (3) of them, or two (2) teams of the nature above mentioned, shall receive credit on the screen for the authorship of the screenplay.

Producer's input. In this example, the producer gets to say which writers have made a substantial contribution. The producer also gets to decide where to put the credit and what the credit is for. When the credits start to role, the frame of film in which the credit appears is called a "title card." Think of the old vaudeville stage shows where the credits were placed on a card on an easel on stage. A "single card credit" is one name appearing alone on screen at one given moment. In this example, all writers are placed on the same card. The producer can decide to have one card for writers ("Screenplay by Kelly Crabb"), one for original story ("Story by Kelly Crabb") and one for source material (for example, "Based on the novel *The Quest,* by Kelly Crabb"). The producer can, if he wants to, let the public know that other writers, who didn't get credit, worked on the project.

Producer shall have the right to determine in which one of the following places the screenplay credit shall appear on the screen: (i) On the main title card of the picture; (ii) on a title card on which credits are given only for the screenplay; (iii) on a title card on which credits are given for the original story; (iv) on a title card on which credits are given for the source(s) of the material upon which the screenplay was based.

A writer whose contribution is judged by Producer to represent a substantial portion of the completed screenplay shall be considered a substantial contributor. As a substantial contributor, such writer shall be entitled to participate in the procedure for determination of screen credits. The screen credits and also the work of writers making substantial contributions but not receiving screen credit may be publicized by Producer.

Writers' protest procedures. If the substantial contributors don't agree on who should get credit, then the producer decides on a tentative basis. He mails out a notice to the writers and gives them a chance to read the finished script and then make a written protest. The actual procedures are more complicated than those listed below, but these steps will give a flavor of the process. In the final analysis, in this case, the producer makes the final determination after hearing all the evidence. If the writers are guild members, the guild itself employs similar rules and makes the determination.

Before the screen credits for screen authorship are finally determined, Producer will send a written notice to each writer who is a substantial contributor to the screenplay. This notice will state Producer's choice of credits on a tentative basis, together with the names of the other substantial contributors and their addresses last known to Producer. Producer will keep the final determination of screen credits open until a time specified in the notice by Producer. If by the time specified a written notice of objection to the tentative credits or request to read the script has not been delivered to Producer from any of the writers concerned, then except as otherwise provided herein, the tentative credits will become final.

However, if a protest or request to read the script is received by Producer from any writer concerned within the time specified in said notice, Producer will withhold final determination of credits until a time to be specified by Producer.

Producer not liable. The prudent producer will get all parties involved to sign off on this procedure which provides that, in any event, the writers will have no claim against the producer related to the producer's decision.

> The writer shall have no rights or claims of any nature against Producer growing out of or concerning any determination of credits in the manner herein provided, and all such rights or claims are hereby specifically waived.

Use of credits by distributors and exhibitors. In addition to the determination of credits, the contract deals with their use. The writer will want some assurance that the credits will show up on the movie itself and in advertisements of the movie and, most important, that those responsible for distributing the movie will comply. Thus, the writer obligates the producer to cause the distributor to comply. Note that in this example, the producer is under an obligation to cause the initial United States distributor to comply by contract, but the producer only has to use "reasonable efforts" to get the distributors outside of the United States (and even then only in the "major" foreign territories) to comply.

> Producer shall contractually require the initial U.S. theatrical distributor of the Picture to comply with Producer's credit obligations hereunder with respect to such distributor's exploitation of the Picture in the United States. In addition, Producer shall use reasonable efforts to instruct the initial theatrical distributors of the Picture in the major foreign territories to comply with Producer's credit obligations hereunder with respect to such distributors' exploitation of the Picture in such territories.

No casual or inadvertent failure. After the credit is finally determined, the producer's concern turns to a list of bad things that might happen if the credit somehow gets left off the movie. The following provision says, in essence, that unless the producer purposefully omits the credits there will not be a breach of contract. Rather, the producer will simply have to give it a reasonable shot to make it happen next time. The derivation of this standard term is not difficult to imagine. Adding credits to a movie is not cheap and the cost of a print keeps going higher.[7] Poster art and media advertising are expensive and, well, you get the idea. In this context, to give a writer the right to declare a breach and risk that such writer will cause all the prints, posters, and media promotions to be pulled in and redone would be unwise to say the least.

> No casual or inadvertent failure by Producer, and no failure of any third party, to comply with its obligations under this paragraph with respect to such credit shall be deemed a breach of this agreement by Producer. Notwithstanding the foregoing, upon receipt by Producer of written notice from Writer specifying such failure in reasonable detail, Producer shall use reasonable efforts prospectively to cure such failure for prints and advertisements prepared after Producer's receipt of such notice.

Services.

There are writers and then there are writers. Producers have learned this lesson over time and, therefore, have found it necessary and appropriate to clarify the nature of the writer's activities.

Doing your best and taking directions. The producer clarifies that the writer will not flake out and shirk his writing duties. He has to do his best. Lawyers know that the term "best efforts" has real legal meaning. With this standard, taking the money and declaring a three-month writer's block will not get the writer off the hook. In addition, the writer agrees to take reasonable directions from the producer. This is important, because some writers don't like to take directions. Put yourself in the position of a producer who spends a lot of money and time to acquire the rights to a famous novel and then spends a lot of money and time to acquire the services of a famous screenwriter, who turns in a screenplay that does not follow the plot points and characters of the novel. It happens. And when it does, the producer needs something to hang his hat on.

> Writer shall devote Writer's best time, attention, talents and capabilities to the service of Producer pursuant to this agreement. Writer shall comply with all reasonable requirements, directions, requests, rules and regulations made by Producer in connection with the Picture or the conduct of its business and shall render services hereunder whenever Producer may reasonably require in a competent, diligent, efficient, conscientious, artistic and professional manner and as reasonably instructed by Producer in all matters, including those involving artistic taste and judgment.

Place of services. The producer also designates the place of services. For instance, the producer may want to meet with the writer from time to time and have him show up for creative meetings with the director and others. If the writer disappears to his Alaska cabin with no phone service, you'll wish you'd put in a provision like this.

> Unless Producer shall agree otherwise, Writer shall perform all writing services hereunder in the Los Angeles metropolitan area.

Fit for a given purpose and delivery complete. The producer also wants to get across the idea that the writer is writing a screenplay for a certain type of movie. Thus, the producer will describe the movie in industry standard terms—here the movie is a "feature-length movie" (meaning that it is about two hours long) and that it is a "first-class movie" (meaning, I suppose, that it is not an off-market movie—pornography or chainsaw murders).

The term "delivery" in the context of a writer's deal is important because it triggers a payment. Here the producer warns that the producer doesn't have to accept the draft (that actual delivery doesn't constitute legal delivery) unless it complies with all of these standards.

> Writer shall ensure that all material delivered hereunder is full and complete in substance and in form, is suitable for use in connection with the production of a first-class feature-length theatrical motion picture and otherwise conforms to the requirements of this agreement. No submission or purported delivery to Producer of any material shall be deemed an actual delivery hereunder unless and until such material shall fully comply with the foregoing provisions.

Exclusivity. When the producer is paying a lot of money for a writer, he doesn't usually relish the thought of the writer working on someone else's script. Therefore, producers like to clarify that the writer is working, at least for a time, for producer and nobody else (including the writer). After the writer has turned in the draft, the producer may reasonably allow the writer to work on other projects—in other words, be nonexclusive to the producer; but even in these cases the writer must work for the producer on a "first-priority" basis (if the producer calls, the writer will drop whatever else he is doing and come running) and an "in-person" basis (the writer can't send over his uncle John or best friend Moe).

During all periods that Writer's writing services are required hereunder, Writer shall render services exclusively for Producer and shall
not render any services for Writer's own account or for any other
person without obtaining the prior written consent of Producer in
each and every case, and during all Reading and Option Periods
hereunder, Writer shall render services for Producer on a non-
exclusive but first-priority, in-person basis.

Rights.

If you have been snoozing, it's time to wake up. Here is where we
talk about chain of title stuff again. The principles are the same as our
previous conversation, but the context is slightly different. Here the
producer is not purchasing rights, he is purchasing services. Thus, as
with the treatment, the producer can be the author of the screenplay
for the purposes of United States copyright law.

Work made for hire. No, I'm not going to repeat the whole
discussion about the work-made-for-hire doctrine here.[8] But I am
going to remind you about the major points. First, special statutory
language is helpful in establishing the context. The example provision
below contains that special language. The result of establishing that
the services are rendered under this doctrine, as recited in this provision, is that the producer is the author for the purposes of the copyright. The producer then lists his or her name (or the name of the
production company) on the USCO form. Note also the broadness
of the scope of this language—"all material of whatever kind or nature created, written or furnished by Writer hereunder and all results
and proceeds of Writer's services." There is no reason to be restrictive.
The producer wants and needs "all" rights.

All material of whatever kind or nature created, written or furnished
by Writer hereunder and all results and proceeds of Writer's services hereunder (collectively, the "Material") shall constitute "works
made for hire" specially ordered or commissioned by Producer for
use as part of a motion picture or other audiovisual work, and accordingly, Producer and Writer acknowledge and agree that Producer is and shall be considered the author of the Material for all
purposes and the sole and exclusive owner, throughout the universe
in perpetuity, of all right, title and interest in and to the Material
and each and every part thereof (including all incidents, plots, dialogue, characters, action and titles forming a part thereof), including all copyrights therein, all renewals and extensions of such

copyrights and all other proprietary rights of any kind, nature or description (including all motion picture, television and allied rights), that may be secured under the laws now or hereafter in effect in the United States of America or any other jurisdiction.

Assignment of rights. First the belt and now the suspenders. As noted above, the work-made-for-hire doctrine has some tricky aspects, so the prudent approach is to get the writer to assign whatever rights the writer might have by virtue of the fact that he or she is, well, the writer. This is a contract action—assigning rights from one party to the next—but it is still effective assuming there is no breach of contract by the producer.

Without limiting the foregoing in any way, Writer hereby grants, assigns and sets over (and, to the extent that the same shall be impermissible or ineffective in any jurisdiction, hereby exclusively licenses) to Producer, throughout the universe in perpetuity, any and all right, title and interest which Writer may now or hereafter have in and to the Material and each and every part thereof (including all incidents, plots, dialogue, characters, action and titles forming a part thereof), including all copyrights therein, all renewals and extensions of such copyrights and all other proprietary rights of any kind, nature or description (including all motion picture, television and allied rights), that may be secured under the laws now or hereafter in effect in the United States of America or any other jurisdiction.

Further assurances. This clause follows a pattern that may be becoming familiar to you. First, the producer recites the two major methods of obtaining rights (work made for hire and assignment) and then says, in essence, in case I forgot to have you sign any piece of paper or take any action, you agree to do it or let me do it for you as your attorney-in-fact.[9]

Upon Producer's request, Writer shall perform (or cause to be performed) such further acts and execute, acknowledge and deliver (or cause to be executed, acknowledged and delivered) to Producer such further documents as Producer shall deem reasonably necessary or advisable in order to carry out the intent and accomplish the purposes of this agreement. If for any reason Writer shall fail to do any of the foregoing within ten (10) days (reducible to as few as five (5) days if Producer determines that business exigencies so require) after Producer's written request therefor, Writer hereby irrevocably appoints Producer as Writer's true and lawful attorney-in-fact (such appointment being a power coupled with an interest), with full power of substitution and delegation, with the right (but not the obligation) to perform any such acts and to execute, acknowledge and deliver any such documents on Writer's behalf.

Name and likeness.

Because of concerns with the laws governing an individual's right of publicity and privacy, producers will always want to clarify that they have a broad right to use the name and image of the writer in connection with the production and exploitation of the movie.

Uses. The provision below contains a broad list of uses. The producer can use the writer's name and approved biographical data in connection with the movie, the advertising and marketing of the movie, and the commerce related to the movie. The only restriction usually asked for, and granted here, relates to product or service endorsements. This requires the writer's prior written consent.

Writer hereby grants to Producer the right, throughout the universe in perpetuity, to use and reproduce and license others to use and reproduce the name, approved likeness and approved biographical data of Writer in connection with the following: (i) the Picture and/or any other production in which the Material shall be used in whole or in part; (ii) the advertising, marketing, publicizing, promotion, exhibition, distribution or other exploitation of the Picture and/or any other production in which the Material shall be used in whole or in part; and (iii) any commercial tie-ins, merchandising and/or the advertising or publicizing of any commodities, products or services relating or referring to the Picture and/or any other production in which the Material shall be used in whole or in part, provided that Writer shall not be represented as using, consuming or endorsing any such commodity, product or service without Writer's prior written consent (except that Producer shall be entitled to use or permit use of Writer's name in the billing block and/or credit list in any such connection).

Throughout the universe and in perpetuity. Contracts like this used to say throughout the world, but why be restrictive? The producer's lawyer may envision his client promoting this movie on a space station some day. And the producer's descendants may be exploiting this property for a long time. To be precise, as a practical matter, in perpetuity means until the copyright protection runs out.

Limitation on remedies.

The producer will want to limit the scope of damage the writer can inflict in case the producer breaches the contract. There are some actions that a grieving writer can take that would stop progress on the movie. When any delay means that the high-priced cast and crew members are standing around collecting checks, while no progress on the picture is being made, the producer will need to avoid the ability of anyone to cause such a delay. The producer will also want to make sure that the writer can't do things that interfere with the financing or distribution of the movie.

No interference, lien, or encumbrance. The producer wants to clarify that the writer will not do anything to interfere with the producer's efforts to get the movie made. He gets the writer to acknowledge that the writer has no lien or other encumbrance on the screenplay that would act as a chill on the producer's efforts to obtain financing and distribution initiatives. The producer also seeks to clarify that even a breach of the agreement will not give the writer the right to take back his screenplay—the producer will continue to have "sole and exclusive" ownership of the screenplay. Remember our discussion about the difference between the work-made-for-hire doctrine and an assignment of rights—the producer's lawyer knows the risks inherent in an action by the writer for breach, in the context of a grant of rights, and drafts the agreement appropriately.

> Writer agrees not to make any claim or bring any suit, action or arbitration or other proceeding which will or might interfere with or derogate from Producer's rights in and to the Material, it being expressly understood and agreed that Writer shall not have or be deemed to have any lien, charge or other encumbrance upon the Material or any rights therein or proceeds derived therefrom and that neither the breach nor alleged breach of this agreement by Producer, nor the termination of this agreement, nor any other act, omission or event of any kind, shall terminate or otherwise adversely affect Producer's sole and exclusive ownership of the Material and all right, title and interest therein.

Law favors money damages. There is an axiom lawyers learn in law school that "the law favors money damages." There are some problems that can't be fixed by money alone (a seller fails to deliver a priceless and one-of-a-kind original painting, for example), but most problems can be. Thus, the producer wants the writer to acknowledge that this is one of those cases. By acknowledging that money will be acceptable as a remedy for breach, the writer is agreeing that other remedies will not be sought. For example, an injunction is not a remedy at law. An injunction would allow the writer, if he otherwise has the grounds, to stop the picture. Given the sensitive and fickle nature of releasing and promoting a movie, this could have a disastrous impact on the producer.

> Writer further agrees that Writer's sole remedy for any such breach or alleged breach shall be an action at law to recover such money damages as may have been actually suffered by Writer as a result thereof. Producer acknowledges that Writer's bringing an action at law solely for damages shall not be deemed a breach by Writer of this agreement.

Representations and warranties, etc.

The writer's deal also includes a full set of representations and warranties on the part of the writer to the effect that all the material provided by the writer is original and will not infringe the works of others. These representations and warranties are similar to those given by the author of a work being optioned or purchased. An indemnity, similar to the one described above, is provided in case of a breach.

Obtaining an Existing Screenplay

PROS AND CONS OF USING A "SPEC SCRIPT"

It may be obvious, but a producer can also purchase a "spec script"—
a screenplay that is already finished. It is a common joke in Los
Angeles that everyone who lives here is writing a script. (As far as I can
tell, however, this is most likely true.) Naturally, not all of these scripts
will win an Academy Award; most of them will not be made into
movies at all. But there are stories about the proverbial diamond in
the rough.

There are some pros and cons to this approach. Now that you
are familiar with the writer's deal, you know that the producer can
control (most of the time) the direction of the writer. Thus, if you
are basing your big breakthrough on a novel, the rights to which
you have obtained, or a treatment that reflects your great idea for a
movie, unless you want to write the screenplay yourself, hiring a writer
is the only way to accomplish your goal.

However, producers (including major motion picture studios) are
always on the lookout for a great script. The clear advantage of purchasing a screenplay is that you can read the finished draft. You can
see if the story is good and whether the characters are well developed.
You can assess the budget. Of course, great screenplays out there on
the open market are rare. And when they do arise, some of them actually start bidding wars—the price goes up and, alas, a young producer
may find himself out of the bidding.

DOING THE ACQUISITION OR OPTION DEAL

You won't be surprised (and perhaps you will be relieved) to hear that optioning a screenplay is very similar to optioning a book. The major differences relate to writer's issues, many of which are found in the writer's deal just discussed. The issues related to the publishing company will be absent in a screenplay option/purchase. The issues related to chain of title, including representations and warranties and indemnification, will be the same. As in the book deal, the grant of rights will be an assignment—as it will be impossible to make the argument that the screenplay was specially commissioned by you.

Buying or optioning from a professional writer.

If you buy or option a screenplay from a professional screenwriter, chances are that writer will be a member of the WGA (Writers Guild of America). Although the basic financial terms and structure of the deal are very similar to the book option, if the writer is a member of the WGA, there will be certain minimums applicable to the various fees and there will also be mandatory contributions to the health and pension funds (we'll talk more about this when we talk later about the WGA).

Separated rights under the WGA agreement.

One of the major issues related to buying or optioning a screenplay from a WGA member concerns "separated rights." Article 16 of the WGA Theatrical and Television Basic Agreement, or WGA agreement, gives writers of *original* material who meet the specified criteria certain rights in material that can be separated from works of others— or separated rights. Maybe it would help to give you an example: Suppose that you come across an original, unpublished screenplay—called *The Quest*—written by a WGA writer on spec. The screenplay contains original characters invented by the writer: Prince Lumine, General Scrivener, Marrianne—the general's fair daughter, Gildemork—the centaur, and other interesting figures. You finish reading this book, raise all the money, and produce the movie. The movie, of course, is a smash hit. Several years later, you read in the trades that the writer has announced his intention of writing a novel and setting up a Broadway musical play based on the screenplay. You call your lawyer, of course. "What's happening here? I own that screenplay! I bought it fair and square!" There is a long pause, followed by the sound "Hmmmm." You don't like that sound. "What does 'hmmmm' mean, exactly?" you say. The lawyer says, "Well, there is this thing called separation of rights." The lawyer's voice trails off as he or she becomes immersed in thought.

Qualification for theatrical separated rights. To qualify for separated rights, a WGA writer must qualify "initially" and "finally." The presence of multiple writers has an impact on the qualification standards.

"Initial qualification" exists when a writer produces an "original story" (treatment or screenplay), if (1) the writer produced such material while in the employ of the signatory production company that commissioned such work or (2) the writer is a WGA member who sells such work to the company prior to its having been published or exploited. Note that original story means a story that the writer comes up with on his or her own. If the producer assigns the writer material to work with, then the writer is not entitled to separation of rights, unless the writer has the approval of the producer to depart from the assigned material or ends up creating a story that can nevertheless be deemed original. The same is true with respect to characters; if the characters are assigned to the writer by the writer's employer, the writer's ability to qualify for separated rights is restricted, especially if the characters are from previously exploited material (for example, a book or treatment that the production company acquired or produced prior to hiring the writer). Also note that a writer who contributes to the writing of a screenplay based on or adapted from another author's original story is not qualified to receive separated rights.

"Final qualification" exists if the writer receives "Story by," "Written by" or "Screen story by" credit on the movie.

When multiple writers contribute to the project (by collaboration with one another or separate contributions to the same work) and are both initially and finally qualified, as described above, all such writers are entitled to receive separated rights.

Exploitation of "theatrical separated rights"—written works. I'm sure you are still asking yourself: "So what is it exactly that the writer gets if entitled to separated rights?" Let's take the example of theatrical separated rights. The WGA agreement provides that if a writer is entitled to theatrical separated rights, the writer has the right, royalty free, anywhere in the world, to publish the separable material (in whole or part) related to the screenplay "in all writing forms and all writing media—excluding only comic books, comic strips and newspaper comics." "Separable material" means, again, material that is original and separate from the material assigned by the producer or production company hiring the writer.

The writer must wait to publish until whichever is earlier: the release of the movie or three years after the writer's agreement is signed. However, this holdback period is extended for one year if principal photography of the movie begins in the third year after the agreement is signed. (This holdback restriction doesn't apply to the publication of hardcover books.)

The signatory production company will always have the right, worldwide and royalty free, to publish and own "synopses, summaries, resumes, adaptations, stories and fictionalized versions of and excerpts from any screenplay . . ." for the purpose of advertising or in connection with the exploitation of the movie.

In our illustration, you (as the producer) may want to publish a paperback novel based on the screenplay (a novelization, in industry parlance), and you may do so if you follow certain procedures for obtaining this right from the writer. In sum, the writer may decide whether he or she wants to write the novelization and negotiate directly with the publisher. If the negotiations are successful within a certain time period, the writer keeps all the payments from the publisher, except for payments related to artwork, the movie's title and logo. If the writer doesn't conclude a deal with the publisher within the time period, the producer may set up a publishing deal by paying the writer an advance, currently, $3,500 against 35 percent of the adjusted gross receipts from such publication, less payments related to artwork and payments to the writer. All these terms are defined in the WGA agreement.

On the other hand, the copyright in published works resulting from a writer's exercise of separated rights goes to the producer. The producer can exercise all rights in the copyrighted works, except for (1) publication rights and dramatic rights (which we will look at next) and (2) any rights expressly retained by the writer in the agreement. The producer may acquire separated rights—in other words, there is nothing in the WGA agreement preventing the writer from granting the producer these rights. The producer must commence procedures to acquire them before the writer exercises the separated rights.

The exploitation of dramatic separated rights—stage plays. Dramatic rights relate to the presentation of the separated material live on stage. The rights start in the hands of the producer, but may terminate and go to the writer under the following circumstances under the 2001 version of the WGA agreement.[1] (1) if the producer starts active development of a bona fide dramatic stage production within three years after the general theatrical release of the movie, but fails to mount the stage production within five years after the movie's theatrical release; (2) the producer fails to exploit the rights within three years of the theatrical release; or (3) the producer does not commence principal photography on the movie within five years following the writer's contract of employment or acquisition.

If the producer does exercise the dramatic rights in a timely way, he must pay the writer 50 percent of certain minimum amounts defined under the terms of the Minimum Basic Production Contract recommended by the Dramatists Guild of the Authors League of America, Inc., unless the writer is considered the author of the dramatic work under that document. In this later case, the writer would get the minimum amount under the document.

Again, when the producer purchases the screenplay, he or she will own the copyright in any dramatic work, except for (1) dramatic rights and publication rights legitimately used by the writer under the WGA agreement and (2) any rights expressly retained in the writer's contract. The producer can obtain the rights described in (1) and (2) above at any time before the writer uses them by negotiation with the writer upon notice to the writer and the WGA.

If the author exercises the dramatic rights, the author must submit a copy of the performance to the producer, abide by any provisions respecting the title, and offer the company the opportunity to provide any needed financing.

Professional writer's rights related to rewrites. Virtually all writers will try to insert a clause in the writer's agreement giving them the right to do rewrites. As you know, it's more than an ego thing. Keep in mind that the production bonus is based on writing credit; the more writers who write, the less chance that the original writer will receive sole writing credit. Moreover, the opportunity to do the rewrite means more work and, of course, more money.

A WGA writer who holds separated rights to a screenplay (which will always be the case when the writer produces an original screenplay on his or her own and sells the screenplay to a producer or production company) must be offered the chance to rewrite at not less than minimum compensation under the WGA rules. In addition, unless the production company previously engaged another writer to do so, the original WGA writer has the right, under the WGA agreement, to perform an additional set of revisions, if needed within three years after the writer's delivery of the last revision because the company changed an element or added a new one.

When a producer or production company options a screenplay from a WGA writer who holds separated rights, the writer has the right to perform any rewrite during the option period, unless that person is unavailable or waives this right.

Sequel payments. WGA writers holding separated rights for a given project are not given sequel rights, but they are entitled to receive 25 percent of their fixed compensation for each theatrical sequel of such project produced by the production company.

Interactive payments. Although WGA writers are not entitled to interactive (computer games, etc.) rights, a writer holding separated rights relative to a given project is entitled to certain scheduled payments under the WGA agreement.

Reacquisition rights. WGA writers are entitled to reacquire material that is original with the writer, provided it has not been exploited in any medium. There are timing and procedural requirements imposed by the WGA agreement. The cost to reacquire the material is generally the company's direct cost in acquiring the project in the first place. Moreover, the writer may also be liable for certain other costs related to the material.

MAKING THE DREAM COME TRUE

Before we move on, I want to backtrack a bit to put the screenplay step in context. Why is it so, that nothing happens until the script is finished? It's not so intuitive, when you stop to think about it. In fact, in other movie-producing countries, it's not even true. It's probably more logical to think that a movie starts when the person with the money says, "Begin."

A wild guess at a historical perspective.

From the reading I have done on the subject,[2] I believe it used to happen like this in Hollywood: A studio executive might listen to a story and then say, "This is a great idea. Let's make a movie." A studio producer would be brought in to develop the idea for Errol Flynn or Rita Hayworth. If everybody still liked the project, the movie would be given a green light and funded, with the development of the script as the first step. That's how they still do it in Japan and Hong Kong, for example. Ah, but, somewhere along the line, somebody had a bad experience. Maybe a story that sounded great in the words of a master pitchman didn't live up to its potential on paper. Maybe the picture's budget got out of hand because the "blueprint" wasn't available to the executives at the time the starting gun went off. And maybe Rita and Errol didn't really like the story—maybe not such a big deal during the "studio system" era, when actors and actresses were exclusive to one studio, but a very big deal as actors and actresses (say, Bette Davis) became more and more independent. And maybe all of these things acted together to cause major problems.

The state of affairs today—the screenplay as a blueprint.

Like it or not, it is true in the American film business today that the screenplay comes first. If you want to make a movie, you had better get a finished screenplay before you start. The script answers the questions that must be asked in order to make a rational decision related to a film's future. For example, the screenplay is the basis for determining the budget of the film and attaching talent to the film.

Budget. The script is essential in making an accurate estimate of the budget. How many actors are there and what is the nature of the scenes? Does this script call for a lot of outdoor or action shots? What about aerial shots? How many extras will be required and for how many days? What types of locations and how many? Should we rent a house in Pasadena or build an interior on a sound stage? How many and what are the nature of special effects called for in the script? What kinds of costumes will be required? Is this motion picture set in modern times (an obvious savings in terms of costuming) or is it a period piece? What kinds of props will be needed? All of these things contained in the script are analyzed in estimating the budget.

Attaching talent. Actors and actresses and directors today as a matter of custom read the script before making a decision to participate in a project. Is this character something that I will be able to do well? Will the role further my career? Will I be required to appear in various stages of undress? Will I be safe? Do I have to handle snakes? Gone, pretty much, are the days when an actor will commit to a project without reading a completed script.

Why they call this development hell.

As we talked about earlier, getting the screenplay finished is part of the development step, another term for which is "development hell." Why? Well, because it is not as easy to write a good script as one might wish or think. One-draft wonders are very rare. The writer's vision may clash with the producer's vision. For example, I know a producer who hired a top writer to create a script based on a lengthy treatment that featured an American involved in a series of historical events. The producer was talking with and was going to show the script, when completed, to a well-known American actor with whom the producer had worked before. The writer, after doing his research and making a trip to the scene of the historical events, decided to write the script from his own (not the producer's) point of view—i.e., without the key character that the American actor was supposed to play. Needless to say, this turned out to be a major problem—just one example of the type of thing that can happen.

Some projects linger for many years before they are ready for production. *The English Patient,* which won the Academy Award for Best Picture, is said to have made the rounds in Hollywood for nine or ten years. Even motion pictures that studios have determined to make, come what may (planned sequels from highly successful motion pictures, for example), may be delayed waiting for the script to take shape. Development can be a long, arduous process with no promise of a successful outcome.

Obtaining Development Money

SOURCES OF DEVELOPMENT FINANCING

Memorize this sentence: "Development money is difficult to obtain, because there is a high degree of risk involved on the part of investors." Got it? Okay, let's have our first heart-to-heart conversation about money.

Because the odds of conquering the development financing step without difficulty are low, development investors, especially those who understand the risks, are hard to find. However, because nothing happens until this step is completed, producers are always looking for development money. For the most part, development funds come from strategic investors—investors who have a reason beyond a mere desire to participate in the equity of the script itself. Occasionally (rarely), foreign distribution companies or television companies will back the development of a script in exchange for the option to obtain the rights to the script in their own territory. More often, in order to feed their distribution machinery, major studios make development investments—purchasing an attractive novel or script and funding high-flying producers with development funds and "housekeeping" arrangements. I can almost hear you say, "If I were a successful producer, I wouldn't be reading this book." Okay—but I'm not going to lead you on: Raising money for development projects is not easy.

STRUCTURING DEVELOPMENT DEALS

The "first money in," high-risk aspects of development investment make these deals tricky to structure. There is no one formula that applies in every case, but it is possible to canvass the basic deal points.

The investment.
The deal will describe the project in some detail and will recite the amount of the investment. Then it will recite the use to which the investment will be put.

Use of proceeds.
The agreement will tell the investor how money will be spent. In the illustration below, the agreement sets forth an allocation of the $300,000 being invested, although the producer can reallocate the money on the various development tasks.

> Producer will use the Investment Amount to develop the Screenplay and make preparations for the production of the Picture. Specifically, the Producer intends to use $100,000 for the completion of the Screenplay, $100,000 for the attachment of principal acting talent, $50,000 to attach the director and $50,000 for legal, re-option and other costs associated with the above; provided, however, that Producer reserves the right to reallocate the proceeds within the stated categories at its discretion.

Creative control.
Development agreements generally clarify that the producer will have creative control. In this agreement the investor gets periodic reports and even has the right of consultation (not always the case). However, the producer agrees that, in any event, no decision will be made that will cause the investor to put more money in the pot. (Note, that the investor really doesn't have a lot of leverage here; if the money runs out, the entire investment will be lost and so the pressure to keep putting money in builds.)

> All decisions, creative and otherwise, regarding the development of the Screenplay will be made by Producer in consultation with Investor. Periodic status reports of the development of the Screenplay will be given to Investor. No decision causing Investor to

make a cash investment of any amount in excess of the Investment Amount will be made by Company without Investor's prior written consent.

Recoupment.

The first money that is made from the exploitation of the screenplay goes to recoup the investor.

Recoupment amount. The development investor may seek, in addition to the investment amount, an interest factor or premium. This premium can range from nothing to 10 to 20 percent or more. The development investor usually seeks full recoupment plus interest at the earliest possible moment—usually the sale of the script or script package to a production financier. If the script is not sold, but held by the producer for production, the development investor will seek recoupment plus interest from the budget of the film; this amount will typically be paid at the start of preproduction, but should be paid no later than the start of principal photography.

> Provided that Investor has fully performed all of its obligations hereunder, Investor will receive 100% of gross revenues received by Producer from the disposition of the Screenplay package (including any amounts from third parties pursuant to the sale of the Screenplay package or the amount allocated in the production of the Picture for the screenplay; provided, however, that such amount shall not be less than 200% of the Investment Amount; the "Package Fee") until Investor has recouped 110% of the Investment Amount . . .

Share of revenues. The investor will also want to have a share of revenues from the exploitation of the screenplay package. Keep in mind that the product of the development step is the screenplay— not the movie itself. In this case, the producer and the investor have decided to split fifty-fifty the amount remaining from the sale or other exploitation of the screenplay package—with the investor's share established at a floor of double the investment amount. Thus, if the investment amount is $300,000 and the producer sells the package for $1 million, the investor receives $330,000 (as the recoupment amount) and 50 percent of the remaining amount or half of $690,000. And since the screenplay sold for more than twice the investment amount, the investor is set. There are plenty of cases, however, where the screenplay package sells for less. In these cases, the investor gets the minimum amount bargained for (or the floor).

> [A]nd, thereafter, Investor will receive 50% of the amount of the Package Fee; provided, however, that to the extent necessary, Investor will cooperate with Producer so that Producer will be able to meet any tax liability related to the receipt (actual or constructive) of development related revenues.

Participation in the movie.

The development financier will also desire a participation in the movie. I have seen this accomplished in a couple of ways. First, if the investor wants to let his money ride—i.e., roll it over into the production budget, then the investor will receive a participation equal to the investment (what happens to the recoupment right is a matter of negotiation). Generally speaking, the producer does not want to give the development financier this right because it becomes a burden on the next financing step—production financing. It is much easier, and more common, for the producer simply to give the development financier a point or two out of his or her own participation.

> In the event that Producer obtains a participation in the Picture, in addition to Investor's right to recoup the Recoupment Amount and share in the Package Fee as set forth above, Investor will receive 2% of 100% of the revenues actually received by Producer from the exploitation of the Picture.

Strategic rights.

For strategic investors, the development deal may include a set of rights related to the investor's business. The most common strategic rights sought by investors are territorial distribution and other exploitation rights.

It is important that the producer not give these rights away. In other words, it is important in the overall scheme of things, that fair market value is paid for the rights even by the development investor. As a producer you may offer the development investor an option to buy the territorial rights at fair market value. It would be acceptable to give the investor a price at the lower end of fair market value (for example, if the territorial rights go for between 10 to 15 percent of the production budget, it would probably be acceptable to let the investor take those rights for 10 percent of budget), but not for free.

As producer, your goal must be to have enough money to produce the film. If a major territory is given away free in the development stage, you may not be able to raise enough outside of such territory to make up the difference. (See the discussion about production financing.) Experienced development financiers will understand this. You should also understand that selling off rights prior to raising the production money can have a negative impact on your ability to raise production financing, since some studios will condition their financing commitment on obtaining all rights. However, this is not always the case and given the difficulty of finding development funding, this cost will probably be worth it.

> Provided that Investor is not in material default hereunder, Investor shall have an option within two (2) weeks of the completion of the Picture to purchase the Japanese rights (including theatrical and television distribution rights) for no less than ten percent (10%) of the final production budget of the Picture, less the cost of any completion bond and contingencies. Investor will exercise such option in writing to Producer within the time limit. After the expiration of the time limit, Producer will be free to sell or otherwise exploit the Japanese distribution rights in his own discretion.

Statements.
A common feature of any deal involving participatory rights is the requirement on the producer's part to keep true and accurate records.

The obligation to keep and the right to audit statements. It won't do the participant much good if the producer's records can't be looked at. This right to audit is customarily at the expense of the party requesting the audit. The person making the request is usually required to give notice. In addition, the audit is usually performed during normal business hours.

> Company shall maintain true and complete records of all material transactions relating to the Screenplay. Investor shall have the right to audit such records at its own expense upon reasonable notice and under reasonable conditions.

Conclusive if not objected to. Typically, the investor will have a limited amount of time to raise an objection. If no objection is raised

within one year, in this case, the statement is deemed conclusive—
i.e., can't be changed. Then, if the investor sits on it for another year
without making an objection, or fails to bring a suit or take other appropriate action within a year after making an objection, the investor
will be contractually barred from bringing an action. (Keep in mind,
that no contractual agreement will time bar an action for fraud—it's
common sense, of course.)

Statements shall be deemed conclusive unless objected to within
one (1) year after being furnished. No litigation or other proceeding
will be maintained in connection with any statement unless commenced within two (2) years after such statement is furnished or one
(1) year after the objection is made, whichever is earlier.

Efforts.

The investor will usually demand some standard of effort in getting the screenplay finished and the project up and running. Best
efforts is the most satisfactory standard from the investors' point
of view. This standard means that the producer must affirmatively
and actively try to accomplish the goals set out in or implied by
the contract. Reasonable efforts is better for the producer. This standard will excuse inaction on the producer's part if the producer can
give any business reason. "Good faith" is meaningful, but somewhat vague as to what the producer has to do. The courts would
probably not find total inaction good faith. In some jurisdictions, such
as California and New York, good faith on the part of all parties is
implied and the covenant of good faith and fair dealing is implied in
every contract.

Company shall use reasonable, good faith efforts to exploit the
Screenplay and set up the Picture.

No right in the intellectual property.

The producer will want to make sure that the investor does not
obtain any ownership right in the screenplay. The investor gets a financial right and that is generally all he gets. This is important, because the producer (surely, you know this by now) must have all rights
to exploit the property.

Nothing in this agreement shall be construed to grant Investor any
right in or to the Picture and/or Screenplay, other than in the rev-

enues derived from the exploitation of the Picture as described in this agreement above, or in any other version or edition of the Picture or Screenplay or any sequel, remake or derivative of the Picture, except and to the extent that all or any portion of the Picture, under license or otherwise, is incorporated or embodied in such sequel, remake or derivative.

Security interest.

Some, but not all, investors will require a security interest in the screenplay. Obtaining a security interest in the screenplay is an advantage to the investor in the event of the bankruptcy of the producer. In such a case, the investor's right to recoupment, especially, is protected in that the investor becomes a preferred creditor in a bankruptcy proceeding. No, we're not going into the depth of bankruptcy law here, but having a security interest in the property in the case of a bankrupt producer is a real advantage to the investor.

> At the Investor's request and at the Investor's expense, Company will grant investor a security interest in and to the assets underlying the Screenplay and, when completed, the Screenplay itself . . .

Priority. Security interests have a priority—for example, "first," "second," and so forth. The producer must take care not to give away a first-priority security interest too early in the game. The Screen Actors Guild (SAG) will demand a first-priority security interest in the picture. Production financiers will also demand a security interest. In this case, the investor agreed to relinquish his or her position when and if necessary.

> [P]rovided, however, that Investor hereby acknowledges and agrees that certain other security interests (for example, interests granted under the Screen Actors Guild and other relevant guilds) may take priority over Investor's security interest; and provided, further, that Investor's security interest, if any, will be released upon receipt by Investor of the Investment Amount.

Perfecting a security interest. In this context it is not your issue; rather, it is the concern of the person seeking the security interest. There are several important court cases and statutory laws governing this procedure. Suffice it to say that the investor should also ask for a further assurances clause.

Other terms.

There are other possible terms, such as miscellaneous boiler-plate about choice of law, amendments, and so forth, but this will give you an idea about development finance. Good luck in finding some.

BOOK THREE

PACKAGING THE ELEMENTS

The next step in your quest is called "packaging." Suppose you just baked a beautiful banana cream pie (my favorite, by the way) and your guests are waiting anxiously to try it. You have several options, of course. You can place a perfectly cut piece of the pie on your best china and serve it with your best silverware with various garnishes on the side. Or, you can put a slab on a paper plate and tell your guests to use their fingers. Or, you can use something in between. (A pie in the face might be a useful idea in some contexts, but that's another story.) The point of this little example is that once you finish your screenplay, there are many ways to serve it up. In this section we'll look at the screenplay from the point of view of the buyer. What makes an attractive (or unattractive) package? That's the question we'll explore.

Identifying the Elements

WHAT DO YOU WANT TO BE?

Before analyzing the packaging step in detail, it is important for you to focus again on your specific goals in filmmaking. Is this project your vehicle to become the producer? Or are you content merely to get your project made and get the best credit you can (for example, co-producer, associate producer, or executive producer) in the process?

In Hollywood, taking a credit in a motion picture is a big deal. A person's credits define in large measure the individual's track record in the film industry—and, as noted, one's track record can be a major factor in determining one's future. As luck would have it, the most opportune time to control your own credit is at the beginning of the packaging step. Keep in mind the subtleties of producer credits as we go through the issues related to packaging. What credit will be yours?

Producer and produced by.

In the book of credits, the producer or produced by credit trumps all other producer credits. It is the most desirable producer credit. (Remember, it is the producer who accepts the Academy Award for Best Picture—need I say any more?) It can be given to (or taken by) the creative producer or by well-known line producers or both (later we'll discuss the distinction between the two). There is technically no limit on the number of producer credits—although there is always murmuring in the Hollywood community from a variety of sources (including, significantly, the folks at the Academy of Arts and Sciences, who hand out the yearly Oscar awards) that there are too many producer credits and that this causes a dilution in the value of the credit. One issue is whether or not a producer will be the sole producer. Certain major producers will normally refuse to accept a shared producer or produced by credit.

"Executive producer."

Executive producer is considered to be the next most prestigious producer credit, but it does carry with it a certain connotation. Historically, I'm told, the executive producer credit was reserved for the agent of the main actor. Today, it is sometimes reserved for a studio executive who oversees the project or the person who is responsible for finding or putting up the money. I often think of this credit going to someone who contributed in some significant way to the film being made—such as bringing the main actor to the table (a nod to history, perhaps) or getting the financing.

"Coproducer."

The coproducer credit is next. The coproducer is usually a working producer, though not necessarily. In the case of a working coproducer, he or she will usually do the bidding of the main producer in connection with the myriad tasks associated with making a motion picture. Honorary coproducers may not actually get involved with production.

"Associate producer."

Associate producer seems to be the least prestigious, but it is better than no producer credit at all. Associate producers may also be working producers and given specific tasks related to the production.

PACKAGING BASICS

In the smallest sense, a "package" is whatever you have to sell to the production entity (either a distribution company or independent financier). As discussed above, in Hollywood, the minimal package is the screenplay. But there are other elements that can be added to make the package more attractive to the buyer. There is no formula for a successful package, but I have listed below some of the elements experienced buyers (production financiers) are likely to look at when making a decision whether or not to put in their hard-earned cash. Also keep in mind that different buyers may have different objectives that affect the way they weigh the merits and demerits of a given package. What may be a plus in one territory, for example, may be a minus in another. A fully completed package will contain six elements: script and story, genre, main cast, director, producer, and budget.

Script and story.
The script and the story embedded therein are the blueprint of the motion picture and the foundation of every package.

Coverage. Believe it or not, some people in Hollywood actually read scripts. No, the president of Paramount Studios will probably not take your script home and read it with all the others submitted (but don't rule it out, either). Studios, agencies, and independent film companies will usually first have the scripts read by someone who is trained to read scripts. In Hollywood parlance, the script is being "covered." Studio executives usually read the coverage. If the initial coverage is good, more and more people will read the script. Coverage on most scripts (I have heard from various studio executives that the figure is 90 percent) is negative. When a reader says it is good, it might even be sent to another reader. What do they look for?

Story. It is an obvious point, but one that bears noting: "The play's the thing" (or so said William Shakespeare).[1] There are many filmmakers today who emphasize style and effects over story. This emphasis may appeal to a certain group, but ultimately a strong story will be the most important element in the package. Does the story entertain—does it embody certain traditional dramatic elements (for example, a protagonist, a conflict to overcome, a motive that drives the protagonist's action forward, and so on)? How does the story make you feel at the end? Has this story been effectively told before? Are there interesting characters? Can the viewer relate to them? Does the viewer care what happens to them? In other words, the script will speak for itself. With few exceptions (I suppose there are still some financiers who will buy without reading), someone will actually read the script and expect to be entertained.

Writer. As noted above, some writers have celebrity status and this status can help enhance the value of the package. This is not always the case, however. Unfortunately, there are famous writers who have produced unimpressive scripts. And Hollywood executives also know that there have been wonderfully commercial scripts by unknown writers. The fame of the writer might entice the potential buyer to read it (even if the coverage is bad), but if the story puts the buyer to sleep—well, the fame thing might not be enough.

Underlying work, event, or person. In some cases, where the script is based on a famous novel (any of the works of John Grisham or Michael Crichton, for example), comic book (*Batman* or *Superman*), television series (*The Flintstones* or *The Addams Family*) or previous motion picture (the many versions of *Robin Hood,* for instance), the value of the underlying property will enhance your project. In addition, a motion picture might be based on a famous (or infamous) event or person. If the event or person is a hot topic, it could be attractive. But again, there are many examples of successful books (and other properties) that did not make successful movies. Movies about famous people, called biopics (biographical pictures), are especially dicey (see the next heading "Genre").

Genre.

The genre of a story can often affect its value and marketability. The weighing of the genre is subject to many factors, including the slippery meter of current tastes. Rather than trying to state the various genres that are safe—it is sufficient to say that there are winners and losers in every genre—below is a list of "problem" genres, those that may draw close scrutiny from potential buyers. It is important to note that the "problem" list is a dynamic concept. Tastes change, as underscored by the current (as of the date of this printing) disfavor concerning musicals. *The Sound of Music,* released in 1965, was the most successful movie ever made for a long period of time. Today, it is hard to imagine that movie being made at all (but see the discussion coming up on musicals).

Period movies. Period movies, which take place in the past, require costumes and a historic look and feel. All of that costs money—more than projects shot in the current day where extras can show up in their street clothes. That alone would not scare the Hollywood financier (there are many examples of successful period movies—*Sense and Sensibility, Emma, English Patient,* and *Titanic* to name a few), but the extra cost is nevertheless a factor to be considered.

Biopic. The biographical picture is a special form of period movie about the life story of, usually, a famous or infamous individual. Unfortunately for those who have done or are planning to do one, however, some of these movies have been notorious examples of flops (*Hoffa* and *Chaplin* to name two). There have been exceptions as well (for example, *A Man for All Seasons* and *A Beautiful Mind*).

Religion movies. Movies dealing with the subject of religion, especially those that are seen as promoting a religion, are also viewed with caution. There are many exceptions, of course, but this type of movie, especially where the funding comes from a religious organization, have been viewed with skepticism. As a passing note, religion has not always been a taboo subject. Again, think of motion pictures such as *The Sound of Music, Ben Hur,* and *The Ten Commandments.* Recently, there is Mel Gibson's *The Passion of Christ.* Notwithstanding the success of this movie, modern-day examples of successful movies concerning religion are rare.

Musicals. This genre, in disfavor in recent years, is a shining example of how tastes change. Some of the biggest movies of all time (*The Sound of Music, My Fair Lady, Oliver,* and *West Side Story,* to name only a few) were based on Broadway musicals. Now, the musical is represented (and very well) by the animated feature film—such as *Beauty and the Beast, Lion King,* and *Prince of Egypt,*[2] (featuring the talents of noted musical theater personalities, like Alan Menkin, Tim Rice, and Steven Schwartz). The movie *Chicago,* Rob Marshall's film based on Fred Ebb's and Bob Fosse's live-action musical adaptation of Maurine Dallas Watkins's play by the same name, however, may have signaled a trend back to the musical film.

Animation. And while we're on the subject, let's talk about animation. Animation is the most specialized genre category and requires a highly sophisticated approach to development, production, and marketing. I could, but won't, fill up many pages about the animated film industry. But I do want to point out several features of animation that make it a high-risk category for distributors and, therefore, a very challenging area for would-be animation producers.

First, animation can be very expensive. Animation requires highly trained individuals and, more and more, expensive computer equipment and facilities. Disney, the pioneer of feature animation, does not release the costs of its projects. However, based on my own experience and the old reliable industry rumor, I estimate the average range for an eighty-five-minute animated movie in the classic style destined for theatrical release as between $30 and $100 million.

Second, animation takes time to complete—at least a year, most likely two years. Think of the investor in an animated feature film. He must shell out between $30 and $100 million and then wait for a long time until the movie is released.

Third, animation is expensive to edit. This may be changing somewhat with the advent of computer animation, but the point is still valid. The budget of a classic, theatrical animation feature has been estimated to be somewhere in the neighborhood of $30 to $40 million (some people estimate even higher). An animated feature averages about eighty-five or so minutes. That means (and I used a calculator for this part) that one minute of film costs between about $350,000 to $450,000. If something doesn't work and a portion of the film has to be removed or redone—well, get your own calculator out.

Fourth, distribution and marketing of theatrical animated films are specialized endeavors. There is a famous story of a producer who screened his independently made animated feature film before a group of studio executives. After the screening, one of the executives approached the producer and said, "If you could add two words to the beginning of your movie, it would be a success." The producer, encouraged and puzzled at the same time, asked, "What are the two words?" The executive replied "Walt Disney." The Walt Disney Company pioneered theatrical animation and still reigns supreme in this area in the United States. Other studios have made substantial inroads in this area (à la DreamWorks with *Shrek*).

There are also advantages to animated projects: Video sales and merchandising make these projects potential big-scale winners. Some of the most successful films of all time are animated feature films. However, the animated feature is a highly specialized and competitive business and this genre requires a special approach to get the movie launched.

Comedy. Comedy is a very popular genre, but I have a word of warning here—comedy doesn't travel. In other words, things that are funny in America, tend not to be funny in Japan or elsewhere.

Part of the problem, of course, is language translation. Often, humor takes the form of word play—puns, secondary meanings, and so forth. These things are very difficult to translate into a foreign language.

Another problem is cultural context. As a young man, I lived in Japan for awhile. One day, I went to the theater with a group of American boys my own age to watch an American Western movie (my favorite genre, which unfortunately has seen its better day). In the movie (the title of which I have forgotten), a city-slicker man from the East Coast comes out of a hotel on his first morning in the Wild West. "Hello," he says to the first person he meets. That person replies, "Howdy." Venturing on, the Easterner tips his hat to another man in the town. "Hello," says the Easterner. "Howdy," comes the reply. With firm resolve, the Eastern man approaches the next townsman and with his best Western accent says "Howdy." The polite reply comes back, "Hello." Now my friends and I thought that this was very funny and we laughed out loud—but stopped when we realized that no one else in the Japanese theater was laughing. "Must be the culture," I thought. And so it is.

Some physical comedy—a pie in the face or a man falling down, making a fool of himself—does in fact translate to other cultures. However, as a general matter, although comedy is always a possibility at home, this genre will limit your international audience severely. Keep this in mind when you are making money forecasts for your movie.

Cast.

The cast element is often a package's most focused-on aspect.

Star power. Many of the foreign distributors and independent film financiers I have worked with on motion picture prospects ask for a cast list first. The issue is marketability. If the motion picture in question does not have a marketable, "marquee name," distributors and financiers may be skeptical about its possibility for success. On the other hand, the presence of recognized and experienced talent adds to the motion picture's credibility. A successful actor's willingness to appear in the movie makes a statement to the film community; it is an endorsement of sorts by the actor. The attachment of certain stars—the so-called "A-List"—is seen by many to virtually guarantee a certain level of consumer interest (but does not always guarantee success). The importance of the cast is magnified in the international market. Certain stars have enormous appeal in certain countries and films with these actors that have mediocre success in the United States will often do well internationally.

Bars at the door. Getting the star to attach to your project can be a daunting proposition, however. Consider the following obstacles potentially lying in the way of a producer seeking to attach a star actor or actress:

One of them, many of you. It isn't a big point, but it is sometimes overlooked. There is only one Tom Cruise, but there are many (maybe hundreds of) producers who would like to develop a project with Tom Cruise in mind. Thus, the competition for the attention of actors with box office draw is severe. These actors have many quality projects to choose from and have many projects in their pipeline. Don't be surprised if your project doesn't make it to the top of the stack.

Making contact. Moreover, all major talent have many sentinels to keep the masses away. Have a heart, these people must get hit on for everything that comes along. Their managers, publicists, agents, and attorneys have all learned that to constantly pester the star with projects that won't fly will make them the former manager, publicist, agent or attorney, as the case may be. To keep their jobs, all of these gatekeepers must seriously screen the projects that come in the door. Many times, only projects presented by the studios or a famous producer or director or writer will make it through.

The price tag. As of today, the "A List" acting talent get $20 to $25 million for a studio-financed picture. Some will act for less (I mean, they will take less up front), if the script turns them on. But now we are back to square one—how to get the script in front of them.

The demise of the "interest letter"—Boxing Helena. Time to learn the word "attach" as it pertains to a star becoming part of the package. It used to be a common practice for an actor or actress to write a letter of interest to a producer. The letter, whatever the wording, was designed to give the general impression that the star was planning to act in the movie subject to financing and the star's availability. The producer would then use the interest letter to induce financiers to put their money behind the package. I say, "It used to be a common practice," because a legal case related to the motion picture *Boxing Helena* seems to have changed that part of the packaging process.

The case pitted the producer of the movie against actress Kim Basinger. The producer sent a copy of the script to Miss Basinger with a letter offering her a lot of money to play the leading female role. Miss Basinger's manager (and Miss Basinger herself apparently) liked the sound of "a lot of money" so they sent an interest letter back to the producer, who used the letter to secure financing. There were also apparently conversations and meetings between the producers and Ms. Basinger's management consistent with the interest letter. Then, somewhere along the way, Miss Basinger (or someone close to her at least) actually read the script. The script called for Miss Basinger to play Helena, the love interest of a demented doctor who decided that Helena was so nice to have around that he cut off her arms and legs and put her in a box. So, Miss Basinger, who apparently did not like the thought of being associated with this movie, decided that she would not act in it after all. When she told the producer this, he sued her and pulled out the interest letter and made reference to the discussions and meetings as evidence that Miss Basinger and he had made a contract. Ms. Basinger and the rest of Hollywood were quite stunned to find out that the court agreed with the producer. The court found that Miss Basinger knew that the producer was going to go raise money on the letter and that her letter and other communications constituted an implied promise to be in the movie. The court supposedly ordered Miss Basinger to pay the producer $8.1 million in damages.[2] So much for the interest letter.

The offer. If you want to attach a star to your movie after *Boxing Helena,* you probably will have to guarantee the actor's fee in the form of a firm offer, often with a pay-or-play provision.

Firm offer. A firm offer, as every first-year law student learns, is an offer that can be turned into a contract by the party who receives it. All the recipient has to do is accept the offer. The offer is called firm because on its face it cannot be withdrawn for a specified time period. For example, I can send a letter stating that I offer the role of the prince to Leonardo DiCaprio for $20 million and that the offer is firm and is being held open for four days. What I am really saying is that I am giving Leo a chance to say yes for four days. If he does say yes—without making a counterproposal (i.e., without changing the terms of my offer)—before my offer expires, there may be a contract. (Actually, fortunately for lawyers, all this stuff is complicated with rules and exceptions, so don't try this without one.)

"Pay or play." In plain English, the term pay or play means that the actor will be paid no matter what—whether the movie is made or not, whether the actor acts or not. In other words, the actor says: "Your choice, either play me [in which case I will act for my fee] or [don't play me, in which case you will have to] pay me anyway." In actuality, the negotiation is somewhat complicated. But at least the rationale should be clear. Actors and actresses who are in demand want to pro-

tect themselves from last-minute cancellations due to lack of financing or last-minute changes in the mood of the decision makers. Their decision to act in your movie means that they have to say no to another movie. If your movie doesn't go, they lose money. This is bad for the actor, his agent, his lawyer, and others who are riding the train of the actor's success.

The issues for negotiation concern the following questions: (1) When does the producer's commitment to the actor turn pay or play; (2) Will force majeure (commonly referred to as Acts of God) release the producer from the obligation to pay or the actor from the obligation to play; and (3) What are the other terms of the engagement (production schedule, etc.)? The important thing to know about pay-or-play commitments is that they are real on both sides. The producer is locked in, as described above. The actor, too, once the star accepts, is legally obligated to perform and has to go through all the steps to decide whether or not to be in the movie. If the actor doesn't show up then he or she expects to be sued.

In most cases, a pay-or-play commitment means X, but in some cases, it can mean Y: (X) Producer A has a pay-or-play commitment with Actor B. Producer A decides not to use Actor B in the movie. Producer A pays Actor B 100 percent of Actor B's promised fixed compensation. (Y) Producer A has a pay-or-play commitment with Actor B, but decides not to use Actor B in the movie. Producer pays Actor B that portion of the promised fixed compensation that the actor has earned.

Although it is not necessary to add an escrow provision in your first offer, you should be aware, for most independent producers and certainly in the case of a first-time producer, that the actor's agent may insist on the actor's fee being escrowed at the time of the first-deal memorandum (see the discussion on the "deal memorandum").

In any event, you had better be prepared, financially and otherwise, to make the movie before making a pay-or-play offer. Some producers might rationalize by thinking that making a pay-or-play offer is not a big risk, because once the big star is locked in the financing will surely follow. This thinking is dangerous, because it is not always true. Even with big names, you may not be able to raise the money. I know of many examples of screenplays packaged with Academy Award–winning actors that have languished in the fickle market of movie financing. Maybe financiers will perceive that the actor's fee is too much. Perhaps financiers will perceive that this actor is not right for this role. Maybe the star is a huge draw in America, but has relatively little cachet internationally. And so on.

WANNA B. PRODUCER PRODUCTIONS, LLC
Term Sheet Offer
THE QUEST

OFFER:	Firm offer, made April 6, 2006. Expires at 11 A.M., Friday, April 21, 2006.
ARTIST:	Eyre A. Star
AGENT:	The Big Talent Agency Move R. Shaker
ROLE:	"The Prince"
CREDIT:	Star billing, first position.
START DATE:	On or about June 5, 2006. Specific dates to be mutually agreed.
SHOOTING:	Shooting on location in Scotland. Ten weeks for production, two free weeks, one rehearsal week, plus three days of looping in post.
SALARY:	$5 million for schedule plus other pre- and postproduction required time.
BONUSES:	A bonus of $100,000 will be paid when the gross domestic box office receipts exceed $50 million. An additional bonus of $100,000 will be paid when the gross domestic box office receipts exceed $75 million.
CONTINGENT COMP.:	10 percent of net profits (same definition as the Producer's), to be negotiated in good faith.
OTHER:	SAG fringes will be applicable.
ELEMENTS:	Writer, Fame S. Writer Producer, Wanna B. Producer
CONTACT:	Kelly C. Crabb, Esq., at 310-555-5555

The form of the offer. The offer usually takes the form of a list of terms (appropriately referred to as a term sheet).

The example above is typical, where—

Offer. This defines the opening and closing date, and expiration time, of the offer. *Note:* If you want or need to make the offer pay or play, one way to do it is to adjust this provision to read: "Pay-or-play offer, made April 6, 2006 . . ." There are other ways to do it, including adding a new sentence that reads: "This offer is made on a pay-or-play basis."

Artist. States the artist's name.

Agent. States the name of the agency and agent of the artist.

Role. Clarifies the name of the role being offered.

Credit. Specifies the type of billing and position.

Start date. Refers to the start of principal photography or the date on which the actor must show up on the set. Sometimes, when the offer is made, the specific dates will not be known, but the actor nevertheless will have to schedule a general time frame. In those instances, the parties will negotiate the specific dates at a later time (see the discussion about the "deal memorandum").

Shooting. Tells where the principal photography will take place (it can specify more than one location, of course), how many weeks (or days) principal photography will last, how many "free" weeks (meaning additional time without any additional payment), the amount of rehearsal time, and the number of days the actor will need to be available for postproduction "looping" (taking all the naughty words out and punching up the dialogue where needed, etc.).

Salary. Describes the fixed compensation that the actor gets for performing services. This is also the pay-or-play amount, if the obligation is made or becomes pay or play.

Contingent or deferred compensation. Describes the contingent compensation of the artist. There are several possibilities here—including leaving this provision out altogether. If you want (or need) to give the actor additional incentives, the choices generally are bonuses or deferred compensation (either contingent or noncontingent).

Bonuses. Bonuses can be structured in many ways, but one common structure for awarding a bonus is to give "bumps" (the stated bonus amount) at certain box office thresholds (in the example, the two bumps come at $15 million and $25 million, respectively).

"Contingent Deferment." Sometimes the actor will accept a deferred payment of some specified amount that is conditioned on there being sufficient revenues generated to cover it—a contingent deferment. For example, suppose the following: "Contingent deferment of $500,000 out of 5 percent adjusted gross revenues." In this case, the actor gets $500,000 from the defined pool, *if,* and only if, 5 percent of

the defined pool is equal to or greater than $500,000. In a way, of course, the bonus bumps referred to above are also contingent deferments, because they are paid only if the defined threshold is met or exceeded. The major difference is that the traditional deferment is designed by the actor's agent to be paid out of earlier revenues.

"Noncontingent deferment." Although not used in the firm offer illustration above, the producer can also consider offering a noncontingent deferment. Some actors may accept a lower fee, with the understanding that out of the first moneys in from the exploitation of the motion picture they will be paid an additional amount. If this amount will be paid without condition (for example, even if the picture does make sufficient money to cover the amount of the payment), it is referred to as a noncontingent deferred payment. This payment is usually expressed in the following way: "Noncontingent deferment of $500,000 from 5 percent of adjusted gross revenues." This means that the actor will get $500,000 from 5 percent of a certain defined pool of revenues. If the revenue pool runs short, the actor will still have a claim against the producer for the remainder. The actor's agent will usually make sure that there is a viable distribution commitment or other source of postproduction revenues and that the definition of revenues from which his client will draw is an aggressive one (i.e., closer to gross revenues than net revenues).

"Participation." A participation is, simply stated, a percentage of the revenues generated from the exploitation of the motion picture. Not all actors can expect to receive a participation in a movie, but it is fairly customary now for the main actors—especially an actor who is attached during the packaging step in order to make the movie go— to get a piece of the action. It will be absolutely imperative to give an actor a substantial participation if the actor takes a fee lower than the usual quote (the fee the actor does or can reasonably expect to receive with reference to the success of the actor's last movie or series of movies). For example, it is rumored that Nick Cage took a guild minimum fee (an amount that would be substantially lower than his normal fee at the time) in connection with the motion picture *Leaving Las Vegas*. In return, Mr. Cage apparently received a substantial participation in the picture—rumored to be in the range of 30 percent or more of the movie's profits. Participations are usually in perpetuity (for as long as the motion picture makes money), but some are limited to a capped amount or a set number of years. Participations are often described as a piece of net proceeds (gross revenues less distribution

fees and costs, including from time to time an allocation for the company's overhead), but more powerful actors will demand and get participations of "adjusted gross" or even gross proceeds. The most aggressive participation is said to come from "dollar one gross," which means that the actor gets to start taking money from the time a dollar reaches the producer's hands. (We'll talk in more detail later about the workings of revenue formulas.)

Other (guilds, etc.). This section describes other relevant terms to be included in the offer. In the example, the producer wants to confirm that the contract will be governed by the rules of the Screen Actors Guild (SAG), which requires certain minimum rates, contributions (called "fringes") to the pension fund and the health and welfare fund, and other matters. (Note again that if you hire a SAG member, you must either require your production company to become a signatory to the Screen Actors Guild Basic Agreement (or other applicable agreement) or use a loan-out SAG signatory (an independent production company set up to hire SAG actors).

Elements. Describing the other elements of the package: the writer, producer, other actors, and director. The actor will care who is directing and acting in the movie, as this will determine the credibility of the project.

Contact. Telling who to contact with a response. In this case, note that the term sheet came from a lawyer. It could also come from a casting director or the producer directly.

A note about the existence of a binding agreement. A relevant question at this point is whether or not a binding contractual obligation arises or can arise on the basis of a term sheet like the one above. What if the actor takes the view that there is a contract and you are not ready? To solve this concern, some attorneys do not send firm offers (in other words, they word the offer as a proposal for discussion purposes only) and add a line that "this term sheet does not constitute a legal agreement" and that a formal deal memorandum or agreement is needed. I do not recommend the automatic use of this language, because I think it works against the producer in a majority of the cases. The addition of this language suggests, of course, that the parties are not finished with the negotiations and that another instrument is required to form a contract. What happens, however, is that, because letters of intent are disfavored, the actor's agent and lawyer will respond only verbally; they will try to keep their options open in order to accommodate a better offer coming in. The answer may be yes or "my client is interested" and the actor may rearrange his or her schedule, show up for fittings and readings, and do other things that indicate intent to act in the movie, but if the above "it's only a proposal" language is inserted and the actor wants to get out of the deal, the actor and the actor's handlers will have a strong argument that there is no real contract, because there is no additional signed agreement. On the other hand, without that type of language, the producer (you) might be able to argue—assuming that the actor and the actor's agent does the types of things that would normally indicate an agreement to perform on the terms set forth in the term sheet—that there is indeed a contract. It depends a lot on the facts of the situation, but every first-year law student knows that it is possible for a contract to spring into existence on the basis of a written instrument and a series of actions consistent with it. Keep that in mind as you think through the likely scenarios—remember, you are the one wishing and hoping that the actor will attach to the package. You are the one who will start telling others that so-and-so's agent said the actor was in. You will stop going out to other actors and making plans with this actor. It is the actor who is likely to have other offers coming in and who may want to go in another direction at the last minute. If the actor's agent calls on the day before principal photography begins to say that the actor is out, you could incur significant losses and will want some recourse.

If you are really worried about having a contract before you are ready, then you should *not* make firm offers (because keep in mind a firm offer can be turned into a contract by a letter that says we accept). Certainly, you would have no business making a firm offer on pay-or-play terms. If necessary, concerns can be addressed by adding provisions in the term sheet under the headings *Other* or *Conditions*. But I advise my clients to think carefully about adding a general statement in the term sheet or offer that no contract exists.

Independent financing and the star. Many stars will not appear in an independently financed film, unless the producer is someone they know personally or by reputation. Since an actor's star status can be affected by the next movie that individual makes, the risk that the movie will not be made or, even worse, made poorly is enough to make actors shy away. Compare this situation to the independent producer's main competition—the studios. The studios not only have the credibility with respect to production issues, they have the power to get the movie distributed. Sure, you may be able to offer the actor a piece of the ownership of the project (something that the studio is not likely to do), but you cannot offer the actor the security of a studio deal.

Scheduling. Then there is the actor's schedule. Even if all the other hurdles can be overcome the actor may simply not have time to work on your project. Do you want to wait for two years to start? That's what it might take in some cases.

No guarantee. Then finally consider this—the history of the film business is riddled with examples of failed motion pictures featuring big stars (*Cleopatra,* with Richard Burton and Elizabeth Taylor, *Last Action Hero,* with Arnold Schwarzenegger, and *Judge Dredd,* with Sylvester Stallone, are examples that come to mind). Obviously, it is important to remember that an actor who may have been a superstar at one time may not command any particular attention at the box office today. There is a well-known example of a Japanese tycoon who self-financed a motion picture, *Solar Crisis,* featuring Charlton Heston. Although Mr. Heston was at one time an undisputed major draw at the box office, at the time *Solar Crisis* was released, Mr. Heston's prime years were behind him. The motion picture was a financial disaster—for reasons other than Mr. Heston's performance. Even where the star is current there is no guarantee. For packaging purposes, however, it is helpful to have a recognizable name.

Minors. Most if not all states in the United States have laws about the ability of minors to legally enter into contracts. (We learned this dramatically in the movie *Liar Liar,* with Jim Carrey—remember he got his client out of a prenuptial agreement because his client had lied about her age when she signed it; in actuality, she was a minor when she signed and now had the right to disaffirm the contract.) Under California law, for example, if a person enters into a contract when he or she is a minor, when such person becomes an adult (eighteen years old, in California), that individual can terminate the contract. This is bad for producers and distributors who would like to believe that they can exploit the movie for many many years. If you want to use a minor in your movie in the state of California, you must have the contract between the production company and the minor approved by a court. Each state has its own requirements. For example, some states require the signature of both parents or legal guardians and the stamp of approval of a judge. Some states require only one parent. Moreover, in some states, like California, there are laws dealing specifically with minors in the entertainment industry. These laws deal mainly with how the minor's salary must be handled; it is a good idea for producers to familiarize themselves with these provisions.[3]

Director.
Some directors have star power equaling or rivaling that of the cast.

Star power of celebrity directors. Steven Spielberg and James Cameron are examples of directors who rival or even surpass famous actors in their ability to attract production financing and box office success. However, high-level directors are usually not willing to join someone else's project. If you could accomplish the impossible and get one of these "A List" guys to do your project you can skip all the rest of the packaging steps. They will get the cast and the money for you. (They might even invite you to one of the private screenings too. As for spending time on the set with them—don't push your luck.)

Industry reputation. The status of any director within the film community is important to your package. A certain level of director will attract a certain level of talent. Actors want someone who can make them look good. Many actors will look to see who the director is before attaching themselves to a motion picture. Many, perhaps most, high-level actors will not attach themselves to a film with a first-time director.

Producer alliances. Many directors have aligned themselves with a producer and will insist on this producer getting sole producer credit. If your dream is to fill that credit slot, this type of director will not work for you.

Producers.
Aligning yourself with an established producer might help you reach your goals, but since this role is what you have been seeking—please read carefully.

Creative producers, coproducers, and associate producers. There are two basic meanings associated with the word producer. If the director is the captain of the ship, the producer, in the general sense, is the ship's owner. The owner/producer (sometimes referred to as the "creative producer") is often the visionary who initially conceives of the project (even projects brought to the producer by others require his visionary support), establishes or clears the rights to the story, raises or supplies the financing to develop a screenplay that captures the producer's vision, and hires the director and others to execute it.[4] Creative producers who have a track record for identifying and developing successful motion pictures (for example, Jerry Bruckheimer and Mace Neufeld, to name two of many) can be a very attractive package element. If a producer has no track record in getting a film made, the other elements of the package take on added significance. Sometimes, if a person (and this could be you) does not have the appropriate contacts or background, that individual will approach a well-known producer with a project and negotiate a minor producer credit, such as coproducer or associate producer. The thought is that this will be a stepping-stone to future status as a full producer.

"Line producers." Another type of producer is the so-called line producer. The line producer, when separate from the creative producer, is the creative producer's administrative executive in charge of physical production and has the task of managing all finances and the logistical matters related to the production of the movie in accordance with the established budget and schedule. The watch words for a successful line producer are on time and on budget. Thus, the attachment of a line producer who is well regarded can be an important plus. It may not by itself, however, be a key to raising production financing or securing distribution.

Executive producers. The executive producer credit is used for various purposes. Common uses include someone who helps procure the money or the major talent. Sometimes this credit will be given to a studio or other executive who plays a role in the production of the movie. Occasionally, today, this credit will go to a principal cast member.

Budget.
An important part of the package is, "How much will the picture cost?"

Making a profit. Profit is calculated by comparing revenues derived from the exploitation of the movie to the costs of making and distributing it. Thus, the budget is an important element of the package. Budgets are normally prepared for a fee by production accountants and others who have the training. Eventually, if you pursue a career as a producer, you will need to develop the ability to analyze and perhaps even prepare budgets yourself. The following are a list of terms related to film budgets:

"Negative costs." The negative cost is the cost of producing the negative of the movie—from which all positive prints of the movie are made. The costs of producing motion picture negatives have been steadily rising. The average cost of producing a studio movie has gone, in the last ten years, from an average of about $25 million to over $50 million. The negative cost is comprised of the "above-the-line costs" and the "below-the-line costs." The origin of these two terms is apparent when you first look at a traditional "top sheet" movie budget—a budget that summarizes the essential cost elements of a movie. The first items listed on the budget are the principal people involved in the movie. Then there is a line, below which all the rest of the movie's cost will be detailed.

Above the line. The above-the-line budget sets forth the fixed compensation of the principal cast and producers (sometimes referred to as the producers unit) and the director (and sometimes the director of photography, who is also referred to as the DOP or the cinematographer). The deferred and contingent compensation of each of these major players will not be included in the budget, but will be a factor in determining whether or not the movie will turn a profit.

Below the line. This term refers to all other costs of making the movie, including the following items: other cast (including extras) and crew, equipment, set design, costumes, location fees, catering, makeup, travel, insurance, guild costs, and so on and so forth.

Releasing (P&A) costs. There are two major cost elements in releasing a movie: the costs of prints of the movie and the cost of advertising. These are referred to as P&A (prints and advertising) costs. Obviously the strategy to be employed in releasing a movie will determine the P&A costs. Distribution strategies are discussed in detail later on. However, note the following variables affecting the budget:

"Prints." A print is a copy of the movie distributed to theaters for exhibition. The average cost of a print ranges from $2,000 to $3,000. (It may be worth noting in this digital day and age that some persons are predicting the eventual end of the print as we now know it.) With

the advent of digital cinema (where movies are made in or converted to a digital format) it is possible to think of theaters equipped with sophisticated computer projectors or satellite receivers. But for now, releasing a motion picture requires one print per screen.

"Screens." The term screen refers to each screen within a movie theater on which a movie can be projected.[5] In this day of multiplex theaters (movie theaters with more than one screen), theater owners can schedule motion pictures they choose to exhibit on one or more screens on any given day. The number of screens to be employed and the release pattern will determine the number of prints to be made.

"Release pattern." The distributor, within the limits imposed by the demand for the movie in question, can decide whether to start big (the widest release patterns start on two thousand to three thousand screens out of about thirty-five thousand total screens in the United States) and try to stay that way for a long period of time, or start on a lesser number of screens (sometimes targeted to a specific geographical area or demographic) and try to build an audience for the movie by advertisement and word of mouth. This second approach is sometimes referred to as a "platform release." The narrowest release pattern would be to rent one theater in one city; a practice that is included in the concept termed "four-wall." (Later we will discuss distribution agreements in detail.)

Traditional advertising costs. The marketing of a motion picture can, and often does, include the following activities: television advertisements, newspaper and magazine ads (often referred to as "print ads"), billboard ads, and radio ads. These traditional methods all cost money and lots of it.

Why packaging is difficult—a summary.

If you have been paying attention, you know that the packaging step is more difficult than it may appear at first blush. After the *Boxing Helena* case, it has become difficult to get an actor to attach to a project without putting up the actor's fee in the form of a pay-or-play offer followed by the escrow of the entire fee. Even with a money backer, a first-time producer may have a hard time attaching a top actor or director. A high-level producer might be able to attach a top actor or director, but the producer may insist on being the sole producer and a director might insist on his producer partner stepping into the role of producer—leaving you out. Added to all of this is the complex and growing financial risk attendant with producing a motion picture.

Papering
the Package

The Deal Memorandum—an Overview

At the end of the packaging step, if you have done your job correctly, you will have a collection of paper. In addition to the screenplay, with its concomitant writer's or acquisition agreement (discussed above), you may have some signed agreements signifying the commitment of important people to your project, including a major cast member, director, and perhaps a producer or two. The standard approach to documenting attachments is a short-form agreement often referred to as a "deal memorandum."

The deal memorandum will usually contain the following terms consistent with and adding substance to the items listed in the term sheet associated with the offer (see above). Unlike the term sheet offer, the deal memorandum is a real contract—there should be no ambiguity about the legal enforceability of the deal memorandum against either party. Let's take a quick look at the deal memorandum terms; however, just as in real life, I'll save the detailed discussion on the long-form agreement for later.

The Structure of the Deal Memorandum

The parties to the deal memorandum.
The deal memo will recite who is hiring who in a legal sense. During the offer stage, the producer may not have formed the production

company or, after the offer is made, the producer may wish to change the contracting entity. The deal memo will be specific about who or what entity is contracting for the actor's services.

Likewise, the deal memorandum will specify the party on the other side of the deal. Although actors often enter into contracts in their own capacity, actors will some times insist on using a "loan-out company," which means that the deal memo will be between the producer's production company and the actor's company, which is obligated to loan out the services of the actor. In the case of a loan-out structure, the actor executes an inducement letter in favor of the producer that states that the actor has read the agreement and agrees to perform the applicable services. Let's take a look at a typical deal memo incorporating a loan-out structure.

> This Deal Memorandum sets forth the mutual agreement by and between Star Vehicle, LLC ("Loanout Company") f/s/o Mr. Eyre A. Star ("Actor") in connection with the production by Wanna B. Productions, Inc. ("Producer") of the feature-length motion picture tentatively entitled "The Quest" (the "Picture") based on the screenplay by Fame S. Writer of the same name (the "Screenplay"). Producer's obligations hereunder are conditioned on Actor's execution of an inducement letter substantially in the form of Exhibit A attached hereto and incorporated herein by reference (the "Inducement Letter").

Loan-out structure. The loan-out structure is commonly employed by actors, directors, and others for a variety of purposes. For example, using a corporation can shield the actor from individual liability—one of the main reasons that producers opt for corporations as production companies. The law of corporations generally provides that liability is limited to a corporation's assets. The actor keeps the corporation generally free from assets (i.e., the actor keeps his house, his money collected from other jobs, and other assets out of the loan-out company). There could also be tax-planning benefits to the actor that are outside the scope of this book. Note that the term "f/s/o" which stands for "for the services of" is used when entering into a contract with a loan-out company.

"Inducement letter" (loan-out structure only). A separate inducement letter, delivered by the actor to the production company, is required when using a loan-out structure. In the inducement letter, the

actor personally signs a letter stating that he or she has read the agreement, understands it, and agrees to abide by its terms, so far as the agreement applies to the actor. Please note that without the inducement letter, there is no real commitment on the part of the actor to act—only on the part of the company to provide the actor's services. It's not a small point. If the actor doesn't show up, without the inducement letter, your only recourse is against the loan-out company (which, as you know, has no assets).

Services: role, start date, and duration.

The deal memo contains a description of the services to be rendered and where they are to be rendered. For example, in the case of an actor, the deal memorandum would refer at least to the name of the character to be played.

> Loanout Company will provide the services of Actor to play the lead role of "The Prince," as portrayed in the Screenplay, a copy of which has been received by Actor. Actor will provide such services in a manner consistent with first class productions. Actor's service will be rendered on ten consecutive weeks commencing on or about June 5, 2006, with the actual start date to be mutually agreed in good faith. Actor will also provide two free additional weeks, one week for rehearsal and three days during post-production for looping, the actual dates of which shall be negotiated in good faith.

Role. If it is a leading role, that fact might be added, as in this example. The only risk in doing so, of course, is that you may have a hard time convincing the actor that he should take less pay than someone else. Thus, use the designation "lead actor" only when you really mean it and mean to stay with it.

Standards. Sometimes, the deal memorandum will have a recitation of the standard under which the person being hired will perform the services (for example, "in a manner consistent with first class productions," although I, and most lawyers I know, would be hard-pressed to tell you exactly what that means).

Start date. The deal memorandum will always recite the approximate start date and the number of shooting days required during "principal photography" (or the "shooting period"). If the days are consecutive, which they usually are, that will also be noted. The actor's actual start date (which will be negotiated over the course of the preproduction period) is a critical date, as most actors understand, because other cast and all the crew will show up on that date and the clock will start running. If the actor doesn't show up—causing a delay or a cancellation, the cast and crew members get paid any way. This could cost a tremendous amount of money and cause problems with the schedule—producers do not like this.

Additional days/weeks. The producer will usually want a couple of extra weeks at no cost, hence the term free. This time is not centered around a certain date, because the operative idea is flexibility.

Rehearsal days/weeks. The producer will want the actor to rehearse for so many days. These dates are also negotiated in good faith.

Postproduction days. At the end of the movie, the producer will need the actor for various purposes: The actor will have to fix any dialogue problems (including doing overdubs to take the naughty words out for television and airline versions). This process is called looping.

Fixed compensation (salary).
The deal memorandum next recites the amount of the actor's fixed compensation and fleshes out the method and timing of payment. It is not part of this deal, but there are other variations on the theme of fixed compensation, including noncontingent deferred payments, which come out of the gross revenues of the project but which are not subject to the movie's success.

> In consideration of Actor's full and complete services hereunder, Producer shall pay to Loanout Company the amount of $5,000,000.00, payable in equal installments on a weekly basis from the commencement of principal photography to the conclusion of principal photography.

Payment schedule. The general custom in the industry, as noted here, is to pay the actor's salary on a weekly basis, starting with the commencement of principal photography and ending at the conclusion of principal photography. If the producer has enough bargaining power, his attorney will sometimes try to hold back a portion of the fee through the release period, as an incentive for the actor to provide the postproduction services and also promotion services, if applicable.

Pay or play. As discussed above with regard to offers, after *Boxing Helena,* the actor's agent is likely to insist that the terms of any binding agreement include a pay-or-play commitment for the payment of the actor's fixed compensation. Lawyers sometimes shorthand this commitment by adding language similar to "Actor's compensation hereunder shall be on a pay-or-play [as such term is generally understood in the filmed entertainment industry] basis." However, the producer would do well to think through the issues here. As noted above, the producer may want to mitigate the effect of the pay-or-play provision by providing contingencies to its effectiveness. For example, the producer may wish to condition the pay-or-play provision on financing (this usually doesn't work, because this is the very thing the agent is concerned about), the absence of a force majeure event, the attachment of a director (or a director being made pay or play), and so on. (See "actor specific terms" below.) One common approach is to offer pay-or-play status, but make the trigger some other person on the project being made pay or play. This might work well in the event of an actor who has less than superstar status. This is, in essence, giving the actor a "most-favored-nation" status with respect to pay or play. The producer may be able to get away with making no one pay or play using this method.

"Escrow." Even assuming that the screenplay turns out to be a winner, actors are generally leery of independent producers (and certainly first-time producers) and may request that part (or more, sometimes all) of the fixed compensation is placed in escrow. In this case, the producer and the actor will select a mutually acceptable third party (usually a bank) to act as escrow agent. There will be a three-party contract—an escrow agreement—laying out the terms of the escrow and providing detailed and objective instructions for the escrow agent to follow in paying the money out. The escrow agent will not agree to make subjective choices. For example, the escrow agent will not be put in a position to decide whether or not one of the parties is in breach of the contract. The instructions usually require payment to be made on the passing of time or on some event (such as the end of principal photography) or on the certificate of one of the parties (such as the certificate by the actor's agent that the actor was in attendance at the required shooting dates, and so on).

Contingent compensation.
Again, we will address this topic in greater detail when we get to the long-form agreement. There are several forms of contingent compen-

sation and not all forms will apply in every situation. In this deal, the producer offered a bonus, but in other deals, the contingent compensation can take the form of contingent deferred payments, which are paid out of various definitions of postrelease revenues.

Box office bonuses. One common form of bonus is a bonus triggered by the box office receipts hitting a certain threshold. In this example, the first threshold is $15 million. Some of the theories underlying the bonus are: (1) The actor is performing for below his or her normal fee—the bonus is a good way to allow the actor to catch up. (2) The actor is willing to defer on this basis because the producer is betting on the actor's performance to bring in the dough. (3) Assuming that the costs of production are low enough, the producer will be so pleased when the movie's box office gross hits $15 million that he will be thrilled to give the actor another $100,000.

> Provided Actor is not in material breach of this Deal Memorandum, Loanout Company will be paid a bonus of $100,000 when and if the gross domestic box office receipts exceed $15,000,000 as reported by Daily Variety. An additional bonus of $100,000 will be paid when and if the gross domestic box office receipts exceed $25,000,000.

Other forms of contingent compensation. There are other contingent payments. For example, a deferred contingent payment might be structured as follows: "Actor may also receive $100,000 from 5 percent of adjusted gross revenues (as defined in Appendix B)." Essentially, this means that the actor may also receive more money from revenues generated by the exploitation of the picture. In this case, the actor's take, if any, would depend on the definition of adjusted gross revenues (a better definition than "net revenues," generally) and the actual performance of the movie at the box office.

Participation.

If the actor has enough leverage, he or she may also be able to negotiate a percentage of the revenues of the picture. These revenues are often referred to in the movie industry as back-end revenues. The possibilities are many. For example, an actor might be able to negotiate participation of the (1) gross revenues (which is the best possible position for the actor), (2) adjusted gross revenues (the next best for the actor), and (3) net revenues (the worst definition, but still better than no participation at all). With regard to each of these definitions, especially adjusted gross and net, there are many possibilities, which we will look at when we get to the discussion on the long-form actor's agreement.

> Provided Actor is not in material breach of this agreement, Producer shall pay Loanout Company a participation, in perpetuity, in the amount of ten percent (10%) of the "net proceeds" derived from the exploitation of the Picture. For the purposes of this Deal Memorandum, the definition of term "net proceeds" shall be no less favorable than the definition used by the Producer.

Net proceeds. Net proceeds and net revenues are terms used to describe the pool of revenues from which most participations are taken. Generally speaking, the net is derived from the following formula: gross receipts less all of (1) distribution fees, (2) distribution expenses, (3) the cost of the picture, and (4) all participants except for net proceeds participants. In the long-form agreement, it takes about twenty pages or so to explain how this works (so we'll discuss it in greater detail later). That kind of detail is naturally avoided in the deal memo.

Producer's definition. Note that in the deal memo, in order to avoid a lengthy discussion on the subject, the producer is sometimes willing to give the actor the same definition that the producer is taking. This is generally an acceptable practice, as most independent producers realize that their definition will have to be fairly standard—otherwise the studio or other financier will not buy it. Nevertheless, the producer's definition (since it is the producer who more or less determines it, in the first instance, alone) will be as good as the producer can make it and, therefore, the actor is usually willing to rely on the fact that the producer will not negotiate against himself or herself. Thus, this approach is not normally used for secondary actors, producers, and the like.

Expenses.
There are four elements of expenses: travel, living accommodations, ground transportation, and per diem. If the production is being done under one of the SAG agreements, the provisions of the applicable agreement will set the minimums for this category, but people typically ask for more than the minimum (for example, it is common

for persons to require first-class travel and hotel accommodations). Some of the usual amenities sought by actors, directors, and producers alike include an on-set trailer, a rental car or limousine, and expenses for a travel companion. In addition, some will seek airfare, accommodations, and tickets to world premieres, and so forth.

Three expense-related issues. The issue, as always, is money. With regard to travel and hotel, the negotiation point will be first-class versus some more moderately priced option. You will see a lot of strange stuff here—actors can be pretty demanding (like the color of the room, whether or not the windows open, etc.). In a film shot on location on a remote Pacific island, one actress demanded a first-class hotel room—sorry, there were no hotels. She got a first-class tent instead. Regarding per diem, the amount is the thing; cash is the thing. (With cash, however, make sure you have a good accountant.) With ground transportation there are also many options: Will the actor have his or her own car and driver? Have a car without a driver? Be forced to ride in the production car?

> First class air travel from New York to Los Angeles or other location required by Producer and accommodations (if in Los Angeles in a regular room at the Five Star Grand Hotel) will be provided by Producer for Actor with respect to Actor's services hereunder. For each day that Actor provides services hereunder, Loanout Company will receive a per diem of $300.00. In addition, if the shooting location is Los Angeles or the Los Angeles vicinity, Producer will supply Loanout Company a luxury rental car for Actor's use for the duration of the shooting on schedule.

Most-favored nation. We'll talk about this again. Basically, this is a shorthand way of saying that if somebody else gets something better than set forth in my contract, I'll get it too. Producers should be careful when using this approach to negotiation, because of the obvious potential for a domino effect if some large person comes to the party at a later date.

> Actor will be on a "most favored nations" status with respect to expenses.

Credit.
In the case of an actor, the following are possible issues to be addressed: (1) if the billing will be star billing, such should be stated;

(2) the position of the billing should be stated (whether the actor's name will be listed before other actors or otherwise); and (3) whether the billing will be above or below the title (usually optional, but some "A-List" talent will demand credits above the title). Look at the illustration below:

> Provided that Loanout Company is not in material breach hereof, Producer shall accord Actor credit in the main titles of the Picture and, subject to Producer's standard exclusions in all paid ads. The Actor's credit will be below the title of the Picture, on a separate card, in first position vis à vis all main cast members. The size and other characteristics of Actor's credit shall be at Producer's good faith discretion, but no less favorable than any other actor's credit on the Picture.

"Main titles." As used in this illustration, the main titles usually appear at the beginning of the movie, but sometimes occur at the end. The most prestigious position for an actor is above the title; here, the actor's title is below the title.

Separate card. The term separate card has been discussed before; essentially, it refers to whether the credit will be alone or grouped with other similar credits. Here, when the actor's credit is shown, it will be the only credit on the screen.

First position. Actors will also negotiate for position, with the first and last positions generally being the most prestigious. Here, the actor gets to be listed before any other actor.

Size and other characteristics. Actors and producers will sometimes dicker over the size of the type and other matters. Here, the producer gets to decide.

No less favorable (most favored nation). With language like this in favor of the actor, although the producer will decide the size and other characteristics of the credit, the producer will not be able to make any other actor's credit bigger or better than this actor.

Uses and rights (chain of title), etc.
The deal memo will contain a recitation that the producer has certain rights related to the actor's services and name and likeness and that the results and proceeds of such services will be owned by the

producer. In the deal memorandum, this is sometimes a mere summary of the longer, more detailed provisions of the long-form agreement. Therefore, producers often supplement this deal memorandum summary by having the actor sign a certificate of authorship. This is a prudent approach, even though the deal memorandum stage is considered preliminary, because of the importance of the chain of title issue and because one never knows for sure that the long-form agreement will ever be finished. Even if a certificate of authorship is used, this deal memorandum provision should contain sufficient language to accomplish the basics of chain of title, name and likeness and the basic intended uses, as well as standard language dealing with the problem (particularly in civil law jurisdictions—such as France and elsewhere in the EC) of "moral rights of authors." See the illustration below:

> The services provided by Actor hereunder shall be used in the Picture and in the worldwide exploitation of such. Loanout Company shall cause Actor to grant Producer the right to use his name and likeness in this connection. All results and proceeds of Actor's services hereunder shall be deemed a work made for hire for Producer and Producer shall own (and Loanout Company hereby grants and assigns, and shall cause Actor to grant and assign, to Producer) all rights therein, including all copyrights and, in this regard, Actor agrees to execute and deliver to Producer the certificate of authorship substantially in the form attached hereto as Exhibit B which is incorporated herein by reference. Loanout Company shall also cause Actor to waive any and all rights related to moral rights of authors.

Uses. It is necessary to explain in the broadest terms what the scope of producer's rights are.

Name and likeness. Producers want the right to use the name and likeness of the actor in the promotion and exploitation of the picture. This is important, because you will want to tell people about the people who acted in and made your motion picture and show their photograph or likeness in advertising the movie. Many persons, certainly actors, insist that they have the right to approve the photographs used or any rendering made of their likeness.

Results and proceeds. As noted above, this provision and the certificate of authorship approaches the task of putting any copyrightable material created by the actor into the hands of producer in two ways: (1) by reciting that the services are a work made for hire (with all the magical language we discussed) and (2) that nevertheless the actor makes an assignment of any and all rights he might have to the producer.

Moral rights of authors. This provision, as well as the certificate of authorship, should deal with that set of civil law jurisdiction rights called moral rights of authors (see above). The appropriate detail is covered in the certificate of authorship and/or the long-form agreement.

Guild references (if applicable).

If the actor is a guild member, a recitation to the effect that the SAG basic agreement will apply and that other obligations under that agreement will be met. The SAG agreement, like all industry guild agreements, form the minimum obligations of the producer, but allow the guild member to negotiate a more favorable deal.

Producer acknowledges and agrees that the SAG Agreement (defined below) shall apply to this Deal Memorandum and that Producer shall pay the applicable fringe benefits payments. Producer shall be entitled to the maximum benefits and maximum rights permitted under the SAG Agreement. To the extent the SAG Agreement requires additional payments to Actor hereunder, such additional payments shall be paid at the minimum rate required. As used herein, the term "SAG Agreement" refers to the current Producer Screen Actors Guild Codified Basic Agreement for Independent Producers.

Fringe payments. The so-called fringe-benefit payments (discussed in detail later) are payments to the guild pension and health and welfare funds. These contributions currently amount to about 13 percent of the actor's compensation and are over and above any other form of compensation.

Maximum benefits and rights. The producer, especially one who pays well above the minimum rate, wants to make sure that there is nothing in the deal memorandum that serves to limit the producer's rights; in other words, if the guild agreement grants some minimum rights to producers, the producer wants to make sure that these minimum rights are available to him or her.

Minimums. One of the features of the guild agreement is that the actor is entitled to the minimums established by the guild basic contract, but the actor can always negotiate a better deal.

Other deal memorandum provisions— looking forward to the long form.

As noted above, the deal memorandum's main purpose is to lock the actor in and get started. The idea is that a detailed long-form agreement will be negotiated and drafted. However, it is often the case that the long form never gets done (although studios will often insist on this happening, even if it happens after the movie is completed). Therefore, the question is where to draw the line.

> The parties hereby acknowledge and agree that they intend to negotiate and enter into a more formal written agreement consistent with the terms of this Deal Memorandum but incorporating other terms and conditions customarily included in agreements in the filmed entertainment industry (such as representations and warranties of the parties, covenants to indemnify, obligations regarding publicity as soon as practicable after the execution and delivery of this Deal Memorandum; provided, however, that unless and until such formal agreement is executed and delivered by the parties hereto this Deal Memorandum shall be a binding agreement between the parties hereto.

Here are some additional considerations for the deal memo.

Representations and warranties. Representations and warranties are an important part of any agreement, but are often left out of the deal memorandum with the idea that they will be negotiated later on. I recommend that some basic representations and warranties be added to the deal memo. They are made by both parties to the agreement. Both parties will represent that they have the right to enter into the agreement and that by doing so they will not violate any agreement with any third party. This is important to you, for example, because you want to make sure that the actor doesn't have a conflicting commitment with some other producer. The production company represents that it has the right to make the movie and agrees to hold harmless the actor or other person for claims made or losses incurred because of a breach of this representation. For example, the actor's agent will not want to put the actor at risk for a gap in the chain of title, so if there is a problem with copyright infringement the obligation will be on the production company to hold harmless the actor from a claim or loss.

Publicity. Producers generally seek an agreement with the actor, director, or other persons to proactively publicize the movie. You've seen actors make the rounds of the late-night talk shows and plug (or promote) their upcoming movies. You will also want to obligate the actor and others to agree to do certain things to promote the movie. Some actors and directors take particular pride in being willing to make personal appearances to plug movies in which they appear; others avoid this responsibility as an inconvenience (a position I find startling, since the success of the movie impacts directly on their career).

No obligation to proceed. The production company will try to protect itself by reciting in the agreement that it has no obligation to actually make the motion picture or use the actor's or other person's services. This is important, even in a pay-or-play situation, because it protects the producer from claims based on anticipated benefits arising from the completion and release of the motion picture. It also allows the producer some degree of flexibility if possible, but unanticipated, circumstances. For example, let's suppose you hire Bobby B. Rate to play the leading role, because Artie A. Actor is busy. But then, low and behold, Artie's schedule suddenly clears and it is worth it to you and your investors to pay Bobby his fee and get Artie to act in Bobby's stead.

Miscellaneous. The deal memo will also state the governing law (for example, the law of the state of California), the fact that the agreement is not assignable by the actor (but that it can be assigned by the production company to a major studio or to an affiliate of the production company party), that it cannot be orally modified, and other standard provisions that lawyers know and love.

BOOK FOUR

GETTING THE MONEY TO MAKE IT HAPPEN

In order to move from the packaging stage (and, more and more, in order to do the packaging tasks) you will need money—and lots of it. For example, you would not be wise to make offers that immediately become pay-or-play obligations without having the money to cover such offers. And, whereas, you will make a lot of promises during the packaging stage to pay money, as you move into the next stage—production—you will actually start paying the money. This means, that you will need to have the money in an account controlled by you. You (or someone hired by you) will write a lot of checks. And if you ever hope to make it out of this process alive, with your sanity and reputation intact, you will need people who know how to handle production spending. Hiring a line producer and others with experience and integrity will be critical. If you stumble here, all the nice agents and other people with whom you just bonded, will become your undoing.

Production
Money Rules

SOME WORDS OF WARNING

I cannot tell you where to find the money, but I have already told you how to raise it. You present your package to someone who wants to invest in film properties.

If somebody becomes interested in your package, you will need to know what you are doing. Now here is where you need some strong words of warning related to some of the pitfalls that are ever present in raising money. The United States government and the governments of each of the fifty states have laws (so-called "blue sky" laws) protecting citizens from losing their money in investments that they don't understand or appreciate. Therefore, raise your right hand and repeat after me—now do it, dang it!—"I promise that I will not attempt to raise money without consulting an attorney who knows about the laws related to raising money." Okay, I feel better.

Use a lawyer to help you.
However, I don't feel good enough to leave this subject alone yet. I want to help you understand why it is important to use a lawyer at this stage. Raising money is a sensitive subject under the law. The commercial history of the world (including the United States) is full of problems caused by shady guys raising money on false promises from people who cannot distinguish a good deal from a scam. There are too many stories about retired people and widows who give up their

life savings to such guys. Therefore, a comprehensive body of law exists, complete with penalties and punishments, for those who do not comply. Moreover, when people lose money, they usually don't hesitate to resort to the sanctions provided by these laws. Don't fudge on the realities of these risks. Get the advice of an experienced lawyer to help you.

Comply with federal securities laws.

There are two major federal laws that relate to the offering of "securities"; they were enacted after the stock market crash of 1929 and have been amended and supplemented over the years.[1] A threshold issue under these laws is what constitutes a security. Since the purpose of this book is not to make you securities lawyers, I will skip a lot of deep philosophical points and tell you that shares of stock in a corporation, membership units in a limited liability company, and limited partnership units are without question securities under those laws. In fact, the scope of the term securities is very broad and there is virtually no way around the fact that any attempt to raise money will implicate the rules under these federal statutes.

There are essentially two major implications of these laws: either you will have to register your offering with the Securities and Exchange Commission (SEC) or you may be able to escape this requirement by fitting into an exception, such as Regulation D.

Public offerings—registration. Registration is required for offerings to the public at large. Because the public includes the widow and her life savings, the SEC will be very protective. Comprehensive and technical documents requiring the disclosure of all the facts related to the investment, including all the risks, must be filed with the SEC. Now here is where I can help you a lot. Doing a public offering on a single movie is too expensive! You can't do it alone, and lawyers will spend a lot of time helping you. In the legal business, time is money and so a lot of time means you will owe them a lot of money. The money you will have to pay them could have gone into the movie. Don't go there. (Now, you have already recouped the price you paid for the book.)

Private placements. United States securities laws provide for exceptions from the requirement to register with the SEC. Under Regulation D, for example, a person (including a movie producer) can make an offer to a small number of persons (and therefore the offering is not public, but private). At present, this number is thirty-five or less. "Ac-

credited investors" (or persons who meet certain financial criteria defined by law)[2] are not counted in this number and, therefore, the offer
can be expanded by targeting accredited investors. In fact, I advise
clients to focus only on accredited investors and to avoid the unsophis-
ticated retirees or those who cannot bear the risk of losing their money.

Generally this means that they are experienced in making investments and can afford to lose all their money. There is a vast difference
between approaching a person who makes investments for a living
or who has experience in making investments and someone who is
doing it for the first time. Moreover, there are risks associated with all
investments (especially movie investment) and only persons with experience will know how to look for and appreciate those risks. Do
not ask Aunt Maggie (unless she is a billionaire) or any other person to
whom the loss of their money would be a life-altering event.

Comply with all applicable state laws.
An experienced securities lawyer will not miss this point, but Uncle
Joe, who practices family law, might—so you should understand that
the federal law is not the end of the issue. All states have laws governing the offering of securities within their borders. Some states are
more restrictive than Regulation D, so be careful. These laws have to
be looked at and complied with too.[3]

Policies to adopt.
At the risk of repeating myself, you should consult a lawyer to help
you use the guidelines contained in the federal and state laws to guide
your plan to raise financing. Generally speaking, there are two areas
of concern: what you say and who you target.

Go after a small, but qualified group. Your attorney and you
should consider the persons who will get your money pitch. Make sure
they are accredited investors. They must be rich (not just richer than
you—rich enough that if your great project goes down without a trace
and they lose 100 percent of their investment, they won't be affected
economically—they may still not be happy, mind you, but they will be
able to go for a long drive in their new Ferrari to work it out). They
should be experienced investors. The best targets are those who make
all types of investments all the time—those who cannot argue, when
things go wrong, that they had no idea of the risks involved.

Industry experience is best. If a person is rich and an experienced
investor, that is good and may help avoid any problems, but it is al-

ways better to have someone who understands the film industry specifically. The film business has certain peculiar risks associated with it. Persons experienced in this area, are less likely to complain if things go wrong. Therefore, motion picture studios and sales agents who are in the business of selling off the foreign rights to movie projects should always be on your list of potential investors. Sure, these investors may have a lot to say about the script and other elements of the package—such as cast and the director—but by and large their experience with movies in general will be a plus. It doesn't hurt that these investors are usually film distributors or people who have intimate relations with distributors, since distribution is a key to making money with your movie. If the investor doesn't have any film experience, the investor should hire a lawyer who does.

Be up front about the risks associated with your project. Now, I know your idea is great and that you have high expectations. It is nice to be positive and excited about your prospects. But you must be realistic. If you are a first-time movie producer, there is no reason to believe that your movie will be successful—in other words, there is a risk because of your inexperience. There are no guarantees—don't make or promise any.

In fact, when you and your lawyer set about contacting people for your project, you will disclose the "risk factors" in making the investment. Examples of such risk factors include: (1) This is a new company with no operating history (by the way it doesn't matter whether you have experience or not—since you are offering investments in your company, it is the company, not you, that needs to make the disclosure); (2) there is no market for the "securities" (this means that the little pieces of paper that represent ownership in your company, which is making the movie, are not being sold on any stock exchange); (3) no market is likely to develop (so unless you have big plans to take your company public—list those pieces of paper on a stock exchange—no market will likely materialize and the investor won't be able to unload his or her investment on someone else[4]); (4) the film business is risky and, therefore, the investors might lose all their investment; (5) the offer contains "forward-looking statements" (which means that the financial projections you make concerning the movie are guesses—they may be good guesses or they may be bad guesses, but they are guesses); (6) there will be a lot of competition (which means that your movie will not be the only one out there); (7) you will have to depend on other people (meaning that you will not be able to make the movie yourself and you will need the skills of others); and (8) so forth.

Be sensitive to the business deal. We will talk about the realities of the business deal later. For example, it is a matter of common sense that making a motion picture without a distribution commitment is more risky than making one with a distribution commitment. Likewise, all distribution deals are not created equal—some are good and some not so good. In addition, it is more risky to make a picture with no recognized talent than it is to make a picture with an established star. It is more risky to use a first-time director, than one who is experienced and who has a bankable reputation. Remember all the packaging issues we discussed above. These are all real issues and must be dealt with. Ignoring them will make a producer lose credibility and affect his or her ability to raise money.

Make sure the investor has legal representation. It is unlikely that a person who has a lot of money, and, therefore, qualifies to hear your pitch, will do the deal without a lawyer. But if the investor fails to consult a lawyer, you should suggest—no insist—that he or she do so. A lawyer experienced in entertainment finance is best.

The difference between a PPM and a business plan.

As we have discussed, the securities laws say, in essence, that unless you follow all the requirements of a public offering (a very expensive proposition) or qualify under the "safe harbor" rules of Regulation D, you cannot engage in a "general solicitation" of securities. Let's look at what that actually means to you.

In the case of a private placement under Regulation D, the producer is making an offer of securities to a qualified group of potential investors—accredited investors and/or a limited number (at this time, 35 or less) unaccredited investors. The investor gets a copy of the producer's PPM, reads it, and, if the investor likes what he or she sees, fills in the appropriate information (how many shares or units—referred to under the law as "securities"—the investor wants to buy) on the enclosed subscription agreement, signs the subscription agreement, and submits it, with the investor's check, to the producer. If the appropriate number of securities are subscribed for (most PPMs have a minimum investment), the producer then issues the securities in accordance with the terms of the subscription agreement. The checks are then cashed and the movie is made.

Is there another way to raise money? The answer is technically yes, but you need to be careful here.

It is possible for a producer to prepare and use a "business plan." The business plan may look a lot like a PPM—it may describe the producer's career and the careers of any other attached persons; it may describe the movie business and the risks associated with movie investments; and it will describe the movie to be made and exploited. However, a business plan will not describe the characteristics of the deal—how the parties will interact to take advantage of the business opportunity posed by the business plan. A business plan is designed *not* to be an offer of securities. For example, business plans will almost always include prominent disclaimers (often in all caps), such as: "THIS BUSINESS PLAN IS NOT AN OFFER TO SELL OR A SOLICITATION OF AN OFFER TO BUY SECURITIES, NOR SHALL SECURITIES BE OFFERED OR SOLD TO ANY PERSON IN ANY JURISDICTION IN WHICH SUCH OFFER, SOLICITATION, OR PURCHASE WOULD BE UNLAWFUL PRIOR TO REGISTRATION OR QUALIFICATION UNDER THE SECURITIES LAWS OF SUCH JURISDICTION." The business plan's underlying assumption is that a particular investor and the producer are going to engage in a negotiation of an agreement, the terms of which will be determined by the negotiation. The agreement involves the sale of securities, of course, but the business plan approach to investors does not implicate the securities laws, because securities are not being offered for sale.

Why be careful? Well, although there is nothing illegal about bringing an opportunity to and concluding a deal with a person, the business plan approach can be abused. Producers who send business plans indiscriminately to dozens of potential investors might easily enough violate the securities laws. A mass mailing of a business plan could be viewed as a general solicitation, for example. Therefore, I advise clients who use a business plan to: only target a limited number of accredited investors (and not to take a chance on unaccredited investors), make sure that the investor hires a lawyer to advise him or her about the deal, and ensure that full and truthful disclosure of the risks is made in the business plan and during the negotiations.

THE BASIC INDEPENDENT MOVIE INVESTMENT DEAL

The basic motion picture financing deal for an independent movie is this: The investors get 50 percent of all net revenues, plus prior recoupment (usually with interest) of their investment, with obligations to third parties coming out of the producer's side.

And here's how it works: The producer shows the investors that he has a corporate vehicle that owns or controls the package—the right to make the motion picture based on the screenplay along with the elements (director, producer, and main actors), if any, he was able to secure during the packaging step. The investor puts up (or makes it possible for the producer to obtain) 100 percent of the amount of the production budget. The producer then causes the production company to make and exploit the movie. From the revenues generated from this exploitation, the amount of money put up by the investor or investors is recouped or paid back (usually with a little extra to account for the interest the investor would have made if he had kept the money in the bank). Once the investor has been fully recouped, the net revenues are split equally between the investor and the producer forever. If there are third parties who are entitled to a participation in the picture, these third parties are paid from the producer's 50 percent of the net revenues.

THE DETAILS BEHIND THE BASIC INVESTMENT DEAL

From this general arrangement, there are a number of subtleties that need to be explored.

Choosing a structure.

The first issue involves the selection of an appropriate production vehicle. The objectives in choosing a structure include limiting your (and your investor's) liability and providing an appropriate mechanism for owning and operating the business of exploiting the intellectual property that will spring into life as a result of you taking the steps discussed in this book. I'm going to take a shortcut here and say that there are four basic structures that you can choose (actually, of course, there are more choices, but, as I said, I'm taking the shortcut): a corporation, a partnership, a limited partnership, and a limited liability company. Here is a summary of each of these vehicles:

Corporations. Every state in the United States provides for the creation of various types of corporations, each a so-called juridical person, with a legal life of its own. Corporations (as juridical persons) can buy and own property and enter into contracts. One of a corporation's most important features is that it is responsible for its own liabilities.

Advantages. The major advantage of a corporation is limited liability for the owners. If someone sues a corporation and wins a judgment against the corporation (with some exceptions), the person can look only to the assets of the corporation to satisfy the judgment—the judgment cannot be satisfied by the assets of the owners of the corporation (regardless of how rich they are and even if the owners control and/or operate the corporation). Because of this, corporations are said to be "limited liability" entities. Corporations can also be owned by more than one person (or entity). These features make the corporate structure a candidate for producing your motion picture.

The corporation can hold the rights and other assets of your package. It can hire people to make and exploit the movie. It can own the movie. It can be owned by you and by your investor. Ownership of a corporation is evidenced by holding shares of stock. All of the shares added together will equal 100 percent of the stock. Thus, by holding the appropriate number of shares, you can own 50 percent of the stock and your investor can own the remaining 50 percent.

Disadvantages. Although for foreign investors a corporation may be the clear (and only rational) choice,[5] there are several significant disadvantages in using a corporation for the purposes of motion picture finance. The main disadvantage is the requirement that money paid to the owners of the corporation must be in the form of "dividends" and, in paying dividends, generally speaking, all shares of stock are treated in the same way. For example, suppose that a corporation has a hundred shares of stock outstanding (meaning that one hundred shares have been issued and are in the hands of owners). If you own fifty shares of stock and your investor owns fifty shares of stock, when the company goes to distribute money it must treat you and your investor the same. There is no simple way (although there are ways—using preferred stock, for example) to allow the investor to recoup its investment first, as described above.

Another disadvantage relates to the fact that, under current tax law, the corporation is taxed on the revenues it receives (remember the corporation is a separate person under the eyes of the law) and the owners of the corporation are taxed again when they receive their dividends. If you think about it, from the point of view of the stockholders, it feels like two levels of tax. It's okay to pay tax, of course, but twice on the same revenue stream is neither efficient nor fun.

Also, corporations have elaborate control mechanisms (the stockholders elect boards that appoint officers). Since one of the producer's major goals is to maintain control, the fact that the shares of stock are divided evenly between the investor and the producer makes it cumbersome to effectuate that control.

Finally, when the corporation is dissolved, each shareholder is treated the same. This sounds innocent enough, but imagine that you, as producer, put in the script and a few thousand dollars to get it written and your investor puts in a few million to get the movie produced. Now let's suppose a disaster happens and that the company needs to be liquidated. Well, you own 50 percent of the stock and so 50 percent of the value of the company will go to you. That sounds like a good deal to you, but it won't to your investor.

Fixes. There are ways to get around each of the disadvantages of corporations. The corporation laws of every state allow for the issuance of different classes of stock. For example, corporations can issue preferred stock to the investors, which allows them to have a preferred position on certain distributions of revenues and on the dissolution of the company.

The corporation can also issue nonvoting stock (even nonvoting preferred stock). This allows the producer to have total control over the operational affairs of the corporation. The terms of the nonvoting stock can be structured so that it will be converted into voting stock, if something untoward happens (such as the producer tries to sell the corporation to someone else for peanuts).

In addition, respecting the double taxation issue, the government allows for the existence of special corporations under Subchapter S of the Internal Revenue Code (so-called Subchapter S corporations), which eliminates the double taxation problem by taxing only the stockholders. It is important to note, however, that only natural persons (not corporate entities) can be stockholders of Subchapter S corporations and thus this structure will not work in certain circumstances.

There are also ways to get around the other problems, the most viable of which is to set up a special purpose corporation to house the motion picture assets and form a contractual relationship between your corporation and the investor (or more likely your investor's corporation). Contracts are quite flexible in terms of structure and the fact that the parties to the contract are corporations gives the limited liability feature prized in corporations.

Foreign investments. As noted above, where the investor is from a foreign country, a corporation may be the clear choice. Generally, the reason that the corporation works so well in these situations is that corporations do not allow the earnings to "pass through" to the stockholders and, therefore, the foreign stockholders can choose, by clever structuring, to leave the earnings outside of their home jurisdiction in order to avoid being taxed there on revenues earned in another country. (In a pass-through entity, such as a partnership or limited liability company, the earnings are often deemed to be received by the partners or members, as the case may be, when received by the partnership or limited liability company. It is way beyond the scope of this book to try to describe how to structure investments by foreigners for tax purposes; such matters need the assistance of a tax accountant or tax lawyer experienced in structuring international film-financing deals.

Partnership. On the other end of the spectrum is the partnership. From the point of view of the law, the partnership is the most simple form of juridical person and, in fact, if you do nothing to structure it otherwise the law will generally see the joint activity of you and your investor as a partnership. Partnerships can also be created in a formal way with official status under the eyes of the state and federal government.

Partnership pluses. Partnerships solve the main problems with corporations. Partnerships allow for the payment of money to the partners in any way the partners agree. In addition, partnerships are not taxed at all—the individual partners are; so, there is no double taxation problem with a partnership.

A standard scenario using a partnership would be for you to contribute the package and for the investor to contribute capital to the partnership. In both cases, you and the investor would receive a capital account based on the value of what you contributed. The capital accounts are returned to the partners in the event of the dissolution of the partnership. Therefore, the problems encountered by shareholders of a corporation on liquidation of the corporation's assets are not faced by partners in a partnership.

Moreover, the partners can split the profits of the partnership in any way they want to. For example, Partner A can put in $1.00 and Partner B can put in $1 million and they can agree to split the profits of the partnership 99 percent to Partner A and 1 percent to Partner B (needless to say, it doesn't happen often, but it is possible).

Partnership problems. The major flaw of a partnership is that it has no limit on liability. If someone sues the partnership and wins a judgment (as described above), the winner can have the judgment satisfied from the assets of the partnership and from the individual partners, who are jointly and severally (meaning as a group and as an individual) liable for the partnership's obligations. To put this another way, the winner of the judgment can potentially take any partner's house or car! This fact is a show stopper for most investors, who are rich guys. If something goes wrong—let's say that your music supervisor borrows a piece of music from the Lennon-McCartney song library and fails to clear the rights—the plaintiff (in this case the publishing company that owns or controls the catalog) will go against the deepest pockets around—your investor (because if you had the money to produce this movie you would, wouldn't you?). The investor won't like this.

Fixes. One possible way around this flaw is to have the partners be corporations. But this could pose other problems and it still allows judgment creditors to reach inside the corporate partners' assets.

Limited partnership. The limited partnership was until relatively recently the structure of choice for independent film financing. A limited partnership is a partnership with two classes of partners: There is one general partner and any number of limited partners. The general partner controls the operations of the partnership and is liable for the limited partnership's problems. The limited partners' only function is to contribute money (in fact, a rule of the limited partnership is that limited partners cannot participate in its management) and receive in return a portion of the profits generated by the actions of the general partner. Limited partners can have prior recoupment and this structure accommodates other typical features of the standard deal discussed above. Limited partners have limited liability; thus, only the assets of the general partner can be reached to satisfy any judgment against the limited partnership. The general partner, who is liable, is usually a corporation and derives limited liability protection for its shareholders from its corporate structure. It holds the rights to the movie and makes all the deals. Limited partnerships can be and are still used for film financing, but because they are subject to fairly rigorous state statutory requirements they have largely given way to the more straightforward and modern limited liability company.

Limited liability company. The limited liability company (LLC) is a popular vehicle for film financing today. When there are two or more members, it can be treated as a partnership and has all the features and flexibility of a partnership, so the members of the LLC are in function partners: they have capital accounts and a negotiated share of the profits (without regard to the size of their contributions). Like a partnership, LLCs are not taxed. There is no double taxation; rather, the members are taxed as individuals. But unlike a partnership, the LLC has a corporation-like shield. This means that judgments must be satisfied only from the assets of the LLC. The assets of the individual members cannot be reached. The rules governing the LLC do not prohibit the members from participating in governance matters, like limited partnerships—all issues like this are negotiated and incorporated into an agreement among the members (called, logically enough, a membership agreement or operating agreement). Moreover, corporations and other LLCs can be members. In sum, the LLC is a partnership with limited liability and is more or less ideal for film financing.

Prior recoupment.

The investor will (or should) insist on the custom of being able to get his or her (its) money back before your production company starts getting its share of the profits. The investor might ask to be paid 100 percent of the "gross" revenues from the exploitation of the movie until 100 percent of the investment plus some percentage (usually approximating an interest rate) has been received. The producer might ask that the investor recoup the investment plus interest from 90 percent or some other percentage less than 100 percent. This gives the producer a chance to start receiving money to cover overhead and for other such purposes. This argument often fails, however, especially if and to the extent that the producer takes an up-front fee at the beginning of the production of the movie (a common practice). Since money is scarce, unless you have a lot of leverage, recoupment will probably come from 100 percent (or some other high percentage) of the gross proceeds. There are two situations, however, that the producer might argue fall outside the prior recoupment rule:

Tax distributions. One of the problems with prior recoupment, for the producer, is tax. During the time that the financier is recouping money, the revenues coming into the LLC or the partnership are considered income to the members or partners, as the case may be. For example, imagine that you form an LLC and attract an investor to finance a $10 million motion picture. Let's suppose, also, that you and the investor agree to split the profits fifty-fifty after the investor recoups his or her money. Then, suppose that the motion picture makes

$12 million at the box office. Under the tax laws, you and the investor could both be deemed to be receiving revenues (and, thus, incurring a tax liability) from the time the money starts coming in. Your problem, in this scenario, is that you will have no money coming in to pay tax—since the first moneys coming in are going to the investor. The fix for this is to provide in the LLC operating agreement or partnership agreement for distributions to be made to the party not receiving prior recoupment in an amount necessary to pay his or her taxes.

Third-party gross participants. Another problem is the third party who gets to participate from gross or adjusted gross revenues. Remember the big star or big director who became attached to your project for less than the normal asking price? Remember too what you had to promise to get such a person to join your merry band. That's right—you promised a piece of the pie and, if you also agreed to participation from the dollar one gross or adjusted gross pools, the income from which the investor can recoup will be reduced. Where this financial reality is part of the package that the investor was able to examine before putting money into your project, you should be okay. But you will have to be careful in the case of negotiations that take place after the financing deal is set. The fix for this is to define such third-party participants as coming off the top (i.e., before the money is deemed to come into the company[6]).

In the money.
The movie is out there in the theaters and, later, in Blockbuster video. People pay to see it and to rent it. And then here comes the money. Like water flowing down an irrigation canal. But hold on—before the water reaches you there will be some diversions. First, before the money even enters the stream of revenues, the theaters take their share, sixty cents of every dollar. What is left is called "theatrical rentals." But wait. From theatrical rentals, the distributor recoups its distribution (often referred to as "P&A"—prints and advertising) expenses and takes a distribution fee (traditionally around 25 to 35 percent, depending on several factors) and, sometimes, a portion to cover its overhead. What is left—sometimes referred to as producer's gross—is what we have been talking about. It goes to recoup the investor's investment plus interest. And then—drum roll please—it is divided between you and the investor. The standard deal, of course, is 50 percent to the investor and 50 percent to you (with you being responsible for third-party participants).

Participants.

It is an axiom of the standard deal that all third-party participants come from the producer's (not the investor's side of the deal).
But the reality of that statement deserves a closer look. Although we
will discuss this in greater detail later, it is necessary to understand in
general how this works. This is a dynamic concept, but for the sake of
simplicity, I will divide participants into three categories: gross, adjusted gross, and net participants. Think of these three participants as
three farmers staking out their positions along the irrigation canal.
The farmer with the most favorable position, a gross participant, diverts the water for his fields near the head of the canal, where there
is most likely to be sufficient water. The next most powerful farmer,
an adjusted gross participant, diverts the water later on down the
canal, before the stream dissipates further. The least powerful farmer,
a net participant, takes from the end of the canal—where there is
the greatest risk that there won't be any water left for irrigation. And,
of course, that is the point. Since some movies don't make a lot of
money, the closer to the headwaters you are the better your chances
of getting your participation; the longer you have to wait, the greater
the chance that there won't be any at all. What does all this mean
to you, the producer? The producer is by definition a net player. Thus,
if the gross and adjusted gross participants take too much of the
stream, there won't be a lot left.

Bringing the
Money Home

Unfortunately, the "angel" investor who puts up all the money in one transaction is a rare thing—which makes the term angel quite apt. But there are other ways to get your motion picture financed. Let's look at some other structures:

THE SPLIT-RIGHTS DEAL

One of the most common ways is to split the distribution rights of your movie up by territory and sell, or presell, those rights one at a time to territorial distributors.

The so-called "split-rights" deal can take several structures, but the most common is perhaps where the producer does a deal with a sales agent. Sales agents make it their business to know the distributors in each territory in their part of the world. If a sales agent likes the producer's package, it will enter into a contract that essentially gives the agent the right to sell the distribution rights in a specified territory or territories. The contracts generated by the efforts of the sales agent promise to pay advances against a distribution fee and the rights granted are distribution rights. Thus, the form of these agreements is, in essence, a distribution agreement. These contracts, in turn, are used as collateral to get the movie fully financed. We will take a quick look at a typical sales agent agreement, but because we discuss distribution agreements in greater detail later, the discussion below is abbreviated.

Territory.

The sales agent will ask for the right to distribute (directly or through subdistributors) your motion picture in a defined territory. Sometimes this territory is the world outside of North America (Canada and the United States). Sometimes the territory will be delineated by naming the actual countries or language-speaking areas (for example, "U.K., Benelux, Germany, and France").

The word "Territory" refers to all territories of the universe, excluding the United States of America (including its respective territories) and the (English- and French-speaking) territories of Canada.

Term.

The sales agent will have these rights for a prescribed term, which can run from a few years to in perpetuity.

The "Term" of this agreement is ten (10) years commencing with the initial theatrical release of the Picture in North America. Sales Agent agrees that it will not permit the distribution or exhibition of the Picture beyond the expiration of the Term for the Picture without the prior approval of Producer.

Rights.

The sales agent, for the purposes of the contract, is treated like a distributor. Indeed, some sales agents do in fact distribute the movie in certain areas, but many merely subdistribute the rights the producer grants to local distribution companies. Sales agents like all rights deals—where all the rights related to the movie (theatrical, television, merchandising, and so forth)—are parceled out, but sales agents will also take limited rights deals in certain circumstances.

License.

Sales agent agreements are usually (almost always) licenses. There are basically two legal approaches to disposing of intellectual property. You can sell (assign) the property or you can license it. In the second case, the original owner of the property (the licensor) keeps title or ownership, but allows the second party (the licensee) to use it in certain ways. In a sale, the owner transfers ownership. The advantage of a license is that the licensor can impose all kinds of stipulations or conditions of use. If the licensee fails to live up to the conditions of use, the licensor can terminate the license; and, upon termination, the rights automatically reside exclusively again in the licensor's hands. In the case of a grant, the termination of the agreement would not necessarily result in the rights reverting to the grantor. This is a big legal difference.

> Producer hereby licenses to Sales Agent for the Term in the Territory the sole and exclusive right to distribute, license, lease, rent, subdistribute, market, advertise and otherwise exploit in any manner whatsoever, in its sole discretion, the Picture and any and all elements thereof and rights therein including any and all versions and trailers thereof, in theatrical, television (all forms), video cassettes and disc media and any other media whether now in existence or hereafter developed. Sales Agent must secure the prior written approval of Producer before attempting to sublicense the Picture for any term extending beyond the date on which this Agreement expires.

Distribution rights. The contract provision above states specifically the uses that the licensee has the right to pursue. Here, those rights include distribution, subdistribute, or exploit in any manner. However, these rights are virtually always limited in that certain rights are held back or restrictions imposed.

Marketing rights. The sales agent also needs the right to promote and market the movie.

Media. The sales agent will want the right to distribute in all media—i.e., theatrical, television, video, DVD, videocassettes, and other media—even media that is developed in the future (see the discussion on distribution deals later on).

Additional rights—aren't you glad you have a clear chain of title? Since we will discuss in great detail in book six a standard distribution contract, I will refrain from reciting here all the specific rights the sales agent wants in the agreement. Rather, here is a sample list: (1) music rights; (2) the right to use the title or titles of the movie, (3) the right to dub the movie in another language or add subscripts; (4) specific rights of publication—including the right to publish summaries of the plot (remember when the producer reserved this right from the original author of the novel—well, now you know why); (5) broadcast rights; (6) use of the name and likeness of the performers that appear in the movie for the purposes of promotion; and (7) the right to prosecute others for copyright infringement. The reason the sales agent wants you to list these rights is largely because the agent wants you to represent and warrant that you have the ability to grant the rights and that if the agent is sued exercising any of these rights you will indemnify him or her. Now you understand why it is important to pay attention to all those "chain of title" matters that I have been harping about.

A special note about music. Write this down somewhere—or get a yellow marker and smear it all over this next sentence: Music is a problem. We will deal with it in detail later, but note the complexity in this context. There is a difference between clearing the rights to have music play in the movie and selling the music on a separate sound track. There is a difference between clearing the rights to a composition and a master recording of that composition. In clearing the rights to music, you must do it one composition at a time—there is no central clearing house for music clearances in America. Producers seem to learn this lesson slowly. Some learn it at great expense.

Reserved rights.
Producers will always want to think about reserving certain rights. For example, a sales agent usually cannot make a persuasive argument that he is better qualified to seek a novelization deal for the screenplay. Sometimes, producers will have a chance to make a worldwide deal for merchandising or even television.

> All rights not expressly licensed herein to Sales Agent, including, without limitation, all theatrical distribution rights to the United States and Canada, merchandising and commercial tie-up, novelization and publication rights, stage rights and any other ancillary or allied rights in the Picture, or the underlying literary, dramatic or musical material contained in the Picture or upon which the Picture is based, are hereby expressly reserved by Producer.

In making this type of deal, the producer will often analyze the situation by looking at the sales agent's capabilities. As noted above, a sales agent who specializes in making foreign distribution deals may not be in the best position to do a print publishing or merchandising deal, which are usually best done by other specialists. The same may also hold true for a commercial tie-up deal (where a manufacturer of goods pays money to be associated with the movie), although one can easily imagine how this might work on a country by country basis as well. Sound-track albums are reserved, because they are better handled by specialists—and because the right to use the music in a sound track might not be clear. Stage rights are rarely given away by the producer—assuming of course he got them.

Advance.

The real point of this exercise is to get an advance payment (or at least a firm commitment to pay) from each territory. It is this advance that you, the producer, will use to finance your movie. Here's how it works: For each territory, you can expect to get a certain percentage of the budget. Suppose, for example, that your sales agent sells the distribution rights to Japan. The territorial rights to Japan (which includes all rights—to wit, theatrical distribution, television broadcasting, and all other rights that the producer has) customarily equals 10 percent of the final production budget, so if the movie budget is $10 million, the advance distribution fee or advance would equal $1 million. The sales agent will procure written commitments from each of the territories or, in some cases, the sales agent will issue a written commitment for all or part of the amount of the advance.

The term advance—applied against the net. The term advance as used in the following illustration is derived from the fact that the producer's compensation structure has two parts: one part is paid up front (or advanced) to the producer and the second part is paid at the back end (net after the deduction of costs and miscellaneous payments). The amount that flows to the producer—sometimes referred to as overages (because this is the amount of revenue that is over and above the amount required to recoup the advance plus the cost of distribution)—is calculated in accordance with the explanation below.

> Sales Agent shall use its best efforts to distribute the Picture in the Territory and to obtain advances in the amount equal, in the aggregate, to at least 60% of the total budget, less completion bond and contingency costs, set forth on Exhibit A attached hereto and incorporated herein by reference, which amount shall be amended to conform with the final budget of the Picture (the "Budget Amount"). If Sales Agent fails to obtain advances from the Territory equal to at least 60% of the Budget Amount within six (6) months from the date of this agreement, Producer shall have the right to

terminate this agreement and all rights granted herein by Producer to Sales Agent shall revert to Producer.

Obligation to distribute. As noted above, the sales agent is treated like a distributor for the purposes of the contract. Believe it or not, some distribution contracts don't actually require the distributor to distribute. In this example, the distributor has to give it his or her best efforts—a real commitment, as discussed above. But suppose that the distributor tries hard, but the movie never makes it to the theater. To make the commitment real, the producer will try to pin the distributor down to a specific number of screens in specific markets (or cities or regions). What makes the provision tolerable in this example, as drafted, is the producer's ability to terminate the contract if the sales agent fails to get the required amount of presales.

Marketing and advertising.
The sales agent (and its distributor licensees) will spend money to market and advertise the movie in the territory. Further, although the sales agent will advance the money for marketing and advertising, the sales agent will insist that the costs be recouped (or paid back) out of the revenues generated by the exploitation of the movie in the territory—moneys that would otherwise go to the producer.

Sales Agent shall market and advertise the Picture in the Territory using customary means (including, without limitation, print ads and television and radio ads) and shall advance the costs of such marketing and advertising and shall have the right to recoup its marketing expenses as provided below.

Obligation to market. The sales agent also agrees to take on the responsibility to market the movie. This is important to the producer, because without some type of marketing, the movie will not be likely to find an audience in the territory.

Recoupment. This word is used in all film-financing contracts. As you know, it means simply the right of a person (payor) who advances a payment to another person (payee) to be reimbursed for the advance, usually out of a stream of payments the payor controls in some way. Here, in addition to the advance referred to above, the sales agent advances the marketing and advertising expenses and recoups the amount advanced.

Sales agent's fee and distribution expenses.

The sales agent, for his or her part, will have the right to charge a distribution fee against the revenues that are derived by exploiting the movie.[1] This fee is usually in the 20 to 25 percent range. This fee, like the expenses discussed above, will be deducted from certain revenues generated in the territories covered by the sales agent. Any revenues left over after the deduction of fees and expenses (overages) belong to the producer. The contract, therefore, starts with gross and carefully explains what can be deducted by the sales agent (including the sales agent's fee); what remains belongs to the producer (or the producer and his merry band of investors and other participants).

The definition of gross receipts. The following contract illustration starts with the basic definitions of gross and net receipts. The definition of gross receipts is simply everything that the sales agent (and the sales agent's affiliates) receives from the exploitation of the movie.

> For the purposes of this Agreement, "Gross Receipts" shall mean all revenues of whatever nature received by Sales Agent from any and all sources derived from the exploitation of the Picture.

The problem with affiliates of the sales agent. An important point in any sales agent agreement is the treatment of the sales agent's affiliates. For example, suppose that the producer enters into an agreement with a distributor for the territory of Japan. The agreement allows the distributor to take a 20 percent distribution fee from the revenue it receives from subdistributors in Japan. Now suppose that the distributor allows its own subsidiary to act as a subdistributor. If the sales agent takes a 20 percent fee and the sales agent's subsidiary also takes a 20 percent fee, the amount of gross receipts to the producer will be reduced and the sales agent will in essence be taking a double fee. A fix, illustrated in the example below, is to define gross receipts in such a way as to include any revenues received by an affiliate (without deductions, of course). Typically, affiliate means a company or firm (including, for example, a subsidiary) in which the sales agent or any officer, director, or shareholder (owning a certain percentage, say 10 percent or more, of the outstanding stock) of the sales agent has any direct or indirect interest. The producer's goal is to make sure that all revenues received by any affiliate of the sales agent, without any deductions of any kind, shall be included in gross receipts.

Any revenues received by any affiliate of Sales Agent shall be deemed included within Gross Receipts for the purposes of this Agreement.

The definition of adjusted gross receipts. Sales agents are usually allowed to deduct certain required payments, such as taxes that the sales agent must pay. The remainder after these more or less automatic deductions is commonly referred to as adjusted gross receipts.

From all Gross Receipts for distribution and exhibition, Sales Agent may deduct all taxes, government or local, required to be paid or payable by Sales Agent based upon or related to the moneys derived from the distribution and exhibition of the Picture in the Territory whether such taxes are denominated as turnover taxes, sales taxes, film hire taxes or similar taxes ("Adjusted Gross Receipts").

Sales agent's compensation—calculation of the net receipts. From the adjusted gross receipts, the sales agent is allowed to deduct compensation and allowed expenses. What is left is net and belongs to the producer.

As compensation, from the Adjusted Gross Receipts, Sales Agent may deduct a Distribution Fee ("Distribution Fee") of 20% of the Adjusted Gross Receipts derived from the theatrical release of the Picture in the Territory . . .

The parties will usually clarify, however, that certain items are not deducted from adjusted gross—for example, box office receipts (meaning the money retained by the theater owners; these amounts are not received by the sales agent); unearned advances and guarantees (typically these are security deposits that may have to be returned to the subdistributor; if they are not returned, however, they will be included within the meaning of gross); rebates, refunds, and adjustments (meaning moneys returned of money previously included in gross receipts); collected taxes; and salvage (amounts received from the disposal of prints) are not deducted from adjusted gross.

Other allowed deductions (distribution costs). There will also be a discussion about other possible deductions from gross. Producers will do well to remember that any allowable deduction will take away from overages, because what is left after taking away the allowable deductions is what the producer gets to keep. Typical allowable deductions include: money transmission costs; the cost of collecting money owed; payments to guilds; the cost of making a foreign language version; reediting costs (where reediting is required); the costs of making prints and trailers; royalties payable for rights related to the exhibition and promotion of the movie (music performance and other rights, for example); insurance and litigation costs; the costs of procuring copyright protection for the film and policing the copyright (going after copyright infringers); and advertising and promotion costs.

Capped distribution expenses. Unwary producers have missed this point and have paid a price. If the distribution expenses aren't capped, the sales agent (and his or her sublicensees) will have the ability to continue making the producer pay for all marketing. This, if you think about it, isn't exactly fair. The producer is not the only party making money here. This is one of those points, like the point about affiliates (discussed above), that the producer should not give in on. Most sales agents, if pressed, will agree to cap distribution fees.

> From the Adjusted Gross Receipts remaining after deducting the Distribution Fee, after full consultation with and the prior written consent of Owner, Sales Agent may deduct and retain a sum equal to all reasonable costs, expenses and charges paid, advanced or incurred by Sales Agent in connection with the derivation of Gross Receipts ("Distribution Expenses"; provided, however, that Sales Agent's right to recoup Distribution Expenses shall be capped at the total aggregate amount of $200,000).

Completion bond.

Some of these distributors will insist that you purchase a completion guarantee or completion bond for your movie. Remember, the movie is not yet completed and so the risk of the movie not being finished, or falling behind schedule, is the most significant risk a distribution company granting an advance will undertake. There are speciality insurance companies that will guarantee the completion of the picture for a fee. If you go this route, therefore, you must include the price of the completion bond or completion guarantee in the budget. In essence, the completion bond provides that if the picture starts having trouble (cost overruns or delays, for example), the bonding company will have the right to step in and solve (or help solve) the problem. The bonding company's solution may be to take over the project and start editing some of your precious scenes out or something similar (that's why you'll want to hire a good line producer). As you can imagine, in this connection, the producer is required to make progress reports and allow the bonding company to examine the budget and look over the producer's shoulder.

Chain of title representations.

And you thought I was just kidding. Nope—now is when people start getting serious about chain of title issues. You will have to make representations and warranties (along with a covenant to indemnify the distributor in case of a breach, intentional or not) that you own the project and have the right to grant the rights you are granting under the contract.

E&O insurance.

In addition to representations and warranties, you will be required to take out errors and omissions (E&O) insurance, covering problems in the chain of title. In some cases, the sales agent will require you to cause the insurance provider to name the sales agent as an additional insured on your E&O policy. Some insurers will do this and some will not. Check it out.

Other points.

The standard sales agent agreement also includes other provisions found in distribution agreements (see the discussion about distribution agreements later on). Such other provisions might include the right of the producer to consult about distribution decisions, the rights related to publicity, including the use of the director's and the actors' names and likenesses, technical delivery requirements, and other miscellaneous provisions.

Sales agent agreements for a flat fee.

In contrast to the foregoing sales agent contract that seeks to "presale" the distribution rights to the movie, some sales agents work for a flat fee plus a participation in the movie going forward. In this type of an arrangement, the producer pays an up-front fee (of somewhere between $10,000 and $20,000) and promises the agent a percentage, perhaps 5 or 10 percent of producer's gross revenues from the distribution contracts procured by the sales agent. This type of arrangement is common where the movie is completed and still without worldwide distribution. The producer must carefully define the usual terms—territory, rights being exploited, reserved rights, and so forth.

THE FILM FESTIVAL ROUTE

You should note that some producers take on the task of preselling all or some of the territories directly. The most common way to do this is to do as the agents do and visit the various film festivals (or film markets) around the world. The most famous film festivals are the Cannes (pronounced, I am assured by those who claim to know, "can"—as in "tin can") Film Festival, held at the city of Cannes on the French Riviera (which is why it is so popular, I suppose); the American Film Market (AFM), held in the city of Santa Monica, California (right next door to Los Angeles, in case you didn't know); the Sundance Film Festival, held in Park City, Utah (up the road from Sundance, Utah, where Mr. Robert Redford, the founder of the Sundance Institute, lives); and others (notably the Toronto and Berlin festivals). Regardless of the locale, they afford an opportunity for sellers of films (sales agents and producers) and buyers of films (distribution companies) to meet and do business. Therefore, with your package in hand, you can approach foreign distribution companies. If there is enough interest in your movie, they might give you the same written commitment that the sales agent procures.

FINANCING THE "GAP"

In the example above, even if either your sales agent or you is successful in obtaining prerelease commitments from foreign distributors, there may still be a gap in the financing—meaning a shortfall between the aggregate amount of the advances you have collected and the budget of the film. There are a number of ways to fill the gap.

Domestic rights.

One way is to sell the domestic distribution rights to the movie. Remember, up to this moment we have only been talking about selling off the foreign distribution rights. There are a couple of reasons for this. The most obvious reason is that you may have tried to approach the domestic studios/distributors (the major studios) and have been turned down. In addition, some producers try to hold on to the domestic rights for themselves, so that they can sell the movie directly to the domestic distributors (including the majors) once the movie is made. Also keep in mind that the North American market (the United States and Canada) is the largest market in the world. By removing the sales agent from the middle, the producer stands a greater chance of making money from this market.

Banks and gap financiers.

The most common way to finance the gap is by going to banks or professional organizations that specialize in this type of lending. These institutions will have several demands that you should recognize and understand.

Completion bond. Gap financiers will insist that you have a completion bond in place.

Chain of title and E&O coverage. Gap financiers will also require you to make certain representations and warranties and obtain appropriate E&O insurance coverage.

Collateral. The gap financiers will insist that the loan covering the gap be collateralized by the written commitments from foreign distributors and by the film itself.[2]

THE COPRODUCTION DEAL

A coproduction is a production by more than one producer.[3] The key concept in a coproduction is ownership or equity. Compare a coproduction to a sales agency agreement, discussed above, where the producer licenses the rights he or she owns to various distributors in order to obtain enough funds in the form of advances to produce the movie. One example of a coproduction deal would be a book company and an animation production company getting together to make an animated movie based on a book, the rights of which are owned or controlled by the book company. The book company puts in the rights to the book and perhaps some cash and the animation company puts in production services and perhaps cash.

Mutual Films, established in the 1990s by several foreign distribution companies, is another example of a coproduction structure.

Apparently, these foreign distributors wanted to join together to help finance and produce first-run movies—movies that would work in their respective territories. Whatever the motivation, coproducers start by forming one of the production entities mentioned above (usually a limited liability company or corporation) and then contribute rights and/or cash and/or services to the entity and decide by contract how the revenues are to be applied and divided up.

The production entity.

The parties to the coproduction first decide on a structure. In the example above, the producer and distribution company have selected a limited liability company as the structure of the deal.[4]

Name, place, and duration. The name of the company can be and often is the same name as the movie, but this is not a matter of great importance, as the company will typically not be used again. Production companies are often single-use entities. The place of business and the term of the agreement (which in turn determines the duration of the production company itself) will be contained in the agreement.

> The "Company" was organized under the laws of the State of Delaware under the name Quest Production, LLC. The principal place of business of the Company will be located at Los Angeles, California, or such other place as the Managing Member may designate from time to time. The Company's existence will continue until terminated, dissolved or liquidated in accordance with this Agreement and applicable law.

Limited purpose. Most production companies are single or special purpose vehicles and, therefore, the legal purpose is narrowly defined in the agreement between the joint venturers. In this case, the parties have decided that the limited purpose is to make and exploit a single movie and do whatever else is needed to further this objective.

> The Company will not engage in any business other than the following: (a) Owning, developing, producing, distributing, exhibiting, transmitting, disseminating, performing and otherwise exploiting a feature-length motion picture and the ancillary rights related thereto (the "Picture") based on the treatment entitled

"The Quest" by Kelly Crabb ("Author") pursuant to that certain rights assignment agreement between Quest Production, Inc. ("QPI"), as assignor, and Company, as assignee, which shall be executed and delivered by QPI and Company as soon as practicable hereafter and (b) such other activities directly related to and in furtherance of the foregoing activities as may be necessary, advisable, or appropriate.

Assignment agreement. Notice the reference to an assignment by the producer to the production company. This is a critical step, because the production company must have the rights in order to produce the movie.

Major terms of the coproduction deal.

The coproduction agreement tries to accommodate the respective objectives of the coproducers. It answers the following critical questions: Who will control the creative direction of the movie? Who will make the business decisions related to the movie? How will the coproducers split the revenues generated by the movie? Who will get what type of credit on the movie? Who will own the copyright of the movie? What strategic rights will the coproducers get (if any), and on what terms?

Control. One of the chief issues in a coproduction deal is control. There are a couple of options: One of the parties to the production controls the creative direction of the movie, or all the parties to the company control, with an appropriate means for breaking tie votes or other deadlocks. If one of the coproducers has developed and is contributing the property, he or she usually tries to maintain creative control. The argument to the money or strategic investor partner is that it is best to entrust the creative decisions to the person with filmmaking experience. This argument doesn't work well, of course, if the coproducer seeking control is a novice or the other coproducers have experience. On the other hand, if the creative producer doesn't win this battle, he or she risks having a third party interfere with the original creative direction of the project. Here, the final creative control goes to the "managing member" (who is appointed by the agreement of the coproducers) with very little management participation by other members.

The management of the Company will be vested in the Managing Member, who will hold office until his death or resignation or removal as provided below in this agreement. The Managing Member may appoint officers to run the day-to-day operations of the Company. The Managing Member will consult fully with the Members of the Company regarding all material decisions, subject to the Managing Member's right to resolve all deadlocks. Unless authorized by the Managing Member or this Agreement, no Member will have any power or authority to bind, act or purport to act on behalf of the Company in any manner.

It is common to allow the coproducers who don't have control to consult on the various decisions that must be made. To avoid the logistical burden of having to file frequent reports or engage in time-consuming creative and other meetings and/or conference calls, the coproducer in control will sometimes try to limit the consultation rights. For example, the coproduction agreement might provide that other members be allowed to attend only key meetings or that their suggestions be in a certain form (for example, in writing). On the other hand, the parties might well agree that consultation rights are "full." In other words, the parties agree to consult with each other on every aspect of the process and try to work out any differences of opinion by mutual agreement or even by arbitration. Usually, however, one of the parties will have the right to make final decisions or break deadlocks. This can be important to all the parties, even to financial coproducers who have no great interest in controlling the creative process; obviously, unresolved deadlocks could delay or even stop the production process to the detriment of all.

Initial capital contribution. The coproducers (each referred to as a member of the company in this LLC structure) agree to make contributions to further the objectives of the company. The most common contribution is cash, but it is not uncommon that one of the parties will contribute the rights. For example, remember our illustration of the publishing company that controls the rights to the novel on which it wants to develop and then produce a motion picture. The publishing company might well agree to contribute the rights, in addition to cash. A studio might contribute its facilities and production personnel. A postproduction facility might agree to do the postproduction work in exchange for a piece of the company. It is even possible for talent (an actor or director) to become coproducers by contributing services. All these contributions—whether cash, materials, or services—have a value. At any rate, when added together, the various contributions will equal the amount of the budget of the movie or some other agreed-upon amount.

> Each of the Members agrees to contribute to the Company the amount of capital set forth opposite such Member's name on Exhibit "A" in exchange for the Economic Interest and Voting Interest set forth opposite such Member's name on Exhibit "A."

"Economic interest." In this context, economic interest means that percentage of the profits that the member is entitled to receive once the money starts rolling in. Remember that in an LLC the economic interest or profit share is determined by negotiation among the parties—it is not always a mathematical proration (as it would be in a corporation).

Voting interest. In an LLC, as in a partnership, voting interest is not necessarily reflective of economic interest (as they are in a corporation). As discussed above, a person can put in $1.00 and get 99 percent of the profits—although this does not normally occur (even in Hollywood). However, because of the flexibility of the LLC structure, it is possible for one party to contribute less money and get creative and business control. In fact, this is often the case in the movie industry, because one of the parties (for example, the one who contributes the rights) may be the only one with real experience in making movies. It is a negotiation.

No additional contributions. In a coproduction deal, one important issue is whether the party in charge of the production has the right to require the other party or parties to put in more money. This right is sometimes referred to as a call. In this example, the party in charge of the production does not have a call on the other parties for more money.

> No Member shall be required to make any additional Capital Contributions. Except as provided in this Agreement, no Member will have the right to withdraw or receive any return of, or interest on, any Capital Contribution or on any balance in such Member's Capital Account. If the Company is required to return any Capital Contribution to a Member, the Member will not have the right to receive any property other than cash.

The issue is a real one, because running out of funds can cause a significant problem—failure to complete the picture. Ironically, this problem affects all of the coproducers directly; if the picture isn't finished, of course, the coproducers won't have any chance to recover their investment or make a profit. One option is to require all coproducers to put in more money in accordance with some formula (perhaps pro rata to their economic interests). The coproducers have options other than putting in more money, the most common of which is to purchase a completion bond.

In addition, it is common that the parties will agree that the capital contributed to the production entity will not be returned prematurely. In other words, the parties who contributed the money won't be able to ask for their money back. The rationale behind this provision is obvious; if the money contributors can pull their money out, the movie might never get made.

Many financiers require that their money bear interest (a charge for the use of funds). In this example, the LLC, the capital contribution does not bear interest.

Capital account. In an LLC, as in a partnership, each member gets a capital account. The capital equals the value of the contribution. The capital contribution is returned to the contributor at a set time in the future (for example, upon the liquidation of the company).

> The Company will establish and maintain an individual Capital Account for each Economic Interest Holder.

Completion bond. As discussed above, a common provision of coproduction deals is the requirement of a completion bond, protecting the coproducers from the risk of the movie not getting made.

> To induce Members to enter into this Agreement, Company agrees that, in connection with the production of the Picture, it will procure out of the budget of the Picture a standard completion bond with respect to the completion of the Picture.

Credit. Coproducers are usually companies and so, as in this example, the credits granted are production company credits. A typical coproduction agreement credit might be in the form of a presentation credit (Crabbapple Entertainment, in association with Four Winds Distribution and Seven Seas Films, present . . .) or a production credit (Your Lucky Day Studios presents a Crabbapple Entertainment, Four Winds Distribution, and Seven Sea Films production of . . .).

> Subject to each Member's full performance of its material obligations hereunder, and further subject to any customary exclusions and exceptions of any distributor of the Picture, each Member will be accorded joint production company credit on the Picture and in all paid advertising, with QPI's credit in first position. Each credit will be the same size as any other main title credit, with all other aspects of each credit in the sole discretion of the Managing Member.

Ownership. A major issue, of course, is ownership of the copyright and other rights in the picture. Like all other matters, this issue is resolved by negotiation based on the various strengths and objectives of the parties. In this case, the parties decided to let the LLC own and control the copyright. It is possible that the copyright to the screenplay is held by one of the coproducers (who licenses—not assigns—it to the production company) and the rights to the picture belong to another party (perhaps the company). It is also possible that a party may be satisfied with its financial interest in the picture, as described in the coproduction (or, in this case, the LLC operating) agreement, without having any copyright ownership. Ownership, among other things, may determine how certain rights are exploited. There is also intrinsic value in building a "library" full of film copyrights. Note, however, that in a coproduction deal, some form of financial equity (or ownership) for all coproducers is inevitable. Even if the cash-contributing members agree to let the producer license the rights to the production company, such members' attorneys will ensure that the license is very long (in perpetuity) and durable (irrevocable); ownership in the production company under such circumstances will approximate equity ownership of the movie itself.

> Upon completion of the Picture, all right, title and interest in and to the Picture (and the Screenplay) shall be owned in the name of the Company.

Strategic rights. As noted above, in a coproduction deal, often the major objective is to obtain certain strategic rights related to the movie. A toy manufacturer might invest in a movie to obtain the rights to manufacture and sell a line of toys derived from the movie, for example. In the following example, two distributors have joined up with the producer to finance part of the production budget in order to gain certain territorial rights (theatrical rights included) in the movie.

> The Members agree that Seven Seas shall have the first right of ne-gotiation respecting a license for all rights related to the Picture for the territories of Japan, Korea and Hong Kong (the "Asian Strategic Territories") and Four Winds shall have the first right of negotiation respecting a license for all rights related to the Picture for the terri-tories of Germany and the United Kingdom (the "European Strate-gic Territories").

Charging for strategic rights. There are two ways to conceptual-ize the deal for strategic rights. For example, the producer can presell the strategic rights to a foreign distribution company. As stated above, I don't really think of this as a coproduction deal, because the producer is merely licensing (or selling, as the case may be) off his as-sets to produce the movie as in the sales agent agreement discussed above. Another example is for the producer and the distribution companies to combine their assets (rights and money) to produce the movie and then, when the movie is finished, sell off the various rights to gain revenue. In this case, two distributors put in money and the producer contributes the rights to produce the movie. The distributors naturally want to obtain the rights to their own territo-ries, but the rights must be paid for, even though the distributors invested in the production. And there is even a minimum price for these rights. The payment for these rights will be treated as revenue to the production company and will go to recouping the produc-tion investment or be divided among the parties as revenue. In the first case, the investors receive no equity (ownership) in the movie. In the second case, the investors do receive equity.

> Anything in this paragraph to the contrary notwithstanding, the parties hereto agree that (x) the minimum advance required for the Asian Strategic Territories shall be 15% of the final shooting budget of the Picture (without regard to any contingency or completion bond costs) and (y) the minimum advance required for the Euro-pean Strategic Territories shall be 15% of the final shooting budget of the Picture (without regard to any contingency or completion bond costs).

Other terms of the coproduction deal.

Like all other financing transactions, the coproduction deal should also set forth other terms and conditions. If distribution rights are part of the deal, the terms of the distribution (for example, the amount of the advance, the distribution fee, the ongoing royalty rate, the term of distribution, territorial restrictions, language restrictions, and the like) should be set forth. In addition, representations and warranties should also be included, along with the usual miscellaneous provisions (the choice of governing law, whether or not arbitration should be used for the resolution of disputes, etc.).

THE "NEGATIVE PICKUP"

One traditional structure for motion picture financing is referred to as a negative pickup deal. The word negative in this phrase means the negative of the motion picture or the master film from which the prints are made. The term pickup is used because of the basic format of the deal:

- In the first step, the producer introduces the movie to the studio that decides to distribute it.
- The studio doesn't give money to the producer. Instead, the studio gives the producer a piece of paper that says in essence that "if you deliver the negative of the picture by [a certain date] we will pick the negative up for [a certain amount of money]."
- Then the producer takes that piece of paper to the bank. The bank makes a loan based on the strength of the piece of paper (i.e., the strength of the studio's credit).

When the bank loans the money, it looks at the same factors noted above: There must be a completion bond (since a huge risk to the bank is that the movie might not be made), there must be representations and proof of chain of title, and E&O insurance. Collateral is less of a concern to a bank in this situation, since it is looking to the credibility of the studio. However, the bank will often take a security interest in the movie.

Note too that the word "deliver" in this context has a special meaning. The producer must meet the delivery requirements of the studios in order to satisfy the terms of the negative pickup deal—something that the bank is vitally concerned about. A producer satisfies the delivery requirements by delivering the negative, all the elements related to the negative, *and* the chain of title documentation.

KNOWING AND APPRECIATING YOUR INVESTOR(S) RISKS

Before we leave this topic, I think it is critical that you appreciate the position of the person(s) you are inviting to your little party. I also think it is important that you do not try to fudge these issues with your investor(s). Your investor(s) are taking substantial risks and here are some of them:

First-time producer.
If you are fortunate to control your own destiny and produce your movie, you need to appreciate the risk that this poses to the investor(s). A producer will make hundreds of decisions and must solve hundreds of problems throughout the course of producing a movie. The way these decisions are made and these problems are solved can easily affect the viability and ultimate success of the project. It's hard enough for an experienced producer. Investing in a first-time producer can be risky.

Distribution.
For investor(s) who don't truly understand the film industry, distribution may be an overlooked element of success. And while it is true that the price could be high for a completed motion picture (indeed, selling the movie after it is produced might be the only course of action open to you), making a movie without a distribution commitment is a very risky proposition. Without distribution, there is no revenue and no way for the investor(s) to recoup the money invested in the movie. And, notwithstanding that you are absolutely convinced your project will bring 'em to the theater in droves, unless you are able to get some executive at the distribution company to agree to make prints of and advertise your movie, it doesn't matter what you think.

General risk of the film industry.
Remember William Goldman's phrase: "Nobody knows anything"? It is an obvious fact of the entertainment industry that art is a subjective thing. Good scripts sometimes make bad movies; mediocre scripts sometimes make successful movies. Movies that would work last year, won't work this year. Movies that would work in the fall, might fail against the Christmas blockbusters. Audiences are fickle. And all of this boils down to risk. A risk that there will be no profit or even that the production money will not be recouped.

The Studio
as Financier

THE STUDIO DEAL

Raising money from independent sources is not the only game in town. There is always the chance that one of the major studios or major production companies will finance your movie. The majors are, after all, the largest dedicated movie companies in the world. Each of them produces over twenty movies a year. Many are developed "in house," but studios also acquire projects from the outside—from independent producers like you.

The steps are familiar: You take your screenplay, along with any packaging elements you have been able to attach, to the studio (usually, the studio's feature development department). If the studio likes your package, the discussions will begin with—you guessed it—chain of title. The company will stand directly in the line of fire of any claim for infringement, if it picks up the project. It will want to know up front that there is no chain-of-title defect. Eventually, if things progress, you will have to deliver proof of a clean chain of title.

When the studio acts as financier, the rules—all determined by the studio, of course—are a bit different. As a general rule (unless you are one of the handful of the top producers in town—and even then some of these will apply):

- The studio, not you, will own the copyright to the movie.
- You will lose some if not all creative control of the movie.

- Your biggest chance to make money is on the fixed, up-front fee; the back-end participation will not likely amount to much.
- Your compensation package will be greatly influenced by the fee level established in your last producing deal—your "quote."
- Your credit on the picture will be negotiated, as there are pressures that the studio faces against credit inflation.
- The studio will not guarantee that the movie will be produced. Rather you will get a "turnaround" right which allows you to get the movie back under certain conditions.

YOUR DEAL WITH THE STUDIO

The essence of the studio deal is that you, the producer, will assign your rights in the package to the studio in exchange for a producer deal. The producer's contract contains your reward for all of your hard work to this point: your compensation and credit. The basic outline of the deal looks like this:

The assignment of rights.
The first part of the studio deal is that you (the producer and captain of the project to this point) assign your rights in the project.

Chain of tile. The assignment is backed by evidence of a clean chain of title and by your representations and warranties related to the chain of title. For example, if the project is based on a screenplay that in turn is based on a novel, you will be required to show both the contract with the novelist (or publishing company or literary agent—whoever controls the movie rights to the novel) *and* the contract with the writer of the screenplay (unless, of course, you wrote the screenplay yourself). When a book is involved, moreover, you will be required to deliver a release from the publisher. If the movie is based on someone's life story (or, to put it more accurately, if real people—and their name and likeness—will be involved), waivers from the persons portrayed may be sought.

> Major Studio's obligations hereunder are subject to the satisfaction of all the following conditions: (a) Delivery of all documents (including a publisher's release) related to the acquisition or optioning of rights related to the novel, *The Quest,* by Kelly C. Crabb (the "Underlying Property"), and (b) Clearance of chain-of-title in and to the "Underlying Property" to the satisfaction of Major Studio's attorneys.

Payment of rights–related obligations. The assignment of rights may also involve the transfer of obligations to the studio. For example, if you have an option agreement with the writer of a novel or short story, you will want to make sure that the studio takes on the obligation to pay any additional option fees (for extending the option, for example) and the purchase price. In addition, you will want the studio to reimburse you for any amounts—option fees, for example—that you have already paid to the writer.

The producer's deal.

Your willingness to assign the package and the underlying rights to the studio, of course, comes with a condition. For your trouble, the studio enters into a producer's agreement with you setting forth your compensation and credit when (and, unfortunately, *if*) the movie gets made.

Services and compensation. The services involved will include producing services, of course. But don't forget the services you have already performed in bringing the package to this point—development services. The following example shows what a producer with a respectable track record might be able to get from a studio:

Development fee. For the producer's efforts during the development stage, he or she can ask for and sometimes receive a development fee (occasionally referred to as a script supervision fee). The range for experienced producers is between $25,000 to $50,000, but like everything else is subject to negotiation. In any event, the development fee is applied against the producer's fee.

> For Development Services, Fixed Compensation: $25,000 ("Development fee").

Producer fee. Perhaps the big moment in time for a producer in a studio deal is the actual fixed producer's fee. There is a custom in Hollywood to base the producer's fee on the producer's last fee—the so-called quote. A producer who has asked for and received a fee of $600,000, for example, can present a request of $600,000 plus as his or her quote. You might ask—and it is a legitimate question—how a first-time producer establishes a quote. The real answer is—it depends. It depends on the past experience of the producer—if the producer has a long history of working as a unit production manager, associate producer or coproducer, the quote will reflect the levels of fixed income for these jobs. It may also depend on the value of the package—if the story is well crafted, based on a famous book, or has attracted the attention of a well-known actor or director, the producer, even a first timer (the Academy Award-winning movie *The Sting,* with Paul Newman and Robert Redford, is said to have been the project of first-time producers, for example) might be able to get a favorable fee deal.

For Production Services: $600,000, less the Development Fee.

Deferments. For various reasons, usually as a compromise, the studio will offer or the producer will propose a deferment. The concept of deferred compensation is like this: The studio says to the producer, "Look, we are making this movie for a small budget and we can't really match your last quote, which was for a more expensive movie." The producer counters, "Okay, I'll come down off my quote if the budget is low, but if the movie makes a lot of money, I would like to be paid accordingly."

Sometimes the deferment is expressed as a certain amount paid out of a certain percentage of the net or adjusted gross proceeds: "Producer will be paid deferred compensation in the amount of $150,000 out of 5 percent of net proceeds," as such term is defined in the agreement.

Another approach to deferred compensation is illustrated below. In this example, the producer gets $150,000 if the North American box office receipts equal or exceed $50 million. The studio and the producer decide to use the box office numbers reported in *Daily Variety.* These types of payments I like to refer to as bumps, and they are not necessarily limited to a one-time event as in this illustration. Producers and other participants like bumps, because the payments are triggered on reaching objective numbers ascertainable by reference to a publicly available source—and *not* by reference to the studio's internal accounting process.

Deferred Compensation: The sum of $150,000 at such time, if ever, as the box office receipts derived from the theatrical distribution of the Picture in North America as reported by *Daily Variety* ("Domestic Boxoffice") equal $50 million or the box office receipts derived from the theatrical distribution of the Picture worldwide as reported by *Daily Variety* equal $125 million, whichever shall occur first.

Participation. Finally, a producer with a track record can ask to participate in the revenues generated by the movie. We will talk later about the details of how the definitions of terms like gross, adjusted gross, and net work in this context. For now, let's look at the basic structure of a participation in a studio deal. Recall the basic structure in an independent deal, where the producer waits for the financier to recoup his money—or break even—before the profits are split on some basis. In the studio deal, the producer's payments are triggered by a series of hypothetical break even points (or breakpoints). In the following illustration, there are four tiers of payments. Each tier is defined by referring to a hypothetical breakpoint—a point at which the studio has recouped an amount equal to the budget of the movie or has, in fact, broken even—and each increasing in favor of the producer.

The basic notion of participations—as we have discussed before—is that the producer should be asked to wait until the studio gets its investment back; after that, the producer should be allowed a greater portion of the revenues. In a studio context, however, the battles over the way this actually works are fierce. In a perfect world, the formula would be as simple as the standard deal discussed earlier. Over the years, however, the studios have developed accounting formulas that are favorable to the studio. The term net, in a studio context, doesn't really mean what it means in a nonstudio context. The studios are famous for taking substantial "overhead" deductions, for example. I know several producers who have told me that their net positions on movies making several hundred million dollars have not generated any back-end income for them. Because of this, producers who have the power, will not settle for net participations and, instead, will bargain hard for participations out of gross revenues. The studios have countered with concepts, such as adjusted gross—a term that allows the parties to argue about what deductions the studio can take out of gross for the purposes of defining the pool of money from which the producer can draw his or her share. It is, therefore, possible that adjusted gross may have more in common with net than gross. But enough of that for now.

Let me try to put this in *simplified* plain English (as opposed to the shorthand jargon used in the illustration below): "Mr. Producer, you will get 5 percent of the money the studio gets from theaters—less an assumed distribution fee of 10 percent of this amount—once the studio has recovered the cost it paid to produce the movie—and some other costs—using these hypothetical numbers. We will increase your percentage to 7.5 percent of the amount the studio gets—less an assumed distribution fee of 17.5 percent once the studio recovers the cost of the movie and other costs using these revised hypothetical numbers. We will increase your percentage, yet again, to 10 percent of the studio's revenues—less an assumed distribution fee of 22.5 percent—once the studio recovers the cost of the movie and other costs at these numbers. When the studio has actually broken even—using the studio's actual distribution fee—not a hypothetical one—we will give you the greater of 50 percent of net—but you have to be responsible for all third parties who get to participate—and 15 percent of adjusted gross proceeds, however we define that term."

> Participation: A sum equal 5% of "Adjusted Gross Proceeds" (as defined below) Commencing at "First Breakpoint" (when "net revenues" first occur assuming a distribution fee of 10%), increasing to a sum equal to 7.5% of Adjusted Gross Proceeds at "Second Breakpoint" (when "net revenues" first occur assuming a distribution fee of 17.5%), increasing to 10% of Adjusted Gross Proceeds at "Third Breakpoint" (when "net revenues" first occur and assuming a distribution of 22.5%) and "Initial Actual Breakeven" (when "net revenues" first occur), increasing to the greater of 50% of "Net Proceeds," reducible by all third-party participations, or a sum equal to 15% of Adjusted Gross Proceeds.

Since a normal studio distribution fee is in the range of 35 to 40 percent, this formulation based on adjusted gross is designed to give the producer a chance to see some money earlier than he or she would have if based on net. Of course, as mentioned before, the real debate in negotiations over these terms concerns the costs and other amounts that the studio is allowed to deduct from total revenues.

One way around this, if the studio will accept it, is to provide for advance participation payments at certain bumps (as we discussed a minute ago). Payments may be triggered at various box office benchmarks (again, as noted in industry publications, such as *Daily Variety*) along the way ($150,000 at $50 million, another $150,000 at $75 million, another $150,000 at $100 million, and so forth). These payments are normally applicable to the net participation. Again, producers and other participants prefer the bump approach, because the box office numbers are easily ascertainable.

Credits. If the studio likes your package, there is little doubt that the studio will be happy to offer you a credit. The questions are what credit and how many credits (remember the other people on your team who are hoping for credit). Individual credits include "a Peter

Producer production" (a so-called production credit), "produced by," executive producer, coproducer, and associate producer. Company credits include production and presentation (as well as "in association with") credits.[1]

Studios may offer resistence to your request for credits, because the studio executives understand that they are likely to encounter credit requests from many other people. Directors often require a producer credit for a producer partner. Actors may require some type of producer credit for their agent, themselves and/or another person. It is not uncommon to see movies with seven or eight producer-type credits. On the other hand, the Producers Guild of America,[2] among other forces, have been trying to combat credit inflation—too many producers on a picture, of course, reduces the importance of the producers credit overall. The example below shows only one credit.

> Credits: Producer shall have a "produced by" credit on screen in the main titles (unless there are no main titles, then in the end credits) and in paid advertising, subject to Major Studio's Excluded Ad (as defined). The "produced by" credit shall be substantially in the form "Produced by Peter Producer," with the size, placement and all other matters determined by Major Studios; provided, however, no other non-cast member may receive a larger credit. In addition Producer may elect to receive a production credit, the form, size, placement and all other matters to be determined by Major Studio after consultation with Producer, such production credit shall appear in Excluded Ads in which the director receives a "film by" credit.

Turnaround. Earlier, we talked about the concept of turnaround in the context of a writer's deal. Let's revisit the subject here. Keep in mind that studio deals seldom, if ever, come with a guarantee that the studio will produce the movie. What happens if the studio decides to do nothing with the project after the deal is signed? This can and does happen. The studio wants to fix the screenplay, but can't get it right. The preferred cast is not available at the time the studio wants to shoot the movie. Another studio has a similar project that is due to come out earlier than this one. The studio itself has a competing film. Whatever the reason, if the movie is not made, you won't make money. And even though you will have been reimbursed for your expenses, the hours of work that you spent in getting the screenplay finished will have been for nothing, unless the movie is finished. The purpose of the turnaround, therefore, is to give you, the producer, a chance to get the prospective film back, if the studio decides not to go forward.

A typical turnaround provides that after a period of time—let's say one year—if the studio has essentially abandoned the work, the producer gets a period of time—say two years—to set the project up somewhere else. If the producer is successful in setting it up somewhere else, the producer is obligated to pay the studio back the amount of its investment in the project to that point. This would include the amounts that the studio paid for the rights to the project or to any writers.

BOOK FIVE

PRODUCING THE MOVIE

Okay, you've developed your screenplay, attached attractive elements, and even raised the necessary money for production. Let's return to your nightmare at the beginning of book 2. There you are, screenplay in hand. You have money in your pocket and are ready to spend it. Your director and line producer have broken down the screenplay into a logical and efficient shooting sequence. You are ready to start, right? Well, yes and no. To get the cameras rolling, there is still some work that has to be done. This is where, to use the analogy of a building project, you get your building permits, your equipment at the building site and the engineers and builders together. In a movie project, similarly, you must procure and prepare your locations, put the cast under contract, get the costumes and props and sets ready, and in the right place and the right time, assemble the equipment and get the crew who know how to use it. And then? And then, you can start making magic.

Some Legal
Preliminary Matters

PREPRODUCTION—GETTING READY TO ROLL

Appropriately enough, the first step of production is called preproduction. This is where you get everything ready. And, trust me, there is a lot to do: Assemble your team—in addition to the director and other producers, you will need a cinematographer (referred to as the director of photography or DOP), a casting director, a production accountant, location scouts, a set designer, an artistic director, a costume designer, makeup artists, props managers, travel agents, and a host of production assistants; you will have to find and contractually commit the rest of the cast and crew; find and make arrangements for locations and schedule the dates; attend to living accommodations, and travel; orchestrate payroll and the payment of expenses; take care of props and equipment; procure location permits; obtain insurance, and so forth. And you will need the help of a lawyer, because virtually all of these things require the formation of a contract. In this section, we will look at several of the major contracts that must be completed before principal photography.

CORPORATE ORGANIZATION

The very first task, assuming that you have not already accomplished this during the financing stage, is to organize your production company. Major studios and major independent producers use a subsidiary corporate or other limited liability entity (corporation, limited partnership, and limited liability company or LLC) for each media project. This subsidiary entity acts as a shield against liability on the part of the parent company. For example, if Paramount Pictures produces a movie called *The Quest*, they might set up a limited liability company called The Quest Production Company. If the company thereafter has a problem, liability for that problem will belong to the company and not to Paramount.

THE GUILDS

You will recall from the discussion above that, before you can hire actors who are members of SAG, or directors and other production personnel who are members of the DGA, the production company you plan to use to produce the movie must become a SAG and/or DGA signatory or make arrangements to use an existing signatory company on a loan-out basis. Moreover, if you plan to use union crew members (best boys, gaffers, camera operators, sound technicians, and the like), your production company must comply with the rules of IATSE (International Alliance of Theatrical Stage Employees, Moving Picture Technicians, Artists and Allied Crafts of the United States, Its Territories and Canada, AFL-CIO).[1] Do not procrastinate because these steps require lead time. Here are the basic steps in having your own production company join the guilds.

What does it mean to join the guilds?
Joining the guilds comes with several burdens. We have discussed these burdens before, but it is important to keep them in mind.

Members only. Once you join a guild like SAG, you can hire, with certain well-defined exceptions, only members of the guild.

"Residuals." Learn well the word residual. Under the rules of SAG, for example, production company signatories will be required to pay residual payments to actor members on the exploitation of the movie in supplemental markets (in the case of SAG, pay television and the sale of videocassettes and DVDs, etc.). Residuals are not applicable to the theatrical exhibition of the movie. This will significantly impact your company's revenue projections. The calculation

of residuals under the SAG basic agreement is based on distributor's gross receipts in two contexts: First, if the producer of the movie is also the distributor (in other words, the producer sells video product to Wal-Mart or Target, for example), residuals are paid out of a defined pool of revenues that is a product of the wholesale price of the product paid to the producer/distributor. For example, if the producer sells 10,000 videocassettes to Wal-Mart for $10 each (so that Wal-Mart can sell them retail for $20 each), the SAG formula says that distributor's gross receipts will equal 20 percent of the wholesale price to the producer (or $100,000). If the producer is not the distributor (in other words, the producer makes a distribution deal with a distributor), the SAG formula says that distributor's gross receipts will equal 100 percent of the fees paid from the distributor to the producer (under that distribution deal). Now the actual formula is applied. For pay television, for example, SAG requires that the actors split a pool of revenues that is equal to about 3.6 percent of distributor's gross receipts. For videocassettes, SAG requires that the actors split a pool of revenues that is equal to about 4.5 percent of the first million of distributor's gross revenues and 5.4 percent of all distributor's gross receipts thereafter. The actors share in the pool on a pro-rata basis roughly in accordance with their fixed compensation.

Pension and welfare contributions (fringe benefits). The company will have to pay an extra amount equal to between 12 and 14 percent of the member's compensation to the guild's pension fund and health and welfare fund. Thus, if an actor negotiates a fee of $100,000, you will pay, say $13,000, to the actor's guild pension fund and health and welfare fund, for a total outlay of $113,000.

Security interest. The guild will most likely require a first-priority security interest in the picture. This is an important fact, because you will not be able to grant any investors or bank a first-priority security interest in your film; they will have to subordinate their interests to the guilds. The guilds will not negotiate their priority. The security interest is largely designed to make sure that the actors will be paid their residual payments.

Bond. The guild will most likely require the production company to post a bond or deposit a certain percentage of the total payroll of its members with the guild in order to secure the payment of fixed compensation.[2]

Work rules. Joining a guild gives rise to an obligation on the part of the producer to conform with the workday, overtime, breaks, and other rules related to the performance of services. A producer who doesn't understand these rules should hire a qualified production manager to make sure that the production is in compliance.

Procedures and requirements. Once you make a determination regarding your cast, director, and crew, you will need to contact the guild and follow the specified procedures to become a signatory.[3]

Using a nonguild person in a guild movie—Taft-Hartley.

I will refrain from going into the background of this federal labor statute and the cases that shaped it. Suffice it to say that, even though the basic tenet of the guilds is that signatories are barred from hiring nonmembers, there are ways that you can use nonguild members in your productions. You do this by submitting a form to SAG referred to as a Taft-Hartley form. The gist of this form is to offer a reason why this nonguild person is necessary to the production. For example, suppose you are making a movie called *Dave* about Washington politics and you want to interview some actual politicians and news anchormen on camera for cameo appearances in the movie. Or perhaps you want to use a professional football player to play himself in a movie about high school football. In essence, if the person you want to use has some unique quality or is playing himself or herself, SAG will generally waive the requirement that all actors appearing in your film must be SAG members. You will still have to pay fringe benefit payments to the guild and include such persons in the residual pool for certain revenue streams (even though, as nonmembers, they won't get to share in these benefits).

Assembling the Main Players

LONG-FORM TALENT AGREEMENTS

During preproduction, you will need to complete (or try at least to complete) the definitive agreements of the actors, producers, and director.

Many production attorneys use a two-tiered form—specific terms with standard terms and conditions—but some attorneys use an all in one approach. The form is less important than the substance, but there is one advantage of having the specific and standard terms separate: the standard terms and conditions don't change from contract to contract and can be presented as the "company's" form as a negotiation tactic.

Specific terms: actor, director, producer.

In this section we will revisit (and even repeat) some of the material discussed in the packaging step. However, that is what long-form contracts do—they flesh out the points addressed in the deal memorandum.

Actor-specific terms. Let's look at a sample long-form agreement for an actor. I'll add my comments.

Preamble. The preamble identifies the parties and gives the producer the necessary information to process payroll, including required tax forms. The information about citizenship and residence is necessary in order to determine whether a visa will be required for this actor.

ACTOR AGREEMENT

DATE:	As of February 1, 2006
PRODUCER:	The Quest Production LLC 1234 Sunset Boulevard Hollywood, CA 90000 Facsimile: (818) 555-1234
EMPLOYEE:	Tom Bigstar (S.S.N. 123-45-6789) c/o Big Talent Agency 0000 Wilshire Boulevard, Beverly Hills, CA 90210 Attn: Mr. Frankie Agent Facsimile: (310) 555-9876 Citizen of: U.S.A. Principal Residence: Los Angeles, California
PICTURE:	Feature-length theatrical motion picture tentatively entitled *The Quest*
ROLE:	"Prince Lumine"

Fixed compensation. This provision specifies the amount of fixed compensation. In this case, reference is made to the SAG agreement and the minimum rate. The plus 10 percent is thought of as the agent's commission and is normally not added if the actor is to receive more than SAG minimum.

In consideration for the full performance of Employee's services during the Guaranteed Period (as defined in the "Terms and Conditions" attached hereto) and all rights granted or to be granted hereunder, Producer shall pay Employee fixed compensation in an amount equal to the applicable minimum daily rate provided under the SAG Agreement (as defined below) plus ten percent (10%) thereof for each day for which Employee renders services on a daily basis (the "Daily Rate") and in an amount equal to the applicable minimum weekly rate provided under the SAG Agreement plus ten percent (10%) thereof for each week for which Employee renders services on a weekly basis (prorated for any partial week). For services rendered by Employee at Producer's request in excess of the Guaranteed Period, Employee shall receive compensation at the Daily Rate for each additional day during which Employee renders services, including post-production services.

Pay-or-play/escrow obligations. As you will recall, after the Kim Basinger *Boxing Helena* case, many agents for actors now insist that the producer's commitment be pay or play. The term pay or play, as you know, means that the producer will pay the actor's fee whether the movie is made or not and whether the actor acts or not. In addition, agents in Hollywood are likely to demand that the actor's fee be put in an escrow account and paid out to the actor according to the actor's agreement.

Producer acknowledges and agrees that Employee's compensation hereunder is on a pay-or-play basis. As a condition precedent to Employee's services hereunder, Producer shall place the Employee's fixed compensation amount in First Talent Friendly Bank (the "Bank") in an escrow account under an escrow agreement in the form attached hereto as Exhibit "A".

Starting date. The agreement will provide for a starting date, usually the day that principal photography begins and always the date on which the actor is expected to report.

The starting date for services under this Agreement is July 24, 2006

"Credit." This credit provision takes care of the details of the actor's credit. Note that it deals with the position of the credit vis à vis the title of the movie; below the main title is less prestigious to the actor, but common (only the most powerful actors routinely get credits above the main title). Also, this actor's credit will be on a "separate card," meaning that the actor's name will appear by itself on the screen (this is better than being included in a grouping with other actors). The actor's name will also be mentioned in paid advertising ("paid ad" in the vernacular) in the so-called billing block—the list of credits that appears below the movie's title on posters, newspaper and television ads, with exceptions (normally understood as small ads and other ads that do not display the billing block). It deals with the size of the type print (in this case no less than any other

actor). This provision also contains a common provision making the inadvertent failure by the producer to provide the credit a nonbreach and giving the producer a chance to cure the omission. Imagine the result to the producer if this now common clause were absent—the producer might be subject to a claim based on each poster or print of the movie made without the actor's credit.

> Provided that Employee is not in default hereunder, that Employee performs all services required by Producer hereunder and that Employee actually appears recognizably in the Picture as released, Employee shall be accorded credit on the screen on all positive prints of the Picture, below the regular title, in the main titles (if any), on a separate card, and, subject to customary distributor exceptions and exclusions, below the regular title in the billing portion of paid advertising issued by or under the control of Producer relating primarily to the theatrical exhibition of the Picture. Such credit shall appear in a size of type not less than the size of type used for any other cast member, except in the event such cast member is accorded credit with respect to an artwork title of the Picture. All other characteristics of Employee's credit shall be at Producer's sole discretion. No casual or inadvertent failure by Producer, and no failure by any third party, to comply with the provisions of this paragraph shall constitute a breach of this agreement by Producer; provided, however, that upon the receipt by Producer of written notice from Employee specifying such failure in reasonable detail, Producer shall use reasonable efforts prospectively to cure such failure on future prints of the Picture or future paid advertising.

Still photographs and biography. This provision is designed as a compromise between the producer's need for still photographs of the actor, for advertising and other purposes, and the actor's desire to approve such photographs. Since it is difficult to run the actor down at the last minute, the producer asks the actor to preapprove a certain percentage of the photographs submitted by producer. Although not included in this sample form, most actors will reserve the right to approve 100 percent of all artist drawings of the actor. The actor will also want an approval right concerning the actor's bio used in promoting the movie.

> Employee shall have a right of approval of the still photography in which Employee appears; provided, however, Employee shall be

required to approve at least fifty percent (50%) of each group of still photographs in which Employee appears that are submitted by Producer to Employee's agent for Employee's approval and at least seventy-five percent (75%) of each group of still photographs in which Employee appears with one or more persons that are submitted by Producer to Employee's agent for Employee's approval. Producer agrees to include a reasonable number of still photographs in each group, and Employee shall provide approval within three (3) days (reducible to one (1) day if Producer notifies Employee or Employee's agent that a quick response is necessary) after receipt by Employee's agent; provided, however, that failing such approval within such period, Producer may select and use such still photographs in which Employee appears as Producer in its sole discretion may determine but only up to the number of still photographs required to comprise the balance of the percentage required to be approved by Employee hereunder. Employee shall be entitled to approve any biographical material used in connection with the performance, distribution, advertising, promotion and other use or exploitation of the Picture; provided, however, that Employee shall exercise each such approval reasonably and within five (5) days after request by Producer or such approval shall be deemed given. Upon request by Producer, Employee shall promptly provide Producer with an approved biography of Employee.

Copy. This provision exists so that the actor won't have to purchase a copy of the motion picture in order to get a copy and so the producer will not have to compete with the actor in a commercial context.

If Employee fully performs all of Employee's services and obligations hereunder, then at such time (if at all) as DVDs of the Picture are made available for sale or rental to the general public, Producer will, upon request, furnish Employee, with one such DVD copy at no cost to Employee. Employee shall use such DVD copy solely for personal, library and reference purposes and in no event shall such DVD copy be duplicated or used for any commercial purpose or for profit, including the making of public exhibitions of the Picture.

Premiere. This provision clarifies the terms and conditions under which the actor will be invited to any celebrity premiere of the movie.

If the actor has clout, his agent may insist that the costs of transportation be picked up or at least guaranteed by the producer. Keep in mind that such costs can mount up quickly.

> Provided that Employee is not in default hereunder, in the event Producer plans a celebrity premiere of the Picture in Los Angeles or New York, Producer shall invite Employee to attend such premiere; provided, however, that Producer shall not be required to pay any of Employee's transportation or other expenses incurred in conjunction with such premiere.

Wardrobe and dressing room. Giving the actor the right of consultation on wardrobe can be a burden on the production, although it is certainly understandable why the actor would want to have a say in what he or she wears on camera. Actors with any leverage also care about their dressing room. In the example below, the actor and producer avoid having to negotiate the details by settling for a "most-favored nation" clause—the actor gets as good a dressing room as anyone else.

Changes to actor's role. This is another concession to the actor, but protects the actor from major changes in the project (remember *Boxing Helena* above; maybe the actor doesn't want to start off thinking that she is playing a nun, only to find out later that she is playing a prostitute).

> Employee shall have a right of consultation regarding the wardrobe and makeup for Employee's role and regarding any material changes to Employee's role. On days worked, Employee shall be entitled to Employee's own dressing room, with the dressing room provided to Employee being no less favorable than that provided to any other cast member.

Most-favored-nation clause. When the government negotiates a trade agreement with a foreign country, oftentimes the agreement will contain a clause that says if either country grants any concession or privilege to another nation that is more favorable than the concessions or privileges in the agreement at hand, the other party will get the benefit of such more favorable concession or privilege. In short hand, the parties agree to treat each other as a most-favored nation. This same concept is employed in talent agreements. In essence, agents will insist that their clients be treated as well as the person who negotiates the best deal (be it the trailer accommodations, per diem, fee, definition of net, and so forth; it's like being a parent). Producers have to be constantly aware of most-favored-nation clauses, because giving something away to one actor can have a multiplying effect.

Arrangements with respect to Employee's per diem, hotel or on-location trailer, travel and other expenses shall be no less favorable than that provided to any other cast member on the Picture.

SAG agreement. This provision clarifies that the terms and conditions of the basic agreement of the Screen Actors Guild will apply to this agreement. The following points should be reviewed:

To hire a member of the SAG, your company must become a signatory to the SAG. Signatories may not hire nonmembers (without a specific waiver from SAG). Other restrictions apply.

There are certain minimum fees and privileges accorded to SAG members under the SAG agreement. The actor can negotiate a better deal, but no worse than these minimums.

Producer shall pay to the Screen Actors Guild Pension, Health and Welfare Plan contributions required by the SAG Agreement with respect to Employee's engagement hereunder. Except as expressly provided to the contrary herein, Producer shall be entitled to the maximum benefits and maximum rights permitted under the SAG Agreement. To the extent the SAG Agreement requires additional payments to Employee hereunder, including for the use or exercise of television broadcast rights and other supplemental market rights, such additional payments shall be paid at the minimum rate required.

Terms and conditions. This provision incorporates by reference the general terms and conditions attached to the specific terms (see "Standard Terms and Conditions" on page 238).

The above terms are subject to the additional "Terms and Conditions" attached hereto and incorporated herein by this reference, except that if there is any inconsistency between the above terms and the additional "Terms and Conditions" attached hereto, the above terms shall govern.

Director-specific terms. Let's look at the similarities and differences in the long-form director's agreement. Note that this contract form is quite favorable to the producer. If the director you wish to hire has a track record, don't count on being able to duplicate the terms that follow.

Preamble. Again, here is the contract information.

DIRECTOR AGREEMENT

DATE:	As of February 1, 2006
PRODUCER:	The Quest Production LLC 1234 Sunset Boulevard Hollywood, CA 90000 Facsimile: (818) 555-1234
EMPLOYEE:	Ken Kantoku (S.S.N. 987-65-4321) c/o Big Talent Agency 0000 Wilshire Boulevard, Beverly Hills, CA 90210 Attn: Mr. Frankie Agent Facsimile: (310) 555-9876 Citizen of: U.S.A. Principal Residence: Los Angeles, California
PICTURE:	Feature-length theatrical motion picture tentatively entitled *The Quest*
CAPACITY:	Director

Customary services. The concept of customs or customary is often employed in talent contracts. In general, this concept may be helpful in describing the duties of the director. However, you should note that industry custom is not always a reliable measure of specifics. Therefore, lawyers in drafting these agreements use this general description as well as specific descriptions of services desired by the producer.

Producer hereby engages Employee, and Employee hereby accepts such engagement, to render such services as are customarily rendered by directors of first-class theatrical motion pictures in the U.S. motion picture industry and such other services as reasonably may be required by Producer in connection with the Picture.

Exclusive period. The director works on a part-time basis, except for the period directly before, during, and after principal photography (until the answer print of the movie); during this time the director is exclusive to the movie. Afterward, for certain enumerated services, the director works on a non-exclusive, but first-priority basis (the director can do other things, but he or she must devote major attention to your picture).

> Such services shall be rendered on an exclusive basis during the period commencing six (6) weeks prior to the commencement of principal photography and continuing until delivery of the answer print of the Picture. During such exclusive period, Employee shall not render any services for Employee's own account or for others without the prior written consent of Producer. If Producer requires further services of Employee thereafter for retakes, added scenes, looping, post-syncing, publicity interviews, stills and similar matters, Employee shall render such services on a non-exclusive, but first-priority basis. Time is of the essence in connection with Employee's services hereunder.

Cover shots. Under the rules promulgated by the Federal Communications Commission (FCC), public carriers have a higher standard of duty to guard against objectionable material. Network television and airline motion pictures are good examples of public carriers—the patrons, including children, have no control over the content and, therefore, such content must be free of objectionable material. (Theaters and premium cable television, for example, are not public carriers because there is the element of choice.) In order to exploit these public carrier markets, assuming that your movie might contain objectionable material (certain words, nudity, and intense graphic violence, for example), you will want the director to take cover shots.

> Employee shall photograph and record all necessary "cover shots" for the release of the Picture on television, based on network continuity standards in existence at the time of commencement of principal photography. Employee shall also provide all "cover shots" necessary for airline, military and other non-theatrical exhibition.

Trailers and other promotional materials. You will also want the director to help produce promotional materials, such as trailers and television spots. These services might not normally be included in the director's customary duties, so the point must be clarified.

> Employee shall also render services in connection with promotional (including "making of") films, trailers and electrical transcriptions in

connection with the Picture. Employee agrees to render such services either during or after the exclusive period as Producer may request, but if after the exclusive period, subject to Employee's next professional availability (provided that Employee will use best efforts to be available at a time convenient to Producer), and Employee further agrees to the use by Producer of behind-the-scenes footage and film clips of the Picture in connection with such promotional films and trailers. Employee agrees that no additional compensation shall be payable for such services.

Standard of performance. Read the book *Final Cut,*[1] and you will know why a provision like the one that follows is a good idea. This makes the director legally responsive to the producer's direction, both in terms of artistic taste and temporal issues—such as the budget and the schedule.

Employee shall render services hereunder to the best of Employee's ability, whenever and wherever Producer may reasonably require, in a competent, conscientious and professional manner having due regard for the production of the Picture within the budget and in accordance with Producer's preproduction, production and post-production schedule, and as instructed by Producer in all matters, including those involving artistic taste and judgment.

Payment schedule. The payment schedule represented in this provision is typical (customary) in director and producer deals.

Provided that the Picture is produced and that Employee is not in material default hereunder, in full and complete consideration for Employee's services and for all rights granted or to be granted hereunder, Producer shall pay to Employee fixed compensation in the amount of $250,000. The fixed compensation shall be payable as follows:
Twenty percent (20%) thereof upon the commencement of preproduction or, if later, the execution of this agreement;
Sixty percent (60%) thereof in approximately equal weekly installments over the scheduled period of principal photography;
Ten percent (10%) thereof upon delivery of Employee's first cut of the Picture; and
Ten percent (10%) thereof upon delivery of the answer print of the Picture.

Full compensation and withholding tax. This provision clarifies that the amount specified above is the only fixed compensation to which the director will be entitled. In addition, this provision clarifies that the producer will have the right to withhold from the director's compensation any applicable taxes.

> Employee acknowledges that the fixed compensation as specified above is an all inclusive flat fee and that Employee shall not be entitled to any additional fixed compensation for any services rendered by Employee during the preproduction, production and/or post-production phases of the Picture. No compensation shall accrue or become payable to Employee during Employee's inability, failure or refusal to perform services according to the terms and conditions of this agreement. Employee agrees that as employer, Producer may deduct and withhold from all compensation payable to Employee hereunder all taxes and other amounts required to be deducted or withheld pursuant to applicable law.

Contingent deferment. In this contract, the director is in line to receive a contingent deferred payment of $50,000 from a defined pool entitled Initial Actual Breakeven. Take a minute and look at the definition, which is typical of deferred payments. (Also note the most-favored-nation clause.)

> Provided that the Picture is directed solely by Employee and that Employee is not in material default hereunder, Producer shall pay to Employee a contingent deferment in the amount of $50,000 payable solely out of proceeds of the Picture after Initial Actual Breakeven (as defined below). Such deferment shall be payable pro rata and pari passu with other similar deferments. For purposes of this agreement, "Initial Actual Breakeven" shall mean the end of the accounting period in which the gross receipts of the Picture are sufficient to enable recoupment of the following items relating to the Picture in the following order of priority on a continuing and cumulative basis: (i) the distributor's distribution fees; (ii) the distributor's distribution expenses; (iii) Producer's distribution expenses; (iv) interest (computed at an annual percentage rate equal to 125% of the prime rate of interest on unsecured loans charged by the Movie Money Bank of California from time to time in effect) on the amounts provided in clauses (v) and (vi) below; (v) the cost of production of the Picture; and (vi) an amount equal to the comple-

tion guarantor's advance to the Picture (if any) (all as may be more fully described and defined in the distributor's customary net proceeds definition). As used herein, "proceeds of the Picture" shall mean said gross receipts of the Picture less the items described in clauses (i) through (iii) above. Notwithstanding the foregoing, if any individual producer or any cast member receives a contingent deferment in an amount or payable at a time more favorable than that granted to Employee hereunder, then Employee shall also receive such more favorable treatment.

Participation. This director also gets a participation of 2½ percent of 100 percent of the net proceeds, defined on a separate exhibit attached to the contract. (We will discuss net proceeds in detail later on.)

Provided that the Picture is directed solely by Employee and that Employee is not in material default hereunder, Producer shall pay to Employee an amount equal to two and one-half percent (2½%) of 100% of the "Net Proceeds" of the Picture, if any. For purposes of this agreement, "Net Proceeds" of the Picture shall be defined, computed, accounted for and paid in accordance with Exhibit A attached hereto and incorporated herein by this reference; provided, however, that Exhibit A-2 thereto (relating to royalties from soundtrack records) shall be disregarded.

Sound-track album participation. Although not always included, in this contract the director will receive a participation from the exploitation of the music sound track made and released in connection with the motion picture. Note that the sound-track royalty is not connected to the revenues generated from the movie and vice versa.

Provided that the Picture is directed solely by Employee and that Employee is not in material default hereunder, in the event that a record company or other licensee (the "Record Company") commercially releases a "sound-track record" (as defined in Exhibit A-2 to Exhibit A attached hereto), Producer shall pay to Employee a royalty at the applicable rate indicated below of the applicable "royalty base price" with respect to the record concerned in respect of net sales of records consisting entirely of selections derived from the sound track of the Picture and sold by the Record Company for distribution through normal retail channels in the United States: 1% in the case of LPs and 0.75% in the case of singles and other records. As used herein, "royalty base price" means the "suggested retail list price" for the record concerned less sales or other taxes included in the price and less the applicable container deduction. Such royalty shall be prorated, calculated, proportionately reduced, adjusted and paid in accordance with royalty provisions contained in the agreement between Producer and the Record Company (the "Record Agreement"). In the event that Record Company advances or other moneys are used by Producer to cover recording costs (including conversion costs), artist and producer advances and similar expense items relating to sound-track records hereunder, no royalty will be payable under this subparagraph (c) until such time as such recording and other costs have been fully recouped out of royalties payable to Producer pursuant to the Record Agreement. For the avoidance of doubt, the royalty payable under this subparagraph (c) will not be cross-collateralized with any other costs or expenses relating to the Picture.

Expenses. Expense reimbursement is triggered if the director is required to render services over a hundred miles from home. This is typical of such provisions.

Employee represents and warrants that Employee's principal place of residence is as set forth on the first page of this agreement. If Employee's services are required by Producer more than 100 miles from Employee's principal place of residence, Producer shall furnish and pay for, or reimburse Employee for the cost of, (a) round trip transportation, first-class if available, by air if appropriate, between Employee's residence (or from wherever Employee then may be, if closer) and such location; (b) reasonable hotel accommodations for Employee while at such location; and (c) a reasonable per diem. Producer shall also provide Employee with non-exclusive ground transportation to be shared with other key employees. Producer's obligation to reimburse Employee for transportation and living expenses shall be subject to Producer's usual expense accounting procedures.

Credits. The prudent producer will impose conditions on the director's credit. The director must be the sole director. The director must not be in default. Once the conditions are fulfilled, the director's credit will be placed on the prints of the movie and, subject to customary exclusions and exceptions (for example, a newspaper ad that doesn't have enough room to carry credits), paid advertisements.

Provided that the Picture is directed solely by Employee and that Employee is not in material default hereunder, Employee shall be accorded the following credits on the screen on all positive prints of the Picture and, subject to customary exclusions and exceptions, in the billing portion of all paid advertisements issued by or under the control of Producer.

"Directed By" credit. This is the most common form of credit for the director. Note that this credit always comes after or below the title of the movie and is by custom the last credit to appear in the main credits.

"Directed By" on screen, on a separate card, below or after the title, in a size of type not less than that accorded any cast member or individual producer of the Picture, and in paid advertisements, below or after the title, in a size of type not less than that accorded any cast member or individual producer of the Picture . . .

"Film By" credit. This credit, which is deemed optional, is highly sought after by directors as the sign of the "auteur" (a ten-dollar word roughly meaning a high-level film artist). This credit is known as the "possessory credit" and it always comes before the title. This credit has come under fire by members of the writers' guild, who have objected to directors taking possessory credit for the creation of the movie.

"Film By" credit in substantially the form of "A Ken Kantoku Film," on screen, on a separate card, above or before the title, in a size of type not less than that of any individual producer's production credit, and in paid advertisements, above or before the title, in a size of type not less than that of any individual producer's production credit.

Other characteristics of the credit. The other characteristics of the credit—style of the type, the position of the credit on the screen or page, etc.—are at the discretion of the producer.

All other characteristics of Employee's credit shall be at Producer's sole discretion. Any references to the title of the Picture are to the regular (as opposed to artwork) title unless otherwise specified.

No breach for inadvertent failure. We've seen this provision before. Suppose the producer or the producer's vendors make a mistake and leave the director's credit off the movie or the paid advertisement. In the worst case, the director cries "breach" and forces the producer to redo all the prints and ads. This would be a major expense and could force the distributor to scrap the distribution schedule. Therefore, the producer provides that a casual or inadvertent failure to give the credit will not be a breach and that the only remedy for the director will be to cause the producer to cure the problem on future prints and ads.

> No casual or inadvertent failure by Producer, and no failure by any third party, to comply with the provisions of this paragraph shall constitute a breach of this agreement by Producer, provided, however, that upon the receipt by Producer of written notice from Employee specifying in reasonable detail of such failure, Producer shall use reasonable efforts prospectively to cure such failure on future prints of the Picture or future paid advertisements.

The right not to receive a credit—Alan Smithee. Directors and producers (especially when the producer is a major studio) don't always see eye to eye on the making of a movie. In 1969, Robert Totten, who was hired to direct the movie *Death of a Gunfighter,* clashed with the movie's star, Richard Widmark (whom Totten had worked with successfully a year earlier on the movie *Madigan*), and asked that his name be removed from the movie—in other words, he requested that he not be given a credit for directing. He petitioned the Directors Guild of America (DGA), the directors union, which agreed to promote a lie. The studio could award a director's credit to a fictitious Alan Smithee (the unusual spelling chosen to avoid the possibility that there might be a real person by that name). The right to deny a credit and give it to Mr. Smithee was later arbitrated by the DGA, which decided to allow the award only if the picture is "taken away" from the director.[2]

In 1997, Arthur Hiller asked for an Alan Smithee credit for the movie *An Alan Smithee Film: Burn Hollywood Burn,* based on the Joe Eszterhas book of the same title about a director actually named Alan Smithee. After granting a Smithee credit to Hiller (one has to wonder if this irony was part of the plan), the DGA announced that it was going to end the practice. The DGA may have also been influenced by another Alan Smithee case during the same time period. The DGA refused to let director Tony Kaye use an Alan Smithee credit on the movie *American History X*. The DGA said he could use any name he wanted to, except Alan Smithee, because he had openly criticized the movie. Mr. Kaye submitted the name Humpty Dumpty, but that was also rejected. He ended up taking the credit in his own name and actor, Edward Norton, whose creative leverage was the source of Kaye's irritation, won an Oscar nomination for Best Actor for his role in the movie. After the *American History X* case, the DGA decided to choose a different fake name for each case. The first example seems to be a "Thomas Lee" credit for director Walter Hill on the movie *Supernova*. However, a search of the Internet Movie Database (www.IMBD.com) reveals that Alan Smithee hasn't completely disappeared from the scene.[3]

> Anything in this Agreement to the contrary notwithstanding, Employee shall have the right in his sole discretion to refuse a credit on the Picture.

Budget, schedule, artistic elements. Control over the budget means control over the production of the movie. The producer should try to maintain control over the budget. The same goes for the schedule and the artistic elements of the movie. Directors will also have an interest in these issues, as it will be the director's responsibility to actually make the movie. This tension between the producer and director is a natural subject for negotiation and agreement. In the example below, the producer has the final approval right related to the movie's budget, schedule, and artistic production elements (which includes cast and crew); however, the producer must consult with the director (provided the director is available). Again, the producer is protected with respect to an inadvertent failure to consult with the director by providing that such failure is not a breach of contract (see the following illustration).

> Producer shall have final approval of the budget, production schedule, post-production schedule, release title and all other artistic and production elements in connection with the production of the Picture, including all "above the line" and "below the line" personnel and elements and all commitments and contracts relative to any of the foregoing. Notwithstanding the foregoing, provided that Employee is available as and when Producer shall require, Producer and Employee shall fully consult with respect to, and shall have mutual

approval of, the key members of the cast and crew. If Producer and Employee are unable to agree on any element regarding which Producer and Employee have mutual approval as provided above, then Producer, after consultation with Employee, shall have the right to designate such element in its sole discretion. No casual or inadvertent failure by Producer to consult with Employee or to obtain Employee's approval shall be a breach of this Agreement.

"Director's cut." In this contract, the director has the right to make an edit (referred to as a "cut") of his own liking—a "director's cut." In addition, the director has the right to have his cut previewed or screened first. The director, however, may not cut or edit the original negative—the master—of the film, without the producer's permission.

Provided that Employee substantially directs the Picture through the completion of principal photography and that Employee is not in material default hereunder, Employee shall be entitled to a director's cut of the Picture. If Producer desires one (1) or more additional cuts of the Picture after reviewing the director's cut, Employee shall prepare such cuts in accordance with Producer's instructions. Producer will organize one (1) or more previews or screenings of the Picture. If multiple cuts of the Picture have been prepared and the parties do not agree on which cut should be previewed or screened, Employee shall be entitled to require that the director's cut be the first cut to be previewed or screened, it being understood that Producer shall thereafter be entitled to preview or screen the other cuts of the Picture. The previews or screenings may be free or paid and may be public or private, as Producer shall determine in its sole discretion. In no event shall Employee cut or edit the negative or other original film or sound elements of the Picture without Producer's written consent. All cuts of the Picture shall be delivered in accordance with the provisions of the "Delivery" paragraph below.

"Final cut." Final cut is the term used to describe the final edit of a given motion picture. Simply put, if the producer reserves the right of final cut (in other words, refuses to give that right to the director) he or she will have the ability to have the last say as to the film's content. In this contract, producer has the final cut right.

Producer shall have the right of final cut of the Picture.

Delivery. When you enter into an agreement with a distributor, there will be a list of items (chain of title documents and film elements) that you must someday deliver to the distributor. You will need the director's help with the delivery of the film elements.

The director's cut shall be completed within eight (8) weeks after the completion of principal photography of the Picture. Should Producer thereafter request that changes be made in the director's or other cut of the Picture, Employee shall make such changes and deliver the changed cut of the Picture to Producer as soon as reasonably practicable (but not later than two (2) weeks after Producer requests such changes). Unless Producer has otherwise approved the same in writing, the Picture as delivered to Producer shall (i) be between 90 and 110 minutes in length (including main and end titles), (ii) be photographed on standard 35 mm film, in color, with an aspect ratio of 1.85:1 and without the use of a hard matte, (iii) qualify for an MPAA rating not more restrictive than "PG-13" and (iv) conform in all material respects to the final approved shooting script. The delivery of the Picture shall include delivery of any "cover shots" required hereunder.

Premiere. Here, again, the director will be invited to attend a premiere, but the director has to pay for his own transportation and expenses. The producer agrees to try to get the distributor to pay for these expenses.

Provided that the Picture is directed solely by Employee and that Employee is not in material default hereunder, in the event that Producer plans a celebrity premiere of the Picture in New York or Los Angeles, Producer shall invite Employee to attend such premiere. Producer will not be required to pay any of Employee's transportation or other expenses incurred in conjunction with such premiere; provided, however, that Producer will use reasonable good faith efforts to cause the U.S. theatrical distributor or sub-distributor of the Picture to pay for such expenses.

Producer-specific terms. You are probably asking yourself, "If I'm the producer, why talk about hiring a producer?" Well, remember that there are different types of producers. If you have never produced a movie, you will need a good line producer to supervise the actual production work.

In reality, the producer agreement does not introduce a lot of new terms. We will look at just a few.

PRODUCER AGREEMENT

DATE:	As of February 1, 2006
PRODUCER:	The Quest Production LLC 1234 Sunset Boulevard Hollywood, CA 90000 Facsimile: (818) 555-1234
EMPLOYEE:	Peter Pro (S.S.N. 123-45-6789) 222 Malibu Ranch Road Posh Ranch, CA 90000 Facsimile: (310) 555-0987 Citizen of: U.S.A. Principal Residence: Posh Ranch, California
PICTURE:	Feature-length theatrical motion picture tentatively entitled *The Quest*
CAPACITY:	Line Producer

Services. Note that the services include development services. It is typical for a producer to be exclusive during principal photography and nonexclusive at other times.

Producer hereby engages Employee, and Employee hereby accepts such engagement, to render services as an individual producer of the Picture. In that connection, Employee shall render all development services as are customarily rendered by producers of first class theatrical motion picture projects and, if the Picture is set for production, all production services as are customarily rendered by producers of first class theatrical motion picture projects. Employee's development services shall be rendered on a non-exclusive basis. Subject to Employee's prior contractual commitments at the time that the Picture is set for production, Employee's production services shall be rendered on an exclusive basis during principal photography of the Picture and on a nonexclusive basis at all other times during the production of the Picture.

Fixed compensation. This provision takes a different approach to fixed compensation. In this deal (not all producer deals are like this) the producer gets a percentage of the budget, with a specified floor. The payment schedule is also different. Fixed compensation to producers for hire is not easily defined, as the approach for each is generally on a case-by-case basis.

In full and complete consideration for all of Employee's services hereunder and for all rights granted or to be granted to Producer hereunder, Employee shall be entitled to receive the following:
In respect of Employee's development and production services in connection with the Picture, fixed compensation in an amount equal to 3% of the final approved production budget for the Picture, provided, however, that in no event shall Employee's fixed compensation be less than $125,000 or more than $200,000. Employee's fixed compensation shall be payable as follows: 20% thereof in equal weekly installments over the scheduled preproduction period, 60% thereof in equal weekly installments over the scheduled period of principal photography, 10% thereof upon completion of scoring and dubbing and 10% thereof upon delivery of the Picture.

Participation. This is a standard participation clause for a producer for hire.

In respect of Employee's production services in connection with the Picture, contingent compensation in an amount equal to 5% of 100% of the "gross receipts" of the Picture after initial cash breakeven, with such gross receipts being defined, computed, accounted for and paid in accordance with Producer's most favorable definition therefor (subject to such changes as the parties shall agree to after good faith negotiations).

"Produced by" credit. The "produced by" credit is the most highly regarded of the producer credits. Credit shared on a card with other producers, as here, is not as desirable as credit on a single card, but the producer here gets the credit in first position, which is preferred to any other position. This credit always comes after the title, and, as noted, usually comes right before the "directed by" credit. The credit, in this case, will look like the director's credit (size, type style, etc.).

Employee shall be accorded a "Produced by" credit in connection with the Picture as follows: (i) on screen, in the main titles (if any), on a card shared only with other individual producers of the Picture, and (ii) subject to customary exclusions, in all paid advertising issued by or under the control of Producer and/or the distributor(s) of the Picture (it being understood that if any other person is accorded a "Produced by" credit in connection with the Picture, Employee's name shall appear in first position). Such credit shall be in the customary position therefor (i.e., immediately preceding the director's credit) and shall be on a most-favored-nation's basis with the credit accorded the director of the Picture in terms of size, duration and other aspects.

"Production credit." A highly desirable credit for a producer or producer's production company is a production credit, which comes above or before the title and usually reads "A Peter Pro Production" (and in its full form with the director's possessory credit would read, "A Peter Pro Production of a Ken Kantoku Film"). The credit is often assigned to the production company—especially where the production company has acquired (or the producer wants the company to acquire) good will.

At Employee's election, Employee or an entity designated by Employee shall be accorded a production credit in connection with the Picture as follows: (i) above or before the title of the Picture on screen, and (ii) subject to customary exclusions, above or before the title of the Picture in all paid advertising issued by or under the control of Producer and/or the distributor(s) of the Picture (it being understood that if any other person or entity is accorded a production credit in connection with the Picture, Employee's or Employee's designee's credit shall appear in first position). Such credit shall be in the customary position therefor (i.e., immediately preceding the director's proprietary credit) and shall be on a most-favored-nation's basis with the director's proprietary credit in terms of size, duration and other aspects.

"Presented by" credit. Only occasionally seen as a personal credit, the "presented by" credit is sometimes sought by producers for their production companies (the most common use of this credit is by a distribution company). The credit would read for example: "Miramax Films Presents."

"In Association with" credit. Another common credit to production

companies is the "in association with" credit. This credit is also commonly taken by distributors. The credit, in conjunction with other credits, reads: "Miramax Films presents, in association with Buena Vista Entertainment, a Lawrence Bender production of a Quentin Tarantino film."

Expenses. This provision is tied to the provision in the director's agreement, but notice that the producer gets reimbursed once the location goes seventy-five (not a hundred) miles beyond the producer's residence.

> Whenever Employee's services hereunder are required at a location more than seventy-five (75) miles from Employee's residence in the Los Angeles metropolitan area, Employee will be given one (1) first class round-trip air transportation, if available and if used, between such residence and such location and will be paid a reasonable expense allowance depending on the location (the amount of which shall not be less than the expense allowance provided to the director of the Picture).

"Standard terms and conditions."

Attached to the actor's, director's, and the producer's agreements are the standard terms and conditions. This attachment contains some critically important provisions to the production company, so it must be made part of the deal and, if the other side has the clout and insists on negotiating the provisions of this attachment, you and your attorney will have to pay attention; in all other cases, the hope is that they will merely accept it. The following are sample provisions—it is not an exhaustive list of all the provisions that are typically contained in this type of attachment:

Work-made-for-hire language. In case you are just joining us, this language is typical of the language employed to cover the work-made-for-hire doctrine discussed in book one on page 30. This magical language is pulled from the Copyright Act and in essence is added to clarify that the producer, not the person being paid by the producer, is the author for the purposes of copyright law. This means that the producer's or the production company's name is listed as the author on the copyright form submitted to the USCO. By force of law, under this doctrine, the producer or production company is the owner of all right, title and interest in the results and proceeds of the employee's services. This language also picks up all renewals and extensions of copyright and all jurisdictions in the world.

Employee hereby acknowledges, certifies and agrees that all materials of every kind created or furnished by Employee and all results and proceeds of every kind of the services rendered by Employee in connection with the Picture, including without limitation all ideas, suggestions, characterizations, dialogue, voice, promotional or "making of" films and other material (all such materials and all such results and proceeds being sometimes collectively referred to herein as the "Material"), are and shall be deemed to be "works made for hire" specially ordered or commissioned by Producer for use as part of a motion picture or other audiovisual work or as a contribution to a collective work. Accordingly, Producer is and shall be considered to be the author of the Material and, at all stages of completion, the sole and exclusive owner throughout the universe in perpetuity of the Material and all right, title and interest therein, including all copyrights therein, all renewals and extensions of such copyrights and all other ownership and exploitation rights of any kind, nature or description in, to and with respect to the Material that may be secured under the laws now or hereinafter in effect in the United States of America or any other jurisdiction (collectively, the rights).

Rights. This language clarifies the list of rights included in the "Rights." It picks up (or should pick up) all the uses that the producer (and the distributor later on) will need to fully exploit the movie at home and abroad (including the European Union—EU).

The Rights shall include without limitation the right to authorize, prohibit and/or control the production, reproduction, fixation, adaptation, distribution, renting, lending, performance, broadcasting, communication to the public and other exploitation of the Material in any and all media and by any and all means now known or hereafter devised, including the right to telecast the Picture and exhibit the Picture theatrically and in supplemental markets (as defined in the SAG Agreement) and the right to make such changes therein and such uses and dispositions thereof as Producer in its sole discretion may deem necessary or desirable. The Rights shall further include without limitation any and all so-called rental rights, lending rights, fixation rights, reproduction rights, distribution rights and neighboring rights pursuant to any international treaties or conventions, any directives or other measures of the European Union or its successors and/or any enabling or implementing legislation, laws or regulations relating to the foregoing (collectively, the "EU Rights").

Assignment (in case work made for hire doesn't apply). As we discussed earlier, the work-made-for-hire doctrine has certain limitations. Therefore, just to make sure the producer/production company owns the rights (as defined), this language clarifies that the employee grants a full assignment of whatever rights he or she might have to the producer/production company. Notice that the grant is "irrevocable," "throughout the universe" and "in perpetuity." It is broad and meant to be that way. About the only thing it doesn't cover is exploitation on another galaxy (don't worry, language covering galaxies far far away will appear before long).

> If and to the extent that under any applicable law the Material is not deemed a work made for hire for Producer or Producer is not deemed to be the author of the Material and the sole and exclusive owner of the Material and all right, title and interest therein (including all of the Rights), then to the fullest extent allowable and for the full term of protection otherwise accorded Employee under such applicable law, Employee hereby irrevocably grants, assigns and licenses to Producer throughout the universe in perpetuity all of the Rights and, in connection therewith, all right, title and interest of Employee in, to and with respect to the Picture and any other works now or hereafter created containing the Material.

Buyout of EU rights. Because of legal principles applicable in the EU, this language is needed to clarify that the compensation paid is intended by both parties to be a complete buyout of all the rights the employee might expect to receive in the EU and that the producer/production company will have the right to directly collect any amount payable to the employee.

> Employee hereby acknowledges and agrees that the compensation paid or to be paid by Producer to Employee for Employee's services in connection with the Picture includes adequate and equitable remuneration for the EU Rights (including the rental rights) and constitutes a complete buy-out of all EU Rights. Employee hereby irrevocably grants, assigns and transfers to Producer, throughout the universe in perpetuity, the right to collect and retain for Producer's own account any and all amounts payable to Employee with respect to the EU Rights and hereby irrevocably directs any collecting societies or other persons or entities receiving such amounts to pay such amounts to Producer.

Moral rights of authors. Although the United States does not recognize the legal doctrine known as moral rights of authors or *droit moral,* the worldwide exploitation of films makes it necessary to cover the issues relating to it. Note the last sentence of this provision, which deals with the problem that many civil law scholars hold that moral rights of authors cannot be waived. (See discussion about *droit moral* on page 56.)

> Employee hereby grants to Producer the right to change, edit, add to, take from, translate, dub, adapt, reformat or reprocess the Material in any manner which Producer may in its sole discretion determine, including without limitation for the following purposes: to meet the requirements of any network or non-network television exhibitor of the Picture, to create foreign language versions of the Picture and to satisfy any relevant censorship requirements. To the fullest extent allowable under any applicable law, Employee hereby irrevocably assigns or waives to Producer any and all rights of "droit moral" or "moral rights of authors" or similar rights which Employee may now or later have in the Material and any other works now or hereafter created containing the Material. Employee expressly acknowledges that many persons will contribute to the Picture and other works that will embody all or part of the Material. Accordingly, if under any applicable law the above assignment or waiver by Employee of such rights of droit moral or moral rights of authors or similar rights is not effective, then Employee agrees to exercise such rights in a manner which recognizes the contribution of, and will not have an adverse effect upon, such other persons.

Further assurances. This provision puts the employee under a legal obligation to cooperate in going forward by providing whatever further documentation or take whatever action might be needed to completely fulfill the promises made in the agreement. For example, suppose that during the process of production an actor composes and recites on camera a poem or soliloquy. To avoid any question as to whether the production company has the right to embody this material in the movie, the producer can ask the actor to execute an assignment or license in favor of the production company. This provision goes a step further and provides that the employee appoints the production company as the employee's attorney-in-fact (and adds all the necessary legal language to make that appointment stick) in connection with the further assurances. Thus, suppose that our eloquent actress refuses to sign and deliver the assignment or license, the appropriate officer of the production can simply sign the assignment on behalf of the actress as the actress's attorney-in-fact.

> Employee agrees to execute, acknowledge and deliver to Producer such further documents as Producer may deem necessary or advisable in order to evidence, establish, maintain, protect, enforce or defend its rights in, to and with respect to the Material and the Rights or otherwise to carry out the intent and accomplish the purposes of this agreement (including without limitation a certificate of employment in Producer's customary form). Employee hereby irrevocably appoints Producer as attorney-in-fact (such appointment being a power coupled with an interest), with full power of substitution and delegation, with the right (but not the obligation) to execute, acknowledge and deliver any such documents which Employee fails to execute, acknowledge and deliver within five (5) days after Producer's request therefor.

No action. This is the flip side of the further assurances clause. In this provision, the employee promises that he or she will not do anything to interfere with the production company's claim or enjoyment of the rights. The employee agrees not to, for example, bring any lawsuit or arbitration proceeding, encumber, or take any other action that will interfere with or derogate from the production company's rights under the agreement.

> Employee agrees not to make any claim or demand or to institute, support, maintain or permit any suit, action, arbitration or other proceeding which will or might interfere with or derogate from any of Producer's right, title and interest in, to and with respect to the Material, it being expressly understood and agreed that Employee shall not have or be deemed to have any lien, charge or other encumbrance upon the Material or any rights therein or proceeds derived therefrom and that neither the breach of this agreement by Producer, nor the termination or cancellation of this agreement for any reason, nor any other act, omission or event of any kind shall terminate or otherwise adversely affect Producer's sole and exclusive ownership of the Material and all right, title and interest therein (including all of the Rights). Employee further agrees that Employee's sole remedy for any such breach or other act, omission or event shall be an action at law to recover such damages as may have been actually suffered by Employee as a result thereof.

Name and likeness. In addition to the images taken during production and incorporated into the movie, you will need to have the right to use the name and likeness of the actor, director, producer, or other cast or crew member in connection with all aspects of exploitation of the movie. Think of all the posters (called one sheets), advertisements, flyers, and other promotional materials. Under the so-called "privacy rights" of the United States Constitution, it is illegal to use a person's name or likeness for commercial gain without such person's permission. One would perhaps like to assume that this right would be implied in the fact that the actor is appearing in the motion picture—but, of course, it is dangerous to make such assumptions and so all actor agreements contain provisions similar to the illustration below. Also, note that you may want to use the director's name and the names of all producers in promoting the movie and, therefore, these provisions are included in all production agreements (and, thus, are in the standard terms and conditions).

> Employee hereby grants to Producer the perpetual rights to reproduce, print, publish and disseminate (and to license and authorize others to reproduce, print, publish and disseminate) in any medium the name, voice, likeness and biographical material of Employee in connection with the performance, distribution, advertising, promotion and other use or exploitation of the Picture (including any and all adaptations and versions thereof); provided, however, that Employee shall not be represented as endorsing any product or service other than the Picture (including any and all adaptations and versions thereof) without Employee's prior written consent.

Commercial endorsements. There is typically a limitation on commercial endorsements. Celebrities in today's world are paid a lot of money to endorse products—these arrangements are separate from their acting and thus actors are careful not to allow the production company to use their name or likeness to endorse anything other than the picture itself. In some cases, a celebrity will have a contractual obligation to be exclusive to a given product category (such as shoes or automobiles). The actor's agent will need this limitation in order to avoid violating such contractual commitments. Note, however, that this provision does clarify that certain uses—such as T-shirts and so forth—are not "endorsements."

> For the avoidance of doubt, the use of Employee's name, voice, likeness and biographical material in soundtrack albums and other

recordings, sheet music and song books, commercial and promotional tie-ins, world wide web sites, promotional items such as posters and T-shirts, novelizations, printed or souvenir programs and other publications relating to the Picture and the exhibition of a "trailer" or promotional film for the Picture on a sponsored television program shall not be deemed to constitute an endorsement.

Representations and warranties. Representations and warranties are an important and customary part of most contracts. Note that the production company is to be indemnified for material supplied to the production by the employee that is not original with the employee that infringes the rights of any other person. So, if the actress referred to above recites a poem that was original with her jealous sister, and the sister sues the production company, the production company can make a claim for indemnification from the actress.

Employee represents, warrants and agrees that: (a) Employee has the full right, power and authority to enter into and perform this agreement and to grant the rights granted hereunder without any restriction or limitation whatsoever; (b) Employee is not subject to any conflicting obligation or disability which will or might prevent or interfere with the execution and/or performance of this agreement; and (c) all material written or furnished by Employee hereunder (if any) shall be original with Employee and shall not violate or infringe the copyright or other rights of any third party. Employee hereby agrees to indemnify and hold harmless Producer and its licensees (and their respective successors, assigns, officers, directors, shareholders, partners, employees, agents and contractors) from and against any and all liability, loss, damage, cost or expense (including reasonable attorneys' fees and legal expenses) resulting from or relating to any claim that is inconsistent with any of Employee's representations, warranties and agreements hereunder.

No obligation to proceed. This clarifies that the producer has no legal mandate to use the results of an employee's services in the movie. This is important, not only because the production company will want to have the right to edit the movie however it desires but to avoid a claim by an actor who wants to assert that not appearing in the movie caused emotional distress or damaged the actor's career.

Notwithstanding any other provision of this agreement, Producer shall have no obligation to actually utilize Employee's services or to include the results or proceeds thereof in the Picture or any motion picture, soundtrack or other property created, produced or developed by Producer of any portion of any of the foregoing, or to produce, release, distribute or otherwise exploit the Picture or any motion picture, soundtrack or other property so created, produced or developed, or any portion of any of the foregoing. If at any time Producer elects not to require Employee's further services hereunder, Producer's obligations hereunder shall be fully performed by payment of any accrued compensation.

Suspension and termination. The following verbose provision enumerates the conditions under which the employee may be terminated.

Producer shall have the right to suspend the use of Employee's services and the accrual of Employee's compensation hereunder and the running of any periods herein provided for during all periods that: (i) Employee does not or will not render services hereunder because of death, illness, incapacity, default or similar matters; (ii) production of the Picture is prevented, interrupted or delayed by reason of force majeure events, including without limitation any labor dispute, fire, war, governmental action, third party breach of contract or any other event beyond the reasonable control of Producer; or (iii) production of the Picture is prevented, interrupted or delayed by reason of the death, illness or incapacity of the individual producer(s), director, director of photography or a principal member of the cast. Unless this agreement is terminated, all dates herein set forth or provided for may, in the sole discretion of Producer, be deemed extended by a period equivalent to all such periods of suspension and no compensation shall accrue or become payable to Employee during the period of such suspension. If any matter referred to in (i) above (other than material default on the part of Employee) continues for longer than five (5) days in the aggregate, or if any matter referred to in (ii) above continues for more than eight (8) weeks in the aggregate, or any matter referred to in (iii) above continues for more than two (2) weeks in the aggregate, or immediately in the event of any material default on the part of Employee, Producer may terminate this agreement and be relieved of any further obligation to compensate Employee (except for accrued compensation for services already performed) or to give credit to Employee. However, if Producer elects to use Employee's services in the Picture, Producer shall remain obligated to compensate Employee and to give credit to Employee, as provided in this agreement. Notwithstanding anything herein contained, if any suspension under (ii) or (iii) continues for two (2) weeks or more, Employee may render services on Employee's own behalf or for others during the continuance of such suspension, subject to immediate recall on the termination of such suspension. If any suspension under (ii) or (iii) above, other than as a result of a labor dispute called by the collective bargaining organization of which Employee is (or, pursuant to this agreement, is required to be) a member, continues for eight (8) weeks or more, Employee may terminate Employee's engagement by notice to Producer but such notice and termination shall have no effect if, within five (5) business days after receipt thereof, Producer gives Employee notice that such suspension is ended.

Suspension and Termination for Change in Appearance. This provision clarifies that if the actor or the actor's appearance changes during the shoot—for example, the actor breaks out with a rash—the production company can suspend or terminate the actor.

Unless otherwise specified herein, in the event that the facial or physical appearance or voice (collectively, "appearance") of Employee materially changes prior to or during the course of Employee's employment hereunder to the extent Employee is not suitable to perform the role as originally contemplated by Producer at the time of casting of Employee in the role, then the use of Employee's services and the accrual of Employee's compensation hereunder, and the running of any periods herein provided for, shall be suspended upon notice to Employee during all periods that Employee does not or cannot adequately render services due to Employee's changed appearance; and Producer may terminate Employee without further obligation (other than the obligation to pay any accrued compensation for services already performed) if the changed appearance continues or cannot be remedied to Producer's satisfaction within two (2) days of such notice to Employee.

Suspension and termination for failure to procure a visa. This provision allows the production company to suspend or terminate an employee for failing to obtain the necessary work permits or visas.

Producer may terminate this agreement without further obligation if any work permits, visas or proof of Employee's right to work required in connection with Employee's services hereunder cannot be obtained in a timely fashion. Whether or not Producer in its discretion agrees to obtain such a work permit or visa for Employee, the responsibility therefor shall rest with Employee.

Producer shall confirm in writing any termination or suspension of this agreement pursuant to this paragraph as soon as practicable thereafter, but in no event shall such written confirmation be deemed a condition subsequent to the effectiveness of such termination or suspension.

Dubbing. The production company will want to have the right to bring in a voice double to do dubbing work. Imagine having to schedule Tom Hanks for a recording session so that you can correct a mispronunciation or, for the purpose of creating a sound track suitable for viewing on an airplane, replacing a naughty word; with this provision, you can get someone in to impersonate Hanks's voice. Notice, too, that the producer can get a singer in to overdub a singing performance that doesn't cut it (hence, for example, Audrey Hepburn's singing performance in *My Fair Lady* can be replaced by Marnie Nixon's).

Producer shall have the right to use a double to represent Employee's physical appearance and to dub or simulate Employee's voice and other sound effects, in whole or in part, in English and all other languages, in connection with the Picture or any part thereof or in any exhibition, advertisement, promotion, marketing, publicity or exploitation thereof; provided, however, that Producer will not dub Employee's voice in the English language or use a double in lieu of Employee except as follows: (a) when necessary to expeditiously meet the requirements of foreign exhibition; (b) when necessary to expeditiously meet censorship or broadcast requirements, both foreign and domestic; (c) when Employee shall fail or refuse to tender the required services, or when Employee is not readily available when and where Employee's services are required; (d) when Employee fails or is unable to meet certain requirements of the role (such determination to be made by Producer in its sole discretion), such as singing or the rendition of instrumental music or other similar services; and (e) when the failure to use a double for the performance of hazardous acts might result in physical injury to Employee.

Publicity. The producer does not want to lose control of the publicity related to the movie and the producer does not want the employee out there saying negative things about the movie.

> Unless Employee has received Producer's prior written approval, Employee shall not issue or authorize the publication of any news stories or publicity relating to the Picture, this agreement, Employee's performance of the services hereunder, or Producer; provided, however, that Employee shall be entitled to issue personal publicity relating solely to Employee in which incidental references to the Picture or Producer are made so long as such references are not derogatory.

Specific performance. Under the law of contracts, the favored remedy is money damages. That means, if an actor decides to breach a contract, he or she can pay you an amount of money to make you whole (the goal of legal remedies). If you think about this in the real world of movie production, money may not make you whole. Actors are unique—there is only one Tom Cruise. And when someone's services are "special, unique, unusual, and extraordinary," the producer may have a claim that money damages won't be good enough and that the producer should have the right to the specific performance (to compel the actor to act). This is the stated purpose of this provision. (Good luck. Compelling someone to act used to be called slavery and the Thirteenth Amendment to the Constitution may have something to say about this.)

> Employee acknowledges and agrees that Employee's services and the rights granted to Producer are of a special, unique, unusual, extraordinary and intellectual character which gives them a peculiar value, the loss of which cannot be reasonably or adequately compensated for by damages in an action at law and that a breach of this agreement will cause Producer irreparable injury. Producer shall be entitled to injunctive and other equitable relief to prevent or cure any such breach or threatened breach, which relief shall be in addition to any other rights and remedies which Producer may have, whether for damages or otherwise.

Assignment. This provision clarifies that the producer may assign its rights under the agreement to another company—an affiliated company (remember our discussion about corporate structuring, where it is recommended that a separate production company be established for the production of the motion picture) or other production or distribution company. This right of assignment cannot be given to the actor— think about it.

> Producer may assign this agreement or loan to furnish Employee's services to any parents, subsidiary or affiliated corporation of Producer, or any entity with or into which Producer merges or consolidates, or which succeeds to all or a substantial portion of Producer's assets, or to any entity which produces the Picture for release and distribution by Producer or which supplies financing or studio facilities for the Picture, or which has the right to distribute the Picture, or which may be or become the owner of the Picture or of the underlying literary property and screenplay. Producer may assign and/or license any of its rights in the Material and/or its rights to use Employee's name, voice, likeness and biographical data and/or its rights in connection with any representations and warranties hereunder, to any persons or entities whatsoever, and this agreement shall inure to the benefit of all such assignees and licensees.

NET PROFITS AND VARIATIONS

Whether or not a participant actually gets to share in the profits that the movie makes depends largely on the contract definition of such profits. Also, since the producer, or person or company that controls the definition of profits, often takes what is left after everyone else has taken his or her share, the definition of profits determines the size of the ultimate profits of the producer or such person or company. There are many stories of motion pictures that were reported to make many millions of dollars in excess of their production budgets that did not yield a profit participation—at least to contract participants. These stories and other factors have created a cynicism in Hollywood about participations—especially participations described as net.

The money, like water over the falls, comes in from ticket sales and other defined sources. First, roughly 60 percent of the water is diverted by the theater owners. The remainder continues down the falls. Next, certain players (those who have the power) divert more water from the falls at various heights. The remainder continues down the falls. Then those persons who have the pull to get a participation, but not the power to cause a diversion from any vertical height, take from a pool at the bottom of the falls—if any. Sometimes the producer takes from that same pool. However, if the producer has enough clout, that pool will be defined for the participant in such a way that it is dry as to that participant, notwithstanding that the water continues to fall into the producer's pool.

Basic definition of net.

Below, is a common definition of net proceeds. For the sake of brevity, this definition has been abridged. Let's look at each of the aspects.

Definition of "distributor." The term distributor is a key part of the calculation of net proceeds, as the moneys received by the distributor constitute the first stage of the waterfall.

"Distributor" shall mean Distribution Co., Limited. If at any time Distributor assigns all or substantially all of its rights to distribute and license the Picture to a "major" U.S. motion picture company (as such term is then commonly understood in the U.S. motion picture industry); provided, however, that such term shall not include any other persons, firms or corporations licensed by such major U.S. motion picture company to distribute motion pictures in any part of the world, nor shall such term include the following: any person, firm or corporation distributing the Picture for purposes other than exhibition in theaters or by television stations; exhibitors or others who may actually exhibit the Picture to the public; radio or television broadcasters; cable operators; manufacturers, wholesalers or retailers of video discs, cassettes or similar devices; book or music publishers; phonograph record producers or distributors; manufacturers, distributors, wholesalers, retailers or operators of any types of merchandise, goods, services or theme park or other attractions; whether or not any of the foregoing are subsidiaries of such major U.S. motion picture company. As used herein, a "subsidiary" of refers to an entity in which a company has at least a 50% interest.

Note that the term does not include:

(i) Any licensee of the Distributor, as the inclusion of any licensee would significantly and artificially increase this pool; in other words, moneys received by licensees of the Distributor are not to be counted in the definition of net proceeds;

(ii) Any non-theatrical or non-television distributor, as moneys from other sources (e.g. from the sale of videos, etc.) are not covered; this definition deals only with theatrical and television revenues;

(iii) Actual exhibitors (i.e., the theater owners, television broadcasters, etc.), as revenues received by exhibitors are also not part of the pool;

(iv) Book or music publishers, as such revenues are handled separately;

(v) Phonograph record producers and distributors, as such revenues are handled separately; and

(vi) Manufacturers and distributors of merchandise, as such revenues are also handled separately.

Definition of "participant." The definition of participant tells who is entitled to receive a piece of the action.

"Participant" shall mean the party under the Agreement who or which is entitled to participate in the Net Proceeds of the Picture and the successors and permitted assigns of such party.

Definition of net proceeds. And now for the moment of truth—the definition of net proceeds describes the pool from which the participant will take his or her money. Thus, if you are a participant and your take is 5 percent of net proceeds, you will get 5 percent of whatever this definition yields. In summary form the formula is simple: Gross receipts less all (1) distribution fees, (2) distribution expenses, (3) cost of the picture, and (4) all participants except for net proceeds participants. All of these terms, of course, are defined elsewhere in the document. Here we go—

Net Proceeds: As used herein, "Net Proceeds" means the excess, if any, of the Gross Receipts of the Picture (as that term is defined herein) over the sum of the following, which shall be deemed recouped by Distributor in the order listed:

"Gross receipts." Gross receipts are the total revenues (less, in most cases, certain off-the-top deductions[4]) from all sources from the exploitation of the movie and are made up of film rentals, revenues from videograms, revenues from the lease of the picture for a flat fee and for miscellaneous licenses of portions of the picture, subsidies and prizes, music-related royalties and merchandise.

As used herein, the term "Gross Receipts" means the aggregate of:

"Film rentals." The gross amount received by theater owners from the sale of tickets is referred to as the "box office gross." The theater owner takes his or her share—roughly 50 percent—and sends the rest, referred to as film rentals, along to the distributor. Similarly, moneys received from television broadcasters are also referred to as film rentals. Thus, exhibitor in this provision means theater owner or television broadcaster—a point which is usually more specifically elaborated. At this stage in the definition of gross receipts, there are usually certain clarifications regarding theatrical rentals mainly dealing with the problem of subdistributors. It is often the case that distributors will grant a portion of the distribution rights to other distributors (referred to as "subdistributors"). The question is how to count rentals received by such subsidiaries. The normal way is to count in gross receipts either the film rentals received by subdistributors that the distributor accepts for accounting purposes or the amount distributor actually received. The distributor usually decides which approach will apply.

All film rentals actually received by Distributor from exhibitors.

"Videograms." A videogram is a technical term encompassing video discs, videocassettes, DVDs, or similar devices embodying the movie. Since, to the distributor, the exploitation of videograms is a separate profit center, gross receipts are enhanced only by a negotiated percentage of distributor's income in this area. Note that in this case the amount is 20 percent of distributors gross "wholesale" rental and sales income. Note also, in the case of sales, that the distributor will deduct an amount to allow for returns. This avoids the burden of having to render an accounting after the fact for actual returns. Note also that the percentage is lowered to 10 percent for sell-through videos. Sell-through videos are sold through to the public (as opposed to the rental business, such as Blockbuster).

Where Distributor directly engages in the manufacture, distribution and sale or rental of videograms, an amount equal to 20% of Distributor's gross wholesale rental income therefrom and 20%—10% in the case of sell-through video devices—of Distributor's gross wholesale sales income therefrom less a reasonable allowance for returns and credits.

Revenues from the lease of the picture for a flat fee, etc. The provision below is pretty much self-explanatory. The point is that any income generated from the movie should (at least from the participant's point of view) fall into gross receipts.

All amounts actually received by Distributor from the following: (i) trailers (other than trailers advertising television exhibitions of the Picture); (ii) licenses of theatrical distribution rights in the Picture for a flat sum; (iii) licenses of exhibition or distribution rights in the Picture other than as described below, specifically including licenses to cable operators; (iv) the lease of positive prints of the Picture (as distinguished from the licensing thereof for a film rental); (v) the sale or licensing of advertising accessories, souvenir programs and booklets relating specifically to the Picture; and (vi) recoveries by Distributor for infringement of copyrights of the Picture.

Subsidies, aid, and prizes. If the distributor receives a governmental subsidy or aid or wins a prize, these should also be included in gross receipts. In this case, local income taxes are deducted.

All moneys actually received by Distributor on account of direct subsidies, aid or prizes relating specifically to the Picture, net of an amount equal to income taxes based thereon imposed by the country involved, if any.

Music publishing, sound-track albums, and merchandising. Each of these three areas of revenues are handled separately in an exhibit to the definition of net. We will look at the basic elements of each right here:

The sums to be included in Gross Receipts under Exhibits "A-1 (Music Publishing)," "A-2 (Sound track)" and "A-3 (Merchandising)" attached hereto.

Music publishing. Distributors don't automatically get music publishing royalties, but to the extent that they do a certain percentage will fall into the definition of gross receipts. Typically, distributors will license or grant the music publishing rights to a music publishing company (it could be a subsidiary or affiliate of the distributors) and take back a royalty. Rather than haggle over the actual percentage that the distributor gets, for the purposes of calculating gross receipts, a negotiated percentage of certain income streams are included. For example, the distributor will be deemed to receive (1) 20 percent (or some other percent) of the "publisher's share" of the "mechanical" and "public performance" royalties in North America, and (2) three cents per copy of sheet music piano or piano vocal copies sold and paid for and not returned in North America. Publisher's share (which is, of course, described in detail in the actual contract provision) is a music industry term meaning 50 percent of the music publishing rights. This term arises from the industry custom that the publisher and the writer each take 50 percent of the total music publishing income. Mechanical royalties are publishing royalties, the rate of which is set by the federal copyright statute, paid to the owner or owners of the music publishing rights respecting songs embodied on phonorecordings (CDs, vinyl records, etc.). These royalties are customarily gathered and accounted for by specialized organizations, the most prevalent of which is the Harry Fox Agency. "Performance royalties" are paid to the owner or owners of the music publishing rights by broadcasters for the right to publicly perform the song. Performance royalties are collected by specialized organizations: ASCAP (American Society of Composers and Publishers), BMI (Broadcast Music Incorporate), and SESAC (Society of European Stage Authors and Composers).

Sound-track royalties. If the distributor obtains the right to make and exploit a sound-track album and actually exercises this right, then gross receipts will be enhanced by any amounts received by the distributor in that regard. Income for inclusion would exclude all royalties and other amounts payable to any artists, conductors, musicians, producers, engineers, or other third parties granting rights or rendering services in connection with such sound-track album and all costs, expenses, and fees related to the sound-track album incurred by the distributor under any agreement with any guild or union and all other recording (including reuse fees), production, and delivery costs of the master recordings. All of the terms, including "sound-track album" have specific detailed definitions. For example, sound-track album includes phonograph records, tapes, CDs, and other devices for audio-only playback. The term reuse fee is a music industry term referring to fees paid to union musicians when the results and proceeds of their services are used in ways other than contemplated in the original contract (for example, the master recording made for the motion picture is used in a separate television program). Production cost is, of course, the cost of producing the sound-track album. Delivery cost is the cost of delivering the master recording to the manufacturer.

Merchandising. If the distributor obtains merchandising rights (the right to make and sell merchandise based on the characters or other elements from the motion picture—for example, action figures, T-shirts, etc.), a certain portion of the royalties received from the exploitation of such rights will be included in the definition of gross royalties. The typical formula is 50 percent of the net receipts from the exercise of merchandising rights. Net receipts means all amounts actually received by the distributor from the exploitation of merchandising rights, less the costs expended by the distributor in such exploitation (such as shipping costs, licensing agents' commissions, royalties, and participations to third parties, etc.).

Less distribution fees, expenses, costs, and certain participants. Now that we have defined gross receipts, we can calculate net proceeds by deducting four categories of costs: (1) distribution fees, (2) distribution expenses, (3) the cost of the picture, and (4) all participants except for net proceeds participants. We will look at each one.

(1) *Distribution fees.* Distribution fees range from about 15 to 40 percent of gross receipts of theatrical rentals, depending on the circumstances. In this example, the distributor takes 30 percent from North America, 35 percent from the United Kingdom, and 40 percent from all other territories.

> Distributor's fees in connection with the distribution of the Picture, shall be as follows:
>
> 30% of the Gross Receipts of the Picture derived by Distributor from all sources in the United States and Canada.
>
> 35% of the Gross Receipts of the Picture derived by Distributor from all sources in the United Kingdom.
>
> 40% of the Gross Receipts of the Picture derived by Distributor from all sources other than those referred to above.

(2) *Distribution expenses.* Deductible expenses include costs and expenses related to the promotion and exploitation of the motion picture. These are the so-called P&A (prints and advertising) costs. Such expenses may include any of the following:

> The cost and expense of creating "prints" and other necessary materials related to the release of the Picture.

The costs and charges for "advertising," including costs of publicizing and exploiting the Picture.

The costs of preparing and delivering the Picture for distribution.

Sales and other taxes applicable to the prints and other materials related to the release of the Picture. This does not relate to income taxes.

Expenses relating to the transmission of money from foreign countries to the Distributor in the United States.

All costs and expenses related to protecting the copyright and other rights in the Picture (filing copyright registrations, and so forth).

Amounts payable to the Academy of Motion Picture Arts and Sciences and other trade associations or industry groups.

Amounts expended by Distributor in defending and settling claims.

All "residuals" paid to actors, writers, composers, directors and others, pursuant to applicable collective bargaining agreements, together with all taxes, pension fund contributions and other costs paid or payable in respect of such residuals, and in respect of percentage participations in the Picture.

The cost of all insurance (to the extent that the same is not included in the cost of production of the Picture) covering the Picture, including but not limited to, errors and omissions insurance.

If Producer incurs any costs or expenses in connection with the Picture (including, but not limited to, any residuals and any taxes, pension fund contributions and other costs paid or payable in respect of such residuals) which would be treated as deductible distribution expenses hereunder if incurred by Distributor, then for all purposes hereof, such costs or expenses shall be treated as if they were incurred by Distributor.

Distributor's deductible distribution expenses in connection with the Picture shall include all costs and expenses incurred in connection with the distribution, advertising, and exploitation of the Picture of whatever kind or nature, or which are customarily treated as distribution expenses under customary accounting procedures in the motion picture industry.

(3) *The cost of the picture.* Then the cost of the picture will be deducted. The "cost of production" of the picture means the total direct cost of production of the picture, including the cost of all items listed on the distributor's standard delivery schedule, plus (unless

you have enormous negotiation leverage) the distributor's overhead charge. The distributor's overhead charge is stated as a percentage (such as 15 percent) of the direct cost of production of the picture, with the understanding that any production facilities, equipment, or personnel supplied by distributor (that are not furnished within the overhead charge) are supplied at the distributor's usual rental rates charged for such items, and such charges shall be treated as direct costs of production of the picture and bear a percentage overhead charge. The distributor's overhead charge is then included in the cost of the picture for the purpose of this calculation. The interest amount is normally calculated at a rate per annum equal to a percentage of the prime rate applicable to un-secured loans charged by certain large banks (for example, Bank of America) from time to time in effect. This amount is usually calculated from the respective dates that each item is charged to the picture until the close of the accounting period during which the cost of production is recouped, except that interest on deferred amounts is calculated from the date of payment.

> The cost of production of the Picture, plus an amount equal to interest thereon, all as provided for herein, and plus such other costs, if any, as may have been incurred in connection with the financing of the cost of production of the Picture. Said interest and other costs shall be recouped before said cost of production.

(4) Contingent participations. Finally, you deduct all contingent participations, including to any gross participants. This does not include moneys paid out of the costs of production of the picture (as such moneys are not contingent) or other participations in the net proceeds. Why deduct gross participations? If you didn't deduct such payments, the net pool would allow net participants to share in gross moneys. Why exclude participations in net? If you deducted these amounts from the net pool, the net pool, of course, would be reduced to zero.

> All contingent amounts consented to by Distributor and not included in the cost of production of the Picture payable to Participant or any third party based upon, or computed in respect of, the Gross Receipts of the Picture (as defined in the relevant agreements) or any portion thereof (excluding, however, other participations in the Net Proceeds of the Picture).

Miscellaneous matters related to net.

And, believe it or not, that's it: gross receipts less all of (1) distribution fees, (2) distribution expenses, (3) the cost of the picture, and (4) all contingent participants (except for net participants).

Once this calculation is made, your percentage is applied to the amount of money described by this definition and a check is written to you. Of course, the actual net proceeds definition drones on for several more pages covering various detailed matters, such as earning statements (the form of the statement you will receive with your check), clarification that a participation in the net proceeds does not give you any ownership rights or any input in the control of the distribution or exploitation of the picture, certain important definitions (such as film rentals), the allocation of your share to one of the applicable revenue streams (this is a tax issue to the distributor), and your right to audit the distributor's books.

Looking at the definition from the other side.

When you are the recipient of a piece of the net, the overhead component and other stingy features of the definition can be daunting. But when you are the producer contracting with participants who will take from your share of what's left over, these issues take on a new perspective. You may have to fight an actor's agent to keep in the overhead, for example.

ADVANCED GUILD ISSUES: JOINING SAG AND DGA

Okay, it's time to get serious about guilds. You already know from our discussion above, that hiring a guild member to direct or act in your movie will increase the budget of the movie and lead to other issues. But let's assume that you've already made a decision to use guild actors and a guild director. We'll look closer at how you go about taking the steps to qualify.

The significance of hiring guild members.

Professional film directors and actors (with a few exceptions) will want to become members of the DGA and SAG, respectively. In order to do so, they must sign an agreement which, among other things, requires that members will not direct or act in a nonunion movie. If guild members work on a nonunion movie (referred to as "working off card"), they can be subject to fines and disenrollment—sometimes for life. Serious film actors (and their agents) will not take a chance on being expelled from the guild.

Union pictures.

A "union" movie is a movie made by a production company that is a signatory to the applicable collective bargaining agreement of the relevant union. The guilds negotiate these agreements periodically on behalf of their constituents. The signatory producers also negotiate either by designating a representative or directly participating. Many smaller producers, of course, leave this negotiation to the more powerful producers. Once the agreement is signed, it is take it or leave it to any new producer/production company that wants to sign on. In addition to the myriad terms and conditions governing minimum wage and the logistics of employment, producers are contractually bound to use only guild members (or seek a Taft-Hartley or other exception from the guild rules). For this reason, producers do not become signatories in their individual capacities; rather, the producer's production company becomes a signatory.[5]

Different types of agreements.

DGA and SAG each have a basic agreement that covers the standard terms and conditions under which a signatory in normal circumstances can hire a member. In addition, there are other agreements for various types of special projects. Note the following general examples:

Basic agreement. This is the agreement that governs mainstream motion pictures for theatrical distribution. It states the scope of the guild's jurisdiction, basic terms and conditions of employment (including travel, accommodations, hours, breaks, overtime), minimum wage requirements, and payment of residuals.

Industrial contract. This contract covers educational and training films for businesses and political and religious organizations. The distribution pattern for films produced under this contract is narrow and limited to noncommercial settings. These contracts have lower minimum rates and modified provisions related to residuals and so forth.

Television commercials. This is a contract dealing with the production of commercials. It has separate rules related to the treatment of actors by producers and a separate minimum wage schedule and residual payment scheme.

Low-budget films. SAG, for example, has a number of specialized agreements fitted to the needs of independent film producers who wish (or have) to make films with very modest budgets. The following is a list of agreements in this category: Low-Budget Agreement, Affirmative-Action Low-Budget Agreement, Modified Low-Budget Agreement, Limited Exhibition Letter, Experimental Film Agreement, and Student Film Letter.

Becoming a signatory.

Once you have decided to hire a DGA director or SAG actor and have determined which of the agreements you wish to qualify under, you will need to take the appropriate steps to sign on. Here are the basic steps:

Contact the guild. Contact the guild as early in the process as possible—once you have decided to hire a guild member. It will take time to complete the process and, although the guilds are generally very cooperative and helpful, it is not a good idea to try and accomplish all these steps at the last minute. You will need the guild's approval prior to the commencement of principal photography.

Have an attorney handy. My advice is to have an experienced attorney at the ready to answer questions and assist in accomplishing the necessary tasks. I have found, over the years, however, that it is not always cost effective to have the attorney take over the process entirely. The application and follow-up with the guild can be effectively done by you or a production assistant, with the help of an attorney.

Guild-required submissions. You will be required to make certain submissions to the guilds:
Screenplay. You will be asked to submit a copy of the most recent draft of the screenplay. This gives SAG, for example, a record of the number of roles and the nature (major or minor) of each role.
Chain of title and title search. You will be asked to submit information about the chain of title with respect to the screenplay: Who wrote the screenplay? Was it original or based on an underlying work? If the latter, how were the rights obtained to the underlying work?
You will also be asked to submit a title search, which can be obtained by services, such as Thomson & Thomson. This company specializes in

performing searches of intellectual property in the various public registries, such as the USCO. When Thomson & Thomson searches the title, they will search the title of your project and turn up all works with a similar name description. This report can be submitted to SAG.

Copyright registration. You will be asked to submit proof that the screenplay has been registered with the USCO by submitting a copy of the stamped copyright application. Note that the registration form must also stand as evidence that the production company itself owns or has the right to produce the motion picture. Therefore, if you use a separate company (corporation or limited liability company or limited partnership) to produce the movie, you will have to either transfer ownership or license the rights to that company in some official way in order to show the guild that everything is legally on the up and up. For example, if you wrote the screenplay yourself and registered it under your own name, but now intend to have your production company produce the movie, you may wish to transfer ownership of the screenplay from you to your production company. Organizations, such as Federal Research Corporation in Washington, D.C., will assist you in making the necessary filings on an expedited basis to accomplish this transfer. This organization is used to working with the guilds.

Organization document. You will need to submit the organizational documentation for the company becoming a signatory. For a corporation, this would be the articles of incorporation. For a limited liability company, this would be the articles of organization. For a limited partnership, this would be the registered copy of the limited partnership agreement. Most often, the guilds will accept only copies certified as duly filed by the secretary of state of the state in which the company is organized.

Taxpayer Identification Number. You will need to obtain a federal Taxpayer Identification Number from the IRS for your production company. This can take some time, so apply or have your attorney apply for this number as part of the incorporation (or other establishment) process.

Financing. You will need to submit information about how the movie is being financed.

Cast list. You will need to submit the name of the director (in the case of the DGA) or a list of the cast members (in the case of SAG) you intend to employ. This will give the DGA or SAG a chance to confirm that the director or cast, as the case may be, are members in good standing of the guild. (Nonguild members may be hired in certain situations.)

Bond deposit. SAG requires that you post a bond. For example, currently SAG requires that the producer deposit an amount of money equal to 40 percent of the estimated total cast payroll with SAG.[6] (Thus, you will have to submit the amount you intend to pay each cast member.) SAG purchases a certificate of deposit (CD) or other interest-bearing financial instrument with this money in favor of the production company. The CD is held by SAG until the final cast list is submitted immediately after the completion of principal photography. (Note that SAG will attach a fine if the cast list is late, so get it in on time.) Once the list is in, SAG will release the funds, plus interest, back to the production company. You can use it to get the postproduction tasks completed.

Security interest. As noted above, SAG will also insist that it receive a first-priority security interest in the movie to secure the payment of residuals. This is accomplished by filing two documents: First, the production company must fill out, sign, and submit a UCC-1 form to SAG, which SAG in turns files with the state and, in some cases, the county. Second, because a security interest is being taken in a copyrighted work (intellectual property) and because copyrights are registered under a federal statutory scheme, you will also be required to fill out, sign, and submit to SAG those documents necessary to record the security interest with the USCO. (Keep in mind that because SAG requires a first-priority security interest, you will not be able to grant your financier or any bank a first-priority security interest in the picture.)

Deposits to the health and welfare and pension arms of the guild. For both SAG and DGA, prior to the start of principal photography, you will be required to make a payment to both the health and welfare fund and the pension fund in the name of and on behalf of the SAG and DGA members involved in your production. For SAG you will pay (as of this writing) 13.8 percent of the total actors' budget to the health and welfare and pension funds. For the DGA, the total health and welfare and pension payment (as of this writing) is 12.75 percent of the aggregate fees to the director and other DGA members on the movie. Note, in the case of SAG, that you must make these payments for each cast member, whether or not the cast member is a member of the guild. Remember the discussion above about hiring non-SAG members on a SAG picture under the so-called Taft-Hartley rules.[7] You must pay these fringe payments even in the case of such a cast member. (Unless the cast member actually joins SAG, however, he will not be able to receive this money).

Procuring Everything Else

CREW AGREEMENTS

Hiring a cast is important, but you will need more help to get the movie made. Someone has to operate the cameras, the sound equipment, and the lighting equipment. You will need art designers, set designers, wardrobe specialists, electricians, carpenters, and many others to make the movie happen.

Some of these people have their own equipment and are paid extra for its use. A typical crew agreement follows:

Preamble.

The preamble identifies the parties and gives the producer the necessary information to process payroll, including required tax forms. The information about citizenship and residence is necessary in order to determine whether a visa will be required for this actor.

Services.

The services section is usually generic, simply obligating the employee or contractor to perform his job in a "conscientious manner" and clarifying whether the engagement is on an exclusive basis, the starting date, and other parameters of the engagement.

Producer hereby engages Employee to provide such preproduction, production and/or post-production services as are customarily

---

CREW AGREEMENT

DATE: As of February 1, 2006

PRODUCER: The Quest Production LLC
               1234 Sunset Boulevard
               Hollywood, CA 90000
               Facsimile: (818) 555-1234

EMPLOYEE: Lawrence Camer Lenz
               S.S.N. 123-45-6789
               9999 Any Street, Apt. 00
               Los Angeles, CA 90000
               Citizen of: U.S.A.

PICTURE: Feature-length theatrical motion picture tentatively en-
               titled *The Quest*

ROLE: Cameraman

---

performed by artists in the position specified above and such other services as may be requested by Producer in connection with the motion picture tentatively entitled "The Quest" (the "Picture"). Employee's services shall be rendered on an exclusive basis and shall commence on April 6, 2006 (the "Start Date") and continue until such date as required by Producer. Nothing contained herein shall be construed as a guarantee of employment beyond the time actually worked. Employee's services hereunder shall be rendered in a diligent and conscientious manner under the direction, supervision and control of, and/or in collaboration with, such person(s) as Producer shall designate, and Employee will promptly comply with all instructions, directions and requests made by Producer, including those involving artistic taste and judgment.

Compensation.

This section clarifies the compensation of the employee, required hours, overtime, travel, and other parameters related to payment. Producer reserves the right to withhold taxes.

Provided that Employee is not in default hereunder, in consideration for the full performance of Employee's services and for all rights granted or to be granted hereunder, Employee shall be paid a weekly rate of $6,000 per week (based on a 6-day week for weekly artists), prorated for any partial week, or $1,000 per day (for daily artists), prorated for any partial day, based on an 8-hour day. If Producer requires Employee's services in excess of eight hours on any regular work day or on a Sunday or a holiday, Employee shall be paid overtime premiums for any overtime worked as prescribed by law, based on an hourly rate calculated by dividing the weekly or daily rate by the total number of hours worked per week or per day, as applicable. No compensation shall be payable to Employee for travel time in connection with Employee's services hereunder. Employee agrees that as employer, Producer may deduct and withhold from all compensation payable to Employee hereunder all amounts required to be deducted or withheld pursuant to applicable law. Employee hereby acknowledges and agrees that no other compensation of whatever nature shall be due and owing from Producer hereunder.

Term.
This provision clarifies the "at will" nature of the employment, meaning that the producer can terminate the employee at any time. It is not unusual to give the employee a period of guaranteed employment.

Employee shall render services for a minimum guaranteed period of ten (10) days and thereafter until the completion of all of Employee's required services hereunder. There is no other guarantee of the length of services. At the end of each day, Employee may be terminated at will by Producer upon oral notice to Employee.

Equipment.
It is not unusual in crew agreements to allow the crew member to use his or her own equipment and for the producer to pay a rental charge for such equipment. Note that a purchase order mechanism is used to avoid any question as to whether the equipment rental is part of the deal. Moreover, the crew member must get approval from the producer prior to renting any third-party equipment. A "recoverable item" is an item purchased by the crew member for the producer. At the end of principal photography (or at the "wrap"), the producer takes possession of any recoverable item.

Any and all equipment supplied by Employee for use in connection with the Picture will be rented from Employee by Producer for the amount of $1,000 per week. Rentals will not be paid unless a purchase order for each item of equipment is approved by Producer prior to the start of the rental period. Any loss, theft or damage to Employee's equipment is the sole responsibility of Employee. Employee shall obtain the prior approval of Producer for any and all equipment purchased or rented by Employee on behalf of Producer. Any equipment purchased or rented by Employee without the prior approval of Producer will be the sole responsibility of Employee. Employee shall be solely responsible for any equipment purchased by Employee that is a recoverable item. All recoverable items will be collected by Producer at "wrap."

Chain of title.

Yes, you must worry about chain of title issues even with respect to crew members. The results and proceeds of the crew member's services may, and likely will, appear in the movie. The set designer's designs could very well be copyrightable, for example. Again, the convention is to use both the belt (the work-made-for-hire doctrine) and the suspenders (assignment of rights) to make sure that the producer has complete chain of title.

All materials furnished by Employee and all of the results and proceeds of Employee's services hereunder (collectively, the "Materials") shall be regarded as "works made for hire" specially ordered or commissioned by Producer for use as part of a motion picture or other audiovisual work. Without limiting the foregoing, Producer shall own, and Employee hereby grants and assigns to Producer, forever and throughout the universe, all of Employee's right, title and interest in and to the Materials, and each and every part thereof, including all copyrights therein, all renewals and extensions of such copyrights and all other proprietary and exploitation rights of any kind, nature or description that may be secured under the laws now or hereafter in effect in the United States of America or any other jurisdiction, with the right to make such changes therein and such uses and dispositions thereof, in whole or in part, as Producer may from time to time determine.

Immigration-related matters.

Further assurances clauses are designed to contractually commit one or both parties to cooperate in the future in connection with the delivery and execution of documentation and with the taking of any action that may be necessary to carry out the intent of the agreement. In this case, the further assurances clause specifically anticipates the possibility that the crew member may be subject to the requirement to deliver a Form I-9 (an Employment Eligibility Verification form under the United States immigration laws). If the crew member is not a U.S. citizen, under this clause, moreover, he or she, at such crew member's own expense, must procure and deliver to the producer all required visa and/or other documents required by the immigration laws. Going one step further, if the crew member fails to deliver any such documentation, the producer can act as the crew member's attorney-in-fact to sign and deliver them.

> Employee agrees to execute, acknowledge and deliver such further documents as Producer may deem necessary or advisable to further evidence or effectuate any or all of Producer's rights as set forth herein, including, without limitation, the completion, execution, certification and delivery to Producer of an Employment Eligibility Verification (Form 1-9), together with supporting documentation, in compliance with the Immigration Reform and Control Act of 1986. If Employee is not a citizen of the United States, then Employee acknowledges and agrees that all of Producer's obligations under this Agreement are conditioned upon and subject to Employee obtaining and delivering to Producer any and all necessary visa forms and/or other documents required by U.S. immigration laws or regulations for Employee employment in the United States. Employee understands and agrees that Employee shall be responsible for obtaining any such documentation and that all costs associated therewith shall be borne by Employee at Employee's sole expense. Employee hereby irrevocably appoints Producer as his or her true and lawful attorney-in-fact (such appointment being a power coupled with an interest), with full power of substitution and delegation, with the right (but not the obligation) to execute, acknowledge and deliver on his or her behalf any such documents which he or she fails to execute, acknowledge and deliver within five (5) days after Producer's request therefor.

LOCATION AGREEMENTS AND PERMITS

Movies can be shot at a variety of locations. Wherever they are shot, however, as the producer, you must make sure that you have the right to shoot. When you arrange to go to a sound stage in Los Angeles, for example, you will sign a contract for the use of the sound stage. This contract will cover the schedule (a big issue in times of rampant production), the charges involved, liability for damage to property and injury to personnel, and so forth. The producer can more or less take it for granted that the studio has the right to make movies on that property. However, movies can be, and often are, made on location (meaning out in the real world). If the screenplay calls for an exterior shot of a residential area in an American suburban town, one option is to take a crew to such a town and shoot away. But in that case, what you can take for granted at the sound stage, you will have to worry about. Is filming allowed in this county? Town? In the majority of places, you will need a permit from the city and permission from the property owner in order to film.

With respect to permits by the city or other governmental entity, you can either visit city hall yourself or hire a "permit service"—companies formed to provide this service to producers.

With respect to independently owned property within the city or other government entity, you or your location manager will have to contact each individual landowner and enter into an agreement that provides for the use of the property for the movie. This is called a "location agreement."

Premises.

The agreement will need a definite description of the location to be used. Note that in this case, the agreement is applicable to the grounds, buildings, and other structures. Also note that the agreement covers the right to enter (access) and leave (egress) and parking. All of these issues are critical to the use of the property in question.

> The "Premises" referred to herein and condition of its use are as follows: The Premises are located at 1234 Castle Tower Peak, Suburbia, CA 90000 and include the grounds at said address and all buildings and other structures located thereon, together with access to and egress from said Premises and [specify parking arrangements here, if applicable].

Enter and remain.

The agreement must recite the rights being granted to the producer. Note that the granting clause describes the right to enter and remain and the specific purposes.

> You hereby grant to us the exclusive right to enter into and remain on your property with personnel and equipment for the purpose

of photographing scenes for the Picture on June 25 through July 1, 2006 (subject to change on account of weather conditions or changes in production schedule) and continuing until completion of all scenes and work required (the "License Term").

Persons and equipment.

As you undoubtedly know, movies are not just about people. There will be a lot of equipment as well. The location agreement must cover both.

Time period.

The agreement covers the time period during which you will be entering and using the property. Notice that this agreement allows for some flexibility in the event of weather changes and the like.

Compensation.

The property owner is usually paid for the use of the property. The amount and the timing of the payment are recited. Moreover, if the term of the agreement is extended, because of weather conditions, etc., additional compensation is paid. The producer will also try to negotiate free days for days used only for contracting, "holding" (keeping intact), or "striking" (taking down) the set. This is not always an easy negotiation, because the owner of the property will likely see no constructive difference between these activities and the activities for which he is being paid. Rather, to the property owner, the real issue is the number of days the property will be needed for production (especially if that materially affects the owner's use).

If we use the Premises as herein provided, we shall pay to you the sum of $3,000 per shooting day; no charge shall be made by you for days used only for construction, holding or striking. All charges shall be paid promptly after completion of all work contemplated, unless specified herein to the contrary. In the event we desire to use the Premises for retakes and/or added scenes, the License Term shall be automatically extended (on a nonconsecutive basis) to include the period required for such retakes and/or added scenes, and we shall pay you the daily rate set forth above.

Additional days.

If the property is unique, it is important that the producer reserves the right to reenter the property in case additional shots are needed.

Note that in this case, the price goes up. This may be logical, as the owner will grow tired at some point of the interference. Money seems to ease this type of pain.

> If following the License Term we require use of the Premises for additional use in connection with the Picture, you shall permit us to reenter upon and again utilize the Premises for such purpose. The dates for such additional use shall be subject to your approval, which approval you shall not unreasonably withhold. If we utilize the Premises for additional filming, we shall pay to you the sum of $3,500 per day therefor. We may at any time prior to twelve (12) hours before commencement of the term specified in Paragraph 2 hereof elect not to use the Premises by giving you written notice of such election, in which case neither party shall have any further obligation. If, within twelve (12) hours of commencement of the term specified in Paragraph 2 hereof, we elect not to use the Premises, we agree to pay you $3,000.

Cleanup and equipment removal.
The producer has the obligation of promptly (defined herein as no longer than three days) after the work is complete or the license term runs out to remove the equipment and other materials placed on the property by the producer.

> Promptly following the expiration of the License Term and, if applicable, promptly upon the completion of any additional use by us of the Premises, but not later than three business days after such expiration of the License Term and completion of additional use, respectively, we shall remove from the Premises all structures, equipment and other materials placed thereon by us.

Rights.
Another link in the chain of title involves the property. So, the producer makes sure that the property owner agrees to the uses the producer intends to make of the property: motion pictures, still photographs, sound recordings, and edited and changed versions of these. The producer will also want to make sure that he or she has the authority to exercise these rights respecting the exterior and interior of the buildings and other facilities and any animals and other property on the premises. The producer will include signs and other writing (but be careful of product names, because whether the owner thinks

so or not the landowner is not likely to have the right to grant you permission to photograph and use in a movie a product's logo or name—this right belongs to the product's manufacturer).

> We shall have the right to take motion pictures, still photographs and sound recordings on or of the Premises and we may edit and change the film, photographs or recordings in any manner as we see fit. We shall have the right to photograph and depict the Premises and to take exterior and interior shots of any buildings or other improvements located on said Premises and photograph any animals, automobiles, or any other objects on the Premises as we may choose, either using the actual name, sign and other identifying pictures, or without regard to the appearance or name of the Premises. We shall have the irrevocable right to make any and all uses of such film, photographs and/or recordings, or any portions thereof, anywhere at any time as we may deem fit, including but not limited to, by way of theatrical exhibition, television broadcasting, and any other method of exploitation, whether now known or hereafter devised, together with the right to display and use, and to authorize others to display and use, such film, photographs or recordings for advertising, publicizing, promotion, or otherwise exploiting the Picture, or any of our rights hereunder.

Equipment and construction.

The producer again wants to clarify that he can bring all kinds of equipment onto the property. The owner acknowledges that the producer has explained the intended uses. Also, the producer clarifies that he has the right to set up a replica of the property (inside or outside) on some sound stage.

> We may bring such personnel and equipment as we may determine necessary onto the Premises for the purpose of exercising our rights hereunder. You acknowledge that we have described generally to you any unusual or unlikely manner in which the Premises, the name of the Premises, and/or your name is intended to be used in the Picture. We may also construct on our stage a replica of the interior or exterior of the Premises as we may determine and we shall not be required to depict the Premises in any particular manner.

No obligation.

Here again is the old standard warning that the producer reserves the right not to make the movie or, more important, not to use the property in the movie, and, therefore, the property owner should prepare himself not to be disappointed when his property isn't in the movie.

> Nothing herein shall obligate us to take motion pictures, still photographs or sound recordings, or to use said pictures, photographs or recordings, or to otherwise use the Premises, but we reserve the right to complete any photography or recording commenced on the Premises.

No interest.

The producer clarifies that the owner of the property, come what may, will not get any interest in the movie itself or the film, photographs, sound recordings, or anything else. The only thing that the producer promises is to remove the equipment when the shoot is finished.

> You hereby acknowledge that you have no interest of any kind or nature whatsoever in such motion pictures, still photographs or sound recordings, made or taken by us on or off the Premises, and you agree that we shall have all rights therein. All sets, props, equipment and other paraphernalia brought upon the Premises by us shall be and remain our property and none of said sets, props, equipment or paraphernalia shall become fixtures by reason of their installation on the Premises; we agree to remove all sets, equipment and other paraphernalia and debris brought upon the Premises by us upon the completion of such use.

Due care.

The producer promises to use due care. First-year law students know that this is a standard for a normal tort claim, so the producer is giving away nothing and by inserting this provision the producer avoids a claim that the standard of care is any higher.

> We agree to use reasonable care to prevent damage to the Premises and we shall indemnify you for any legal liability arising out of bodily injury or property damage (ordinary wear and tear excepted) as a direct result of our negligence on the Premises to the extent such li-

ability or loss is not otherwise covered by any insurance policy, and subject to written notice from you specifying the precise nature of such bodily injury or property damage within forty-eight (48) hours following the occurrence thereof.

Representations and warranties.

Here again is the lawyer's favorite. This is where the producer and his or her lawyer ask the owner to acknowledge that he or she has the authority to enter into the agreement and grant all the rights and privileges that the producer is asking for. In addition, the producer wants the owner to know that there would be a big problem if these rights were invalid; this is to avoid the argument that the owner had no idea of the extent of the damages the producer might incur.

> You hereby warrant that you have the full right to enter into this agreement, that you are authorized to grant us all of the rights set forth herein and that the consent of no other party is necessary to enable us to use the Premises as herein provided. Any or all of the rights herein may be exercised by us, our successors, licensees and assigns. You realize that in taking any motion pictures, still photographs and sound recordings of or on the Premises, which is at substantial cost to us, we are relying upon the rights granted to us hereunder.

Restrictions on remedies.

Lawyers representing producers do not like the possibility that anyone could file an injunction to stop the movie. Therefore, they try to restrict the owner's remedies to actions for money (or, in the parlance of lawyers, actions "in law"—as opposed to actions "in equity," where the owner could ask for an injunction).

> Your rights and remedies in the event of any breach by us of this agreement shall be limited to your right to recover damages, if any, in an action at law, and you hereby waive any right or remedy in equity, including without limitation any right to terminate or rescind this agreement, or any right granted to us hereunder, or to enjoin or restrain or otherwise impair in any manner the production, distribution, exhibition or other exploitation of the Picture or any parts or elements thereof or the use, publication or dissemination of any advertising in connection therewith.

PRODUCT PLACEMENTS

Cash payments for product placements.

Product placements are used to cut down on the outlay of cash toward the budget of the movie. For example, BMW reportedly paid a significant amount of money to have the modern-day James Bond drive a BMW (rather than the British-made Aston Martin prominently driven by the early permutations of James Bond) in several 007 offerings. The idea, of course, is to promote the sale of products by associating them with the movie, the movie hero, or simply by exposing the product to the audience in a positive or interesting way. The product line isn't limited to cars. It can be anything. (Think of Tom Hanks and Meg Ryan sending instant messages back and forth to each other via AOL in *You've Got Mail*—come to think of it, even the title of the movie could very well have been part of a commercial tie-in.)

Value in kind.

Sometimes, the consideration for a product placement is not cash, but so-called "value in kind" or "VIK." For example, Toyota Motors might, as opposed to paying cash for the product placement in the movie, offer a number of Toyota vehicles to the producer for use during the production of the movie. Producers always have need for vehicles to transport people and things from one location to another and having the free use of VIK trucks and automobiles saves money from the budget and goes directly to the bottom line. The same can be said for computers and a host of other things that might be useful to the producer during the production stage.

Movie comes first.

Many producers and their directors take (and should take) the view that product placements take a backseat to the continuity of the story and other things more to the point of the movie. I know of situations where the company paying for the placement became very aggressive in trying to dictate to the producers and directors exactly when and how often the product placement shots were to appear. Producers normally do (and again should) resist this strenuously as the appearance that the movie is a gigantic ad for a single product could seriously jeopardize the artistic quality and integrity of the project. Product placement agreements generally provide that the producer will have the sole right, perhaps in consultation with the product manufacturer or ad agency, to make creative decisions about the product placement. Moreover, I know of several situations where the product placements shots wound up on the editing room floor and were never integrated into the movie. In these instances, of course, the producer returns to the manufacturer the money paid for the product placement. Of course, the producer's lawyer must negotiate for the right to do this and a provision to this effect has to be placed in the contract.

Filming
the Movie

THE POINT OF NO RETURN?

"Lights, camera, action!" The day finally arrives and the director begins the process of shooting the scenes. As we have noted above directors rarely shoot the scenes in continuity (in the order they appear in the screenplay). Rather, the director and the line producer shoot the scenes in an efficient order. For example, they will shoot all the scenes that take place in a certain location, regardless of where they appear chronologically, during the same time period. Likewise, they will shoot all the scenes involving the same cast members at the same time, so as to avoid having people sit around collecting a paycheck while doing nothing.

Once principal photography starts, it becomes a freight train not to be derailed; once the cast and crew and equipment are gathered, it becomes extremely important not to stop. Bad weather, illness, equipment failures, disputes, and any other deviation from the "shooting script" (the version of the screenplay actually used in photographing the movie) will cost money. The more days, the more money.

While it is quite rare that things get so out of hand that the production stops once principal production starts, it does happen. I have heard of an expensive American movie project being shot in Japan being called off by the studio, because the director realized that a significant error had been made in the shooting budget. Stories abound about movies derailed by the illness of a main cast member or star. The point is to plan well and be well insured. Also, have backup plans.

GUILD RULES APPLIED

I'd like to say a few things about the impact of the guilds on the photography process. Because time is money to any producer, if producers could rule the world without any consequences, casts and crews would be forced to work around the clock in order to get the movie done in the minimum amount of time possible. But producers don't rule the world—on the other side of the equation are the collective bargaining units (or guilds). SAG, for example, has established limits on the number of hours that professional actors are allowed to work and describes the terms of overtime work. The SAG agreement also requires certain breaks for rest and for meals. SAG even sets parameters respecting actors' appearance on camera in the buff. DGA, AFTRA, and IATSE also limit in specific ways the abuse their members are allowed to take at the hands of producers. Your unit production manager should have a thorough knowledge of these limits; they should ensure your production company's compliance with the guilds' rules and operating procedures.

THINGS THAT HAPPEN DURING PRINCIPAL PHOTOGRAPHY

Ongoing script clearances.

We talked about the importance of clearing the screenplay of problems with copyright infringement, defamation, and trademark infringement. But this is often not good enough. Actors occasionally ad lib their lines, adding copyrighted (but uncleared) material. I am familiar with an actor who recited a poem on camera during a shoot; the poem wasn't in the script, but it fit perfectly with the actor's character and was in fact a wonderful addition to the actor's dialogue. The only problem was that the actor wasn't making it up—he was reciting it from his childhood memory and couldn't remember its provenance. It took the producers of the movie many months to run the origins of the poem down and to determine, finally, that the poem dated back to the 1800s (alas, and lucky for them, the poem was in the public domain).

Producers hire a person—a script supervisor—to track all the changes that happen along the way. The updated screenplay needs to be checked for problems like the one described above.

Ongoing releases (people, places, things).
In the normal course of a shoot, there is an ongoing need to clear people (such as extras), places (such as locations), and things (such as trademarks), where contractual rights haven't been cleared. A clearance form must be obtained for each such situation. For example, extras must sign a release. Location agreements must be obtained for each location. And a release must be obtained for each trademark focused on by the camera. Therefore, the producer and unit production managers should keep standard forms to be signed and should be trained to identify the situations that require the forms. A sample list of possible situations follows (note, this is not a test—all the situations below require a release):

Fifty extras are needed for the scene in the Wolf's Lair Inn on Day 3 of the shoot.

A new cameraman is called in to replace Joe, who called in sick.

Ken Kantoku, the director, decides to shoot a "pickup" scene on the lot behind the house that has been rented for Day 7 of the shoot. The lot is owned by Larry Landowner, who hadn't been contacted before the shot.

The prop master decides to put bottles of Shanassee Ale, a popular drink in northern Wales, on the tables of the Wolf's Lair Inn for the shoot.

The set designer, in an emergency, calls up a local design company not currently under contract and hires a local designer/artist to make a backdrop for a scene in Wolf's Lair Inn on Day 4 of the shoot.

Finishing All
Production Details

DUBBING

At the end of the movie, the sound track of the movie usually has places that have to be fixed. Perhaps during an action scene the sound recording was muffled by other noises. Perhaps a word or two was dropped. In order to fix these problems, the producer will need either the original cast members' availability at the end of the shoot or the right to overdub the original cast members' voice with another voice. Both of these approaches have to be provided in the appropriate contract, which of course is negotiated before the shooting begins.

EFFECTS

The special visual and sound effects are added after the principal photography. These effects are created by specialists—from individuals working at their individual computers to large and famous institutions, such as Industrial Light & Magic and Imageworks. Whatever your choice, like all other aspects of the movie, it is better to get started early. Often, the special visual effects have to be coordinated with the regular scenes. Think of *Jurassic Park*, for example, where the audience has to believe that the cyber dinosaurs are actually tromping around in the meadow where the cameras were shooting film.

MUSIC

Music is added to the sound track during the postproduction stage. By this time, however, the producer has (or should have) all the documentation in place to prove chain of title related to the music being added. Failure to do this is asking for major trouble. During this stage, producers should make sure that the music supervisor or music producer doesn't add any new music that has not previously been cleared.

FINAL CREDITS

The credits are added to the prints as one of the last steps. And, of course, there are legal rules. The SAG rules[1] dictate that the end credits contain, on at least one card, a list of performers and roles played. All the credits on the card(s) are to be the same size and style of type. The producer, however, has the final say on the arrangement, number, and selection of cast members portrayed.

Some individual credits, as you know by now, are governed by contract. As producer, you must make sure that you or somebody on your team(preferably an attorney) examines the applicable agreements for a list of contractually required credits.

Otherwise, the order of the credits is largely governed by custom (which is not followed invariably). As we have discussed above, the current standard is for certain credits (called the "main credits") to come at the beginning of the movie and for certain credits (called the "end credits," appropriately enough) to come at the end. The best advice I can give you is to rent a couple of recent movies and take note of the order and other characteristics of the credits.

The Legal Details

WHAT'S IN A NAME? MPAA TITLE REGISTRATION

Titles not protected.

It is well established in the United States that movie titles are not protected by copyright law. It is possible, under certain circumstances (if the title has acquired "secondary meaning"—i.e., the title is sufficiently well known—*Star Wars*, for example—so that the movie becomes identified as originating from a unique source), that you might be able to register the title of a movie as a trademark, but that process can be expensive and is not always appropriate.

Background.

From 1922, the Hays Office (the shorthand name of the Motion Picture Producers and Distributors of America, which was made up of mainly the major studios of the time) maintained the Title Registration Bureau, which allowed members to reserve titles for movies that they might make. The basis of the protection was contract law—a binding agreement among members. Independent producers (yes, they existed even way back then) found themselves at a disadvantage because the studios hoarded titles. The most famous of these early cases occurred in 1938 when Charlie Chaplin tried to name his newly finished movie *The Dictator* only to discover that Paramount had already reserved the name. Paramount was agreeable to sell the title to Chaplin for a mere $25,000 (a sizable sum in those days), but Chaplin opted to rename his movie *The Great Dictator*.

Registration process.

The title registration system, as it has evolved today, is governed by the Motion Picture Association of America (MPAA), a trade association whose members include all the major studios. Below can be found some basic information about how title registration works under the MPAA's rules. Note, however, that the following discussion is not intended to cover all the exceptions and detailed information contained in the rules, which can be obtained from the MPAA.[1]

The MPAA's Title Registration Bureau administers the program and promulgates its rules, which are binding on all MPAA members and each of their subsidiaries (thereby eliminating one of the major loopholes present in the old system, where members circumvented the rules by creating nonmember subsidiary companies, which could act outside the system) and nonmembers (or independent producers who sign up voluntarily). An annual fee is required for each subscriber.

When a subscriber registers a title, the subscriber indicates whether the title is for a theatrical feature (a feature of more than thirty minutes) or theatrical short feature and whether the title is (1) a copyrighted work title (a movie title that is the same as a copyrighted and published work on which the movie is based—for example, *Gone with the Wind* is a movie title taken from the copyrighted and published book, *Gone with the Wind* by Margaret Mitchell); (2) an "original work title" (titles that are the original brainchild of the subscriber—and not a copyrighted work title or public domain title); or (3) a "public domain title" (a title taken from an underlying public domain work—such as *Romeo and Juliet*, which, of course, is based on Shakespeare's play *Romeo and Juliet*).

When a title is registered, depending on whether or not the movie has been distributed or released, it is placed on the Unreleased Film Index or Released Film Index.

Protection on the Released Film Index.

Titles on the Released Film Index (of priority titles of movies that have been released into the public) are protected titles. The protection lasts permanently (with some technical exceptions). The owners of released titles have authority under the system to either prevent or allow others to use an identical or similar title.

General rules for establishing priority on the Unreleased Film Index.

To win priority for a title, so to speak, a subscriber must establish and keep priority for the title on the Unreleased Film Index until the film is released. The MPAA currently employs a complicated set of rules to establish priority in the event of identical or similar titles. Generally speaking, a "copyrighted work title" receives priority status on the Unreleased Film Index. If a subscriber tries to register a subsequent identical original work title, the registration is denied. Where there is no copyrighted work title (and there is no identical or similar title on the Released Film Index), the original work title that is first in time receives priority over subsequent original work titles and public domain titles for a period of time (currently one year). An original work title that is identical to a previously registered original work title receives a "reserve position."

If there is no reserve position title, a registered original work title will be automatically renewed for additional one-year terms. If there is a title in reserve, the title in priority position will nevertheless be renewed for six months if the priority subscriber has a bona fide intention to produce or release a movie with the title and either (1) all the reserve title subscribers consent to the renewal; (2) the priority subscriber notifies the MPAA that principal photography is scheduled to commence within one year; (3) principal photography has begun; or (4) principal photography is finished and a released date for the movie has been set.

Reserved position titles are listed in the priority received by the MPAA and move up in priority as prior positions are vacated.

Special rules for public domain titles.

Public domain titles work in basically the same way as original work titles, except that the MPAA imposes certain additional qualifications for acceptance. Public domain titles must not be identical to either (1) a "protected title" on the Released Film Index that was commercially released prior to the effective date of the MPAA rules (the Rules) where the protected title is within the longer of twenty-five years from its original commercial release or within one year after the date of the Rules or (2) a protected title on the Released Film Index that was commercially released after the effective date of the Rules and is within twelve years of its original commercial release.

Challenges and disputes.

As you might expect, participation in the MPAA's system does not eliminate conflict or controversy. What if the titles aren't identical but are simply similar? What if you are ready to go, but a prior registrant won't budge, even though that project is not ready?

The MPAA's title registration system provides for protests and challenges and even arbitration. A prior registrant who has established his or her rights may protest subsequent titles on the basis that a conflict exists. A conflict exists if the newer title is so similar that it will likely confuse the public as to the identity of the origin of the movie; you need both similarity and likelihood of harm.

Once the protest is made, the question may be settled through negotiation or arbitration between the parties. If the parties settle their negotiation, they report the settlement to the MPAA Title Registration Bureau and the protesting party withdraws the protest. If negotiation doesn't work, the parties may pursue arbitration before a panel of the Title Registration Bureau. The parties can challenge any arbitrator on the basis that such arbitrator may be interested in the outcome. When at least three disinterested arbitrators are selected, the arbitration proceeding goes forward. The arbitrators are free to set the rules of the proceeding and are not bound by legal rules of evidence, discovery, or other common features of court proceedings. The arbitrators consider whatever evidence they want and consider the "equities" involved. Majority rule prevails.

Under the Rules, the party who looses may appeal. The appellate procedures are similar to those described above. The appeals board's majority decision is binding.

Outside the system.

I am often asked whether or not it is necessary to join the MPAA. On the one hand, refusal to join ensures that the producer won't be contractually bound by the MPAA's rules. If the producer is outside the system, since titles are not protected by copyright law and, under normal circumstances, trademark law does not apply, the producer can use any title desired. Thus, at least in the development stage, the producer doesn't have to worry about titles. It is also possible to research titles and obtain title insurance. However, since the goal of every producer is to have his or her movie distributed in theaters, and since most distributors (certain all of the major ones) are members of the MPAA, title registration may become an issue down the road. If it is important that your movie have a certain title, therefore, you should at least look into the MPAA system. If you are flexible on the title, then this is an area that you might consider letting the distributor of your movie handle.

TITLE CLEARANCE/TITLE REPORTS

Clearing the title of your movie, whether or not you use the MPAA title registration system, is an important step. You will need to prove that you have the right to use the title you have chosen in order to obtain E&O insurance, for example. Moreover, your distributor will be concerned about whether or not you have this right.

A common way to approach this task is to conduct a title search or obtain a title report from a service, such as Thomson & Thomson. The title is researched in the USCO, the Library of Congress and certain other common law databases to see if there are any matches, the absence of which is good news for you. The exact title, and all logical variations of it, are searched in a variety of categories, such as: Motion Pictures, Television, Radio, Books (fiction and nonfiction), Stories and Articles, Dramatic Works, Screenplays, Record Albums, Musical Compositions, Music Videos, and Additional Uses. Even if there is no exact match, the report will comment on titles with similar phrases or words.

The research should also involve a search of federal and state trademark registrations in entertainment classes for the exact title and closely related similar titles. Newspapers and trade notices are also consulted.

If the search identifies identical or closely related similar titles, you will need to consult an entertainment or trademark attorney to help you analyze the legal feasibility of continuing with your choice of title. This area of law is very complex and a discussion of the issues involved is beyond the scope of this book. As a matter of common sense, of course, the closer the titles you find is to your chosen title, and the closer the use of those titles is to the use of your title, the more problems.

COPYRIGHT REPORT

A copyright report is also a common requirement of E&O insurance carriers and is useful in securing distribution. Copyright research helps identify ownership information and assignment history of a specific work. A full copyright search determines copyright status and ownership of a movie and reveals underlying and derivative works, copyright registration and renewal data, and assignments. The research covers the following sources: USCO records, entertainment trade publications, Library of Congress records, online and CD-ROM entertainment databases, and other applicable databases.

A copyright report might also cover characters, including the first and subsequent appearances of an existing character and may provide the information needed to determine the owner of the rights. The report identifies underlying and derivative works. The sources of this search are the same as for a full search.

Special searches can also be done. A "screening search" looks at registration and renewal and in process data for a particular work. An author search examines registration, renewal, assignment, and in process data for all works in the name of a certain entity or individual. A "registration/renewal search" looks at registration, renewal, and in process data for a certain work. An "assignment search" shows transfers of rights, licenses, liens, and mortgages recorded with the USCO, in the name of a particular work, individual, or company.

The purpose of these various searches is to support your claim of a viable chain of title. If problems are discovered, you will need to consult an attorney to help you analyze the possible fixes.

SCRIPT REVIEW AND CLEARANCE

Once the screenplay is finished—I mean really finished (as in ready to shoot, with due attention paid to the changes made during the shoot), it must be reviewed by a lawyer who understands the legal issues inherent in movie scripts. There are persons who specialize in this type of script review. Established producers and production companies will know them. Here is a general list of what issues to look for in a script:

Defamation.
Look for characters based on real people whose reputation is being trashed in the screenplay. Drama requires heroes and villains, so virtually every script portrays someone as a bad guy. Even the protagonist will have flaws, in today's world of the antihero. Under certain circumstances, the portrayal of moral and other defects in the characters of your movie could lead to a claim for defamation.

Defamation (sometimes referred to as slander or libel) is a claim based on the injury to one's reputation. The law of defamation is complicated and since I'm not running a course in law school here, I will stick to the basics. Generally speaking, the plaintiff can prevail in a defamation case if another person publishes a false statement about the plaintiff that causes actual money damages. Law professors spend hours discussing the fine points of publication, false statement, and damages (for example, whether or not it is necessary to prove such[2]), but we need not go into that detail here. As a producer, you can avoid the most obvious problems by understanding the basics and taking a common sense approach; and, of course, you must have a lawyer examine the script for things that are not so apparent.

Real person. The first issue, as obvious as it may seem, is whether or not the person is a real or fictitious person. Even if a fictitious name is used, if the identity of a real person can be reasonably ascertained by circumstances, there could be a problem. Thus, as you examine the screenplay for this issue, be on the lookout for thin disguises. This is one of the main reasons that lawyers include a standard disclaimer at the end of each fictional movie to the effect that persons and incidents portrayed in the motion picture are made up and any resemblance to actual persons or incidents is merely coincidental.

By the way, under United States law, the heirs of a deceased person can bring an action for defamation. A deceased person is real for these purposes. However, the heirs must satisfy the other elements of the cause of action for defamation.

Publication. Although the subtleties of publication may be a ripe topic for law school exams, I can pretty much assure you that a statement or portrayal that appears in a movie playing in theaters, released on video, and broadcast on television has been published for the purpose of making out a cause of action.

False. The statement or portrayal must be false. The statement may be rude, obnoxious, hurtful, mean, and nasty, but if it is true the target of the statement is out of luck. Truth is an absolute defense against a claim of defamation. Therefore, if your movie trashes the reputation of a real person, but you have undeniable proof that the person is as portrayed, you need not worry.

Standard of care. One of the complexities of defamation law relates to the type of victim. Remember the Paul Newman, Sally Field tour de force *Absence of Malice*? (Just remember the title.) If a person is a public figure, then the individual must show malice in order to win a defamation case. This means that the person who publishes the false statement or portrayal literally intends to (or knew or should have known that it would) injure the victim—a mere showing of negligence (failing to do thorough research, for example) isn't good enough. The rationale is that someone who has been thrust into the public eye (actors and politicians, for example) should have less expectation of privacy. The obvious corollary is that a higher standard of care (more research) is needed in the case of the average citizen. Notwithstanding this legal distinction, it would be wise to exercise due care in every case. If a negative allegation about a real person portrayed in the movie is made, you should check it out. Find substantiating evidence of the portrayal.

Damages. Generally, an individual must prove that the statement caused actual money damage. Suppose the movie falsely shows that someone had an extramarital affair; the victim would have to show that the depiction affected the person in some real way—that no one would buy the book the victim wrote about making a happy marriage; that his wife divorced him, etc. Actually, under United States law, there are certain categories (the so-called slander per se categories[3]) where the plaintiff may not need to prove damages. As a practical matter, however, the mere threat of a defamation suit can have a chilling effect on financiers and distributors and can be difficult to deal with. The script reviewer will therefore raise questions about any possible problem.

Privacy violations.

In addition to defamation, as a legal matter, the Constitution provides persons with a right of privacy in certain contexts. You already know, if you've been reading this book in chronological order, that a person's name and likeness cannot be used to promote products or services, unless that person consents to such use. This is part of the right of privacy.

Another branch of this right is known as "false light." In a defamation case, as noted above, a person must prove that statements made are false. However, it is possible to create a false illusion about someone without making a false statement (or without making any statement at all). Thus, if the screenplay places an individual in a highly offensive light by embellishing, distorting, or fictionalizing the story elements or simply by placing someone in a suggestive context, that person might win a claim under this theory.[4]

Moreover, even though you can make the life story of a person, as we discussed above, you can't obtain information related to someone by overly invasive means. For example, it would be unwise (actually, illegal) to place cameras and listening devices in an individual's home (or point them through a window) to gather information about a person. You can't hire people to tail someone (although there may be more leeway in the case of a public figure—even there, however, a paparazzi who trespasses on the public figure's property would be in trouble).

Trademark infringement.
The rule is this: Generally speaking, in making your movie, you cannot prominently feature a trademark owned by another person or company without that individual's or company's consent. Let's break this down.

Trademark defined. The commercial history of the world has demonstrated that brands can be extremely valuable. Think of any successful product, like Coca-Cola. (I like to use this example, because a high school buddy of mine went on a tour to the former Soviet Union years ago. His group traveled for many hours outside Moscow by train without seeing any sign of the West, but when they reached their destination they saw—all by itself—the familiar red dot with the words Coca-Cola inside. We used to joke that when man lands on Mars he will likely encounter a Coca-Cola trademark.) The Coca-Cola Company has spent a hundred years and millions of dollars building its brand. It takes great care to ensure the quality of its products. And to let people know that they are buying a genuine Coca-Cola product, the company puts its brand name and a mark or symbol (called a "trademark") on each product.

Governments around the world, including the United States, have instituted trademark registration procedures. Trademark registration is somewhat complicated in that marks are registered for different classes and the requirements from country to country are different. To do it right, a company employs trademark lawyers and agents to oversee this work. A full-blown international registration is very expensive.

Companies who have built up a successful trade name and trademarks at great cost protect them at great cost. The reason is simple; if just anyone could put the Coca-Cola trademark on a drink, people would become confused. They would buy beverages thinking they were buying a genuine Coca-Cola product, but the Coca-Cola Company wouldn't be making any money. Even worse, suppose that a counterfeit beverage manufacturer makes a product that doesn't taste good or that has harmful ingredients. The value of Coca-Cola's trademark is injured. Therefore, Coca-Cola, like all companies with valuable trademarks, goes after counterfeiters and trademark infringers with fearless abandon.

Trademarks in movies. So what has all this got to do with moviemaking? Well, if you shoot a scene that prominently features a trademark, you might have trouble. And here comes the question that almost all producers want to ask: "By showing the trademark in the movie, I am giving the company free advertising! What's wrong with that?" It's a fair question and producers often have this point of view, but it is dangerous. The problem is this: Owners of trademarks like to control their use. Maybe the movie in question makes an unpopular political statement (drinking Coca-Cola, for example, is not a political decision and the company will want to stay away from such issues) or in other ways espouses an unpopular theme or becomes the subject of criticism or ridicule. By showing the mark in the movie, for good *and* for bad, the mark becomes associated with the movie. This association must be agreed upon and, since the owner's consent was not obtained, the owner is aggrieved in the eyes of the law.

Street shots. What are we talking about here? Okay, let's suppose you show your hero running through Times Square chasing a bad guy. The camera follows them, in and out and round about, picking up literally hundreds of trademarks in its lens. No, I am not saying that you need to go to a special effects lab and have all the marks removed. Nor am I saying that you have to get a release from each of the trademark owners. The uses that are dangerous are the close-up shots and shots that are scripted. Suppose you have your hero stop and purchase a soft drink from a street vendor. The vendor gets out a can of Coke and the camera shows the hero, branded can in hand, taking a drink. That's a dangerous shot. Producers generally use generic cups and unbranded beverages and other products in their movies to avoid this problem. James Bond does not, for example, identify the branded ingredients of his famous shaken-not stirred martini.

Commercial tie-ins. Ah, but James Bond makes no secret of his newly acquired love for BMW automobiles (in certain 007 installments, BMWs replaced the original Aston Martin as the official James Bond–mobile). That is because BMW and the producers of the movies that feature James driving BMW automobiles have a written agreement. BMW pays the producer for this association—it's something they want. No infringement here.

Copyright infringement.
And, yes, the reviewer of the screenplay will look for copyright issues, even though you have been careful to complete your chain of title. And here is what the person will look for.

General. The kinds of copyright issues that arise in the context of reviewing the screenplay are many and can arise in a variety of contexts. To date, we have taken care of several of the most important chain of title issues outside the screenplay: The agreement for the underlying work, the writer's agreement for the screenplay, an agreement locking in the major cast, a director's and a producer's agreement. At this point, the reviewer will look in the screenplay itself for possible references to works by other parties. For example, the writer may have someone quoting poetry or prose written by other authors. Designs and artwork are also subject to copyright and the portrayal of such items will also be questioned and somehow resolved.

Film clips. The use of film clips in your movie is dangerous and involves special consideration. For example, I once received a call from the agent of a famous film director who wanted to show a couple watching a Japanese monster movie; ten seconds was all he needed. The Japanese company, at first, did not want to grant its consent. The director did not want to give up and eventually, after calls from the likes of me and others (including the director's famous friends), the Japanese company gave its permission. Why the fuss?

First, the film clip itself can be and usually is a copyrighted work. If so, you must get clearance from the owner—usually a studio. Studios will invariably charge you for the use of the clip.

There is a persistent misconception that I've heard over the years to the effect that footage from "trailers" (the promotional short that plays in the theaters and sometimes on television as a movie preview) is not entitled to copyright protection. This is not true. Trailers incorporate footage from the movie and that footage is entitled to the same protection as the movie itself. Even if the footage never shows up in the movie because it is taken by a separate camera, that separate footage is owned by someone and cannot be used in your movie without the permission of the owner. Of course, footage from movies created years ago could be in the public domain, but this will require research on the part of you and/or your attorney. I once had the pleasant experience of being told by the owner of a library of films that the film clips I wanted to clear were in the public domain. Don't count on the studios always being so forthcoming.

Second, even if you obtain the copyright owner's permission to use the clip, you must obtain permission from the primary actors in the footage. Although the actors may have granted rights to the producer of the movie from which the clip has been taken, the producer may not have the ability under the agreement or under the SAG agreement, which has special provisions regarding the licensing of film clips for use in a second production, to grant a license without payment to the actors in the clip or without their consent. Generally, the consent of SAG actors in footage taken prior to the 1960s is not required, but again there are significant exceptions (for certain major stars who had the clout to cut special deals).

Finally, and don't forget this, please, film clips generally come with music in the sound track. This music is likely to be protected by copyright law and, if the sound track is being used, the rights have to be cleared in the same way as explained below.

MPAA RATING SYSTEM

The MPAA also oversees the ratings of movies. With the political unrest of the 1960s came a new type of movie. Films with explicit language and nudity were given a green light and scheduled for distribution. Up until this time, the Production Code promulgated in the 1920s by the so-called Hays Office (the forerunner to the MPAA) had been the standard for self-regulation. The Production Code, in the 1960s, was virtually a mandate for censorship. Jack Valenti, newly appointed in 1966, caused the MPAA to dump the code in favor of a new standard for self-regulation. In November 1968, Valenti announced a new voluntary film ratings system with four categories: G for general audiences (all ages admitted), M for mature audiences (parental guidance recommended, but all ages admitted), R for restricted audiences (no one under seventeen admitted without an accompanying parent or guardian), and X for adult fare (no one under seventeen admitted). In 1984, the M rating was changed to PG for parental guidance (PG-13 was also added to give emphasis regarding children thirteen and under). In 1990, "NC-17: NO ONE 17 OR

UNDER ADMITTED" replaced the X rating, which had over time taken on a "surly" meaning (to quote Valenti).

The MPAA emphasizes that the ratings have nothing to do with the quality of the movie. Rather, the ratings are meant to be parental guides.

How ratings are decided.

The ratings are decided by a full-time Rating Board located in Hollywood. There are eight to thirteen members of the board, chosen by the MPAA president, who serve for periods of varying length. They work for the Classification and Rating Administration, which is funded by fees charged to producers/distributors for the rating of their films. The MPAA does not challenge or overturn decisions made by the Rating Board.[5]

Submissions to the Rating Board are voluntary.

Whether or not to submit a movie to the Rating Board for rating is a voluntary choice. Most producers and distributors, however, do in fact submit their films for ratings. A producer can go to market without the MPAA ratings, but producers cannot attach the G, PG, R, or NC-17 ratings by themselves. The rating symbols are federally registered certification marks of the MPAA and cannot be used without going through the process.

How the rating is applied.

In reviewing submissions, the members of the Rating Board are supposed to apply the rating they think most parents would apply. They must report their reasoning in writing. The rating is determined by a majority vote.

Right to reedit.

The producer who doesn't like the rating given to the movie can request an explanation from the board. The producer can reedit the movie and submit the modified movie again to the board for a second review.

Appealing the rating.

If a producer is unhappy with the rating and doesn't want to edit the movie, he can appeal the decision to the Rating Appeals Board, which sits as the final arbiter of ratings. The Appeals Board comprises fourteen to eighteen members who serve terms of varying length.

After the movie is screened, the producer whose film is being appealed explains why he or she believes the rating was wrongly decided. The chairman of the Rating Board states the reason for the film's rating. The producer has an opportunity for rebuttal. After both sides of the argument are heard, the Appeals Board discusses the appeal and then takes a secret ballot. It requires a two-thirds vote of those present to overturn a Rating Board decision.

Using the ratings in advertising and trailers.

All advertising for rated movies must be submitted to the Advertising Administration for approval prior to its release to the public. This includes, but is not limited to, print ads, radio and TV spots, pressbooks, videocassette packaging, and theatrical and home video trailers.

Trailers must be approved for "all audiences," which means they may be shown with all feature films, or restricted audiences, which limits their use to feature films rated R or NC-17. There will be, in all audience trailers, no scenes that caused the feature to be rated PG, PG-13, R, or NC-17. Each trailer is preceded by a tag that tells two things: (1) the audience for which the trailer has been approved and (2) the rating of the picture being advertised. The tag for all audience trailers will have a green background; the tag for restricted trailers will have a red background. The color is to alert the projectionist against mismatching trailers with the film being shown on the theater screen.

MUSIC CLEARANCE

Music can be a source of trouble. There are several reasons. First-time producers treat music as an afterthought. The musical score is usually not completed or laid into the sound track until the postproduction phase. With all the other stuff going on, the inexperienced producer turns his attention to music only when he or she comes to it. This is not a good idea, because music-related issues can be complicated.

There are two types of music, each with its own set of problems. First, many movies employ music that exists in a prerecorded format. The most obvious example of this is the use in a sound track of a popular song that has (or had, as the case may be) a life on the radio. The second type of music is specially commissioned for use in the movie. We will talk about the special aspects of both types below.

Prerecorded music.

Suppose the producer finds a popular recording that he feels would be great in the last scene of *The Quest*. It should be obvious by now, but you cannot legally take a recording without permission and drop it into your sound track. Moreover, you will normally need the permission of at least three persons (or entities).

Copyright in the composition—sync license. Just like your treatment or screenplay, a musical composition is protected by copyright. The protection springs into life the moment the composition is fixed in a tangible form (recorded or written down in notation, for example). When I say composition, I am talking about the melody, lyrics (if any), and arrangement. In the case of popular music, the term song is also used. Note also that music, lyrics, and arrangements can be created by collaboration, so there may be more than one person with ownership. You must get their permission to use their composition.

Music publishing—administration rights. Happily, many composers grant the right to control (or administer) the composition to a music publishing company. Music publishing companies enter into licensing agreements for the composition, collect royalties paid pursuant to these agreements, and distribute such royalties to the composer(s), after deducting its share (the publisher's share, which is usually 50 percent). This means that your attorney can usually clear a composition by contacting the publishing company, which is identified on the recording (if there is one) or on the liner notes contained in the packaging or by a number of different other means.

Sync license. Licenses related to the use of a composition or song (as opposed to a master recording) in a movie are referred to as "sync licenses" (or synchronization licenses), because they give the producer the right to synchronize the composition in timed relation with the visual images on the film. The sync license is often a flat fee (i.e., it does not normally bear an ongoing royalty). The fee is typically paid in one payment prior to the beginning of principal photography or sometimes on the date of the agreement.

This letter, when countersigned by you below, shall constitute an agreement (this "Agreement") between Righteous M. Uzak ("Composer") and Quest Productions, LLC ("Producer") related to the musical composition, including music and lyrics written by Composer (the "Composition"). The motion picture or television

296 THE MOVIE BUSINESS

production covered by this license is entitled "The Quest" (the "Picture").

The composition can be used in the picture and in separate soundtrack albums. This later right is a benefit to the composer, who makes money (in the form of mechanical royalties) every time an album is sold and every time that the song plays on the radio (in the form of performance royalties). The mechanical royalty, which is paid to the owners of publishing rights, is fixed by statute and is either calculated on a per song basis (for example, $0.085 per song) or, if the music is score and not a single song, on a so-much-per minute basis (for example, $0.0165 per minute), whichever is more.[6] The sync license also clarifies the duration and scope (in this case, "throughout the universe" and "in perpetuity"). Note also that the license is nonexclusive, meaning that the composer (or the composer's publisher) will be able to license the use of the composition to other producers. The composition can also be used in all media—including the now famous "any form whether now in existence or hereafter devised."

For good and valuable consideration, the receipt and sufficiency of which are hereby acknowledged, Composer hereby grants to Producer, and Producer's successors and assigns and licensees, the non-exclusive right, license and privilege and authority, throughout the universe, to record and cause the fixation of the Composition in synchronization or in timed-relation with the Picture and in a separate sound-track album or albums and to make copies of such recordings and import such recordings and/or copies thereof throughout the universe and to exhibit, distribute, sell, lease, license, use, exploit and market such Picture and sound-track album(s) throughout the universe in any and all media now known or hereafter devised (including without limitation all forms of theatrical and non-theatrical exploitation, all forms of television and all forms of video and audio exploitation). The recording and synchronization rights granted above shall endure for the periods of all copyrights in each country throughout the world in and to the Composition, and any and all renewals or extensions thereof in each country throughout the world that Author may now own or control or hereafter own or control without Author having to pay any additional consideration therefor.

In the case below, the composer limits the use of the license. The producer is not allowed to make derivative works (the producer can't make a dramatic work based on the lyrics, for example), change the lyrics, use the title of the composition as the title of the movie, or use the composition in any way not contemplated by the license.

> This license does not include any right or authority: (a) to dramatize or to use the plot or any dramatic content of the lyrics of the Composition; (b) to alter the lyrics or music of the Composition; (c) to use the title of the Composition as the title of the Picture; (d) to make any other use of the Composition not expressly authorized herein.

The composer is required, of course, to make representations about the origins of the composition and the composer's legal ability to grant the rights granted.

> Composer hereby warrants, represents and agrees that it has the legal right to enter into this Agreement and grant the rights granted herein. To the Composer's best knowledge, the Compositions do not contain any copyrighted or other proprietary material belonging to any person or entity other than Composer.

The composer, on his part, clarifies that rights not granted are reserved.

> Subject only to the non-exclusive rights granted herein above to Producer, all rights of every kind and nature in the Composition are reserved to Author, together with all rights of use thereof.

Finally, the composer gets a credit. Note the difference in how the credit provision is handled in the synchronization license (a simple reference) and the master use license below (the explicit language of the credit).

> Composer shall be given a credit on the Picture in form and substance satisfactory to Composer.

Copyright in the phonorecording—master use license. Okay, you've signed a sync license and the song is yours to use in the movie. Ah, but you are not finished. If you want to use the original recording in your movie you must also get a license from the owner of the master recording. Pursuant to the recording contract with the artist, the record label owns the master recording. You can usually tell the copyright in the composition, which is indicated by the © mark, from the owner of the master, which is indicated by the Ⓟ mark.

Master use license. The license is referred to as a master use license. The financial and other terms are similar to those in the sync license. The owner of the master, usually a record label, grants the producer the right to use a master recording (you know, the original recording of a golden oldie) in and in connection with the movie. Note the familiar "timed relation" language. The agreement recites that the music may be used in the movie and in trailers and other advertising. The amount of time is usually specified in the license, because the record label does not want the song to be overplayed or used as underscore. The license is nonexclusive; the label can grant a license to other producers.

> Company hereby consents to Producer's use of the master recording ("Master") embodying the performances of John B. Goode, Badde B. Oi and Gee Tarman p/k/a The Dreamers (the "Group") of the musical composition entitled "Follow Your Quest" as a featured vocal over the end titles (for up to three (3) minutes twenty-eight (28) seconds in duration) in Producer's motion picture entitled "The Quest" and all in-context trailers, advertisements, featurettes and promotional material therefor, as well as excerpts therefrom (collectively referred to herein as the "Picture").

Rights being sought—movie and sound track. The granting clause of the agreement recites the basic parameters of the license—who gets it (the producer and the producer's successors and assigns), on what basis (nonexclusive), where (worldwide), and for what purpose (exhibiting, distributing, exploiting, and performing the movie). One critical aspect of this license is to clarify that the song can be used in both the movie sound track, in videograms of the movie, and in a separate sound-track album. This is some times a bone of contention with the record label, because it means that the track might find its way onto a sound-track album distributed on a competing label.

> For good and valuable consideration, the receipt and sufficiency of which are hereby acknowledged, Company hereby grants Producer, and Producer's successors, assigns and licensees, the non-exclusive worldwide right, license and authority in perpetuity to reproduce and perform the Master in the sound-track of or in timed-relation

with the Picture for the purpose of exhibiting, distributing, exploiting and performing the Picture throughout the world in any and all media now known or hereafter devised and in any and all manners or formats now known or hereafter devised (including without limitation all forms of theatrical and nontheatrical exploitation, all forms of free, pay and other television, and all forms of home video exploitation, whether by means of cassettes, discs or otherwise) and, further, in a separate original sound-track album containing other master recordings from the sound track of the Picture released in connection with and as part of the release of the Picture.

Credits. Of course, the producer has to give credit where credit is due. In the case of a master use license, credit goes to the performers and the producer, at least. Moreover, the record label may have an agreement with the composer and lyricist to provide them credit; the label will pass that duty along to the producer (and, of course, the producer may have incurred this obligation in the context of the sync license discussed above). Finally, it is customary in the music industry to give a provided courtesy credit to the label. Look at the following example:

Producer shall accord Company and the Group appropriate credit on all prints of the entire Picture which include the Master, together with similar credit for other recordings included therein, as follows:

"Follow Your Quest"
Performed by The Dreamers
Written by Gee Tarman and Righteous M. Uzak
Composed by Righteous M. Uzak
Produced by The Dreamers and Prough Dooser
The Dreamers appear courtesy of Cooperative Records

All other characteristics of such credit shall be at Producer's sole discretion. No casual or inadvertent failure by Producer and no failure by any third party to comply with the provisions of this paragraph shall constitute a breach by Producer of this Agreement.

Reuse fees. If the master recording was made using guild musicians—for example, musicians who belong to the American Federation of Musicians (AFM)—reuse fees may apply. A "reuse fee" is applicable where the music was recorded for a specific purpose (for example, for use in the sound track of Movie A) and is then used again for another purpose (for example, in the sound track of Movie B). The producer will generally have the obligation to pay these fees in any master use agreement and therefore, as in the example below, the producer will need the record label's cooperation in providing information concerning the applicability and payment of reuse fees.

> Upon Producer's written request, Company shall provide Producer with all the necessary information to enable Producer to pay all reuse fees which may be required by any applicable unions, in accordance with such unions' contracts and regulations. Producer hereby agrees to pay all such reuse fees and any and all pension and/or welfare payments required with respect to Producer's use of the Master as provided herein. Producer hereby agrees to indemnify and hold harmless Company from and against any and all claims, demands or actions with respect to such fees and payments.

Sync license. The record label's lawyers know what you know—that the use of a master recording requires both the label's permission and the permission of the owners of the composition embodied in the recording. Therefore, those nice lawyers will make sure that the producer understands and takes care of this obligation, so that it won't come back to bite the label.

> Producer shall be solely responsible for obtaining the appropriate synchronization and performance license from the copyright owner or controller of the musical composition embodied in the Master and for paying all fees with respect thereto, and Producer shall indemnify and hold harmless Company from and against any and all claims, demands or actions in connection therewith.

Artist. One more point for the master use license. For the most part, the recording label, as copyright owner, will have the right to control the use of the master recording. The recording artist will usually have granted all rights to the label and so it will be unnecessary to get the artist's permission, except perhaps to obtain the right to use the artist's name and likeness to promote the movie. Compare this situation to civil law jurisdictions where "neighboring rights" (one of which is called performing rights) give the artist certain rights in and to his or her performance.

Music libraries.

Most movies, whether they use individual songs or not, use score, underlying music selected because it enhances aurally the mood portrayed with the dialogue and pictures. Some score music is prerecorded and available through music libraries. Music libraries stock prerecorded music of all types—whatever mood you and your music supervisor are looking for. The folks who own and operate these establishments understand the movie business. Therefore, the music is available in the technical formats that musical supervisors demand. Moreover, and most important, the rights to these pieces are usually cleared from a legal perspective. I say usually because you and your lawyer will want to get the appropriate documentation (including representations and warranties about chain of title and the whole bit). Granted, the selection will not include a lot of famous melodies and it's doubtful that you will find any original-artist hits, but it should be less expensive than the alternatives.

Commissioned music.

Or, if you have the money, you can hire a music composer to score the movie on a custom-made basis. Virtually all major motion pictures use experienced composers, some of whom (John Williams, James Horner, Jerry Goldsmith, and others) are famous in their own right. A full-blown composer agreement will contain all of the issues discussed above, plus the usual chain of title concerns.

Loan-out structure. The following example is in the form of a loan-out structure. Note that the composer's company is lending the composer's services. It is possible, of course, to engage a composer directly.

> The following will confirm the agreement between Quest Productions, LLC ("Producer") and RMU, Inc. ("Lender") for the services of Righteous M. Uzak ("Composer") in connection with that feature-length motion picture tentatively entitled "The Quest" (the "Picture").

General services. The composer will usually do more than simply compose music. The producer will generally count on the composer to select and conduct the orchestra, arrange the music he or she composes, and adapt the music the artist doesn't compose (the music licensed pursuant to a sync license, for example). This provision lists the customary duties of a film composer and then clarifies below, the specific duties.

> Subject to the provisions of this agreement, Composer shall perform in connection with the Picture all services and duties customarily performed in the motion picture industry by a composer, scorer, conductor, orchestrator, arranger and adapter (collectively, the "Services").

Score. The producer wants to make sure that the composer agrees to supply a complete score. Merely composing pieces of music will not get the producer where he needs to be at the end of the day. The producer will need the composition and the accompanying orchestration, arrangement, and so forth.

> Without limiting the foregoing in any way, the Services shall include all of the following: Composing, orchestrating, arranging, preparing, packaging and submitting to Producer, and if requested by Producer, collaborating with others in the composition, orchestration, arrangement, preparation, packaging and submission to Producer of, music suitable for use as the complete background score for the Picture (the "Score") . . .

Performance. The producer can't hand the audience a copy of the score and expect them to sing along in their heads. Therefore, it would be good to get the music performed. The composer is expected to select the orchestra, rehearse with the orchestra, and then, when ready, record the music in sync and in timed relation with the picture images of the movie.

> Conducting an orchestra in the rehearsal, performance and recording of the Work in synchronism and timed relation with the Picture . . .

Master recordings. As you know from our discussion above, the original recording is referred to as the "master recording." This is a bit of duplication (the kind of duplication lawyers are famous for), but it does in fact narrow the process down to a concrete item. Note the use of the word "producing"; a record producer is more akin to a director in movie business parlance. Thus, the composer-as-producer is expected to make the creative decisions related to getting the performance down on tape or a hard drive (or whatever it is producers use nowadays).

> Recording and producing original completed master recordings of the Work (the "Masters," and together with the "Score," the "Work");

Music supervision. As the music producer, the composer is expected to supervise the processes involved in making the master recording as required by the movie producer (who usually allows the director to supervise this work). This is a major collaboration in the making of a movie and when done correctly is magic. Think of Randy Newman's score in *The Natural;* Jerry Goldsmith's score in *A Patch of Blue;* and James Horner's score in *Titanic.* Note too that the role of music supervisor may be performed by a person other than the composer. One possible way to divide their duties is to let the music supervisor select the individual musical pieces (including a smattering of Golden Oldies) and then work with the composer to fill in the rest of the score.

> Supervising the music editing and dubbing of the recording of the Work in connection with the Picture, including any and all changes or modifications required by Producer;

Delivery. Delivery is a term of art and refers to that moment in time when the music elements are made available to the movie producer so that they can be put into the movie. Delivery specifications are important because they get everyone working on the same page. Here, the composer has to deliver seven items, from the conductor's part (the master score in printed form) to the masters and beyond. The reference to the DA-88 in the sample provision below dates this material (because the technology of sound changes more rapidly than the weather). And believe it or not, a competent music composer will actually understand what all this terminology means.

> Delivering the Work to Producer in the forms customarily delivered in the U.S. motion picture industry including the following items (collectively, the "Delivery Items"): (i) the original copy of the conductor's part; (ii) two (2) copies each of all lead sheets for the original music and for the arrangements, cues, bridges and derivatives of the Work; (iii) one (1) copy of the music cue sheets, which cue

sheets shall set forth the nature, extent and exact timing of the uses made of the Work in the Picture, and such other information as is customarily included in music cue sheets of motion pictures; (iv) one (1) 8-track, stereo audio cassette Master in the DA-88 format (or such other format as Producer shall specify), which cassette shall contain the recording of the Work suitable for mixing with the other sound elements of the Picture and shall not be recorded with any electronic reverberation added unless Producer otherwise requests; (v) one (1) stereo digital audio tape Master of the Work mixed by or under the direction of Composer for inclusion in a sound-track album of the Picture; (vi) one (1) stereo digital audio tape Master of the Work mixed by or under the direction of Composer for inclusion on phonorecords other than the sound-track album; and (vii) all other sound recordings produced hereunder, whether or not included in the final Masters; and . . .

Incidental services. And alas, because people might actually take such a list literally, the producer clarifies that the composer may have to do things related to but not described in the list.

Rendering such other incidental or related services as Producer shall request in connection with the Picture, including services in connection with any added scenes, changes, additional sound recordings or retakes.

Nonexclusive, first-priority basis. The producer may not need to tie up the composer's time on an exclusive basis, but he will want to clarify that during the critical time his job comes first—before any other job, be it for a third party or the composer himself.

During the Term, Composer shall render services for Producer on a nonexclusive but first-priority basis for Producer and shall cause Composer not to render any services for Composer's own account or for any third party which might conflict or interfere with the timely completion of any or all of the Services.

Best time; creative control. This is similar to provisions in other agreements with creative people in that it sets a standard for the services to be rendered. In addition, this provision clarifies that the producer calls the shots, including with respect to creative matters.

Composer shall devote Composer's best time, attention, talents and capabilities to the service of Producer pursuant to this agreement, comply with all requirements, directions, requests, rules and regulations made by Producer in connection with the Picture or the conduct of its business and render services hereunder whenever and wherever Producer may require in a competent, diligent, efficient, conscientious, artistic and professional manner and as instructed by Producer in all matters, including those involving artistic taste and judgment.

Schedule; right to reject. The producer establishes the schedule for delivery. But the key concept here is that the producer has the right to accept or reject all or part of the composer's work product. If the producer does reject the work, then the composer agrees to make changes and to do it to the satisfaction of the producer. Of course, the law will impose some reasonableness standard to the producer's discretion. The producer cannot just keep rejecting the work product, causing the composer to write and write without end. But it is clear that the producer doesn't have to accept the music if he doesn't like it. Whether the producer accepts the music or not, payment of some kind will be necessary.

Composer shall perform the Services and deliver the Work in accordance with such schedule as Producer shall determine from time to time in its sole discretion and shall ensure that the Work and all of the Delivery Items and other materials delivered hereunder are suitable for use in connection with the production of a first-class motion picture. Upon any purported delivery of the Work or any other material hereunder, Producer shall have the right to accept or reject in its sole discretion the Work or other material as submitted. Should Producer reject any portion of the Work or other material as submitted, Composer shall change or modify such rejected portion to Producer's satisfaction as soon as reasonably possible after Composer receives notice of such rejection. Composer agrees that failure to secure on a timely basis Producer's acceptance of the Work and the Delivery Items and other materials to be delivered as part of performing the Services shall constitute a Default (as defined below) by Composer and shall entitle Producer to exercise any and all remedies available to Producer under this agreement or under any applicable law or otherwise.

Other musicians. As the music producer, the composer will have the opportunity to engage other musicians. In this case, the movie producer has the right to approve (or disapprove) these other musicians. The composer must procure fully executed chain of title documents from these other musicians.

> Prior to employing, engaging or otherwise utilizing the services of any musicians or other persons in connection with the performance of the Services, Composer, in each and every case, shall consult with Producer (it being agreed that Producer shall have the right to approve any such persons) and shall procure fully executed copies of such consents, releases, certificates and other documents as Producer in its sole discretion shall require.

Fixed compensation. The composer is paid fixed compensation for providing the services. In this contract, which is a standard approach, the composer is paid in three installments: when the artist signs the agreement or starts work, when he or she starts recording the score, and when the artist's services are finished under the agreement. The fees vary from composer to composer and can range from the hundreds to the millions of dollars. Again, the "to Producer's satisfaction" condition embedded (see clause [iii] in the sample provision that follows) in clause (iii) is difficult to negotiate if the composer is famous. At the very least, the composer's attorney will ask for the insertion of "reasonable" before the word "satisfaction" in the last sentence.

> On condition that Composer fully and faithfully performs all of the Services, as full and complete compensation for all of the Services hereunder, all of the results and proceeds of the Services, all rights granted or to be granted to Producer hereunder and all representations, warranties, indemnities and agreements made or given by Composer in connection herewith, Producer shall pay to composer the sum of Fifty Thousand Dollars ($50,000), payable as follows: (i) Twenty Thousand Dollars ($20,000) upon the later of the execution of this agreement or the commencement of the spotting of the Picture, the receipt of which is hereby acknowledged; (ii) Fifteen Thousand Dollars ($15,000) upon the commencement of the recording of the Score; and (iii) Fifteen Thousand Dollars upon the completion to Producer's satisfaction of all of the Services.

Other's compensation included. An important feature of composer agreements is that the composer's compensation is meant to cover any persons the composer brings in to help him and the cost of equipment and studio time. Thus, composers are on guard to budget for such other persons and things and the producer is free from having to pay extra for them.

> Composer acknowledges and agrees that the compensation payable hereunder shall include any and all compensation, fees and other sums payable to musicians and other third parties in connection with the Work and the preparation, rehearsal, performance, recording and synchronization thereof, including the following: (i) music; (ii) copyists; (iii) orchestration; (iv) studio rental; (v) engineering services; (vi) musicians and vocalists; (vii) cartage; (viii) instrument rentals; and (ix) tape stock.

Producer expenses. Not so fast. The composer gets a chance to push back on costs. Below, the composer clarifies that the music editor will be paid by the producer. The implication is that the music editor will be hired at the discretion of the producer.

> Notwithstanding the foregoing, Composer shall not be responsible for costs related to the post-production services of a music editor, if any.

Credit. The composer will want his credit and so the composer agreement, like all the others we have looked at, will have a credit provision. There is only one point we haven't seen before, and that is the wording of the credit itself. Here the credit is "Original music composed by . . ." There are other possibilities: "Music by . . ." or "Musical score by . . ." for example.

> Provided that Composer fully and satisfactorily performs all of the Services pursuant to the terms and conditions of this agreement and that all of the original music contained in the Picture as released is the product of the Services, Producer shall accord Composer credit on screen, on a separate card, in the main titles (if any), in the form of "Original Music Composed By Righteous M. Uzac" or a phrase substantially similar thereto. Except as set forth in the preceding sentence, all other matters pertaining to Composer's credit shall be determined in Producer's sole discretion. Producer may,

but is not obligated to, give Composer credit in paid advertisements (subject to customary exclusions) issued by or under the control of Producer. No casual or inadvertent failure of Producer, and no failure by any third party, to comply with the provisions of this paragraph shall constitute a breach by Producer of this agreement. Notwithstanding the foregoing, upon receipt by Producer of written notice from Composer specifying any such failure in reasonable detail, Producer shall use reasonable efforts prospectively to cure such failure.

Rights. Look at the rights provision below and think how impressive it is that you can read this dense legal language and understand all of it. First, the provision invokes the work-made-for-hire doctrine and bolsters that position by the statutory work-made-for-hire language—"specially ordered or commissioned by Producer for use as part of a motion picture or other audiovisual work." As such, the language clarifies that the producer is in fact the author under copyright law. The term rights is defined as ownership, including under the law of copyrights. Then the provision recites all the things one can do with the rights and in what media—essentially, the producer can do anything he or she wants in whatever media the producer wants to do it (even media that hasn't yet been developed). The rights also include the rights that exist under the laws of the European Union, because the rights will be exploited there (and everywhere). And, sure, if the work-made-for-hire doctrine is ever found not to apply, the composer grants all his rights to the producer. And, this is a rights provision from a "loan-out" agreement. Easy, isn't it?

> Composer hereby acknowledges, certifies and agrees that all material of whatever kind or nature created, composed, prepared, performed, recorded, packaged or delivered by Composer hereunder and all results and proceeds of Composer's services hereunder (all such material and all such results and proceeds being sometimes collectively referred to herein as the "Material"), including the Work and the Delivery Items, shall constitute "works made for hire" specially ordered or commissioned by Producer for use as part of a motion picture or other audiovisual work. Accordingly, Producer is and shall be considered the author of the Material for all purposes and the sole and exclusive owner, throughout the universe in perpetuity, of all right, title and interest in and to the Material and each and every part thereof, including all copyrights therein, all renewals

and extensions of such copyrights and all other proprietary rights of any kind, nature or description that may be secured under the laws now or hereafter in effect in the United States of America or any other jurisdiction (collectively, the "Rights"). The Rights shall include the right to authorize, prohibit and/or control the production, reproduction, fixation, adaptation, distribution, rental, lending, performance, broadcasting, communication to the public and other exploitation of the Materials in any and all media and by any and all means now known or hereafter devised and the right to make such changes therein and such uses thereof as Producer may deem necessary or desirable. The Rights shall further include any and all so-called rental rights, lending rights, fixation rights, reproduction rights, distribution rights and neighboring rights pursuant to any international treaties or conventions, any directives or other measures of the European Union or its successor and/or any enabling or implementing legislation, laws or regulations relating to the foregoing (collectively, the "EU Rights"). If and to the extent that under any applicable law the Material is not deemed a work made for hire for Producer or Producer is not deemed to be the author of the Material and the sole and exclusive owner of the Material and all right, title and interest therein (including all of the Rights), then to the fullest extent allowable and for the full term of protection otherwise accorded Composer under such applicable law, Composer irrevocably assigns, grants and transfers, to Producer throughout the universe in perpetuity the Rights and, in connection therewith, all right, title and interest of Composer in, to and with respect to the Score and the Masters and any other works now or hereafter created containing the Material.

EU rights. Under European Union law, it is important for producer to buy out the EU rights. This gives the producer the right to collect all moneys (except for music performance royalties in connection with the public performance of the score) payable to the composer with respect to the EU rights.

Composer hereby acknowledges and agrees that the compensation paid or to be paid by Producer to Lender in connection with the Work includes adequate and equitable remuneration for each and every one of the EU Rights (including the rental rights) and constitutes a complete buy-out of all of the EU Rights. In connection with the foregoing, Lender hereby irrevocably assigns, grants and transfers, and shall cause Composer to irrevocably assign, grant and transfer, to Producer, throughout the universe in perpetuity, the right to collect and retain for Producer's own account any and all amounts payable to Lender with respect to the EU Rights and hereby irrevocably directs and authorizes Producer to direct any collecting societies or other persons or entities receiving such amounts to pay such amounts to Producer (it being understood that this section shall not be deemed to apply to any music publishing royalties payable to Lender in respect of the public performance of the Score).

Right to edit, modify, etc. As is the case with all other basic works, the producer must have the right to use the work in any way the producer needs. The producer clarifies that the producer will edit and modify the work to conform to technical requirements, use it as a replacement for other music, use it as background music, in commercials, and so forth. By the way, this right will be required by the issuer of the errors and omissions insurance.

Without limiting the generality of the foregoing, Composer hereby acknowledges and agrees that Producer and its licensees shall have the unlimited and exclusive rights to do the following: to change, edit, add to, take from, dub, mix, remix, adapt, reformat or reprocess the Masters in any manner for any reason, including to conform to technological or commercial requirements in various formats now or hereafter known or developed and to eliminate material which might subject Producer to any legal action; to use and authorize the use of the Masters for background music, synchronization in motion pictures (including the Picture) and television sound tracks and other similar purposes, including use in means of transportation and in commercials for any product in any and all media, without any payment other than as provided herein; to manufacture records by any and all methods now or hereafter known embodying any portion or all of the Work; and to delay or refrain from doing any or all of the foregoing.

Moral rights. Moral rights of authors, of course, is an issue with music, just as it is with any other creations. Thus, this provision will find its way into a composer agreement.

To the fullest extent allowable under any applicable law, Composer hereby irrevocably waives or assigns to Producer any and all rights of "droit moral" or "moral rights of authors" or similar rights which Lender or Composer may now or later have in the Material and any other works now or hereafter created containing the Material. Composer expressly acknowledges that many persons will contribute to the Picture and other works that will embody all or part of the Material. Accordingly, if under any applicable law the above waiver or assignment by Composer of such rights of droit moral or moral rights of authors or similar rights is not effective, then Composer agrees to exercise such rights in a manner which recognizes the contribution of and will not have an adverse effect upon such other persons.

Further assurances. This is a rather complete version of the further assurances clause. It covers additional documents that help bolster the producer's position. It also covers the execution of a "composer's certificate," which, of course, is virtually identical to the certificate of authorship (see above). And it appoints the producer as the composer's attorney-in-fact so that, if the composer is not around when the producer is feeling insecure about whether or not he or she actually has the rights, the producer can sign the documents and do whatever is needed to get them.

Upon Producer's request, Composer shall perform (or cause to be performed), such further acts and execute, acknowledge and deliver (or cause to be executed, acknowledged and delivered) to Producer such further documents as Producer shall deem necessary or advisable in order to evidence, establish, maintain, protect, enforce or defend its rights in and to the Material or otherwise to carry out the intent and accomplish the purposes of this agreement. Without limiting the foregoing in any way, Composer shall execute, acknowledge and deliver to Producer a composer's certificate in Producer's standard form therefor in connection with Composer's delivery of the Delivery Items and any other materials hereunder. If for any reason Composer shall fail to do any of the foregoing within five (5) days after Producer's request therefor, Composer hereby irrevocably appoints Producer as Composer's true and lawful attorney-in-fact (such appointment being a power coupled with an interest), with full power of substitution and delegation, with the right (but not the obligation) to perform any such acts and to execute, acknowledge and deliver any such documents in Composer's name and Composer's behalf.

Name and likeness. The producer will want to use the composer's name and likeness to promote and exploit the movie. The producer is not able, however, to use the composer's name and likeness in a way that makes it look like the composer is promoting or endorsing a product or service.

> Composer hereby grants to Producer the right, throughout the universe in perpetuity, to use and reproduce and license others to use and reproduce the name, likeness, attributes and biographical data of Composer in connection with the following: (i) the Picture and any other work in which the Material shall be used in whole or in part; (ii) the advertising, marketing, publicizing, promotion, exhibition, distribution or other exploitation of the Picture and any other work in which the Material shall be used in whole or in part; and (iii) any commercial tie-ins, merchandising and/or advertising or publicizing of any commodities, products or services relating or referring to the Picture or any other work in which the Material shall be used in whole or in part, provided that Composer shall not be represented as directly using, consuming or endorsing any such commodity, product or service without Composer's prior written consent.

No claim or interference. Because of the nature of copyright law, when things go wrong, it is possible that the composer might be able to conjure up some type of claim related to the composer's work on the project. These claims could have a negative impact on the producer's ability to move forward with the project. Therefore, the producer wisely exacts a promise from the composer that the composer will not make any claim that interferes with producer's rights or his or her ability to make the movie. Even if a valid claim arises on the part of the composer, the producer tries to limit the composer's rights. For example, the producer may breach the agreement after the composer has created some music that has already found its way in the movie score. In that case, the producer doesn't want to go to the expense of pulling the music out. Therefore, the composer's remedies are limited to a claim for money damages "actually suffered" and do not include the right to seek an injunction.

> Composer agrees not to make any claim or bring any suit, action or arbitration or other proceeding which will or might interfere with or derogate from Producer's rights in and to the Material, it being ex-

pressly understood and agreed that neither Lender nor Composer shall have or be deemed to have any lien, charge or other encumbrance upon the Material or any rights therein or proceeds derived therefrom and that neither the breach nor alleged breach of this agreement by Producer, nor the termination of this agreement, nor any other act, omission or event of any kind, shall terminate or otherwise adversely affect Producer's sole and exclusive ownership of the Material and all right, title and interest therein. Composer further agrees that Lender's or Composer's sole remedy for any such breach or alleged breach shall be an action at law to recover such damages as may have been actually suffered by Composer as a result thereof.

Music publishing royalties. Okay, here is something novel to music agreements. Let's review how the music industry works. As we noted above, the exploitation of musical compositions is generally handled by music publishers, which often administer (control) the music rights. In the case of a commissioned score, the producer cares most about whether the music is fit for the purposes the producer envisions, but it is quite possible that the music might find a market outside the movie. Down the road, other producers might want to use it for their audiovisual works. Directors of commercials might want it. People might want to buy sheet music and play it at home on the piano. If you get lucky and your score turns out like the score from *Breakfast at Tiffany's* (which featured the song "Moon River," one of the most often "covered"—a music business term that means to record a new version of a song after it has already been released— songs in pop music history), there might be a chance for other performances. All of these uses bring publishing revenues into the bank.

> Provided that Composer is not in default hereunder, should Producer or Producer's direct music publishing administrator(s) exploit music publishing rights in connection with the Score, then Lender shall be entitled to the music publishing royalties as set forth below:

Mechanical, synchronization, and other rights. The composer gets to keep 50 percent of the revenues generated from mechanical, electrical transcription, and sync licensing. Mechanical royalties are royalties paid to the publisher and composer on the sale of recordings (called "phonorecording" under the copyright law) for allowing the composition to be embodied in the phonorecording. Sync rights, described before, are fees and/or royalties to publishers and composers for allowing the composition to be laid in the sound track of the movie. Note that the composer's share is net of taxes, commissions, or servicing fees. This, of course, is a benefit to the producer, who keeps everything that the composer or publisher doesn't get. Performance rights are excluded, because they are covered separately in the next section.

> Fifty percent (50%) of any and all net sums, after deduction of any commissions or fees charged by any applicable rights society, collection agent or subpublisher, any costs of collection and any taxes, actually received by Producer (or credited to Producer's account against an advance) in the United States in United States dollars from the exploitation in the United States and Canada by Producer's licensees of mechanical rights, motion picture and television synchronization rights (other than with respect to the Picture, any sequels or remakes thereof or any other work created or owned by Producer in which the Score is used), print rights and all other rights (except those rights relating to the public performance royalties covered below) in the Score, whether or not such licensees are affiliated with, owned in whole or in part by, or controlled by Producer.

Performance royalties. In the case of performance royalties, the composer gets to keep all (100 percent) of the writer's share, which, if you recall, is 50 percent of the total revenues from the performance of the composition. The other 50 percent is called the publisher's share. Each time a composition is performed on the radio or on television, for example, the radio and television broadcasters must pay a performance royalty. (Significantly, no performance royalties are paid to the composer when the movie plays in the theaters in the United States.) The collection of performance royalties is a big job and falls to one of the several performance rights societies or guilds, who take on this job for the publishers and writers. The largest performance guilds are ASCAP (American Society of Composers and Publishers), BMI (Broadcast Music Incorporated), and SESAC (Society of European Stage Authors and Composers). Composers and publishers who meet certain qualifications (for example, composers who publish one of their songs) can join. The guilds then collect the royalties and send the money where it is supposed to go. In this case, the producer allows the composer to sign up for 100 percent of the writer's share, with the publisher's share going to the producer. However, the writer gets to take any complaint up with the guilds directly.

One hundred percent (100%) of the "writer's share" of any public performance royalties received directly from Composer's own affiliated performing rights society; provided, however, that Lender shall not be entitled to receive any part of the moneys received by Producer from ASCAP, BMI or any other performing rights society from which Producer shall receive payments for the use of the Score in all countries of the world. Accordingly, Producer shall not be required to pay Lender royalties for public performances of the Score, and Lender agrees, and shall cause Composer to agree, to look solely to such society for such royalties and waive any claim against Producer for the "publisher's share" of such royalties received by Producer.

Free goods. Since the composer gets to receive money based on records and performances, the producer must think ahead. The producer will want to give copies of the sound-track album away or allow radio stations to play the songs without remuneration; therefore, the producer wants the composer to understand that there will be no payment to the composer on such items.

Notwithstanding any other provision hereof, Producer shall not be required to pay any royalties in respect of professional or complimentary printed copies of the Score or copies of mechanical derivatives of the Score which are distributed gratuitously to performing artists, orchestra leaders and disc jockeys or for advertising, promotional or exploitation purposes for which Producer receives no payment or credit.

Accounting statements. The producer's obligation to pay royalties involves keeping records and making such records available to the composer. Here, the producer agrees to provide accounting records twice a year. The producer also sends along the royalty check. If the payment due is a low amount (here the threshold is $50), the producer can add the de minimis payment to the next accounting period.

Producer will render semi-annual accounting statements by September 30 for the half-year ending June 30, and by March 31 for the half-year ending December 31. Such statements shall be accompanied by the appropriate payment; provided, however, that if the balance due is less than $50.00, Producer shall have the right to carry forward the balance until the end of the next subsequent accounting period during which the balance due exceeds $50.00.

Returns. Now here is an important concept, so time to wake up again. In some cases—records and sheet music, for example—there is an industry custom that allows customers to return products that they don't like (there are signs, in the digital world we live in, that retailers are bucking this custom, but for now, it is a concern). When that happens a lot, the stores might return them to the producer and then the producer might have to give money back. This is bad, because the producer has to pay royalties on the original sales. Therefore, the producer will create a reserve—a pool of money used to pay for returns. The reserve is removed from the gross revenues and, therefore, reduces the composer's royalties. A composer's attorney may accept the reserve, but will usually insist that it be liquidated (disbursed to the parties) after a reasonable time period.

> Producer shall have the right to retain as a reserve against returns such portion of payable royalties as shall be necessary in Producer's best business judgment.

Record royalties. In addition to sync license fees and mechanical royalties, paid with respect to the music publishing rights, the composer may be able to negotiate a separate record royalty for performing on the recording as a musician or the conductor of the orchestra.

> Provided that Lender and Composer are not in default hereunder, if any of the Masters is included in a sound-track album or other phonorecord (a "Record"), Lender shall be entitled to receive the following record royalties, as applicable:

The formula. The provision below sets forth the royalty formula used in the music business. Take a look and we'll discuss the formula and various facets of it.

> A basic "all in" royalty at the applicable rate indicated below (the "Basic Rate") of the applicable suggested retail list price ("SRLP") for the Record concerned less sales or other taxes included in the price and less the applicable container deduction (the "Royalty Base Price") with respect to the Record concerned in respect of net sales of Records and sold by Producer or its licensees for distribution through normal retail channels: (i) on Records sold for distribution in the United States, 9% in the case of "topline" LPs (such rate being referred to herein as the "U.S. Basic Rate"); (ii) on Records sold for distribution in Canada, 75% of the U.S. Basic Rate; and (iii)

on Records sold for distribution in any other country, 50% of the U.S. Basic Rate; provided, however, that record royalties with respect to sales of Records in the United States and Canada shall only be payable to Lender if such payment is consistent with the terms and provisions of the Distribution Agreement. In all events, such basic royalty shall be computed in the same manner as Producer's record royalty is computed pursuant to its agreement with a record company which distributes such Record ("Record Company") and shall be subject to the same prorations, reductions, deductions, adjustments and computations as is Producer's record royalty. For the avoidance of doubt, such basic royalty shall be inclusive of all royalties (other than mechanical royalties) payable to Composer and all musicians and other persons granting rights or rendering services in connection with Masters hereunder. In addition, Lender shall not be paid or credited with record royalties or other sums in respect of any exploitation of the Masters for which Producer does not receive payment or credit. Neither Lender nor Composer shall be entitled to any part of any advances or guarantees received by Producer from any Record Company.

The formula derived from the provision above is essentially this:

> **Basic Rate x SRLP – taxes – container deduction = Royalty Base Price**

"Basic Rate." The basic rate is a percentage spelled out in the contract applicable to certain categories of products in certain markets. For example, in the sample provision below, the basic rate for "topline" product (the current market stuff) sold in the United States is 9 percent. In Canada, the basic rate is 75 percent of the United States basic rate. For other countries the basic rate is 50 percent of the United States basic rate. The idea is to get to a base number that represents profit.

SRLP. SRLP stands for suggested retail list price, a term of art that means the price that the record label would like to see the product sold for.

Sales tax. The formula allows for the deduction from SRLP of sales and other applicable tax.

Container deduction. The container deduction is an amount approximating the actual cost of the manufacture of the recording.

Normal retail channels. The producer is not willing to give this formula in specialty markets (where the price is much less than SRLP). For example, record clubs sell product for much less than SRLP.

Record company contract prevails. The producer clarifies that, regardless, the formula in the producer's contract with the record label will trump the one in this contract, if it is different. The reason for this is obvious. Record companies may think up new tricks, which the producer will want to pass along to the composer.

Actual revenues. The producer in this case prudently clarifies that the composer will not be entitled to payment unless the producer actually receives payment.

No advances. Finally, it is critical that the producer clarifies that the composer will not receive any royalty compensation from any advance that the producer receives from any record label. The way this is drafted, however, leaves some doubt about whether or not the composer will be entitled to receive royalty payments during the recoupment-of-the-advance phase. This should be clarified. Obviously, the producer doesn't want to pay royalties during this phase, because the advance probably has been used toward the production of the movie. (See the discussion of recoupment of costs below).

Proration. Since a sound-track album might contain the works of several composers and artists, the producer clarifies that the composer who is a party to this agreement will only receive payment for the "selections" (sometimes referred to as "tracks") that person has composed. Thus, if there are ten selections on the album and the composer wrote five of them, the composer will receive five-tenths of the total royalties (or 50 percent). Try the formula out; it works.

> The otherwise applicable royalties payable to Lender above shall be prorated by the total number of record royalty bearing selections contained in the applicable Record (i.e., the applicable royalty shall be multiplied by a fraction, the numerator of which is the number of masters embodied on the applicable Record conducted by Composer and the denominator of which is the total number of record royalty bearing selections embodied in such Record).

Recoupment of costs. The composer doesn't get anything until the producer recoups the total cost of producing the master recording of the score and the master of any sound-track album (including reuse or new use fees, as applicable). Remember my note above about the advance? Well, this provision may indeed fix that problem. If the producer uses the advance to pay for the recording and mastering costs, then this provision allows the producer to recoup that advance without paying royalties to the composer.

> No record royalties shall be payable to Lender unless and until the Record Company or Producer, as the case may be, has recouped (i) all recording costs incurred in the recording of any Masters containing the Work, which for purposes of this provision shall be deemed to equal at least one-half ($\frac{1}{2}$) of the compensation payable to Lender pursuant to paragraph 4 hereof and (ii) the actual recording costs for converting the Masters for use on a sound-track album and/or other Records (including reuse or new use fees, and editing, transfer and so-called "sweetening" costs) from the record royalties otherwise payable to Lender hereunder. After such recoupment, the record royalties shall be paid prospectively (i.e., on all Records sold after such recoupment).

Direct payment. The operative word here is best efforts. As we have discussed before, in the law, the duty of best efforts in fact does require affirmative action on the part of the producer—that person can't just sit and watch events take their course. But best efforts also do not constitute a guarantee. Thus, the producer says he or she will try, but the producer is not guaranteeing that the record label will account to and pay the composer directly. If the record label won't pay directly (an accounting burden), the producer agrees to pay.

> Producer agrees to use its reasonable efforts to cause the Record Company to account for and pay Composer's record royalties directly to Lender, and if a Record Company agrees in writing to so account directly to Lender, Producer shall be relieved of such obligations hereunder and Lender shall look solely to such Record Company for such record royalties. Should a Record Company not agree to directly account to Lender, Producer shall render accountings and accompanying record royalty payments to Lender within thirty (30) days after Producer's receipt of corresponding accountings and record royalty payments from said Record Company; provided that, no such accounting shall be required for any periods in which no Record Royalties are due to Lender.

Audit rights. The composer, along with all other parties who have the right to receive licensing revenues, will want the right to audit the records of the party responsible for paying such revenues. The producer wants to make sure that the audit right doesn't turn into a huge burden of time and money. Thus, the producer imposes some restrictions and ground rules. For example, if the composer gets a statement and doesn't complain about it for a year, then the time for complaining is over. Audits have to be done on advance notice during normal business hours at the place where the records are normally kept. The composer is also limited to a two-year period to bring an action based on a certain statement.

Except to the extent that Lender or Composer objects by written notice received by Producer within one (1) year after a specific statement is rendered to Lender, an accounting rendered hereunder shall constitute an account stated, and shall be final and binding between Lender and Composer and Producer. Lender, or a certified public accountant acting on Lender's behalf, may examine Producer's books and records with respect to a specific statement concerning the Score or the Masters once during the one-year period following the rendition of such accounting. Such examination shall be conducted upon reasonable advance notice, during normal operating hours, at the office at which such books and records are regularly maintained. No action or proceeding may be brought with respect to a specific accounting statement or the period to which it relates more than two (2) years after such accounting statement is rendered. For the purpose of calculating such time periods, Lender shall be deemed to have received an accounting statement when due unless Producer receives written notice of non-receipt from Lender within sixty (60) days thereafter. However, Lender's failure to give such notice shall not affect Lender's right to receive such statement (and payment, if applicable) after such sixty-day period. If Producer shall make an overpayment to Lender for any reason, Lender shall repay such overpayment to Producer promptly following Producer's request therefor or Producer may deduct such overpayment from future amounts due to Lender and/or pursuant to this agreement or any other agreement.

Rerecording restriction. The composer agrees, in this case, not to produce or rerecord the score or any part of it (or allow anyone else to do the same) for five years following the movie's release. This protects the producer from having to compete with the composer over the music that the producer paid for.

Lender represents, warrants and agrees, and shall cause Composer to represent, warrant and agree, that Composer shall not produce or rerecord or authorize the production or rerecording of the Score or any part thereof for any third party within five (5) years following the later of the initial release date of the Picture or the initial commercial release of a Record hereunder.

INSURANCE

Errors and omissions (E&O) insurance.

The E&O insurance policy covers problems with chain of title and violations of publicity and other rights. It is, therefore, important. What if the book you optioned wasn't really written by the purported author? What if you thought you had cleared the rights to a given musical composition, only to find out that some third party had a claim related to that composition? What if you obtained permission from a major studio to use a film clip in your movie, but forgot to obtain the permission of the persons who appear in the clip? An E&O insurance policy is designed to cover problems like these.

Applying for E&O insurance. The insurance companies that write E&O policies are experts at what this risk entails. Therefore, the application to obtain an E&O policy reads like a review course of the things that we have been discussing relative to chain of title. The insurer looks (or rather has its law firm look) at the application for potential problems. If the problems are too severe, the policy may exclude certain types of risks or the application might be rejected outright.

"Clearance procedures." Some applications require the producer to hire an attorney to examine the insurer's clearance procedures and declare the actual steps taken in connection with the production as adequate. A sample list of clearance procedures covers the points that we have been talking about in this book, so let's take a look for the sake of review:[7]

Script clearance. As discussed above, the script needs to be read with an eye to avoiding material that is defamatory, invades privacy, or in other ways gives rise to a cause of action by some third party. (See discussion above.)

> The script should be read prior to commencement of production to eliminate matter, which is defamatory, invades privacy or is otherwise potentially actionable.

Monitoring. Clearance of the screenplay alone will not avoid all the problems that might arise. Remember the trademark issues and other issues discussed above that might arise during the filming or postproduction.

> Applicant and its counsel should continuously monitor the production at all stages, from inception through final cut, with a view to eliminating material which could give rise to a claim.

Copyright report for published works. If the work has been published (like a novel or other work that has been released into the general stream of commerce), the insurer will insist on a formal copyright report (both domestic and foreign) being obtained from Thomson & Thomson or a similar service. This report will identify the validity of foreign and domestic copyrights, including required renewals. If the published work is a completed film, the copyright report should also include any underlying work (such as a published novel or original screenplay).

> Unless work is an unpublished original based on any other work, a copyright report must be obtained. Both domestic and foreign copyrights and renewal rights should be checked. If a completed film is being acquired, a similar review should be made on copyright and on any copyrighted underlying property.

Chain of title for unpublished original screenplays; submissions. For original screenplays that are unpublished, the applicant producer will need to describe the chain of title from the basic idea, sequence of events, and characters. Remember our discussion about submissions? The insurer wants to know if you accept submissions and, if you do, whether or not you have received any similar properties. If you have, the insurer wants you to explain why you think the submittor isn't going to make a claim. (If you use a standard submissions agreement—discussed on page 22—you won't have to worry about this.)

> If the script is an unpublished original, the origins of the work should be ascertained—basic idea, sequence of events and characters. It should be ascertained if submissions of any similar properties have been received by the applicant and, if so, the circumstances as to why the submitting party may not claim theft or infringement should be described in detail.

Title report. The insurer will insist on a final title report (which you can also obtain from Thomson & Thomson) before the final title goes on the movie.

Prior to final title a Title Report should be obtained.

Dealing with real people. As discussed above, the producer and the producer's lawyer must obtain written releases from persons who appear in the movie or explain why the releases are not needed. (This makes you happy that your talent agreements have been signed and delivered, right?)

> Whether production is fictional (and location is identifiable) or factual, it should be made certain that no names, faces or likenesses of any recognizable living persons are used unless written releases have been obtained. Release is unnecessary if the person is part of a crowd scene or shown in a fleeting background. Telephone books or other sources should be checked when necessary. Releases can only be dispensed with if the Applicant provides the company with specific reasons, in writing, as to why such releases are unnecessary and such reasons are accepted by the Company. The term "living persons" includes thinly disguised versions of living persons who are readily identifiable because of identity of other characters or because of the factual, historical or geographical setting.

Right to edit, modify, etc. All rights acquisition agreements, including writer's agreements, talent agreements and personal releases, composer agreements, and so forth must obtain a provision allowing the producer to edit, modify, and amend in any way he or she wants. (This is why we talk about having this right.)

> All releases must give the applicant the right to edit, modify, add to and/or delete material, juxtapose any part of the film with any other film, change the sequence of events or of any questions posed and/or answers, fictionalize persons or events, including the release and to make any other changes in the film that the applicant deems appropriate.

Minors. Producers have to be on the lookout for minors and, if minors are to be used, they must follow the court procedures to have the contracts affirmed by a court or otherwise as required by law. (Remember the movie *Liar Liar*?)

If a minor, consent must be obtained to be legally binding.

Music. You must obtain the sync and performance licenses and master use licenses. (Aren't you glad you took care of all of this?)

If music is used, the applicant must obtain all necessary synchronization and performance licenses from composers or copyright proprietors. Licenses must also be obtained on prerecorded music.

More about chain of title. Get those rights agreements and connect the chain.

Written agreements must exist between the applicant and all creators, authors, writers, performers and any other persons providing material (including quotations from copyrighted works) or on-screen services.

Property. You've got to get the location and property releases.

If distinctive locations, buildings, businesses, personal property or products are filmed, written releases should be secured. This is not necessary if non-distinctive background use is made of real property.

Independent sources. If you don't get the rights to a book about an actual event (one that has been cleared for copyright issues), then you've got to get independent original sources—so-called primary sources (newspapers, contemporaneous diaries, etc.).

If the production involves actual events, it should be ascertained that the author's sources are independent and primary (contemporaneous newspaper reports, court transcripts, interviews and witnesses, etc.) and not secondary (another author's copyrighted work, autobiographies, copyrighted magazine articles, etc.).

A final check of the script and the film. As part of the E&O insurance application, you will agree to continue your review of the script updates and the film to see if any problems pop up during the shooting.

Shooting script and rough cuts should be checked, if possible, to assure compliance of all of the above. During photography, persons might be photographed on location, dialogue added or other matter included, which was not originally contemplated.

Uses. Each rights agreement must have specific language allowing the producer to exploit the movie in any way he or she wants to.

If the intent is to use the production to be insured on videotapes, videocassettes, videodiscs or other new technology, rights to manufacture, distribute and release the production should be obtained, including the above rights, from all writers, directors, actors, musicians, composers and others necessary therefor, including the proprietors of underlying materials.

Film clips. Remember the problems with film clips. Insurance companies also know about these problems and insist on clearance procedures being followed.

Film clips are dangerous unless licenses and authorizations for the second use are obtained from the owner of the clip or party authorized to license the same, as well as licenses from all persons rendering services in or supplying material contained in the film clip; e.g., underlying literary rights, performances of actors or musicians. Special attention should be paid to music rights as publishers are taking the position that new synchronization and performance licenses are required.

Right of publicity. Where there is a lot of fictionalization about real persons, living or dead, releases must be obtained from such persons or their estates. If the screenplay is 100 percent fiction, then all the names should be fictional.

Aside from living persons, even dead persons (through their personal representatives or heirs) have a "right of publicity," especially where there is considerable fictionalization. Clearances should be obtained where necessary. Where the work is fictional in whole or in part, the names of all characters must be fictional. If for some special reason particular names need not be fictional, full details must be provided to the company in an attachment to the applications.

Happy litigants and close calls. If someone has sued in the past, that person is likely to sue again (insurers espouse the lightning strikes twice theory). You should avoid that person. The insurer will also encourage the producer to avoid close calls and difficult circumstances. A good insurance broker will help you manage these risks.

Consideration should be given to the likelihood of any claim or litigation of any claim of litigation. Is there a potential claimant portrayed in the production who has sued before or is likely to sue again? Is there a close copyright or other legal issue? Is the subject matter of the production such as to require difficult and extensive discovery in the event of a necessity to defend? Are sources reliable? The above factors should be considered in your clearance procedures and recommendations.

Cast insurance.

Producers can buy insurance for the cast. Actors are human. They get sick and are injured. We've already talked about the cost of gearing up for principal photography and have taken a conceptual peek at the trouble that would arise if an actor playing a major role didn't (or couldn't) show up. The insurer will insure this risk for a fee.

Faulty stock; negative film, and videotape; camera and processing, etc.

Suppose you have just finished day nine of a twenty-day shoot. Then suppose, as your crew gets ready for dailies, it is discovered that a roll of film used in camera two was ground up in the camera's gears amounting to a total loss of the material shot on that roll. Who's going to pay for the cost of reshooting the lost scenes? Insurance companies will sell insurance to cover this risk as well.

Workers' compensation and liability insurance.

Some states require that the producer procure workers' compensation insurance to cover injuries and other problems that arise on the job. In addition, producers customarily purchase property damage and liability insurance to cover damage to equipment, automobiles, buildings, locations and the like, as well as injury to persons working and standing around on the sets. This insurance can also be purchased.

Completion bond.

We have talked about completion bonds above. A completion bond is an insurance policy that insures the completion of the movie—which includes bringing it in on time and on budget. The companies that issue this type of insurance play an active role in monitoring the progress of the production of the movie and any problems that might occur along the way. In the worst case (for example, if the movie falls substantially behind schedule or the production goes substantially over budget), the terms of the insurance typically give the insurance company the power to come in and take steps to get the movie done (even if that means cutting the movie without certain scenes, for example).

BOOK SIX

MAKING MONEY WITH THE MOVIE

You are in the theater. The lights are dim. Your loyal friends and family, who have believed in you and stuck with you through your travails, are there. Members of the cast and crew are there. Your dream has become a reality. After many months of hard work and careful planning your great idea has been transformed into moving images on the silver screen. I know you are exuberant, but why aren't you feeling relaxed? I think I know what's on your mind. You are thinking about what's coming up next. You are thinking about the mountain of money (somebody else's money) that was spent on your making your dream. And, most important, you are thinking about getting that money back. Well, here is where we talk about how that happens. Every movie has a life cycle that ideally begins with the exhibition of the movie in theaters. For certain types of movies, merchandise licensing and the sale of sound-track albums is possible. The next stops on the journey are home video and pay-per-view. The movie then makes a stop on free television. There might be print publication and even stage play opportunities. Interactive games and the Internet have opened up new vistas and have lengthened the life cycle of motion pictures.

Theatrical Distribution

THEATRICAL DISTRIBUTION BASICS

We now reach one of the culmination points of your dream: the distribution of your movie in theaters—the crown jewel of movie exploitation. This marks the point when your great idea reaches the silver screen with millions of adoring fans standing in line to see and enjoy it, and laying down their hard-earned money for the privilege. This is where the marketing machine goes into full gear, spending all that P&A money to get the word out. The critics will write—good things, I hope—about your movie. The "hype" will start to build.

The importance of theatrical distribution.
Why is theatrical distribution so important? It is a long-standing tradition that theatrical distribution starts the distribution cycle. This is where the movie critics start writing about the movie and where the main cast and director start to make appearances on behalf of the movie. This is a convenient spot to start spending advertising dollars. The theatrical release says, more or less, that this picture is worthy to be counted among the other pictures that played in the local theaters (avoiding the stigma of straight to video and other less-than-worthy projects). Theatrical distribution in the United States, moreover, is the foundation of international acceptability. Foreign distributors will tell you that theatrical distribution in the United States will enhance the value of the film's foreign appeal. I have no

statistics or other data to back up these notions—but I can confidently tell you that most people in the industry think this way. Therefore, get a domestic distribution deal.

Timing of the theatrical distribution deal.

Even though we waited to talk about distribution until we arrived at the point in the process where it occurs, there are several places in the making of a film where you can set the deal: after the treatment is written, after the screenplay is finished, and after the movie is produced.

After the treatment is written. As we have discussed, in today's world of making movies, it is highly unlikely (try virtually impossible) that a distributor will agree to take the movie on the basis of a treatment only. Well, if your treatment is written by Michael Crichton or John Grisham—maybe.

After the screenplay is finished. Once the screenplay is finished, it is possible to put together an attractive package and set it up with a distributor for financing, production, and distribution. As we have noted above, given the realities of today, this is the ideal time from the production financier's point of view at least in which to get this commitment in place.

After the movie is produced. The other possibility is when the movie is finished. This is the most risky point in time for the investor. As you know by now, assuming you believe what you've read above, many things can happen along the way to affect the final product. You might run out of money and not be able to do those killer special effects you have imagined. Your actors might not capture their roles. Your director might turn your masterpiece into something less. In sum, at the end of the rainbow, there may not be a distributor willing to take the picture. If that is the case, your investors have just bought themselves a very expensive, one-of-a-kind, home video.

On the other hand—and it does happen—the stars might line up and everything could go as planned or better and you could have a real gem on your hands. If this happens, you can take your movie to one of the many film markets, submit it to a film festival or shop it around town. If you get more than one bid (the beginning of a bidding war), you may be in the driver's seat to get a great deal from a substantial distributor. You'll be a hero. The odds are not with you, but it could happen.

The distribution world.

As we discussed in the context of raising money, distribution can be divided into two parts: domestic distribution and foreign distribution. Within each of these areas, there are major and minor players, each with their own set of strengths and weaknesses.

Domestic distribution. Domestic distribution, at least from my current viewpoint, means North America (the United States and Canada and their respective territories). One used to be able to say that this territory represented the majority of a movie's expected worldwide revenues. It is now thought that North America represents 30 to 50 percent of the worldwide box office of any given movie. It is true, however, that North America remains the most important single territory. Because North America is the center of the film world (in other words, no other single area represents a larger source of revenues and because the world's most important distribution companies are located in North America), the distribution worthiness of the film outside North America is often determined by the existence and quality of a North American distribution deal.

Foreign distribution. Technically, the territories outside North America constitute the foreign market. However, within the foreign market, there are some important established territories and some that are merely emerging. The major markets outside of North America are Japan, Germany, the United Kingdom, France, Italy, Benelux (Belgium, The Netherlands, and Luxembourg), Scandinavia (Denmark, Norway, Sweden, and Iceland), Spain and New Zealand/Australia. It is generally thought that these areas represent 40 to 60 percent of the world market. This is not to say that there are no other important areas. Latin America is growing in size and importance. Taiwan, Hong Kong, Korea, and, of course, China represent huge potential sources of revenues. (China, for example, is said to have at least 150 million people with incomes that rival the middle classes in Japan and the United States). Eastern Europe and Russia also represent opportunities. Indonesia, Malaysia, Singapore, and India are also potentially large markets. In a real way, the lack of importance of some territories is due mainly to factors that are political in nature. At the current time, China imposes a quota system on movies being imported from outside its borders. India, which produces more movies than any other country in the world, is protective of its local industry.

The independent film world can be more or less defined by surveying the attendees at a series of markets throughout the world. The

Cannes Film Festival (in Cannes, France), the American Film Market (in Santa Monica, California), the Sundance Film Festival (in Park City, Utah), the Toronto Film Festival (in Toronto, Canada), the Berlin Film Festival (in Berlin, Germany), and so forth, are magnets for the world's major film distribution companies and producers from this industry.

The majors. Depending on the winds of fortune, there are five or six major distribution companies. All of them are located in the Los Angeles area[1] (fondly referred to throughout the world as Hollywood—even though, technically, only one, Paramount Pictures, is actually located in Hollywood proper). Each major studio has an interesting history, reaching back to the early 1900s, and each can claim numerous classic films, larger-than-life stars, auteur directors, and visionary producers that provided the foundation of what the movie industry is today.

The major studios have gone (and are going through) many changes. In the Golden Age, the studios were more-or-less self-contained fiefdoms that financed, developed, produced, and distributed their own movies. Each studio hired its own contract writers, actors, directors, and producers. They built their own lots. They owned their own equipment. The independent filmmaking community existed, even back then, but the studio system reigned supreme.

Even in the midst of the studio system's glory, there were significant movements opposing the power of the studios, including the experiment of United Artists—a studio formed by three of the most powerful actors of the time (Douglas Fairbanks, Mary Pickford, and Charlie Chaplain) and director D. W. Griffith, but the studio system survived primarily intact until the early 1950s. Even United Artists, originally a distribution company dedicated to the release of independent films, eventually took on the trappings of the studio system. Reasonable minds can differ on what really brought about the dramatic shift in power from the studios controlling everything in the Golden Age to the balance of power that exists today, but the fact is that certain talent (and the agencies that represent them) share the power with the studios who have decided that distributing films (which includes controlling the theatrical, television, video, and other exploitation rights) is the best business to be in.

In addition to a shift in the system, there has been a dramatic shift over time in the fortunes of the actual corporate entities that dominate the business. MGM, for example, was the undisputed king of movieland during the height of the studio system. Today, according to many, it may be a stretch to list MGM as one of the major distributors (which is nevertheless, for historical means, what I have done below, even though it appears at this writing that it will be acquired by Sony Pictures).

It is also worth noting that, although all of the major studios are located in California in the United States, half of them are now owned by large multinational firms from a variety of countries. Sony Pictures (formerly Columbia Pictures) is currently owned by the Japanese electronics giant Sony Corporation. Twentieth Century Fox is owned by News Corporation, the corporate vehicle of Australian mogul Rupert Murdoch. Universal Pictures, at least partially back in U.S. hands (General Electric, which also owns one of the three major U.S. television networks, NBC), was owned in rapid succession by a Japanese company (Matsushita Electric), a Canadian company (Seagram), and a French company (Vivendi), which still owns a stake in the company.

A highly relevant point for all producers to take note of is the affiliations that the major studios have. As a matter of course, studios acquire formerly independent production companies with successful track records (for example, Disney acquired Miramax Films and Warner Bros. acquired New Line Cinema). Alternatively, studios may offer high-level producers housekeeping deals—which may take the form of granting the producer an office on or near the studio lot and/or some discretionary development funding. The studio will ask for a first look at the producer's product, and the producer benefits from the housekeeping arrangement—which means the producer must offer the film to the studio first. Some producers may even have an output deal, where the studio promises to distribute all or a certain number of the movies made by such producers. These affiliations, however structured, are how the studio guarantees a predictable source of movies to feed the studio's distribution pipeline.

In introducing the studios below, I have tried to give a brief flavor of each studio's beginning, its claim to glory, its affiliations, and how it approaches distribution. Please keep in mind, however, that I have not tried in every case to be 100 percent comprehensive; these things change rapidly as a rule. Still, you should have an idea of how the distribution world works.

Currently, the major distribution companies are:

MGM/UA. The studios began in 1915 as Triangle Pictures, which merged with Marcus Loew's Metro in the early 1920s. It became Metro-Goldwyn-Mayer in 1924, with the combination of Metro, producer Samuel Goldwyn, and producer Louis B. Mayer, who ran the studio throughout the bulk of its glory years (though many historians credit the illustrious producer genius Irving Thalberg for MGM's greatness). During the height of Hollywood's Golden Age, MGM was the most powerful studio, renowned for the glossy style of its films, complete with lavish wardrobes, high-priced sets, and its unmatched stable of superstars. MGM used to brag that it had "more stars than there are in the heavens." [2]

During its heyday, MGM boasted an average of one film a week. In 1939, MGM gave the world two of the most beloved films in history: *Gone with the Wind* and *The Wizard of Oz*.[3]

MGM did not transition well into the 1950s with the onslaught of television. A run of lackluster films (with the notable exception of the James Bond 007 series of movies) made MGM vulnerable to a series of corporate takeovers. The devastating blows to MGM's heritage were the sell off of the studio's back lots to housing developers and, more significantly, the sale of the bulk of its famous film library (including *Gone with the Wind, The Wizard of Oz,* and its famous musical titles) to mogul Ted Turner, in 1986. In 1990, the bulk of its historic studio facilities were sold to Sony Pictures Entertainment and are now home to Columbia Pictures and TriStar Pictures, two of Sony's divisions.

In 1981, MGM and the equally troubled United Artists (the studio that was formed early in the history of Hollywood by a group of antistudio celebrities) merged. Today the company is known as MGM/UA. But even the combined entity is substantially weaker than any of the other distributors listed as majors in this section. Its most important current assets appear to be James Bond and the famed Leo the Lion trademark (which appeared first on a silent film in 1928). In the fall of 2004, Sony Pictures (together with several other companies: Comcast Corp., Providence Equity, Texas Pacific Group, and DLJ Merchant Banking Partners) signed an agreement to acquire stock of MGM for $2.85 billion plus assumption of about $2 billion of MGM's debt. MGM will continue to operate as a private company, although Sony has said it plans to do co-productions with MGM and will distribute its films and television programs.

Twentieth Century Fox. Founded in 1913 by William Fox, the studio began by producing the famous Movietone Newsreels even before it moved to its current location. Fox opened its studios in Century City in 1928, on land that used to be the personal ranch of Western movie star Tom Mix. Seven years later, Fox merged with Twentieth Century Pictures (which had been founded in 1933 by Darryl F.

Zanuck, after he left Warner Brothers), and the company became Twentieth Century Fox in 1935.[4]

In 1950, Twentieth Century Fox's epic, *All About Eve,* was nominated for more Academy Awards (fourteen) than any other motion picture in the history of Hollywood (although it actually won "only" six Oscars, including Best Picture). In the early 1960s, the lavishly produced *Cleopatra,* with superstars Richard Burton and Elizabeth Taylor, almost sank Fox, which survived only by selling off a major part of its studio lot to developers, who turned it into the modern-day Century City. But Fox made a comeback in 1965 with *The Sound of Music,* which was at the time the most successful movie in actual dollar terms ever made.[5]

In 1977, Fox released *Star Wars,* launching its creator, George Lucas, into the stratosphere. Its two sequels and three prequels have made the *Star Wars* series one of the most valuable properties in movie history.[6] In 1997, Fox Studios (in a coproduction deal with Paramount) scored, at the time, the biggest box office hit of all time, with *Titanic.*

The studio is now owned by Rupert Murdoch's News Corporation, which also owns the Fox Television Studio. Fox has several divisions, including Fox Fine Line (which specializes in the art film genre) and Fox Searchlight (which specializes in lower-budget films). In addition to being one of the major United States distributors, Fox has its own international distribution system.

Paramount Pictures. Adolph Zukor, a one-time partner of Marcus Loew (one of the original partners of MGM), started his production company, Famous Players, in 1912 in a rented horse barn near Sunset and Vine. In 1926, Zukor merged Famous Players with a national distribution company, Paramount Pictures, and later brought in producer Jesse L. Lasky. Another merger brought in Sam Katz, a marketing guru, who insisted that the company's name, Paramount-Famous-Lasky, be shortened to Paramount. In 1928, Paramount under Zukor grew to over 1,200 theaters. The year before, Paramount had hired David O. Selznick, the young genius from MGM, to help with the company's production plans.

The list of landmark motion pictures filmed by Paramount Pictures begins with the classic silent films such as *The Sheik* with Rudolph Valentino, in 1921, and includes the first movie to ever win an Academy Award for Best Picture, *Wings,* in 1927. Paramount was the home of such early superstars as Mae West, W. C. Fields, and Mary Pickford, as well as directors, Cecil B. DeMille and D. W. Griffith.

A major studio in its own right, RKO Studios was once located at the southwest corner of the Paramount lot. Begun by Joseph P. Kennedy, the studio produced countless hits, including the classic, *It's a Wonderful Life,* nine Fred Astaire/Ginger Rogers musicals, the original *King Kong, Bringing Up Baby* (with Cary Grant and Katharine Hepburn), Alfred Hitchcock's *Notorious,* and Orson Welles's masterpiece, *Citizen Kane* (which is often mentioned as the most critically acclaimed movie of all time). The decline of RKO began in 1948 when it was bought by eccentric tycoon Howard Hughes, who eventually sold it to Lucille Ball and Desi Arnaz in 1959, who made it part of their Desilu Productions. Eventually, the RKO/Desilu property was taken over by its larger neighbor, Paramount Studios.

In later years, Paramount had major hits and has also had good luck with sequels, releasing the series of extremely popular *Star Trek* movies (starting in 1979 and based on the enduring television series), as well as the *Raiders of the Lost Ark* Indiana Jones adventures and the seemingly endless *Friday the 13th* horror series.

Tom Cruise's production company, Cruise/Wagner, is housed on the Paramount lot. Academy Award winners *Forrest Gump* and *Braveheart* were Paramount releases and Paramount shared the honors, and the profits, with Fox on *Titanic.*

In 1994, the entire studio was bought by media giant Viacom, for $10 billion. In 1999, Viacom bought the CBS television network. And in 2002, Viacom bought the nearby KCAL studios. Paramount distributes its films internationally through UIP, a joint venture among Paramount, Universal, and MGM.

Universal Studios. In 1912, German immigrant Carl Laemmle, created the Universal Film Manufacturing Company to defy the trust—the Motion Picture Patents Company controlled by Thomas Edison. In 1915, Laemmle finished construction on Universal City, a giant hilltop studio, on the site of a chicken farm. In 1918, just barely out of high school, Irving Thalberg joined Universal (later, Thalberg was a major influence on the spectacular rise of MGM).

From the outset, Laemmle shunned the "first-run" market (big-budget prestige films) in favor of low-budget pictures that could be produced in quantity. Universal was responsible for the development of the original classic horror films, such as *Frankenstein* (in 1931), with Boris Karloff, *Dracula* (in 1931), with Bela Lugosi, and *The Wolf Man* (in 1941), with Lon Chaney, Jr. The studio also produced comedies, such as the famous series of movies with Bud Abbott and Lou Costello.

Among the major studios in the Golden Age, Universal remained primarily known as a low-budget, genre-picture film studio. When it failed to keep pace with other studios, a number of its stars and creative talent (including Valentino, Bette Davis, Busby Berkeley, Elizabeth Taylor, and James Dean)[7] left to join different motion picture companies.

Universal's current image is different. In 1969, Universal signed a talented young director named Steven Spielberg. Getting his start with a made-for-TV movie called *Duel,* Spielberg turned out an incredible series of blockbusters beginning in 1975 with *Jaws. Schindler's List* won Spielberg an Academy Award for Best Director and Best Picture in 1994. Spielberg's *ET: The Extraterrestrial* was the box office mark for several years (until *Titanic* won the spot for Fox and Paramount). Spielberg's *Jurassic Park* and *Lost World,* based on Michael Crichton's best-selling novels, are two of the most lucrative features ever made. In 1994, Spielberg joined Jeffrey Katzenberg (formerly of Disney) and music industry giant David Geffin to form DreamWorks.

Imagine Films is one of the primary housekeeping arrangements in the Universal system and Brian Grazer and Ron Howard, of Imagine Films, have established themselves as premier filmmakers with movies like *Apollo 13* and *A Beautiful Mind,* to name just two.

Until recently, Universal was owned by MCA Inc., which was purchased in 1990 by the Japanese electronics giant, Matsushita Electric, and sold in 1995 to the Seagram Company. In June 2000, the Seagram Company (including Universal) was purchased by France's Vivendi for $33.7 billion. In May 2004, Vivendi Universal Entertainment was merged into the National Broadcasting Company, owned by General Electric, to create NBC Universal. Universal's international distribution is carried out by UIP.

Warner Bros. Warner Bros. was founded in 1922 by four brothers: Jack, Sam, Harry, and Albert Warner. The siblings never seemed to get along with each other, but Warner Bros. Studios managed to flourish and produced some of the most memorable movies in the history of Hollywood's Golden Age. Although slow to start, in 1927, Warner Bros. upstaged the more established companies like MGM and Paramount by producing the world's first "talkie" (a movie with sound) starring Al Jolson, *The Jazz Singer.* The risks involved in pursuing sound films proved to be well worth it and Warners propelled itself into the majors.

In contrast to the colorful musicals of MGM, Warner Bros. made black-and-white, gritty, and realistic dramas. The studio put out numerous gangster films, such as *Little Caesar* (with Edward G. Robinson), *The Public Enemy* (with James Cagney), and *I Am a Fugitive from a Chain Gang*. Humphrey Bogart starred in Warner classic film noir such as *The Maltese Falcon*, *The Big Sleep*, and *Casablanca*.

In later years, Warner Bros. seemed to continue its gritty drama tradition with Marlon Brando in *A Streetcar Named Desire*, James Dean in *Rebel Without a Cause*, Judy Garland in *A Star Is Born*, Paul Newman in *Hud*, Warren Beatty in *Bonnie and Clyde*, and Clint Eastwood in *Dirty Harry*.[8]

In more recent years, Warner made a series of acquisitions. It acquired New Line Cinema, which was at the time a so-called major "mini." New Line's recent addition to movie history *The Lord of the Rings* trilogy makes that move look pretty smart. In 1995, Warner purchased Turner Broadcasting, Inc, which gave Warner control of one of the most prized possessions in the industry—the MGM film library (which includes such classics as *Gone with the Wind* and *The Wizard of Oz*), both purchased from MGM by Turner in 1986. In the 1990s, Warner also aquired Castle Rock Entertainment and Village Road Show.

In January 2000, Warner Bros. parent, Time Warner, Inc. (which also owns and controls CNN and HBO cable services, and publishes *Time*, *People*, *Sports Illustrated*, *Entertainment Weekly*, and *Fortune* magazines), was purchased by America Online (AOL), in what was at the time the largest corporate merger in history at a reported cost of $163 billion. Warner Bros. has its own international distribution.

The Walt Disney Company. The Walt Disney Company was formed in 1923 by Walt Disney, one of the true icons of American culture and business,[9] and his brother Roy. The Disney brothers founded their company on the then-emerging art form of animation. In 1928, Disney Brothers produced a successful short film called *Steamboat Willie*, which featured the character Mickey Mouse—whose image is still the logo of the company. The culmination of the development of Disney's art came in 1937 with *Snow White*, the first full-length animated feature film. From the profits of that film, the Disney Studios were built in Burbank. The Disney animation franchise was built on *Snow White* and its progeny.[10]

After the founder's death in 1966, Disney struggled momentarily to find its future, but recovered eventually with a string of very successful animated features in the classic Disney style (*The Little Mermaid*, *Beauty and the Beast*, *Aladdin*, *The Lion King*, and others), as well as some live-action movies (such as *Flubber* and the *Honey, I*

Shrunk the Kids series). Disney, in collaboration with the CGI pioneer, Pixar, also scored with *Toy Story* (for two movies) and *Finding Nemo;* it has taken up the CGI revolution on its own (with efforts such as *Tarzan,* and *Monsters Inc.*).

Disney decided to depart from its pure family slate and make and distribute movies with a different demographic. It established Touch-stone Pictures and Hollywood Pictures, the latter of which is no longer with us. These companies produced some hit movies (such as *Pretty Woman*—where the Cinderella character is a prostitute). And in 1993, Disney executives really raised some eyebrows by acquiring Mi-ramax Films, which has produced some graphic, decidedly not family-friendly movies, such as, *Pulp Fiction* and *The Crying Game,* but which has also won Academy Awards with *The English Patient* and *Shakespeare in Love.*[11]

Disney has its own domestic and worldwide distribution through Walt Disney International and Buena Vista International.

Sony Pictures Entertainment. Columbia Pictures was originally founded in 1920 under the name of C.B.C. Sales Film Corporation by Joe Brandt and the brothers Jack and Harry Cohn (who later changed the company's name to Columbia in 1924). Harry Cohn was the studio's longtime president (until his death in 1958) and his brother Jack handled the successful distribution network from New York (although it was never able to purchase a theater chain like some of the other studios, such as Paramount, Universal, and MGM).

In its early years, Columbia had a reputation for producing low-budget westerns and comedies. In fact, it was the success of its B-westerns (especially those of Tim McCoy, Buck Jones, and Ken May-nard) and its serials *(Batman* and *Terry and the Pirates,* for example) that kept the company profitable during the Great Depression. The studio also seemed to have a knack for successful movie series, like the *Blondie* films, and those about the jewel thief, *Lone Wolf.*

The Three Stooges proved a valuable asset to the studio, as did the services of director Frank Capra, whom Columbia hired in the late twenties to direct many of the studio's comedies. In fact, it was Capra and his relatively large-budget production of *It Happened One Night,* starring Clark Gable (on loan from MGM) and Claudette Colbert (on loan from Paramount), that gave the studio its big break into Holly-wood respectability. In 1934, it became the first picture ever to win the "Big 5" Academy Awards, taking those for Best Picture, Actor, Actress, Director, and Screenplay.

Several other significant Capra films followed, including *Mr. Deeds*

Goes to Town with Gary Cooper and Jean Arthur, and *Mr. Smith Goes to Washington* with Arthur and Jimmy Stewart. Columbia also found profitable talents in director Howard Hawks and the witty, debonair Cary Grant, who contributed to several of the studio's successful screwball comedies like *The Awful Truth, Holiday,* and *His Girl Friday.* Rita Hayworth was to Harry Cohn the studio's biggest star, however, and her pinup value during World War II helped the studio through what proved to be some rather difficult times. After Frank Capra left the studio in 1939, the notoriously difficult Cohn had a difficult time finding quality directors. But Hayworth's musicals helped the studio through the forties.

By joining the trend toward television (it founded the television production subsidiary Screen Gems) and by backing various independent producers such as Elia Kazan, Fred Zinnemann, David Lean, and Otto Preminger, Columbia regained its stature during the 1950s.

After the deaths of the Cohn brothers in the late 1950s, successors Abe Schneider and Leo Jaffe took over leadership of the company and it continued to prosper. Hits of the 1960s included *Lawrence of Arabia, A Man for All Seasons,* Spencer Tracy and Katharine Hepburn's last picture together, *Guess Who's Coming to Dinner,* the musical Best Picture winner *Oliver!* and the surprise blockbuster *Easy Rider,* which cost Columbia less than $500,000 to produce but brought in more than $25 million in gross box office revenue.

Columbia did not do well during the 1970s and even sold its Gower Street lot in a cost-cutting measure, moving some of its operations to Burbank. In 1982, it was purchased by The Coca-Cola Company, which pumped in needed funds. Coca-Cola even launched a new motion picture studio called Tri-Star Pictures, and in 1987 the two were merged to form Columbia Pictures Entertainment, Inc. After only a few minor successes however (*Ghostbusters,* in 1984, being one), Coca-Cola decided to get out of the movie business, and in 1989 the studio was bought by the Sony Corporation of Japan, which officially renamed the parent company of Columbia and Tri-Star, Sony Pictures Entertainment.[12] It was recently announced that Sony reached a deal with Kirk Kerkorian, the major stockholder of MGM/UA, to acquire on some basis the new smaller studio.

Foreign studios and distributors. Foreign distribution companies are in an interesting position. During the last fifteen or so years, the major studios have moved in one way or another to establish their own foreign distribution capabilities. This has created an interesting opportunity for independent producers. In order to compete for first-run American product, foreign distributors have had to keep their eye on Hollywood and are always on the lookout for properties that might have a chance to do well in the United States and carry over to the foreign market in question.

That's the good news, but there is bad news. Apparently, the foreign market for American Films is driven by famous talent. Thus, in order to attract foreign distributors your film should have an amazing package (in which case you might be able to attract a major studio).

Basic distribution points.

With the status of your project and the various players in mind, you are ready to start thinking about putting a deal together. The basic concepts are as follows:

Release pattern. There are several approaches to releasing a movie; I will talk about four: general, platform, art house, and "four-wall."

General release. A general release is a broad release on a certain date. For example, you want to tell someone in the industry about the release of your movie. You say, *"The Quest* is being released in the major markets on November 8 on two thousand screens." The term major markets refers to the size of the geographical area. Los Angeles, Chicago, New York, San Francisco, Houston, Toronto, and other large cities would be considered major demographic markets. The term screens refers to the number of motion picture theater screens that will be used for the release. Gone are the days where the movie theater has only one screen; multiplex theaters have multiple screens. It is possible, of course, for a movie to be shown on more than one screen in a single multiplex theater. There are roughly thirty-five thousand screens in America, including drive-in theaters. The widest releases—reserved for large-scale movies, such as the *Star Wars* series and motion pictures starring Tom Cruise—are in the three thousand- to six thousand-screen range.

Platform release. Some movies are not given a broad, general release. Rather, the distributor, in consultation with the producer sometimes, will select a certain market (or geographical area)—a platform—from which to build a base audience. Suppose a movie that is seeking a family audience is being released. The distributors might well open the movie in the South or other areas where family movies play well. Once a base is built (meaning once the distributor can show that the movie is attracting reasonable numbers—expressed in terms of a dollars-per-screen and average weekend per market box office), the distributor increases the size of the platform into a wider stream of release.

Art house. There are theaters across the land that cater to a certain type of audience—the lover of the so-called "art film." Actually, I tend to think of these films not so much as a separate genre of film but as films suited for a distinctive release pattern. *Shakespeare in Love* and other such movies distributed by Miramax Films, are examples of motion pictures that built their base in the art house circuit. These movies are generally speaking dramas (not action adventures), with relatively modest budgets. Certain foreign movies (such as *The English Patient* [United Kingdom], *Life Is Beautiful* [Italy], and *Shall We Dance* [Japan]) have found a mass audience from the platform of the art house circuit. Because of the success of Miramax and some of the films that began life in the art house theater, many studios have established art house distribution arms (although they may not refer to these films using this terminology). Sony Classics and Fox Fine Line, and of course Miramax, are examples of companies set up to handle these specialized distribution needs.

"Four-wall." The term "four-wall" is derived from the fact that the distributor obtains the entire theater (all four walls of it), as opposed to the screen (one wall). In practice, "four-walling" means that the distributor (or the producer) makes a deal for one or a group of theaters in which to exhibit the movie. This release pattern can be one screen at a time or limited to one region (similar to a platform release). There have been successful runs with a "four-wall" approach.[13]

The nature of screens. There are screens and there are screens. Think of your own theater-going habits. There are the class "A" theaters where the movies getting the big hype always play. There are the "B" and "C" theaters as well. It is likely that the major studios will find their way onto the most popular screens and the independent features will find a home on these other screens. There are even the so-called "dollar" theaters; these are analogous to the bargain racks for CDs at your local record store.

Distribution costs (P&A).

The release of a movie ideally starts with an effective advertising campaign. The obvious techniques are television ads, trailers in the movie theater, posters on buses and at bus stops, newspaper ads, setting up a Web site for the movie, trotting out actors from the movie for appearances, etc. The distributor is typically responsible for marketing the film and paying the costs of the marketing. There are situations, however, where the producer may call the shots (see "Rent-a-Studio Deal" below). As discussed above, the P&A costs are normally recouped in first position, prior to the recoupment of the cost of the negative itself.

Theatrical rentals and distribution fees.

The distributors get paid for their efforts, of course. In a straight-forward independent distribution deal, where the distributor pays P&A, the distribution fee is said to range from 35 to 25 percent (although I have heard of both higher than 35 percent and lower than 25 percent) of theatrical rentals. We discussed the waterfall of revenues in detail above in our discussion of profit participation for talent. From the distributor's point of view, the discussion is fairly simple. A person buys a ticket at the movie theater for $10, let's say. That amount is box office or gross revenues. Then the theater takes its fee (roughly 50 to 60 percent) and gives the rest—called film rentals—to the distributor. The distributor keeps all of it until P&A has been recouped, plus a certain percentage for interest and overhead, and then deducts its distribution fee. Then, if the distributor put up the money to produce the movie, the distributor recoups the production amount, again plus interest and overhead. The rest—the net—goes to the producer.

In the case of a normal studio deal, where the distributor and the investor are one, the producer may be hired as an employee (and the distributor will own the copyright); if that is the case, he or she will get a salary—sometimes substantial—with a contract participation—usually amounting to zero (unless your name is Jerry Bruckheimer). In other words, recalling our irrigation analogy, the studio is the big farmer here. Even the producer will be left without water from the flow of postrelease revenues.

Leverage.

Many producers, therefore, try to position themselves against the major studios. They will try to leverage their position by raising the P&A money separately or by selling off one or two or all foreign territories, hoping to earn profits (referred to as overages—moneys earned after the advance has been recouped) out of those territories. Or, they might sell off some of the ancillary rights. This approach does not always work. Major studios often, as a matter of policy, refuse to take a picture unless they can do an all-rights deal, meaning that all the territories and all the rights are in the package. It seems to ebb and flow, however, and there always seems to be some opportunity to seek some type of leverage.

Rent-a-studio deal.

The so-called rent-a-studio deal is the highest form of leverage for the producer. In this case, the producer raises all the money needed to make, and in some cases advertise, the movie. The producer then goes to the distributor to request distribution services only. Some studios won't engage in rent-a-studio deals, but if there is enough money on the table, the producer can usually find a distributor to take the film.

The good points of a rent-a-studio deal are lower than normal distribution fees (I have seen them as low as 12 percent and as high as 20 percent) and control. Another, not insignificant point, is that distribution can usually be guaranteed in this case. Sure it costs more, but at least there will be a release and a chance to get money flowing in the positive direction.

But, alas, like all things, the rent-a-studio deal has its drawbacks as well. First, although studios do from time to time take these deals (because it makes good sense to feed the distribution machine with product), the movie must compete with product that the distributor owns. I could go into all kinds of inappropriate examples about a mother who elects to save her own child from a burning building before attempting to save the neighbor's child—but I don't need to: Between two movies, the studio is going to be tempted to put its own over yours. Moreover, the lower distribution fee can also be a drawback. I once had an honest conversation with a client regarding how to diplomatically raise the distribution fee offered by a distributor. The client was legitimately worried that the distributor would not be incentivized at 12 percent to distribute his movie.

Another point is control. Even where the producer is putting up the P&A money, the distributor will often insist on being in control of the media spend and other aspects of the distribution exercise, such as toy manufacturer, etc. Distributors cherish relationships with media purchasing companies and with manufacturers and so on. This can be good for you in some ways. But if you have hopes of getting your sleeves rolled up and involved in some of these strategic marketing decisions, perhaps you should think again.

All in all, a rent-a-studio deal has many problems and is not for the tenderfoot. Distribution is, like all endeavors in life, a highly specialized and complex activity. Because there are many facets, there are many chances for something to go wrong. But from the perspective of the investor, it is a lot better than no distribution at all.

DISTRIBUTION AGREEMENT

So here we go. We will examine a theatrical distribution agreement up close in all its glory. We will visit some of these general concerns in a specific way. I have deliberately chosen a hodgepodge of distribution agreement terms in order to illustrate a broader scope of issues. The producer in this illustration has more leverage than might normally be expected; an established distributor will win on many of these points.

I should note that many, if not most, of the issues arising from this agreement have already been discussed in the context of a foreign sales agent agreement—since those agreements are distribution agreements in fact. I will try to avoid too much duplication, but I have saved the more comprehensive discussion for here.

You should also keep in mind that the distribution agreement is the culmination of all the work that has gone on before. At this point, the finished movie and the material documentation that relates to it must be delivered.

The engagement.

The production company which owns the copyright in and to the movie (sometimes referred to as the "producer" and sometimes as the "owner") engages the services of the distributor. The agreement starts out by clarifying the following basic points:

The parties and major terms. The first part of the agreement summarizes who the parties to the agreement are and what their general intention is—here, the owner of or the person who controls the copyright licenses certain rights related to the movie in a selected territory for a certain duration of time based on terms and conditions to be specified.

Exclusivity in the "territory." In the agreement, the producer licenses to the distributor all normal distribution rights exclusively in the territory. This means that no one else (not even the licensor) may exploit the movie in any way there.

Conditioned on performance. Note also in the provision below that the validity of the license is expressly conditioned on the performance of the distributor. This seems like an obvious point, but it could be important. It might be possible for the distributor to argue that the license remains in force, even if the distributor breaches the contract. The producer will want to preserve the argument to move the film to another distributor or to make the license nonexclusive if there is a breach. Again, this provision shows the clout of this particular owner/licensor. This type of condition may be impossible for a first-time producer negotiating against an established distributor.

> This Distribution Agreement is made as of July 7, 2006, between The Quest Productions, LLC ("Producer") and Doughmestic Distribution, Inc. ("Distributor"). Subject to timely payment of all moneys due Licensor and Distributor's due performance of all other terms of this Agreement, Licensor licenses exclusively to Distributor, and Distributor accepts from Licensor, the feature motion picture entitled "The Quest" (the "Picture") only in the territory of North America (the "Territory" as more fully described below), subject to the terms and conditions of this Agreement.

Territory.
The term territory is very important in a distribution agreement. As we have discussed, the owner of a film can split the rights in various ways; splitting up the distribution rights by territory is a major deal point. In this agreement, the licensor is licensing the distribution right in North America, which refers to the United States of America and Canada, defined broadly to include their respective territories, ships, and air carriers. The North American territory remains the most important territory for films that hope to achieve international success, although it no longer represents half or more of the revenues of the movie as it did before.

> The word "Territory" refers to the United States of America and Canada, and their respective territories and possessions, including ships and international air carriers under their respective flags.

Term.
This license is designed for a finite term of years. In the illustration below, the producer is licensing the distribution rights for twelve years. If the producer has clout, a shorter period might be possible. If the distributor is a major, the license period will likely be longer (twenty to twenty-five years is not unheard of; in perpetuity is also

common). Generally, distributors will resist shorter periods of time. Distributors like to build libraries that they can exploit in various ways (for example, distributing videos and licensing television deals); they hire people to work these libraries. Trying to limit the rights to a short period will almost never be favored by a distributor. On the other hand, independent producers may be nervous about allowing their precious project to sit languishing in the hands of a distributor who does nothing with it.

> The License Period for the Picture shall commence on the date of this Agreement and end twelve (12) years from the Producer's delivery to Distributor of the Picture's first 35 mm print. Distributor agrees that it will not permit the distribution or exhibition of the Picture beyond the expiration of the Term.

General distribution rights.

Because licensors generally reserve to themselves all rights not specifically granted (see "Reserved Rights" on page 356), the distributor will be looking for a comprehensive list of specific licensed rights related to the movie, like the list below:

Exclusivity. It probably goes without saying, but the distributor will insist on receiving an exclusive set of rights in the defined territory. The distributor does not want to compete with anyone else in the exploitation of the movie.

Distribute and sublicense. Distributors will always want the right to distribute the movie directly, of course, and to license (technically, "sublicense") this same right to third parties. Perhaps the distributor has the capability to distribute the movie in the United States, for example, but has to sublicense the theatrical distribution rights to another distribution company (or an affiliate) incorporated in Canada. Licensing the right to sublicense is necessary, but may lead to problems discussed below.

All versions. The distributor and owner seek to clarify the scope of the distribution rights in various ways. Here the agreement provides that the distributor can distribute (and all the other verbs listed here) the movie and all "elements" and "rights" constituting or embodied in the picture. Moreover, the agreement clarifies that the producer can use any version (the airline version, for example, can be broadcast on television) and trailers (clips from the movies) can be used to make promotional advertisements.

> Producer hereby grants to Distributor for the Term in the Territory the sole and exclusive right and license to distribute, license, lease, rent, subdistribute, market, advertise and otherwise exploit in any manner whatsoever, in its sole discretion, the Picture and any and all elements thereof and rights therein including any and all versions and trailers thereof, in theatrical, television (all forms), video cassettes and disc media. Distributor must secure the prior written approval of Producer before attempting to sublicense the Picture for any term extending beyond the date on which this Agreement expires.

Media—future media and the Internet. This provision also clarifies the various media through which the movie can be exhibited. The distributor's lawyers will make this list as comprehensive as possible: theaters, on television, videocassettes, and disc media. This list is not totally comprehensive, however, as it is missing two common concepts, reflective of two important issues in current distribution deals:

Future media. Distributors with clout will insist on the addition of a clause that reads something like "and any other media, whether now or hereafter in existence." This phrase significantly expands the rights of the distributor by automatically including future media borne by technologies that may develop in the future. An example we have discussed before would be television—contracts drafted in the 1940s that included similar language would have included television when it became commercially available in the 1950s. Absent this language, television would not have been included. At the rate that technology is being developed today, this phrase underscores a major issue for distributors and owners alike. Distributors will insist on it; owners will fret about granting it.

Internet (broadband) and digital cinema—the concept of exclusivity. Time to wake up! Here comes an important discussion and one worthy of your attention. The established custom, as we have observed, is for owners to license (or grant) rights on an exlusive basis by territory. In this example, the distributor has the exclusive rights for North America. By implication, of course, the owner licenses exclusive rights to other distributors for other territories. Prior to the advent of the Internet, the major concern about the violation of exclusivity was overspill from the signals generated by broadcast satellites. For example, let's suppose the copyright owner licenses all rights for Japan to company JD, which sublicenses the television broadcasting rights to company JTV. That company uses a satellite to beam down the signal of the movie to homes in the territory of Japan. It is impossible of course, to shape the signal in the exact shape of Japan, so the signal also falls on parts of Taiwan and Korea. To counter this problem, the broadcaster scrambles the signal and sells or rents devices in Japan that unscramble the signal. The system is not perfect (some enterprising people from Taiwan or Korea might go to Japan and get their hands on a scrambler), but it works well enough and distributors and producers generally resolve this issue after discussion and compromise.

The Internet, however, poses a new challenge to the system of exclusivity by territory. The Internet (and the expansion by broadband technology of its power to allow for the exhibition of movies) knows few if any boundaries. Releasing a movie over the Internet in France theoretically makes that movie available in China (and elsewhere). Today, motion picture companies either refuse to allow exhibition over the Internet or make the license subject to an indefinite "freeze." For example, a motion picture company might agree to license the Internet rights, but might also restrict its use until the technology is developed that will contain the signal to the defined territory. So far as I know, the state of the art of "containment" technology hasn't thrilled many content owners, so in reality this provision amounts to a "no give" to the distributor. A better approach for the content owner would be, in my estimation, a most-favored-nation approach: The distributor says, "Okay, I give on the broadband grant, but if you do ever grant the rights to a third party you have to give them to me too on the same terms." This at least guards against a distributor in France distributing movies in Japan over the Internet while the exclusive distributor for the Japanese territory can't.

From the distributor's viewpoint, however, there is a significant countervailing concern. Suppose that the owner of the movie refuses to grant the Internet rights, as in our illustration above. The distributor, in that case, has a legitimate concern that the distributor's exclusivity will be violated if the Internet rights are used by the owner or some third party licensee of the owner. Thus, the distributor may insist, as a defensive move, that the owner refrain from using or sublicensing these rights or, alternatively, indemnify the distributor for a loss of exclusivity caused by the Internet broadcast of the movie.

Licensing beyond the term. Note that the distributor must get the producer's approval to enter into a sublicense beyond the term of this agreement.

Specific distribution rights.

The distributor will be looking for specific other ways to exploit the movie. The producer, therefore, may grant any or all of the following rights:

Music performance rights. The distributor needs the right to use and perform any "music, lyrics, and compositions" in the picture or in the sound track. The distributor has the obligation to pay performance royalties, which are irrelevant in the United States with respect to theatrical exhibition, but are relevant with respect to television broadcasts. In other countries, performance royalties might be payable for both theatrical exhibition and television broadcast. Of course, you remember that performance royalties are paid to the music publisher and composer.

> Use and perform any and all music, lyrics and musical compositions contained in the Picture and/or recorded in its sound track. Where required to be paid by exhibitors, Distributor shall pay or cause to be paid all royalties or license fees to any performing rights society or association for the public performance of music or musical compositions recorded in the Picture necessary in the Territory arising out of the exercise of its distribution rights, and shall hold Owner free and harmless therefrom. The rights licensed hereunder are subject in all respects to all rights of composers, authors, music publishers and performing rights societies with respect to the performance of the music synchronized with the Picture, and Distributor shall not knowingly permit or authorize any exhibition of the Picture which would constitute an infringement of any performance rights in any music synchronized with the Picture. Owner shall furnish Distributor with a music cue sheet in customary form for each Picture;

Title. Remember all the talk about title clearance. Well, here it is. You will have to grant the right to use the title to the distributor. You will need to have this right in order to grant it. Notice that some owners insist that the title of the movie cannot be changed (impractical in foreign language territories, where the distributor is in a better position to know whether the title or a direct translation of the title will work in the territory). The owner may nevertheless insist on the right to approve any new title.

> Use the title or titles of the Picture . . .

Distribution. Of course, distributors will need the right to "distribute, exhibit, advertise, publicize and exploit" the movie.

> Distribute, exhibit, advertise, publicize and exploit the Picture in such manner as Distributor may deem proper or expedient, subject to the provisions of this Agreement;

Dubbed versions. The distributor may need to create foreign language versions of the movie. There are basically two ways to do this. A dubbed version is where the vocals on the sound track of the movie are overdubbed by vocals recorded in the foreign language. When the actor's lips move, the foreign language is heard. A titled version is where the original sound track is used, but foreign language subtitles are superimposed on the film.

> Make such dubbed and titled versions of the Picture, and the trailers thereof, including, without limitation, cut-in, synchronized and superimposed versions in the appropriate language or languages;

Publicity. The distributor will need the right to promote the movie in a variety of ways and will need a bundle of rights related to such promotion.

> Publicize and advertise the Picture throughout the Territory during the Term . . .

Printed summaries. Remember our discussion about the rights agreement; in most such agreements, where the movie producer is seeking to obtain the rights to a novel, the author will reserve print publishing rights. On the other hand, promotion often includes written summaries of the story line of the movie. The distributor will need to have the right to make written summaries or abridgments of the movie's story. This need is actually anticipated in the rights agreement. Remember that the author grants the producer the limited right to make summaries of the film's story; these summaries cannot exceed a certain number of words. The provision in the distribution agreement mirrors the one in the rights agreement. In this example, the summary cannot exceed 7,500 words. The producer's lawyer will have to check the rights agreement to make sure that the producer has this right to give.

Publish, cause or permit to be published in all applicable languages and in such forms as Distributor may deem advisable, synopses, summaries, resumes or abridgements of the Picture (not exceeding 7,500 words in length) in newspapers, heralds, magazines, trade periodicals, comic books, programs, booklets, posters, lobby displays, press books and other publications and in all other media of advertising and publicity;

Promotional broadcast rights. Television and radio are primary media for advertising. The distributor needs the right to broadcast portions of the film or depictions of the movie as promotion for the motion picture. This right extends to sound recordings or to living persons. However, in this example, a limit of fifteen minutes is imposed—enough to make a so-called trailer; this is to prevent the distributor from turning the promotional use into a performance. Note also, that the distributor is prohibited from playing the fifteen-minute segments serially; this is to prevent the serialization of the movie on television or video.

Broadcast, or license or authorize others to broadcast, by radio or television, adaptations, versions or sketches of the Picture or any parts or portions thereof, from sound records or with living persons, or otherwise, but not to exceed 15 minutes in running time and in no event serially;

Name and likeness. The distributor will want to use the name and likeness (including photographic images and voices) of the actors in connection with the promotion of the motion picture. This use is limited, however, to the movie. The distributor cannot use the name and likeness of any person to advertise or promote anything else. For example, the distributor can't promote a product or merchandise using an actor's name or likeness. As we discussed above, many actors endorse certain products and are careful to avoid breaching their endorsement contracts. Moreover, since endorsement services are a lucrative source of income for certain actors, these individuals and their agents would frown on giving away endorsements for free.

Use the name, photograph, likeness and reproductions of the voices of any artist rendering services to promote and advertise the Picture, but not for the purpose of any commercial tie-up merchandising or

by-product arrangement, and not for an endorsement, direct or indirect, of any product or service other than the Picture . . .

Distributor credit. The distributor wants the right to designate
itself as the distributor of the movie. The distributor usually shows this
designation at the beginning of the movie in the form of a presentation card (sometimes animated) at the very top (or beginning) of the
movie. MGM's Leo the Lion roars. The Disney Magic Kingdom castle sparkles. The Paramount peak encircled by a wreath of stars comes
into view. The Fox searchlights rotate. Lady Columbia holds her
torch. WB materializes. You've got the picture.

> Announce and include on the main or end titles of the Picture and
> trailers thereof and in all advertising and publicity relating thereto,
> in such manner, position, form and substance as Distributor may
> elect, consistent with standard guild requirements and any contrac-
> tual commitments of which Distributor is notified by Owner, the
> designation of Distributor or any of its subsidiaries and licensees as
> the Distributor of the Picture; and . . .

Going after pirates. The owner will want to protect the property
from "pirates" (no, this does not refer to Johnny Depp and *Pirates of
the Caribbean,* these are people who want to infringe the copyright of
the movie). The owner will insist that the distributor agree to assist in
that process because the distributor is in the best position to discover
the piracy—and the distributor, of course, has an interest in going
after pirates as well. Distributors want the right to go after persons
who make illegal copies, broadcasts, or exhibitions of the movie, because pirates are taking money from the distributor's pocket. Although the distributor may be in the best position to find the bad
guys and go after them, the owner wants to be a party to these actions.
Thus, the agreement between the owner and distributor needs to sort
out the various issues. In a legal sense, however, the copyright owner
must grant the right to sue infringers to the distributor.

> Assert and prosecute all claims or actions or causes of action against
> any and all persons for the unauthorized or illegal use, copying, re-
> production, release, distribution, exhibition or performance of the
> Picture or any part or versions thereof, upon which it is based that
> is used therein, or any part or version thereof, or for the enforce-

ment or protection of all or any rights herein granted together with full and complete authority and power of attorney in the name of Owner to do all or any of the foregoing. Owner hereby appoints Distributor its true and lawful attorney-in-fact for such enforcement or protection. Owner, at its own expense, will have the right to join any action under this provision. No settlement or other disposition of any action hereunder prior to final court . . .

This right has to be granted by contract, because the copyright of the movie, in this context, belongs to the producer. To secure this right, the distributor's lawyers have required the producer to grant distributor a power of attorney, which means that the distributor can sign papers on behalf of the producer (without the producer's further consent).

Reserved rights.
As is common in most license agreements, the producer licensor reserves all the rights not granted.

General reservation of rights. If the producer doesn't expressly grant a right to the distributor, the producer reserves it to himself. That explains why the grant of rights section is so detailed.

Clarification of specific reserved rights. Just to be sure, the producer lists those specific rights that he is most concerned about. Note that some of the reserved rights are not granted to the distributor, because the producer doesn't have the rights. Remember the rights acquisition agreement. If the screenplay was based on a book, for example, the author would not have granted print publishing rights. On the other hand, there are some rights that the producer would have reserved, because it might make more sense to exploit them directly with another distributor. For example, the producer might wish to reserve television rights in order to license such rights to broadcasters. In the example below, the producer clarifies that the theatrical rights outside North America, the free and pay television, merchandising, commercial tie-up, novelization, and publication rights in the movie are reserved to the producer.

All rights not expressly granted herein to Distributor, including, without limitation, all theatrical distribution rights outside the Territory, free and pay television, merchandising and commercial tie-up, novelization and publication rights, and any other ancillary or allied rights in the Picture, or the underlying literary, dramatic or musical material contained in the Picture or upon which the Picture is based, are hereby expressly reserved by Owner.

Hold backs.

Even if the distributor agrees 100 percent to the reservation of rights, the distributor will insist on the producer's agreement not to use (or hold back on the use of) certain of these rights for a set period of time, called the hold-back period. In the example below, the producer agrees to refrain from exercising the free television rights for thirty-six months from the initial theatrical release of the movie. The theory behind the hold back is that allowing the movie to be shown on television within the theatrical release period would negatively impact on ticket sales; why would a person want to go to the theater and buy a ticket when the movie can be seen on television for free. The argument holds water, and so the producer usually agrees to the hold back. Pay television and video rights are not to be exercised within a year from the initial release. The same rationale applies.

> Owner agrees not to authorize or permit the exhibition of the Picture in the Territory: (i) Free Television: thirty-six (36) months from initial theatrical release of the Picture in the Territory. (ii) Pay Television: twelve (12) months from initial theatrical release of the Picture in the Territory. (iii) Video: six (6) months from initial theatrical release of the Picture in the Territory.

Distributor's obligation to distribute.

There is a big difference between receiving a right and using a right. Believe it or not, I have actually seen and heard of distribution agreements that don't require the distributor to distribute the movie. Either the obligation is left out of the agreement or the commitment is actually illusory—the distributor doesn't really have to do anything because of a condition that may or may not be fulfilled or is fulfilled at the distributor's discretion (for example, "We'll distribute it if we like it."). However, despite the disparity in bargaining power between the producer/owner and the distributor in a normal situation, for the sake of the investors and himself or herself, the owner of the movie must insist on an objective standard for measuring the distributor's commitment.

"Best efforts." We've seen and chatted about this phrase before. To a nonlawyer, best efforts might seem pretty vague. Who determines, for heaven's sake, whether or not the distributor has done his or her best. However, every first-year law student knows that best efforts is a real commitment. In 1917, Judge Benjamin Cardozo, one of the most famous judges in American jurisprudence, handed down a decision in the case of *Wood v. Lady Duff-Gordon,* which set forth the principle, still followed today, that an exclusive licensee has a duty to use best efforts to exploit the exclusive license.[14] Thus, courts may in fact read into a distribution agreement with exclusive terms (here the exclusive right relates to the territory of North America) the duty to distribute. In this case, however, the duty of best efforts is not implied, it is stated flat out—the distributor must actually do something toward distributing the movie.

Guaranteed number of screens. The favorite objective standard employed by lawyers to ensure distribution is to specify a set number of screens. There are at this point in time about 35,000 screens in the United States, including drive in theaters. A wide release would be 3,000 to 6,000 screens. In this case, the number is 500 screens. This is a modest release.

Distribution plan. It is typical for the producer and distributor to create a distribution plan. The plan will specify the markets or metropolitan areas targeted and the timing of the release. Both issues are critical. Five hundred screens could mean five hundred screens in out of the way rural America or five hundred screens in the biggest metropolitan areas. In addition, the release could happen on the same day as the new installment of *Star Wars* or in a window when nothing much is happening. The producer may not be able to control all these matters but should certainly be aware of them.

> Distributor shall use its best efforts to distribute the Picture in the Territory; provided, however, that if Distributor fails to cause the Picture to be displayed on at least five hundred (500) screens within the United States Territory before the date of January 1, 2005, Producer shall have the right to terminate this Agreement. For the remaining regions within the Territory, Distributor and Owner shall mutually determine a feasible plan of distribution, including an appropriate number of screens, which Distributor shall use its best efforts to execute.

Distributor's marketing and advertising obligations.
The distributor typically markets the movie. There is a science to this as well, but the producer needs to know at least the basics of how this works in the contract.

Distribution budget. Big studio movies require a tremendous investment in marketing and advertisements. It is not unusual to hear that the P&A cost was half, or the same, cost as the negative. On smaller movies, the marketing budget reflects the modest scale of the release.

Preapproved marketing plan. In this example, the producer has input in the distribution plan by being able to approve the marketing plan and the budget.

> Distributor shall allocate a budget of $500,000, all of which shall be used to market and advertise the Picture, in accordance with the preapproved advertising and marketing plan for the Picture.

The basic money formula—how everyone makes money.
Okay, let's get down to money. There is the art part of movie making too, I know, but let's talk about how the money is going to be divvied up when it comes in the door.

Again, imagine our farmers waiting their turn to irrigate their fields. The water (the money) flows downhill from various sources, (including, for example, the theater owners, the DVD retail stores, and television broadcasters) into the field of the first farmer (the distributor). When the first farmer (distributor) takes everything he or she is entitled to take, the water is released to flow into the field of the second farmer (the copyright owner), who collects it for the benefit of other farmers (for example, the investors and third-party participants) and himself or herself. Generally speaking, the formula looks like this:

> **Gross – Distribution Fee – Distribution Expenses = Net**

Each of these elements deserves our attention. And once we arrive at net we need to review the duties of the copyright owner regarding it. Also, as we know from our discussion above, some farmers (participants) have enough clout that they can connect their irrigation ditch before the water reaches the net pool. We'll talk about how all this works in detail below.

Determination of gross receipts.
We start with the definition of gross receipts. Then, we define what can be excluded from gross. Then we see what the distributor can take from gross. Then, below, we see what's left over for the producer and others to share. Here we go.

Licensor owns all revenues. The agreement clarifies that revenues are the property of the producer (here the owner of the copyright in and to the movie). This is important in a dispute. In a dispute over money—and, yes, there are many—the distributor will have a big advantage, as it will probably be holding the money. However, this paragraph rebuts the old adage that "possession is nine-tenths of the law." Here it is quite clear that the producer owns the revenues and that the distributor has no claim to them.

> Owner is and shall be the sole owner of all "Gross Receipts" payable to Owner under this Agreement. Distributor has and shall have no claim, right or interest therein.

On a continuous basis. This language clarifies that in calculating gross receipts for the purpose of this agreement, the math is done more than once. You keep adding to gross receipts as the money keeps coming in the door, whenever and from whatever source mentioned below.

Gross receipts. This is the sum on a continuous basis of the following amounts derived with respect to each and every licensed right:

All moneys and other consideration. Consideration is a term that first-year law students learn in their contracts class. My explanation won't help you pass the bar exam, but one way to look at this word is to imagine a scale (like the one held high by Lady Justice). On one side of the scale is the bundle of rights being licensed to the distributor. On the other side of the scale is the consideration (usually, but not always, money) given in exchange for this bundle. Here, the producer's attorney wants to make sure that the concept doesn't get lost for the vagueness of the word—he clarifies, therefore, that advances, guarantees, security deposits, awards, and other things qualify as consideration and, therefore, fit in this definition.

Received by, used by, or credited to ... The producer's lawyer now focuses on the verb portion of the sentence. We could say "gets," but that might not pick up the concept of used by or credited to. For example, suppose some money is supposed to come in the door, but before it does the distributor assigns the right to receive such money to a third party in exchange for a new Porsche. The distributor might be tempted to argue that the money wasn't really received, but the producer's lawyer doesn't want to hear that argument—hence the word used. Or suppose that some theater owner has an account with the distributor and from time to time gives the distributor a credit when the movie is shown at the theater, but doesn't actually pay the distributor until later. Again, the distributor would like to argue that the money hasn't been received, but the producer's lawyer doesn't want to hear that either. Thus, the phrase credited to is added to clarify that the money belongs to the producer when the accounting credit is given.

Definition of distributor—including affiliated companies. Distributors like to argue that the receipt by anyone but them is not receipt. Ah, but an experienced lawyer for the producer shouldn't fall for this argument. There is a good reason, discussed and illustrated below (see "Gross Revenues Calculated at the Source"), why the definition of distributor should include the distributor, the parent company, the subsidiaries, the affiliates, and other approved companies (companies likely to be in the sphere of the distributor's influence). Basically, the producer's lawyer wants to make sure that all revenues received by any of these affiliated companies are treated as if they were received by the distributor for the purposes of the agreement.

A focus on verbs—exploitation. The producer's lawyer also wants to avoid any argument that a certain type of exploitation was excluded and, thus, this provision is drafted with a lot of verbs, all of which stand for ways in which the movie can be exploited by the distributor.

Without deduction. Gross means gross. We'll talk about deductions when we talk about net.

Each licensed right. Into the pool called gross we will put in all the revenues from every right licensed under the agreement. All means all.

All moneys or other consideration of any kind (including all amounts from advances, guarantees, security deposits, awards, subsidies, and other allowances) received by, used by or credited to Distributor or its subsidiaries, parents or affiliated companies, or approved subdistributors or agents (collectively "Distributor") from the lease, license, sale, rental, barter, distribution, diffusion, exhibition, performance, exploitation or other exercise of each licensed right in the Picture, all without any deductions; and . . .

Recoveries. Included in gross are all moneys received from infringers (often referred to as pirates). Suppose that Pirate Replicators buys a DVD of your movie and makes a million illegal copies for sale in the U.S. market. Then let's suppose that your distributor catches these bad guys, takes them to court, and wins a $5 million judgment. That $5 million would go into the basket labeled gross.

All moneys or other consideration of any kind received by, used by or credited to Distributor as recoveries for the infringement by third parties of each Licensed Right in the Picture; and . . .

Money made from promotional materials. All money received by the distributor from dealing in enumerated advertising materials, such as trailers, copies, stills . . . and so on. There is a market for these materials and the revenues generated in that market should go into the pot marked gross.

All moneys or other consideration of any kind received by, used by or credited to Distributor from any authorized dealing in trailers, posters, copies, stills, excerpts, advertising accessories or other materials made in connection with or supporting the exercise of each Licensed Right in the Picture.

Gross receipts calculated at source.

This concept is touched on indirectly above in the definition of Distributor. It is an important point, so the producer's (your) lawyer will want to deal directly with the major point—making sure that gross receipts are calculated at source.

At source—a general illustration. Not that any distributor would ever do this, but suppose you were a distributor and wanted to pull a fast one on the producer. Here's something you could do: You could create a subsidiary or two and make them subdistributors. For example, let's suppose that Big Distribution Co. (BD) creates and then sublicenses the rights it has to Big Distribution Japan Co. (BDJ) which then subdistributes to Big Distribution Tokyo (BDT). Let's also suppose that BD owns all the stock of BDJ, which owns all the stock of BDT. In the sublicense agreements, each of the sublicensees charges a 20 percent distribution fee and then remits the balance up the chain. Mr. Yamamoto buys a movie ticket in Tokyo and pays $20 (close to the real price in Japan for a movie ticket). Assume that the theater owner takes $10 and remits the balance to BDT. BDT takes $2.00 and remits $8.00 to BDJ. BDJ takes $1.60 and remits $6.40 to BD, which takes $1.28 and hands over $5.12 to the producer (who, of course, has to share this fifty-fifty with the financier and pay all the third-party commitments). Do you sense something wrong here? Good, so does the producer's lawyer. That is why the contract defines "Distributor" as the distributor (BD in our hypothetical) or its subsidiaries (BDJ), parents or affiliated companies (BDT), or approved subdistributors or agents (any others in the chain of distribution that the distributor can control or manipulate. No double dipping allowed! If any of the distributor's parent, subsidiaries, or affiliates get money, it will be treated as if the money was received by the distributor.

> Distributor may not deduct or charge any fee against Gross Receipts in calculating all amounts due Owner. For the purpose of determining Licensor's share of Gross Receipts, all Gross Receipts must be calculated "at source."

At source—the levels. Producers' lawyers, when negotiating a distribution contract, tend to be a little on the paranoid side. So, just to make sure everyone knows what "at source" really means, the contract describes six different levels of revenue and states specifically how to calculate the revenues.

> By way of clarification, this means that Gross Receipts derived from the exploitation of any of the following rights must be calculated at the following levels; (i) for any Theatrical Licensed Right, at the level at which payments are remitted by local exhibitors of the Picture; (ii) for any Non-Theatrical Licensed Right at the level at which payments are remitted by governmental agencies or institutions which exhibit the Picture directly to their patrons or make the Picture directly available to their patrons; (iii) for any Home Video Licensed Right, at a Wholesale Level or Direct Consumer Level, de-

pending on the level at which the Videogram leaves the control of Distributor; (iv) for any Commercial Video or Public Video Licensed Right, at either the Wholesale Level or Direct Consumer Level, or the level at which payments are remitted by local exhibitors or other persons which publicly perform the Picture directly before the public; (v) for any Ancillary Licensed Right, at the level at which payments are remitted by airlines, ship companies, or hotels which exhibit the Picture directly to their patrons or make the Picture directly available to their patrons; and (vi) for any Television Licensed Right, at the level at which payments are remitted by stations, cable systems or telecasters which broadcast, cablecast or transmit the Picture directly to the public.

Let's look more closely at each of the levels of at source:

Theaters. When revenues are derived from the exploitation of the movie at theaters, the calculation of gross receipts must be made using the amount of money paid by the theater owners (called exhibitors). In other words, the calculation can't be made based on payments down the line through other entities or persons (whether or not they are defined as "distributors").

Nontheatrical. When revenues are derived from the exploitation of the movie to institutions not primarily engaged in the exhibition of movies—governmental agencies or other institutions (for example, distributors may sublicense the exhibition rights to the United States government for exhibition to its military personnel located around the world), the calculation of gross receipts must be made based on the payments by such governmental agencies. The calculation cannot be made based on payments to brokers or subdistributors down the line (whether or not they are defined as "distributors").

Home video. If the revenues are derived by selling home videos (videocassettes or DVDs, for example, sold directly or indirectly to individuals for home use), the calculation must be based either at the wholesale level (when Wal-Mart pays the distributor for a shipment of DVDs that it will sell at its retail outlets, to give one of many possible examples) or at the direct consumer level (when John Q. Customer purchases a videocassette of the movie directly from the distributor online at distributor's Web site). The general rule is that the calculation is made at the level where the product leaves the distributor's control (keeping in mind that distributor is defined broadly).

Commercial video. If the revenues are derived by selling commercial videos (high-quality videocassettes or DVDs, for example, sold or licensed to nontheatrical exhibitors), the calculation is made either at the wholesale level (where the Red Cross purchases videos for exhibition at its facilities worldwide) or the direct consumer level (for example, when Stanford University purchases a copy for exhibition at an on-campus theater).

Ancillary rights. In this contract, ancillary rights has a specific meaning: airline, ship, and hotel. Thus, when revenues are derived from exploitation of the movie in any of these three ways, the calculation is made at the level where the airlines, ship company, or hotel makes payment (when Marriott Hotels makes a purchase for exhibition in its hotels throughout America, for example).

Television. If the revenues are derived from television exhibition, the calculation must be made at the level where payment is made by the station, cable, or other telecaster that broadcasts the movie directly to the public (for example, when ABC pays the owner for a network broadcast of the movie).

Certain items not included in gross.

There are certain items that have the appearance of gross revenues that are nevertheless not included in gross for the purposes of determining who gets what.

The following shall not be included in gross receipts:

Exhibitor's share. In a distribution contract, gross receipts does not mean all box office receipts. All moneys that go to the theater owners are not included in the gross. As you know, the term for the revenues paid by theaters is called theatrical rentals and is not the same as box office.

The moneys derived by any theater or other exhibitor from exhibition of the Picture.

Unearned advances. No advance, deposit, payment, or guarantee received by or promised to the distributor is calculated as part of the gross until it is earned (in other words, until there are no more conditions left to be satisfied for its receipt). For example, if a theater gives the distributor a deposit in connection with the receipt of five prints, but the theater can get back the deposit if it returns the prints in good condition, the deposit cannot be taken into the gross.

Advance payments and security deposits, until earned or forfeited. Nonreturnable guarantees are deemed advance payments and excluded from Gross Receipts until earned.

Rebates, refunds, adjustments. If the distributor makes an adjustment (for example, gives a discount to an exhibitor), offers a refund (for example, returns money to an exhibitor), or grants a rebate (for example, promises to give back money in exchange for the satisfaction of some condition), the amounts in question are not counted in gross.

All adjustments, refunds or rebates given to sublicensees of the Picture by Distributor. To the extent any such amounts represent a return of amounts previously included in Gross Receipts, an appropriate adjustment in Gross Receipts and Distribution Fees shall be made.

Taxes. If the distributor collects taxes or other payments that have to be remitted in turn to the government, such amounts are not calculated in the gross. The examples here are admission taxes, sales taxes, and value-added taxes.

Any amounts collected by Distributor or its subsidiaries or licensees of the Picture as taxes or for payment as taxes, such as admission, sales and value-added taxes.

Royalties for the benefit of authors and others. If the distributor collects money for the benefit of authors, composers, or publishers, for example, such amounts are not included in the gross. Note that often these payments will be collected directly by performing rights societies (such as ASCAP or BMI in the United States). Since the producer is the contracting party with authors and composers, it may be necessary for the producer to reserve the right to receive these royalties. In this second case, the revenues would be counted in the gross, but since the producer would be paying them out again it is essentially a wash.

All amounts collected by any collecting society, authors' rights organization, performing rights society or governmental agency which are payable to authors, composers or producers and which arise from royalties, compulsory licenses, cable retransmission income and music performance royalties.

Salvage. If the distributor receives money from disposal of the prints or other materials related to the movie, these are not considered part of gross revenues. The distributor gets to keep such revenues.

All moneys received by Distributor or its subsidiaries from the scrapping or disposal of copies of the Picture or other materials.

Subsidies treated as a part of recoupable expenses. In certain situations, incentives in the form of rebates or subsidies may be given to the distributor in connection with the release of the movie. These payments are not included in the gross. The distributor gets to keep these amounts, but has to apply them against the amount of recoupable distribution costs.

The following amounts, if received by, used by or credited to Distributor will not be included in Gross Receipts but will be used to reduce Recoupable Distribution Costs: (i) publicity and similar subsidies for the cost of releasing, advertising or publicizing the Picture; (ii) income from publicity tie-ins; or (iii) freight, print, trailer, advertising and other cost recoveries, rebates, refunds or discounts from exhibitors, approved subdistributors or other Persons.

The provision lists three examples:
Publicity and similar subsidies. In certain jurisdictions, the distributor might receive money or other advantages related to the release of the movie. These things will not be included in gross, but will go to reduce the distributor's costs related to the release of the movie.

Income from publicity tie-ins. Money might be received from certain commercial institutions wanting to tie their products or trademarks to the release of the movie (I'm not talking about companies whose products appear in the movie; I'm talking about companies that become associated with the release of the movie). Think of a fast food restaurant that puts the name of the movie on soda cups and bags filled with fries. Again, this money will not be a part of gross, but will reduce the distributor's releasing costs.

Freight, prints, trailer, advertising, and other cost savers. Similarly, distributors might receive money or in-kind value from freighters, the makers of prints and trailers, advertising companies, and the like. Suppose, for example, that a replication facility decides to make a certain number of prints at no cost in exchange for promotional consideration (in brochures or on posters or one-sheets). Again, this money or in-kind value is not part of gross.

Distribution fees.

The distributor deducts its fee from gross receipts.

Fee range. The fee ranges from 20 to 40 percent, depending on the circumstances. Generally speaking, the more money the distributor has in the deal, the higher the distribution fee. For example, in a rent-a-studio deal, the distributor will likely demand a smaller fee (in the 20 percent range), because it did not put up the money for the production of the negative.

Different structures for different rights. This example deals with the theatrical release of the movie in the territory. In a full-blown distribution agreement, there will be different structures for different rights. For example, the distributor will be able to take a fee for the following, in addition to the exploitation of the theatrical rights: nontheatrical rights, home video rights, commercial video rights, ancillary rights, and television rights. (See the discussion above regarding "Calculating Gross at Source.") In addition, the distributor may negotiate for the merchandising, sound track, and other rights. Each right will have its own structure—its own distribution fee arrangement.

> As compensation, from Gross Receipts, Distributor may deduct a Distribution Fee ("Distribution Fee") of 25% of the Gross Receipts derived from the theatrical release of the Picture in the Territory.

Distribution expenses.

The distributor now deducts its permitted expenses incurred in the release of the movie in the territory.

Rationale. The negotiations respecting the deduction of distribution (P&A) expenses can be intense. But let's start with a simple proposition. Since the distributor has an obligation to release the movie, and since it costs money to do so, it is fair and reasonable to let the distributor recoup costs. Tradition allows the distributor to recoup this amount before remitting any money to the owner or anyone else down the line.

Reasonableness standard. Keeping it simple still, from the owner's perspective, every dollar spent on distribution is a dollar that will not reach the pool called net. Thus, while the owner is fully supportive of the distributor's efforts to distribute the movie, and while the owner fully understands that this effort will require money, the owner is not keen about allowing the distributor to engage in unreasonable activities or to incur unreasonable expenses in this endeavor. Notice that in this case (and not a feature of every distribution agreement), the distributor agrees to consult with the owner about the deduction of costs.

> From the Gross Receipts remaining after deducting the Distribution Fee, after full consultation with Owner, Distributor may deduct and retain a sum equal to all reasonable costs, expenses and charges paid, advanced or incurred by Distributor in connection with the derivation of Gross Receipts ("Distribution Expenses"), including without limitation the following:

List of specified expenses. It seems natural that both sides would gravitate toward a list of approved costs. In this example, the words "without limitation" give the distributor some leeway, but the list does form an established base from which the distributor can operate.

> "Conversion/Transmission Costs": All costs of conversion of moneys, including cable expenses and any discounts taken for the conversion thereof directly or indirectly into United States Dollars and all costs of transmission of such moneys to the United States.
> "Collection Costs": All costs incurred in connection with the collection of moneys includable within Gross Receipts, including reasonable fees of attorneys and auditors, and loss, damage or liability suffered or incurred by Sales Agent in the collection of such moneys, whether by litigation or otherwise.
> "Guild Payments": To the extent of the obligation of Sales Agent pursuant to the Agreement, if any, all costs incurred with respect to payments required, including employee fringe benefits and taxes payable with respect thereto, under applicable Collective Bargaining Agreements by reason of or as a condition to any exhibition of the Picture, or any part thereof, or any use or reuse thereof for any purpose or in any media whatsoever.
> "Foreign Version Costs": All costs incurred to make and deliver foreign language versions of the Picture (other than the Italian language version), whether dubbed and/or subtitled in one or more languages including translation, narration, looping, retitling, superimposing, recutting, spotting, rerecording, remixing, redubbing and reediting of the Picture and trailers; transportation, packing and

handling of Motion Picture Copies and parts thereof with respect to the preparation of foreign language versions of the Picture; and registration for copyright in the Territory.

"Reediting Costs": All costs incurred to recut, reedit, rerecord, rescore, remix and redub the Picture, including changes, eliminations or additions with respect to the Picture for Theatrical and NonTheatrical Exhibition, and conforming (voluntarily or involuntarily) the Picture to requirements of censorship, classification and rating by governmental, or local organizations or other Parties, including exhibitors and religious and ethnic groups, and to national and/or political regulations of any Territory.

"Physical Material Costs": All costs of motion picture copies and trailers including laboratory, labor, service, materials and facilities costs in connection therewith.

"Royalties": The costs of all licenses required to permit exhibition, distribution or other use of the Picture, trailers, and motion picture copies thereof, including fees for use of any patented equipment or processes; synchronization, recording and performing royalties and fees with respect to performance of lyrics and music and Literary Material; any reuse fees and costs advanced by Distributor; any costs incurred to acquire, use and publish Picture music advanced by Distributor.

"Insurance Costs": All costs for Insurance coverage of any and all risks of loss with respect to the Picture and any components thereof, including errors and omissions insurance and loss or damage to motion picture copies and physical material insurance.

"Copyrighting Costs": All costs to obtain copyright and the extension and renewal thereof, and other similar protections throughout the world, wherever and whenever incurred within Distributor's sole discretion.

"Copyright Infringement Costs": All reasonable costs incurred to protect the copyright ownership in the Picture and to prevent any infringement of copyright or violation of rights in and to the Picture or any elements thereof (whether by litigation or otherwise) and reasonable attorneys' fees in connection therewith.

"Claims and Litigation Costs": Subject to the indemnification obligations of Owner pursuant to the Agreement, all costs incurred by reason of claims asserted by third parties which arise out of the production, distribution, exhibition, and/or exploitation of the Picture (including claims of infringement, unfair competition, violation of any right of privacy, defamation or breach of contract) including attorneys' fees, litigation expenses, and investigation expenses. Distributor shall have the right, in consultation with Owner and at the Owner's consent, to settle and pay any such claim. After settlement or final judicial determination of any such claim, any reserve taken shall be adjusted to reflect the actual costs paid by Distributor and the net balance after such adjustment, if any, shall be credited to Gross Receipts.

"Advertising/Promotion": All reasonable out-of-pocket costs incurred to promote and advertise the Picture in the Territory, including advertising accessories, publicity, publicity material and exploitation. Distributor shall have no right to deduct any overhead expenses as part of Distribution Expenses. Distributor shall not deduct any cost or expense more than once.

All moneys received by reason of the infringement or interference by third persons with the Picture or any of the rights granted herein shall be added to the Adjusted Gross Receipts remaining after deducting the Distribution Fees and the Distribution Expenses. The amount remaining shall constitute the "Net Receipts."

Cap on distribution expenses. Okay, let's go back and look at the relatively simple propositions discussed above—yes, it is fair to allow the distributor to deduct distribution costs, but such costs should be reasonable. However, like everything else, there is a more complicated side to this. Keep in mind that gross receipts, like water in a pool, is a finite concept. Only a certain number of tickets will be sold. Only a certain number of videos will be sold. Only a certain amount will be received from television and other sources. Therefore, once the money is taken out by one party, the money available to other parties is reduced. The more the distributor takes out, the less there is for you.

> Anything in this Agreement to the contrary notwithstanding, in no event will Distributor be allowed to deduct from Gross Receipts, after the deduction of the Distribution Fee, an amount in excess of 10% of the final production budget (less contingencies and the cost of any completion bond) of the Picture as Distribution Expenses.

Now, let's imagine that the distributor doesn't really care much about how much money it spends for distribution expenses. How can this be? This is money out of the distributor's pocket, right? Not really. The distributor knows, for example, that before any water flows into the net pool (the pool from which you will be taking), it will be allowed to take two deductions from gross receipts. The first deduction is the distributor's fee. The next deduction is recoupment of costs (P&A). It might be possible to suppose that the more money the distributor spends on advertising the bigger the gross. And the bigger the gross, the bigger the fee. And since the distributor gets to recoup the fee and costs out of the gross (before the stream of money reaches you), the distributor has an incentive to spend more and more. The bottom line is that the amount that the distributor is allowed to recoup must be limited in some way. If not, the producer (you) will not see any money (i.e., there won't be any water in the net pool).

The approach we discussed above was to limit the distributor to the recoupment of reasonable expenses and to make the distributor consult with the owner on each deduction. From a lawyer's point of view, this approach is somewhat impractical. Who will ultimately determine what is reasonable? What if there is a dispute? By limiting the distributor to a finite amount of distribution expenses, the distributor is forced to determine for itself what is reasonable.

Another approach is to give the owner approval rights over deductions. This is a satisfactory approach if the owner knows as much or more than the distributor about distribution in the territory—which usually is not the case. I prefer the cap on distribution expenses as an approach, *if* you can get it.

No cross recoupment. Another common limitation on recoupment of P&A expenses is illustrated by this provision. Expenses recouped in connection with the exploitation of one right may not be recouped with respect to the exploitation of another right. For example, let's suppose that the distributor places an ad for the movie in a magazine. If the distributor recoups the cost of the ad out of theatrical revenues, the distributor may not recoup the same cost out of home video revenues, even if the ad promotes home video rentals and sales. Again, the rule is no double dipping allowed.

> Distribution Expenses will be calculated only as incurred with respect to the exploitation of each applicable Licensed Right. Distribution Expenses incurred with respect to the exploitation of any one Licensed Right may not be recouped from the Gross Receipts derived from the exploitation of any other Licensed Right.

Net and what to do with it.

When you finish calculating gross receipts and deducting the distribution fee and the allowable distribution expenses from gross receipts you are left with net proceeds. Let's take a second to review what happens to it. I'd like to say that the owner gets to keep it, but alas it doesn't work that way. We have to remember all the contracts the producer has made to this point.

Recoupment of the negative cost. Somehow or other, the party who put up the money to finance the production of the negative must get back the money. It usually happens at this stage. After the distribution fees have been deducted, the cost of the negative is recouped. The traditional concept, as you recall, is that all of the net goes to the production investor until the investor has been fully recouped. The following exceptions may be true, depending on the negotiation:

Taxes. The producer will want to reserve the right to pay his or her own taxes, if any, arising from the receipt of revenues.

Use of funds payment. The investor may request an interest factor based on the fact that the investor's money has been in use by the producer. A typical scenario is to allow the investor to recoup the negative cost plus prime plus 2 percent (or some similar percentage).

Participations from gross or adjusted gross. Also remember that the producer may have had to agree to give participations to actors or directors out of pools that are actually better than net. For example, the actor's deal may allow the actor to hook up his siphon hose in the gross pool or a pool that is almost gross (i.e., adjusted gross). In this case, the contract must make it clear that the net from which the investor is allowed to recoup is defined in such a way as to take into account these payments.

Postrecoupment division of net—participations. And speaking of participations, remember the producer is responsible for participations; all third-party payments are usually taken care of out of the producer's share. So, even though the general concept is to split the postrecoupment net between the investor and the producer, the producer's share rarely equals 50 percent of the net. Producers strive to keep 20 to 25 percent of the net. Good luck.

Accounting and audit rights.

The right to an accounting and the right to audit the records related to revenues is a standard provision sought by producers in distribution contracts.

Limitations on cross collateralization. Cross collateralization is an accounting concept. The following example shows how cross collateralization works: Suppose the producer licenses the distribution rights to three movies, each costing $1 million to produce, to a single distributor. Then suppose that the first picture breaks even, grossing $1 million, but the second two movies are failures, one grossing $500,000 and the next one a total bust at $0 (obviously not your movie). Suppose also that the distribution expenses for each movie are $100,000. With the ability to cross collateralize the revenues, the distributor has $1.5 million of revenues to work with. Using the formula from the example above, the distributor takes a distribution fee of 20 percent (which equals $300,000) and then recoups $300,000 in distribution costs, leaving a total of $900,000 in the net pool). From this pool, assuming that there are no gross or adjusted gross participants, the producer should pay off the $3 million production investment— but of course the producer (and his or her investors) will fall short by an amount equal to $2.1 million.

> The Picture will be treated separate and apart from any other picture licensed to Distributor, whether in this Agreement or otherwise, and the payments applicable to the Picture will be treated as a separate and independent accounting unit and not cross-collateralized or setoff, unless stated otherwise in the Deal Terms. Amounts due for the Picture or other picture(s) may not be used to recoup amounts unrecouped for the Picture or any other picture(s), or vice versa. Gross Receipts and Recoupable Distribution Costs may only be cross-collateralized among the Licensed Right in a Picture to the extent specifically authorized in the Deal Terms.

Now let's look at the same situation where cross collateralization is not allowed. In this scenario, the distributor must look at and apply the formula to each movie individually. Thus, in the first movie, the distributor takes a $200,000 distribution fee and recoups $100,000 as distribution expenses, leaving $700,000 in the net pool. In the second movie, the distributor takes a $100,000 distribution fee and $100,000 for distribution expenses, leaving $300,000 as net. Finally, the distributor takes $0 and leaves $0. The producer in this scenario is left with $1 million in net (a gain of $100,000 for the producer).[15] Producers, therefore, don't like to let the distributor cross collateralize expenses. This provision prevents the distributor from accounting in this way; rather, the distributor must apply the formula and account for the revenues applicable to one movie at a time.

Limits on allocations. This is another potential for abuse by a distributor. Suppose that the distributor is distributing two movies (one yours) at the same time. The distributor rents the *Queen Mary* and invites a group of exhibitors aboard for a big bash promoting the distributor's slate—the two movies. Since the bash benefited your movie, and because the distributor is spending more money on press coverage for the other movie, the distributor allocates 100 percent of the bash to your movie and 0 percent to the other movie. Not fair you say. And that is the point of this provision.

> If the Picture is exploited in connection with other pictures, then Distributor will only allocate receipts and expenses among such pictures in the manner approved by Licensor in its sole discretion in advance.

Financial records. The producer puts the distributor under the following obligations: The distributor must keep true and accurate records of the billings and collection of gross receipts. The distributor must use "generally accepted accounting principles" (ask your accountant what this means) and must be consistent in the way the books are kept. For home video rights, the records have to show manufacturing data related to individual videograms. The distributor must keep statements, contracts, receipts, and other accounting records related to the movie. These obligations are relatively common in distribution agreements—other than with the majors (which have the legendary power to account on their own terms).

> Distributor will maintain complete and accurate records in the currency of the Territory of all financial transactions regarding the Picture in accordance with generally accepted accounting principles in the entertainment distribution business on a consistent, uniform and nondiscriminatory basis throughout the Term. The records will include without limitation all Gross Receipts derived, all Distribution Expenses paid, all allowed adjustments or rebates made, and all cash collected or credits received. Where any Video Rights are licensed, such records will also include all Videograms manufactured, sold, rented and returned. Unless Licensor pre-approved otherwise in writing, all such financial records will be maintained on a cash basis, except where Distributor permits any offset, refund, rebate or other reduction in sums due Distributor, then the amount will nonetheless be included in Gross Receipts. Distributor will also keep complete and accurate copies of every statement from third

parties, and contracts, vouchers, receipts, computer records, audit reports, correspondence and other writings from authorized subdistributors and agents and all other parties pertaining to the Picture.

Reports. It is customary for a distributor to provide periodic reports of the gross receipts that the distributor collects pursuant to the distribution agreement. The report typically shows, by territory, the amount of gross receipts earned, the distribution expenses recouped, and the exchange rates used. Specific information is required in the case of revenues generated from the exploitation of video rights. Significantly, the distributor is required to send money with the report.

In addition to any other reporting requirements in this Agreement, starting after Delivery of the Initial Materials, Distributor will furnish Licensor a statement in English (and, if requested, supporting documentation) which sets forth from the time of the immediately prior statement, if any, with respect to each Picture all Gross Receipts derived, all Distribution Expenses paid identifying to whom, and all exchange rates used, all on a country-by-country basis. Where any Video Rights are licensed, the statements will also include: (i) all Videograms manufactured, sold, rented and returned; (ii) the wholesale and retail selling prices of all Videograms; and (iii) all allowable deductions taken. Such information will be provided in reasonable detail on a current and cumulative basis. Each statement will be accompanied by payment of any moneys then due Licensor.

Frequency of reports. Typically, as in this case, the reports come more often during the first part of the release cycle and less frequently as time goes on. In this example the reports are given monthly for a year, although they could be made quarterly or semiannually. Afterward, as the release cycle enters into its later phase, the reports can come less often. In this example they slow to quarterly reports, although semiannual, even annual, reports are possible.

Distributor will render statements as follows: (a) monthly within one (1) month of the end of the applicable month for the first twelve (12) months following the First Theatrical Release of the Picture and following the end of each Holdback specified in the Deal Terms; and (b) thereafter quarterly within one (1) month after the end of each calendar quarter, or such other quarterly accounting periods as Licensor may designate, until the end of two (2) quarterly periods after the Term. Distributor may not withhold any Gross Receipts as a reserve against returned or defective Videograms for more than two (2) consecutive accounting periods, and the amount withheld may not exceed ten percent (10%) of the amount of Gross Receipts derived from Videogram exploitation for the two (2) consecutive accounting periods immediately preceding the two (2) consecutive accounting periods for which the reserve is retained.

Audit rights. The producer also wants to have the right to audit the distributors records from time to time. This keeps the distributor honest and is a formidable weapon in the event of a dispute. The distributor insists, on its part, that reasonable notice be given and that the audit be done during normal business hours, thus limiting the producer's ability to harass the distributor with spur of the moment audits done at midnight on Saturday, for example. The expense of the audit is borne by the producer—since the audit is being made at the producer's request; this is designed to eliminate "fishing" expeditions. However, if the producer or the producer's auditors discover a discrepancy greater than an agreed-upon percentage (in this case, the discrepancy is 5 percent or greater), the expense of the audit shall be borne by the distributor.

Continuing until three (3) years after the Term, Owner may examine and copy on its own or through its auditors Distributor's financial records regarding the Picture on ten (10) days' notice. The examination will be done with reasonable notice and at normal business hours and shall be at Owner's expense, unless an underpayment of more than five percent (5%) is uncovered, in which case Distributor will pay the costs of the examination on demand.

Delivery and return of materials.
Delivery is a critical point in the history of your movie. This is when the producer gathers together the works of his or her creation and hands them over to the distributor. Without these materials, the distributor won't be able to distribute the movie.

Delivery items and schedule. Producer/owner promises to deliver all the materials needed for the distribution of the movie. The materials are delivered in accordance with a schedule. Here notification of delivery constitutes delivery, but remember that the following illustration is very pro-producer. In many contracts, delivery means physical delivery—with substantial penalties for late delivery.

> Owner shall deliver to Distributor the Picture and all materials related thereto and necessary for the distribution of the Picture on or before the date that is 60 days after the completion of principal photography of the Picture, subject to events of force majeure (the "Delivery Date") in accordance with the Delivery Schedule attached hereto as Exhibit "DS" and incorporated herein by reference. When Owner shall advise Distributor in writing that a Delivery Item or Items set forth on Exhibit "DS" has or have been tendered to Distributor and/or Distributor's designee, and has tendered such Items, Owner shall be deemed to have made a tender of delivery with respect to that Item(s).

Inspection and the ability to cure. The distributor has the right to inspect the delivered items and make objections. If the distributor does object, the producer/owner has the right to cure any problems within a certain period of time (here within ten days).

> Distributor shall have an "Inspection Period" of fifteen (15) days to inspect and examine the Items so tendered. In the event that Distributor objects to the tender of delivery, in whole or in part, on or before the end of the Inspection Period, Distributor shall notify Owner in writing, which notice shall set forth with particularity Distributor's objections and shall state in what respects the tender of delivery is not complete or is not in conformity with this Agreement. In the event Distributor makes no objection during the Inspection Period, the Item(s) in question shall be deemed delivered in comformity herewith. In the event that Distributor objects, owner shall remedy the deficiencies regarding the Item(s) in question within ten (10) days ("Cure Period"). Distributor shall have the same rights of inspection and cure in connection with the redelivered Item(s) until such time that Owner remedies the deficiencies.

Lab access letter. The distributor will need access to all the materials related to the movie in order to do an effective job distributing the movie. Since it would be impractical to deliver all related materials, the producer/owner will simply give the distributor access to the laboratory where the materials are stored. The terms of access are pursuant to a lab access letter agreement. For example, pursuant to the letter, the producer authorizes the lab to allow the distributor to duplicate the various materials. Moreover, the letter will clarify that the distributor must pay the duplication charges and that the lab may not look to the producer's credit. Another common feature is the clarification that the distributor may have access and make orders for duplication, even if the lab has claims against the producer/owner. Finally, the letter clarifies that the lab may not, without written permission, let the original materials out of the lab.[16]

> During the Term of this Agreement, Owner further grants to Distributor access to all other materials and elements of the Picture pursuant to the terms of the laboratory access letter attached hereto as Exhibit "A" and incorporated herein by reference. Should Owner fail to deliver any of the materials, Distributor, in addition to all of its other rights and remedies, may manufacture such undelivered elements and deduct the cost thereof from Gross Receipts, if any, as set forth in this Agreement.

Possession does not constitute ownership. Just because the distributor is allowed to duplicate and take possession of the prints, preprint materials, and other materials related to the movie does not mean that the distributor has any ownership interest in the movie.

> Legal title to all prints, preprint material and other material of the Picture, including dubbed or superimposed prints, provided to, or created by, Distributor shall at all times belong to Owner, and all rights including copyrights in such materials shall vest in Owner upon the creation thereof. During the Term, Distributor shall have the right to possession and control of such materials solely for the purpose of exercising the rights granted herein, and Owner shall at all times have access to such materials. Distributor shall execute, acknowledge and deliver to Owner any instruments necessary for Owner's ownership of such materials.

USE AND RETURN OF PRINT MATERIALS

Original continuity. The producer wants the distributor to promise not to show modified versions of the movie. The producer may have an agreement with the director that obligates the producer to put the distributor under this obligation. Or the producer himself may push the issue of creative continuity. The distributor promises, there-fore, that the prints will be shown as originally constituted and that there will be no "changes, interpolation or elimination," except as agreed to by the producer (remember that the distributor wants the right to add its own credit to the movie).

No alterations. It is especially important to the producer that cred-its, trademarks, and similar matters that have been contracted for are not altered or eliminated. Imagine the reaction of the car company, which paid money to have its car driven by the star of the movie in the big car chase scene, when it discovers that the scene is missing or that the car's identifying marks have been edited out.

> Except as expressly permitted herein, all prints shall be exhibited in their original continuity, without change, interpolation or elimina-tion, and in no event shall any credit, trademark, trade name, sym-bol or copyright notice be eliminated or altered.

Dubbed versions. In some cases (for example, animated movies), the tradition is to have the movie dubbed—have native speakers of the language overdub the original English language sound track. This may be necessary, in the distributor's opinion, to maximize the rev-enues in a given territory. From the producer/owner's perspective, however, quality will be a big issue. The producer spent a lot of money on the original actors (not insignificantly because they could deliver their lines well); he will not want to sit back and let the distributor bring in a group of amateurs or have the dubbing services done with home equipment. In any event, the producer will want to have access to the new sound track and will want to own it. (Keep in mind that the distribution deal may be over someday and the producer will get the distribution rights back.)

Moreover, the producer/owner will want to know about costs. Even if the distributor has the obligation to front the costs, the dis-tributor will probably have the right to recoup that cost. It all hits the producer's bottom line.

And note that this sound track is new. And because it is new, there could be new material that the producer's lawyers have not cleared for E&O–type issues. In this case, the producer wants the distributor to indemnify and hold the producer harmless for any problem.

> Distributor shall obtain the written prior approval of Owner for the script of any dubbed version of the Picture and for the voices of any

such dubbed version. All dubbing shall be of first-class quality and done at a studio selected by Distributor and approved in writing by Owner. Distributor shall also submit to Owner for its prior written approval the costs of making such dubbed or superimposed version. Distributor agrees to and shall indemnify and hold Owner harmless against any claims or causes of action in any way arising out of and in connection with the dubbing or superimposing of the Picture, provided Owner notifies Distributor in writing with respect to any restrictions. If a dubbed version of the Picture is made, Distributor shall make all sound-track materials of the dubbed version and trailers of the Picture available to Owner. All such sound-track materials shall become Owner's sole property and shall be delivered to Owner as provided herein.

Return of prints. When the distribution contract comes to an end, the producer/owner will want the materials—especially prints and sound tracks (that were added by the distributor, if any)—returned. These materials will retain their value as the movie continues to be exploited on television and in the home video rental market. The producer, however, in an effort to save the cost of storage, may want to have certain of the materials destroyed. If the producer decides to go that way, the producer may want to have his own representative supervise the destruction of the materials and/or receive a certificate from the distributor that the materials were destroyed in accordance with the producer's instructions.

Upon the expiration of the Term for the Picture, Distributor shall deliver to Owner at Distributor's expense at its office, or elsewhere as Owner shall elect, all prints and preprint material and all dubbed sound tracks, subtitled or subtitling material, and all other optical and/or magnetic sound tracks, and/or positive prints of the Picture containing optical and/or magnetic sound tracks, which were made for Distributor, whether or not such materials are actually used by Distributor, and all cue sheets, dialogue lists and other documents delivered hereunder; provided however, that Owner, in its sole discretion, may require that said materials or parts thereof, be destroyed under the supervision of a person designated by Owner, and in such event Distributor shall deliver to Owner a duly authenticated certificate of destruction for each and every such item.

No encumbrances. Since the producer will rationally maintain the position that the producer owns all materials and rights, he or she will want to make sure that the distributor doesn't do anything to encumber these materials and rights. For example, suppose that the distributor wants to get a little more cash out of the movies in his or her library; so the distributor calls up a bank and says, "I need a loan of $20 million. I have a hundred titles in my library, including that great movie *The Quest,* and I'm willing to put up the prints to that movie and the others for collateral on my loan." Then suppose that the distributor declares bankruptcy. The bank will take the prints and other materials for the movies, including *The Quest,* as it will have the right to do under the terms of the loan. That creates an untenable situation as the producer will need the prints back to continue distributing the movie in the applicable territory, but the bank is unlikely to return them as it is out some money. The producer, therefore, wants to clarify that the prints and other materials cannot be encumbered in this way.

> Distributor shall not sell, assign, pledge, mortgage or hypothecate any of the prints or preprint materials of the Picture nor make any other disposition thereof other than exhibiting or granting to others the right to exhibit said prints in the Territory.

Representations, warranties, and covenants regarding chain of title, etc.

Please remember our discussion about the purpose of representations and warranties in a contract of any kind. Well, here we are again. And, although the distributor is not a buyer, the distributor is still stepping into the stream of commerce. By doing so, the distributor becomes a target for parties who believe they've been injured by the movie. No, I'm not saying that the distributor is worried about a print of the movie rolling off a truck and hitting someone—the distributor is concerned about latent defects, including the chain of title of the movie, copyright infringement, trademark infringement, defamation, invasion of privacy, and similar problems. The distributor takes this seriously because distributors make good targets for lawsuits. Many times, the distributor is the deep pocket and the best one to file suit against. Consequently, the distributor will insist on trying to shift the responsibility to the producer/owner by having the producer/owner make representations and warranties about chain of title, defamation, and other matters. In addition, the distributor will demand that the producer/owner make promises or covenants not to do anything that will cause the representations and warranties to become false in the future.

Legal authority, no interference. The producer/owner represents that he or she has the right to sign the contract and perform the
duties that the contract demands—such as grant the exclusive distribution rights in the territory, for example. The clear implication,
which is actually recited in the provision, is that there will not be any
legal claims, liens, or encumbrances on the movie that might interfere
with the distributor's rights under the contract.

> Owner has the right to enter into this Agreement and to grant to
> Distributor all the rights and licenses herein contained and agrees
> that on the Delivery Date of the Picture, there will not be any out-
> standing claims, liens or encumbrances in or to the Picture or any
> part thereof which can or will impair or interfere with the rights or
> licenses herein granted to Distributor.

Exclusive rights. The producer/owner represents, moreover, that
he or she has not granted the rights given to the distributor to anyone else; in addition, the producer agrees that these rights won't be
granted to anyone else in the future and that nothing will be done to
interfere with the rights granted to the distributor. For example, suppose that the producer gives an exclusive right to the distributor in the
specific territory, but later grants the right to another distributor in
another territory to sell video cassettes to a chain of video stores that
have outlets both in that other territory and the original territory.
That would be a violation of this provision.

> Owner has not sold, assigned, transferred or conveyed and will not
> sell, transfer, assign or convey to any party, any right, title or interest
> in the Picture contrary to the rights granted to Distributor and
> will not authorize any other party to exercise any right or take any
> action which will interfere with or compete with the rights granted
> to Distributor . . .

Finished movie. The producer promises that on the delivery date
(the date that the materials are delivered to the producer), the movie
will be finished. It will be completely assembled with a complete
English language sound track and all up to the required specifications.

> On the Delivery Date, the Picture will be completely finished, fully
> edited and titled and fully synchronized with English language, dia-
> logue, sound and music, recorded with sound equipment pursuant

to valid licenses and in all respects ready and of a technical quality adequate for general release . . .

Rating. The movie will also conform to industry standards and norms promulgated by the MPAA. In addition, the movie will have an MPAA rating.[17] In many cases, such as this one, the restrictiveness of the rating will be specified. For example, suppose that the distributor specializes in distributing family-oriented movies, but the rating comes in at R. This would be a problem. Note that if this is an issue, it is always important to understand it in the early going. Producers have to keep track of rights given to third parties, such as directors who, for artistic reasons, may not want to be bound to a certain rating. The producer should think this through during the negotiation of the director's contract because it may be difficult getting the director who has no restrictions to allow editing the film later for ratings purposes.

On the Delivery Date, the Picture will conform to the requirements of the Motion Picture Association of America, Inc., and has, or will, when submitted for a rating, receive an MPAA rating not more restrictive than "PG-13."

Payments made. The producer/owner also represents that there are no material unpaid bills with respect to the movie. Unpaid bills open the distributor to claims by creditors who are owed money. The list of payments include: payments to owners of copyrights (literary, dramatic, and musical rights) for stories, plots, and other creative elements related to the movie; payments to inventors and patent right holders for the use of equipment and technology; payments with respect to exploitation and the payment of all production costs.

On the Delivery Date, all of the following have been fully paid or discharged or the payment thereof shall be secured in a manner reasonably satisfactory to Distributor:
All claims and rights of owners of copyrights in literary, dramatic, musical rights and other property or rights in and to all stories, plays, scripts, scenarios, themes, incidents, plots, characters, dialogues, sounds, music, words and other material of any nature whatsoever appearing, used or recorded in the Picture;
All claims and rights of owners of inventions and patent rights with respect to the recording of any and all dialogue, music and

other sound effects recorded in the Picture and with respect to the use of all equipment, apparatus, appliances and other materials used in the photographing, recording or otherwise in the manufacture of the Picture;

All claims and rights with respect to the use, distribution, performance, exhibition and exploitation of the Picture, and any music contained therein, excluding so-called small performance fees and television performing rights fees payable to the owners of copyrights to the music contained in the Picture; and

All costs of producing and completing the Picture.

No liens. Now back to the representation. The distributor wants to know that there are no liens against the movie. The distributor doesn't want third parties out there taking the producer (and movie) into bankruptcy in order to satisfy the claim. A lien is a word that is usually accompanied by a list of legal words that have a similar meaning—a legal interest attached to a property representing the temporary rights of a third party for the purposes of giving the third party a sense of security. Another term is security interest. For example, you go to the bank and borrow money for a new car. The bank looks at the situation and analyzes its risk; if you default on the loan, the bank could come after you (but, of course, the likelihood is that if you had the money you probably wouldn't have defaulted on the loan) or it will just simply take back the car (the car is collateral and the bank's interest in the car is a security interest). Another example is necessary. Suppose you are an investor in a motion picture that runs into cost overruns. Before long, the producer declares bankruptcy. Ah, but your attorney (a bright fellow indeed) made sure that to protect your position you have a security interest in the movie. What does this mean to you? It means that you move to the head of the line, ahead of the unsecured creditors (i.e., those creditors of the producer who don't have a security interest in the producer's asset). So, while everyone is waiting around to see what assets of the producer can be liquidated to pay them off, you, the investor in this example, stand at the head of the line when the main asset—the movie itself—is liquidated and the creditors are paid.

Except for customary guild liens. We noted this before, of course, but it bears repeating that SAG, at least, will demand a security interest in the movie to satisfy certain of the producer's obligations under the SAG agreement with the producer. There is no practical way to avoid these liens, so the producer/owner must make note of them in this representation.

> Except for customary guild liens, bank liens and completion guarantor liens created in connection with the financing of the Picture's production, there are not now, and there will not be outstanding at any time liens, claims, charges, encumbrances, restrictions, agreements, commitments, or arrangements whatsoever with any person, firm or corporation, or any obligation (past, present or future), or any defaults under, or breaches of, any contact, license or agreement which can, or will, in any way interfere with, impair, abrogate, or adversely or otherwise affect any of the rights granted to Distributor pursuant to the terms of this Agreement, and that (except to the extent hereinafter expressly provided) there are not now and will not be any payments of any kind required to be made by Distributor in respect, or as a result, of any use of the Picture pursuant to the rights and licenses herein granted to Distributor. Owner represents and warrants that any liens of any other third parties which may hereafter attach to the Picture are and will be subordinate in all respects to Distributor's rights under this Agreement, and that Owner has paid and will pay all sums owing to Screen Actors Guild, if any, including residuals, except as set forth below;

No infringement or violation of third-party rights. The distributor wants to know that the movie (including its title and all of its various parts) will not violate the rights of any other person. There are a lot of issues here, but the basic concern is again a desire on the part of the distributor to avoid liability for any of the problems listed. Remember that the purpose of the representations and warranties provision is to clarify who should bear the liability for problems. Of course, in real life, the negotiation is a matter of both logic and leverage (which party is the strongest), but I would like to focus on logic. All of the problems listed here are problems that the producer/owner caused or overlooked (made an error or omission). As between the two, the producer/owner is in the the best position to prevent these problems. Trademark issues, as we have discussed, most likely arise during the shooting of the movie—the failure to clear certain shots with trademark owners, for example. Copyright issues include chain of title problems that find themselves in the final shooting and final conformed script (the script that conforms to the dialogue that actually makes it into the movie. Personal and privacy rights include the failure to clear name and likeness rights from people who appear in the film or in promotions for the film. The distributor wants the producer/owner, as the party who is in the best position to know, to give details related to these possible latent defects in the intellectual property and contractual aspects of the movie.

> To the best of Owner's knowledge, neither the Picture nor any part thereof, nor any materials contained therein or synchronized therewith, nor the title thereof, nor the exercise of any right, license of privilege herein granted, violates or will violate, or infringes any trademark, trade name, contract, copyright (whether common law or statutory), patent, or any literary, artistic, dramatic, personal, private, civil or property right of privacy or publicity or "moral rights of authors" or any other right whatsoever or constitute libel or slander of any person, firm, corporation or association whatsoever . . .

No other distribution. Since the distributor is bargaining for exclusive distribution rights, the distributor wants to know whether the movie has been distributed by any means. A prior release could have a negative impact. For example, suppose that the producer showed the movie around, but it never took hold—it didn't have legs (as they say). This would be information that the distributor would need to know.

> In the Territory, neither the Picture nor any part thereof has been released, distributed, or exhibited theatrically or non-theatrically or by means of television, nor has it been banned by the censors of, or refused import permit or entry into, any nation or political subdivision thereof . . .

Government actions. Likewise, the distributor would like to know whether the movie had been banned for censorship or other reasons by any government. Obviously, if the answer is yes, then that market and perhaps others won't be available for the movie.

No transfer of rights. The distributor would also like to know whether any rights related to the movie have been transferred to another person in the territory. This not only includes the movie, but the material (book, original screenplay, or other work) upon which the movie is based. Remember our discussion regarding sequels in the rights agreement? Look at the same concept from the distributor's point of view. The distributor is gearing up to distribute your movie; that means money for P&A, and so forth. Then, all of a sudden, another company releases *Son of Quest,* based on a grant of rights that you gave that other company. The distributor won't be happy.

> In the Territory for the Term of this Agreement, Owner has not sold, assigned, transferred or conveyed, and will not sell, assign, transfer or convey, to any party, any right, title or interest in and to the Picture or any part thereof, or in and to the dramatic or literary material upon which it is based adverse to or derogatory of the rights granted to Distributor. In the Territory for the Term of this Agreement, Owner further represents and warrants that it has not authorized and will not authorize any party to distribute, exhibit or exploit in any language, in any location, by any method or means, the Picture . . .

All necessary rights. The distributor also wants to make sure that the producer/owner owns or controls all the rights necessary to produce and exploit the movie and that the rights are paid for and are without restriction. There are three types of rights receiving attention here: (1) the rights required to create or produce the movie, (2) the right to exploit the movie (i.e., distribute, exhibit, etc.), and (3) the right to exploit the movie in any media (i.e., at theaters, on DVD, over the Internet, etc.). With regard to the third set of rights, the distributor asks the producer/owner to confirm that the owner owns and controls the full set of rights granted for use in all media and devices now known and "hereafter devised." With regard to music, distributors know that royalties for performing rights relative to music are paid on a per performance basis in the future, so the distributor wants to know that satisfying the normal requirements of paying ASCAP, BMI, or other performing rights organization will be sufficient. If not, the distributor wants to know the story—either the music is in the public domain, so royalties don't need to be paid at all, or the producer/owner controls the rights directly and so the payments under the distribution agreement will satisfy the distributor's obligations related to music.

> Owner owns and controls, without limitations or restrictions whatsoever, all motion picture, performance and all other rights granted hereunder in and to the Picture and all the sound tracks thereof, and has obtained all necessary licenses required for the production,

synchronization, exhibition, performance, distribution, marketing and exploitation of the Picture hereunder (including the music contained therein, subject only to the payment of such performing fees if any, as are customarily payable by exhibitors to such performing rights society as shall have jurisdiction) throughout the Territory and in perpetuity for any and all purposes licensed hereunder and by every means, method and device now or hereafter known or required for full, complete and unlimited exercise and enjoyment by Distributor of each and all of the rights herein granted to it; the performing rights to all musical compositions contained in the Picture are (i) controlled by the American Society of Composers, Authors and Publishers (ASCAP), Broadcast Music, Inc. (BMI), the Performing Rights Society (PRS) or their affiliates or (ii) in the public domain or (iii) controlled by Owner to the extent required for the purpose of this Agreement in which event Owner hereby grants a synchronization license and public performance license to Distributor with regard to all music contained in the Picture throughout the Territory and in perpetuity without additional consideration . . .

No other payments. The distributor wants to make certain that the producer/owner left no payment obligations to the distributor. For example, in this sample provision, the distributor asks the producer/owner to represent that there are no payments that must be made to actors, musicians, directors, writers, or other participants in the movie. In other words, the distributor wants to clarify that these obligations belong to the producer/owner.

There are not and will not be any payments (out of any part of any revenues from the distribution or exploitation of the Picture or otherwise) which must be made by Distributor to any actors, musicians, directors, writers or to other persons who participated in the Picture, or to any union, guild or other labor organization for any right to exhibit the Picture or as compensation in connection with such exhibition or for any other use of the Picture or any of the rights therein and thereto granted hereunder and Distributor shall have no obligation to pay any residuals . . .

Valid copyright. The distributor also wants to know that the movie copyright and the copyright on the material on which the movie is based are valid and will last for a long time—here the provision reads "for the maximum period of copyright protection available . . ." In addition, the distributor needs to be sure that the movie is not in the public domain in any material part, as this again would weaken the exclusivity of the distributor. The producer's lawyer appropriately adds, however, that if the distributor markets the movie in some territory that is not a signatory to the Berne Convention, the representation and warranty will not apply; the producer, in essence, draws the line at taking on the obligation to research the laws of all nations.

> The copyright in the Picture and the literary, dramatic and musical material upon which it is based or which is contained in the Picture will be valid and subsisting for the maximum period of copyright protection available throughout the universe, and no material part of any thereof is in the public domain. Anything in the foregoing notwithstanding, however, if Distributor distributes or sub-licenses the Picture within countries not signatory to the Berne Convention, then the representations and warranties stated in this paragraph shall not apply.

Technical requirements. The distributor also wants to be sure that the producer will take responsibility for any problems caused by a technical defect in the materials related to the movie (for example, negatives, interrogatives, interpositives, etc.) delivered to the distributor.

> All negatives, interrogatives, interpositives and other pre-print material delivered or made available to Distributor are and will be of a technical quality suitable in Distributor's sole discretion for the manufacture therefrom of technically acceptable positive release prints of the Picture and the trailer(s) thereof.

Representations, warranties, and covenants: the producer/owner fights back.

We discussed this briefly above, but let's review. In the representations and warranties section, the producer/owner can typically make several arguments that mitigate responsibility. Remember that the philosophical basis for representations and warranties is that the producer/owner is in the best position to know and should therefore take responsibility. However, distributors will often be willing to allow certain changes in the wording.

"Best knowledge." With regard to certain representations and warranties, the producer/owner will want to say, "to the best of my knowledge . . ." something is true. If the issue is ever decided by a court, this clause will often mitigate the producer's risk. For example, look at the provision under the title "Valid Copyright" on page 389. The producer might prevail in an argument that this provision is modified by a best-knowledge qualifier. There are many countries in the world, each with a slightly different copyright law. The phrase will be less effective in the United States, of course, but in some nations it might remove the producer from liability. There are other provisions where a best-knowledge qualifier will be useful; for example: (1) payments (the producer is saying that he or she may not be directly in control of all payments); (2) violation of third-party rights (the producer may not have knowledge of all possible claims because some of the material might have been gathered by third parties or from sources that have been deemed to be in the public domain); (3) no distribution in the territory (because distributors in other territories might have been illegally distributing in the territory); (4) no restriction on distribution (because the producer may not be able to anticipate all applicable regulatory restrictions); and (5) valid copyright (see above).

Material. Another qualifier used by producer's counsel is the word "material." For example, a distributor may ask the producer to warrant that there are no restrictions to distribution. A simple response might be to add material before the word "restrictions" in the warranty. It doesn't always persuade the distributor, but is worth a try here and there.

Deliveries regarding chain of title and other matters.
Because the distributor is a favored target by potential claimants, representations and warranties alone may not be satisfactory. Often, in addition, distributors will want their lawyers to have a chance to review the chain of title documentation and will require the producer/owner to make copies of all such documentation available to the distributor. Consider this the final word on the topic of chain of title. If the producer has been doing his or her job, the producer's claim of copyright ownership will be superior to all persons who have any creative input into the development or production of the movie.

Chain of title documentation. Sure, the movie is registered with USCO as a separate work related to the original underlying work and/or screenplay. But, as you know, legal title is proved by written contracts, waivers, and executed certificates of authorship, and the like (either employment agreements that rely on the work-made-for-hire doctrine or contractor agreements that require an assignment of rights) and the USCO registration certificates related to all the various creative elements connected with the movie; the distributor may want to see these things.

Documentation related to the clearance of other liability issues. Distributors may also want to have the right to see documentation that the producer has cleared all potential actions unrelated to copyright matters, such as the right to use a person's name and likeness in the movie or in connection with the promotion of the movie. This is especially true in the case of merchandise that bears the likeness of any real person. Distributors' attorneys are sensitive, as we have discussed, to possible claims of defamation and invasion of privacy.

> At Distributor's reasonable request and expense, Owners shall provide Distributor with copies of all registrations, contracts and other documentation evidencing Owner's ownership of all right, title and interest in and to the Picture and each of the elements required to be delivered to Distributor pursuant to this paragraph and all research and other evidence related to the right to use the name and likeness of any person portrayed or appearing in the Picture and of any other documentation of whatever nature related to the clearance of potential or actual third-party rights or claims. In addition, Owner shall deliver true and correct copies of the errors and omissions insurance policy referred to below and a certificate from the insurer that the policy is in full effect during the required period of time.

Indemnity.

One major point of representations and warranties is to exact an indemnity in cases where a misrepresentation leads to a loss of some type. Let's suppose that the producer/owner represents that the distribution rights are exclusive to the distributor, but it turns out that the rights in the same territory have been given to another entity, which sues the distributor and wins a judgment. This loss, then, would be passed along to the producer who made the warranty to the original distributor.

Who is covered. The provision makes clear that the distributor, its subsidiaries and affiliated companies, its officers, directors, and employees are covered by the indemnity. Come on, guys, let's put in "representatives" too. Got to cover the lawyers.

Right of set off. Always a hotly contested provision, the distributor is asking for the right to enforce his or her own indemnity right by simply keeping the indemnification money as it comes in the door instead, of course, of paying the money to the producer. This, believe me, is an onerous privilege and gives the distributor enormous leverage in a dispute. Most producers will resist it.

Owner does hereby and shall at all times indemnify and hold harmless Distributor, its subsidiary and affiliated companies, its officers, directors, and employees, and its exhibitors, licensees and assignees, and each of them, of and from any and all claims, demands, and causes of action, or any thereof, arising out of or relating to the Picture, connected with or resulting from any breach by Owner of any of its representations, warranties, covenants or undertaking under this Agreement. Upon notice from Distributor of any such claim, demand or action being advanced or commenced, Owner agrees to adjust, settle, or defend the same at the sole cost of Owner. If Owner shall fail promptly to do so, Distributor shall have the right, at Distributor's own expense, and is hereby authorized and empowered by Owner to appear by its attorneys in any such action, to adjust, settle, compromise, litigate, contest, and/or satisfy judgments and take any other action necessary or desirable for the disposition of such claim, demand or action. Distributor shall have the right to deduct the amount of any such payments and expenses, or any part thereof, from any sums accruing to or for the account of Owner under this or any other agreement between Owner and Distributor.

Additional insured. Distributors will often require the producer to procure and maintain appropriate E&O insurance for the duration of the release cycle. In addition, the distributor may insist on being named as an additional insured on the policy. Thus, if the distributor incurs a loss related to the insured movie, the distributor can collect on the policy. Most insurers have little trouble with this, since one of the main reasons that producers obtain the insurance is to satisfy the demands of the distributor related to E&O issues. This provision involves an agreement over the limits of the policy. It provides that the producer's insurance will be used prior to any insurance carried by the distributor—the result of this, naturally, will go to lowering the insurance premiums for the distributor.

> Owner agrees to cause Distributor to be named as an additional insured with respect to the Picture under Owner's Errors and Omissions policy for a period of three (3) years from commencement of photography of the Picture, which insurance shall be in an amount not less than $1 Million/$3 Million with a deductible of not greater than Ten Thousand Dollars ($10,000). Owner agrees to cause its carrier to assume primary responsibility, notwithstanding the fact that Distributor shall also have its own insurance coverage. Owner's policy must provide that any insurance coverage held by Distributor is excess insurance not subject to exposure until the coverage of Owner's policy is exhausted. Owner's policy must provide for thirty (30) days prior written notice to Distributor prior to any revision, modification or termination.

Distributor's warranties.

The producer will also want the distributor to make representations and warranties. These provisions are more or less standard corporate representations not specific to the movie business and include things like the distributor's statement that (1) it is duly organized and validly existing under the relevant laws; (2) it has the power and authority to enter into the agreement; and (3) the agreement will be an enforceable legal obligation of the distributor.

Duties of the distributor regarding the copyright.

The producer will be placing the movie in the distributor's hands for an important and critical phase of its existence. Therefore, the producer wants to make sure that the distributor will cooperate in protecting the copyright.

Registration. The distributor will most likely be in a better position to ensure that the copyright is registered in the "territory" (especially where the territory is not the United States). Thus, the distributor is obligated to register the copyright in the territory in the producer/owner's name or, if the producer/owner approves, the distributor's name. Copyright registration in the distributor's name is necessary only if the registration procedures require it; this poses a risk to the producer/owner, of course, so the producer/owner requires that the distributor hold the copyright in trust for the producer/owner.

Distributor shall pay any and all fees necessary or required to protect the Picture and all materials relating thereto by copyright in the Territory, such copyright to be taken in the name of Owner or Distributor, as Owner shall designate in its sole discretion, and to renew or extend such copyright. It is agreed, however, that if taken in Distributor's name, Distributor shall hold the copyright and renewals thereof in trust for Owner's benefit and further that upon the expiration of the rights granted herein with respect to the Picture, all rights in and to such copyright shall revert to Owner.

Infringement. The distributor agrees to give the producer/owner notice of any infringement of the copyright or trademarks and to take charge of any proceedings in the producer's name. The owner nevertheless reserves the right to take whatever action the producer/owner thinks is necessary to protect the owner's (and the distributor's) rights.

Distributor shall promptly notify Owner in writing of any infringement in the Territory of the copyright of the Picture or of the trademarks used in connection therewith, and shall take any and all proceedings in the name of Owner or Distributor, or any other parties, as Owner shall in its sole discretion direct to prevent and restrain any such infringement. Owner is authorized to take such steps as it deems advisable to protect its rights and those of Distributor in and to the copyright of the literary, dramatic or musical material for the Picture and all materials relating thereto.

Merchandise Licensing

MERCHANDISING RIGHTS

Using entertainment property-borne characters as the basis of merchandising is not a new concept.[1] But the concept didn't reach its full-blown glory until the 1970s with the motion picture series *Star Wars.* Today, merchandising is a major consideration of most movie deals. Merchandising obviously works better for some genres than others (*Spider Man* toys, accessories, games, bedsheets, lunch pails, shirts, and shoes, etc., intuitively seem more marketable than the same line of products branded by the logo of a movie like *A Beautiful Mind,* for example. Even I would prefer a Spider Man T-shirt to one featuring Russell Crowe as John Nash—although I wouldn't count the possibility of the Crowe T-shirt out entirely).

Merchandising is a concern often in the development or preproduction stages. If the character is a soldier, for example, even the weapons that a character carries and the vehicles that he rides in are frequently designed with toys in mind.

Promotional tie-ins are another form of merchandising. A noted example is Sears Roebuck's promotional tie-in with Steven Spielberg's animated feature, *An American Tail.* Sears used the movie tie-in to enhance its own exposure. Sears spun off a second-tier promotion to McDonald's, bringing families flocking to this fast food Mecca for branded toys and souvenir cups. The model has been followed many times over.

MERCHANDISING RIGHTS DEAL

A general merchandising rights deal is fairly straightforward. It starts with clarifying the scope of the license. We will discuss later how merchandising is dealt with between the rights holder and the manufacturer (who will exploit these rights with, and, therefore, stands in the shoes of, a distributor—don't get confused).

Merchandising defined.

Merchandising is defined here as tangible goods, meaning all of the things we have discussed above: games (computer, video, and other electronic games), toys, comic books, so-called "making of books," apparel, food, beverages, posters, and other commodities items. These tangible goods are based on or utilize the names, likeness, or characteristics of the artists in their roles in the movie. Finally, these goods are for general sale to the public. Note that services can also be defined as merchandise. If it can be branded, marketed, and sold, it is merchandise.

> Merchandising means exploitation of tangible goods that are based on or utilize names, likenesses or characteristics of artists in their roles in a Motion Picture or physical materials appearing in or used for a Motion Picture and that are made for sale to the general public.

Merchandising rights—general legal underpinnings.

Let's think about the legal requirements of merchandising in light of this definition. In other words, do you have the right to engage in merchandising? Character merchandising relies on a combination of two or three basic legal footings: (1) grant of publicity rights—the right to use a person's name and likeness for commercial purposes; (2) grant of copyright—the right to use a unique design or characteristic of a character's physical appearance or costume; and (3) grant of trademark license—the right to use trademarks (names and logos of popular properties) in the branding of the merchandise.

> In connection with every Motion Picture produced or created under this Agreement, Producer shall have the sole and exclusive Merchandising Rights during the Merchandising Period in and to the Picture-Related Merchandise (as defined below) throughout the

universe, except for the Reserved Territory (as defined below). "Picture-Related Merchandise" shall mean any merchandise, product, service or other merchandising item of any nature that relates to the Property with respect to which either the item itself, or its packaging (or "hang tags") or its marketing or promotional materials, explicitly reference the Picture (e.g., "Now a major motion picture") produced hereunder or contains, uses or incorporates any distinguishable element, artwork, design, logo or other material which first appears in the Picture produced hereunder. "Classic Merchandise" shall mean all merchandise relating to the Property which is not Picture-Related Merchandise. Owner has the sole and exclusive merchandising rights in perpetuity throughout the universe with respect to Classic Merchandise.

Did you and your lawyer take care of obtaining all these rights when the timing was right?

Name and likeness. Remember the artist agreement? We went to great pains to have the artist give us the right to use his or her name and likeness. Imagine an Indiana Jones T-shirt. Suppose that the lawyers for Mr. Lucas failed to get Harrison Ford to grant this right in Mr. Ford's acting agreement. This would not be good, because Mr. Ford is Indiana Jones. People might not be thrilled about buying a T-shirt with some generic guy touting a whip.

Designs. Think of a Darth Vader doll. For this purpose, it may be largely irrelevant that David Prowse was the guy walking around in that black robotic-looking galactic garb and that James Earl Jones was the ominous voice. The real issue here is who owns the character design. Well, again, if Mr. Lucas's motion picture lawyers were doing their job correctly (and it certainly appears that they were), the costume and character designers gave their rights to Mr. Lucas's company, Lucasfilm, in their contracts for the purpose of making merchandise.

Trademarks. The producer will also need to own, in a trademark sense, the names of the properties being licensed. There is very little doubt that Mr. Lucas's lawyers did a fine job registering a trademark for the name and logo seen on official *Star Wars* merchandise.

Combinations. Again, these things can work in combination. A Luke Skywalker doll, for example, implicates the character (including the character's costumes, weapons, etc.) designs, the likeness of the actor (in this case, Mark Hamill) who plays the character, the name of the character itself, and the *Star Wars* brand. If you are serious about merchandise licensing, you and your lawyer will need to care about all these issues.

Picture-related merchandise.

This limitation is usually a critical one in cases where the movie is based on a preexisting franchise. Examples are plentiful. Before it became a 2002 blockbuster hit movie, the Spider Man property was a comic book. Before the movie, there was a Saturday-morning animation series. Spider Man merchandise did not wait for 2002—it was around for several generations prior to that. So, what happens to the preexisting merchandising deals now? Although there is not just one answer to this question, a common approach is illustrated in the example above—the movie distributor's right to merchandise is strictly limited to picture-related merchandise. In this case, the agreement defines this as merchandise relating to the movie being distributed and nothing else. The merchandise must be specifically identified with the movie by its packaging (which includes so-called hang tags—tags sewn into plush dolls or clothing) or by words (such as "now a major motion picture" or by specific elements, artwork (including colors), designs, logos, or other material that appears in and in connection with the movie. The marketing materials must also have this same specific identification.

Limitations and restrictions on the rights.

In the agreement we have been discussing, the producer gets an exclusive merchandising right, with the exception of a reserved territory. Keep in mind that the producer has to sell this to a distributor down the road. Limitations like the reserved territory in our agreement can be difficult—sometimes impossible—to sell to a major distributor. Japan, for example, is a fertile field for comic book and computer game titles that could be made into feature motion pictures. The issue here is often that the merchandising campaign is highly developed at home and, thus, the licensor of rights may either need to (because he has a contract with a third party) or want to reserve the merchandising rights for the home territory. This will result in a struggle (because the distributor will not be happy about giving up the exclusivity), but if the property is famous the owner may have the leverage to get the deal done with the restriction in place.

Style restrictions.

The owner/licensor of a character has a vested interest in the look of the character in the movie. Therefore, the rights agreement may contain guidelines related to the costuming and other design elements of the character. In this example, the producer is required to submit for approval a detailed style guide. In addition to the producer's obligation to follow the guide in creating the characters for the movie, the producer is obligated to give a copy to and require third-party merchandise licensees to follow the guide.

> Producer shall submit to Owner a detailed style guide (the "Style Guide") depicting the character of The Prince along with any other characters contained in the Prince Comics or Prince television programs ("Prior Material") that Producer decides to include therein. Each character contained in the Style Guide shall be in color, and shall illustrate the front, back, sides and size of the relevant character. Within ten (10) days following receipt of any draft of the Style Guide, Owner shall provide Producer with either its written approval thereof, or detailed, specific objections thereto. If a draft of the Style Guide is not approved, upon Producer's receipt of Owner's specific objections thereto, Producer shall use reasonable efforts to address Owner's objections, after which Producer shall resubmit the disapproved portions of the Style Guide to Owner. Producer may amend the Style Guide at any time; provided that Producer submits any such amendment to Owner for its approval. In respect of Producer's third party licensees who distribute Picture-Related Merchandise and with whom Producer is in privity of contract, Producer (i) shall furnish the Style Guide to each such licensee, and (ii) shall contractually require each such licensee to comply with the provisions of the Style Guide; provided, however, that under no circumstances shall a breach of any of the terms of this provision by any such licensee be deemed a breach thereof by Producer.

Hold-back restrictions on licensor.

The producer (who stands now in the shoes of the distributor, because the producer will have to sell this rights agreement, restrictions and all, to the distributor) will spend a lot of money distributing the picture and gearing up for the picture-related merchandising campaign. He knows that the distributor will not want to compete with the preexisting merchandise (referred to in sample provision that follows as "Classic Merchandise"). Therefore, the hold-back mechanism is employed. In this case, the owner has to refrain from licensing merchandising rights for a period that runs from a year before the movie is released to two years after its release. An exception is made for licensing agreements in place at the time the agreement is signed, although the producer makes sure that these preexisting licensing agreements are not expanded in scope and are strictly and narrowly observed. This three-year period is designed to give the picture-related merchandise a fair chance to take hold.

> During the period commencing one (1) year prior to the initial theatrical release in the United States of the Picture and continuing through and until two (2) years after such initial theatrical release, Owner agrees that it shall not distribute, sell, or authorize the distribution or sale of, any items of Classic Merchandise other than those items set forth on the attached Exhibit "A" which are currently being distributed by third party licensees of Owner pursuant to fully-executed license agreements. Owner agrees that such items shall only be distributed in accordance with the provisions of such pre-existing license agreements, and that such pre-existing license agreements shall not be modified or extended after the date hereof without Producer's prior written consent. Exhibit "A" also shall set forth the territory and term of each such license agreement. In this connection, Producer shall advise Owner of the anticipated initial theatrical release date of the Picture.

Rising tide theory.

As an alternative to a hold-back, the producer (again looking out for the distributor's position) will insist that he or she receive an appropriate percentage of any substantial rise in Classic Merchandise revenue due to the marketing of the movie. For example, let's suppose that the owner in our example has a licensing agreement for Classic Merchandise that for the past three years has generated $1 million per year. Then, a month prior to the theatrical release of the movie, right when the movie's ad campaign is getting under way, there is a sudden spike to $1.3 million per year. The owner reaps a similar rise in his participation in the Classic Merchandise. The producer's lawyer will try to come up with a formula that gives the producer a certain percentage of the increase (in this example, in the $300,000 spike). It is not always easy to demonstrate the rising tide and is cumbersome to administer. Still, it may be preferred, when compared with a hold-back restriction.

Merchandising compensation.

There are essentially two approaches to merchandising revenue. One is to include merchandising revenues as part of the definition of gross for the purpose of calculating net. The owner gets a participation by getting a piece of the net. In this example, however, the owner of the rights demands that the merchandising rights be kept separate and that a separate royalty rate apply to merchandising—regardless of how the producer actually decides to treat the merchandise on the exploitation side.

> Notwithstanding any other provision hereof, under no circumstances shall the computation of the Gross Receipts hereunder take into account revenues properly attributable to the use or other exploitation of merchandising license rights. If Producer shall produce the Picture under this Agreement, Producer shall pay to Owner an amount equal to fifteen percent (15%) of the "Merchandising Net Receipts" derived from the Picture. For purposes of this agreement, the "Merchandising Net Receipts" derived from any motion picture produced hereunder shall mean and refer to all revenues actually received by Purchaser from the use or other exploitation of the merchandising license rights respecting such motion picture less any licensing agents' commissions and any other costs and expenses (including collection costs) directly relating to the realization of such revenues.

Merchandising period.

Significantly, the merchandise licensing period starts prior to the release of the movie. That is because merchandise licensing and movie marketing experts know that the promotion of merchandise promotes the movie and vice versa. The rumor is that the prerelease merchandising effort for *Spider Man,* the subject of the most successful theatrical release of all time at this point, generated revenues that rival those obtained at the box office. In the example below, merchandise licensing may begin six months prior to the theatrical release. The merchandising licensee may continue to sell merchandise for a number of years after the movie is finished. Notice that the merchandising period is different for "toys and games" and all other types of merchandise, with toys and games having a window that is twice that of other merchandise. The rationale probably has something to do with the nature of the product inventory—toys and games are produced in greater quantities and take longer to sell off than T-shirts and bed-sheets.

> The "Merchandising Period" means (i) with respect to toys and games, the period commencing on the date six (6) months prior to the initial theatrical release of the First Picture and continuing through and until the date that is five (5) years after the Production Period expires, and (ii) with respect to all other items of merchandise, the period commencing six (6) months prior to the initial theatrical release of the First Picture and continuing through and until the date that is three (3) years after the date on which the Production Period expires.

THE MERCHANDISE LICENSING DEAL

Okay, let's look at it from the other side. You have the merchandising rights and you want to exploit them. As noted above, there are three ways to do this. One way is give the rights to the theatrical distributor and let the distributor run with them. Another way is to go through a licensing agent. The third way is to approach the merchandise manufacturers one at a time, for example, a toy manufacturer, game manufacturer, apparel companies, etc. Whatever way is chosen, it is important to understand the basics of the licensing deal:

Licensing agent.

There are a number of licensing agents out there who will take your property and make licensing deals with various manufacturers. This is a great advantage to producers, especially first-timers, because these agents are experts in the merchandise licensing world. They know what the standard deals are, who the reputable manufacturers are, and, of course, have access to these manufacturers. The downside? A licensing agent takes about one third of the licensing revenues. In some cases, this may be negotiable, but that is where the negotiations will start.

Merchandise—the style guide.

The first step in a merchandising deal, of course, is to identify the merchandise or property being licensed. Merely listing the characters is not sufficient, since other things matter. For example, it is important to standardize the appearance of the character, including the exact design and color of the character's skin (or fur or feathers, as the case may be), and clothing and equipment, and so on. The typical method employed for this is a style guide, which the licensee must follow in manufacturing merchandise. The style guide contains detailed renderings of all the matters that the licensor holds dear: drawings of the characters from several perspectives, a color guide, etc. The licensee must strictly follow the style guide.

> The "Property" consists of (i) the names and likenesses of the Characters (defined below) as depicted in the "Quest" Style Guide, as amended and updated from time to time, a copy of which shall be forwarded to Licensee upon execution of this Agreement; (ii) the Trademarks as set forth in Exhibit "A"; and (iii) such other trademarks (including any trademark applications and registrations related thereto) related to the Property that Licensor develops and/or uses during the Term.

Trademarks.

A trademark is a word or design (for example, a logo) that identifies to consumers the source of the merchandising. Not all names or logos are trademarks, because the name or logo must be used in a trademark sense—in other words, the mark must be used as a brand or in other ways stand for the source of the merchandise. For example, *Peter Pan*, merely as the title of a movie, does not work as a trademark. But Disney works as a trademark, because the word (especially when the stylized lettering registered by The Walt Disney Company is used) has acquired customer good will over the years. When people see the Disney label, they expect a certain type of product.[2] *Peter Pan* would work as a trademark for merchandising if a line of characters were marketed under the *Peter Pan* name (the trademark status of the mark can be reinforced by labeling each character doll or each toy or T-shirt or whatever with a *Peter Pan* label). At any rate, it is important to understand that the characters (with their design elements) are different than the trademarks that identify the source.

Future trademarks and characters.

It is possible in the life of characters and trademarks that the licensor will continue to develop interesting elements to the family. The licensee will sometimes negotiate for the right to add these things to the deal.

Territory.

The territory in a merchandising deal is two dimensional: there is a geographical territory and market type (here referred to as a channel of distribution. Remember that all rights can be split up. Thus, a licensor can give one company the right to make and distribute merchandise in Japan and another company the right in Canada (another good reason for the style guide referred to above). Moreover, the licensor can pick one distributor for one kind of market and another for a different market—even within the same geographical territory.

The "Territory" is the United States and Canada and is limited to the following "Channels of Distribution:" Gift Market, Specialty/Department Market, Mid-Tier Market, Mass Market, direct mail and mail order catalogues, the Internet and television shopping networks.

Channels of distribution.

In the example above, there are several channels of distribution or merchandising markets listed.

Gift market. Here, the term gift market means card shops, gift shops, florists, independent and specialty toy stores (such as FAO Schwarz, Zany Brainy, Mastermind, and Store for Knowledge, but excludes mass market toy store chains, such as Toys "R" Us and KB Toys), hospital gift shops, airport gift shops (excluding duty-free shops), hotel gift shops, novelty shops, and chains (such as Spencer Gifts), high-end department stores (such as Macy's, Bloomingdale's, and Nordstrom, specialty children's apparel and accessory stores, and bookstore chains (such as Barnes and Noble, Borders, Waldenbooks, Chapters, and Indigo).

"Mid-Tier market." Mid-Tier Market usually means mid-tier department stores (such as JC Penney, Sears, and Mervyns).

"Mass market." Mass market means mass-market department stores (such as Wal-Mart, Kmart, and Target), club stores, mass market toy stores (such as Toys "R" Us and KB Toys), supermarkets, drugstores, dollar stores, video stores, and office superstores (such as Office Depot, Staples, and Office Max), but specifically excluding flea markets.

"Direct mail." The term direct mail means going directly to the consumer by way of the postal service (and not by way of a retail store). Mail order catalogs (such as L.L. Bean) are one example of directing marketing.

The Internet. The Internet is another means of direct marketing, but is listed separately, because it is new and specialized. The Internet can be a problem because many movie producers would like the right to sell property on their own Web site. The licensee, of course, doesn't want to compete with the producer. Internet marketing may have restrictions placed on it—hold backs for example.

Television shopping networks. Television shopping networks, such as QVC, are also a potential distribution method.

Royalty. The royalty is the main source of revenue to the producer. The typical range for a royalty rate is between 6 to 10 percent of gross sales. Here is an example of a simple escalating royalty, meaning that the royalty goes up if a certain threshold of net sales (as defined in the agreement) is reached. This example shows only one escalation threshold, but there can be more.

The "Royalty" is as follows: 8% of Gross Sales (as hereinafter defined) of the Licensed Articles (as hereinafter defined) to the extent such Net Sales are equal to or less than $500,000 and 8% of Net Sales of the Licensed Articles to the extent such Net Sales exceed $500,000 but are equal to or less than $1,000,000.

Gross sales. Gross sales is the most common formulation. Gross, of course, means all revenues generated by the sale of merchandise.

Net sales. Net sales is also used for the calculation of royalties. It is defined as gross sales less certain agreed-upon costs (the cost of manufacturing, shipping, and advertising, for example) and perhaps taxes. Obviously, the royalty rate in a net sales context should be higher.

Retail price. The royalty can also be based on the retail price of the merchandise. Instead of calculating the royalty based on net sales, the royalty is a percentage of suggested retail price. Where there is no suggested retail price, the royalty would be a percentage of 200 percent of the actual wholesale price.

Cover price. The royalty can also be based on the cover price (the price actually printed on the merchandise). Again, if there is no cover price, the royalty will be a percentage of 200 percent of the actual wholesale price.

Advance.

A common feature of any merchandising deal is an advance payment to the licensor. The advance payment is negotiable, there is no set formula for determining the amount. Obviously, the more valuable the property, the higher the advance. It is usually nonrefundable. Thus, if no merchandise is ever sold, the licensor keeps it. However, the advance is recouped out of the royalties payable to the licensor. Compare the advance to a fee (another possible payment in a merchandising deal); the fee is neither refundable nor recoupable. A fee, however, may not be accompanied by a royalty (for example, the licensee will offer a flat fee—say $25,000—per character).

An "Advance" in the amount of $100,000 shall be payable by Licensee as follows: $50,000 upon the execution of the Agreement by Licensee; and $50,000 on or before October 6, 2006. The Advance is non-refundable but recoupable from Royalties otherwise due during the Term.

Minimum guarantee.

Another common feature of a merchandising deal, especially where the licensor has bargaining leverage because there is a demand for the merchandise, is the minimum guarantee (or MG as it is sometimes called). The minimum guarantee is simply the lowest amount that must be paid to the licensor for the license. The MG can be calculated per year or per the term of the contract (as here). If it is per contract term, there are usually provisions in the contract providing a new (often increased) minimum guarantee for any renewal term. The rationale for the minimum guarantee is fairly obvious. When the owner of a hot property decides on an exclusive licensee, that owner must take the property off the market to all other distributors and rely on the licensee of choice to bring home the bacon. During the negotiations for hot properties, the licensee makes all kinds of promises about how well the licensee will perform, so the licensor says, "Okay, put your money where your mouth is." It goes without saying that if the property isn't hot, there will be no MG, or the MG will be small.

The "Minimum Guarantee" of Royalties for the Term is $500,000. Not later than thirty (30) days after the expiration of the Term, Licensee shall pay the negative difference, if any, between (i) the sum of the Advance and Royalty payments previously paid, and (ii) the Minimum Guarantee.

Copyright notice.

Remember that this is a license, so, if you have managed to keep ownership of the copyright of the movie, you will want the world to know it. Yes, I know that you do not need the copyright notice to protect your ownership, but when you get to this point—the point of publishing (or making public) your work—the notice is customary.

Each Licensed Article (as hereinafter defined) and all related advertising, promotional and packaging material shall include the following trademark and copyright notices (collectively, the "Notices"):

 TM

© 2006 Crabbapple Entertainment Group. All Rights Reserved.

Trademark notice.

The trademark notice in the United States takes two forms: (1) the ™ mark, which means that a trademark application is pending at the United States Patent and Trademark Office (PTO) and (2) the ® mark, which means that a trademark has been officially registered at the PTO.[3] In either case, the owner of the trademark will insist on the notice being placed on the merchandise.

The Notices must be prominently displayed on all Licensed Articles and related advertising, promotional and packaging material, either (in the case of packaging material) on a hang tag or well situated on the packaging itself. All point of purchase displays must include the Trademarks and Notices as well. If a permanent sewn label of any kind is affixed to the Licensed Articles the "crab and apple" design must be part of the sewn label. No other trademark or logo (including without limitation, . . . Licensee's own house mark) shall be displayed more prominently than the Trademarks. Notwithstanding the foregoing, if the physical limitations of the Licensed Articles do not permit placement of the Trademarks and Notices indicated above, subject to the prior written consent of Licensor, the foregoing may be abbreviated to the following:

© Crabbapple

Licensor approval.

Licensors want to protect the good will built up in their property and, therefore, licensors care about the quality and appearance of the merchandise. Cheap-looking merchandise reflects poorly on the image of the owner of the trademark and on the movie itself. Most licensing agreements, therefore, provide that the licensor will have the right to inspect and approve the merchandise, packaging, and advertising related to the merchandise.

Licensee shall submit for Licensor's prior written approval all samples, prototypes and layouts for the Licensed Articles and Copyrighted Materials at all stages of production. Licensee may not develop, proceed to the next stage of development and/or production, manufacture, use, offer for sale, sell, advertise, promote, ship, distribute or otherwise exploit any Licensed Articles or any Copyrighted Materials, in whole or in part, until it has received Licensor's written approval of such Licensed Articles or Copyrighted Materials. Such approval may be granted or withheld as Licensor, in its sole discretion, may determine to assure the quality of the Licensed Articles and Copyrighted Materials and the reputation of the Property. Licensor agrees that its approval rights with respect to Licensed Articles or Copyrighted Materials will not affect Licensee's freedom to determine its own prices. If Licensor fails to approve in writing any of the submissions furnished to it by Licensee within twenty (20) business days from the date of receipt thereof by Licensor, such failure shall be considered to be a disapproval thereof.

Approval process.

The process starts when the licensor provides licensee the style guide referred to on page 400. The licensee then makes samples, prototypes, and layouts. The licensor looks at these items, at any time during the production process. Before the licensee moves to the next stage of production (in other words before the licensee goes from the sample or prototype to the assembly line or from the layout to the finished project) he or she inspects these items. The example provides that the licensor can approve or disapprove in its sole discretion. Some licensees may argue that the standard should be reasonable approval (in other words, that the licensor should be required to give a reason for denying approval), but licensors will resist this. On the other hand, licensees will want to be free of licensor interference with respect to prices and other business-related matters. What happens if the licensor says nothing or fails to either approve or disapprove? If the licensor has a lot of leverage, silence will be deemed disapproval as in the example above. If the licensor has less leverage, however, silence will be deemed approval.

Quality control.

After the products start rolling off the assembly line, the licensor will still want the right to maintain quality control. This provision, therefore, provides that the licensor will continue to get samples and will have the right to inspect the manufacturing facility. The products must stand up to the standards set forth in the style guide.

> Thereafter, to enable Licensor to determine whether Licensee is maintaining quality, Licensee shall furnish and ship, at Licensee's expense, within thirty (30) days following the close of each Annual Period, samples of each Licensed Article, including all related packaging, advertising and promotional materials, and Licensee's annual catalogue (if any), and one (1) high-resolution digital photograph and/or transparency of each Licensed Article, as follows: two (2) samples of each to Licensor. Licensor shall have the right at all reasonable times, and upon reasonable notice, to inspect the site(s) of production of the Licensed Articles. Such inspection shall occur in the presence of an employee of Licensee, provided that such employee shall in no way interfere with Licensor's inspection rights. All Licensed Articles and Copyrighted Materials, and the manner of sale, advertisement, promotion, shipment, distribution and exploitation of same, shall be of high quality, and in accordance with the high quality standards established by Licensor for the Property as set forth in the "Quest" Style Guide.

Advertising.

The licensing agreement should also deal with the subject of advertising. If the property attracts attention from more than one potential licensee, then the promise to advertise could be a factor for making a decision. Here the licensee promises to spend $100,000 per year (not a lot of money in today's world of media, but better than nothing). Remember that advertising for the merchandise is also advertising for the movie.

> Licensee shall expend $100,000 during the first Annual Period for consumer print and/or television advertisements (specifically excluding co-op advertisements) to advertise and promote the Licensed Articles and the Property. Such advertisements shall be prepared by Licensee in consultation with Licensor. A detailed statement of accounting outlining such expenditures shall be furnished to Licensor simultaneously with the Royalty Report due for the first calendar quarter.

No co-op advertising.

The example above excludes co-op advertising. Co-op advertising is where two or more sponsors get together to create a single advertisement that works for both. For example, suppose Toys from Movies, Inc. (TFM), a toy manufacturer, makes a deal with the producer of *The Quest* to make action figures based on characters from the movie. Then suppose that TFM produces co-op ads with Toys for Sale, Inc. (TFS), a large chain of retail toy stores, where toys from the movie are part of a large montage of other toys and other brands. The point, again, is dilution of the brand and the possibility that the other toys listed in the ad may actually compete. Licensors would like to carefully control this type of situation.

Television advertising.

The most mass of mass media nowadays is still television. Thus, some licensors—those with a lot of leverage (because television advertising is one of the most expensive means of getting the word out)— insist that at least some of the advertising dollars be spent on television ads. A "national spot" is an advertising spot during a program that reaches the entire nation (some spots are sold to regional and local advertisers). "Direct response" advertisements are those that give the viewer a chance to buy the item being advertised directly from the source by calling a number or accessing a Web site displayed on the ad itself.

> In connection with the Marketing Date of the Licensed Articles, Licensee will promote the Licensed Articles and the Property with television advertisements, a minimum of five national spot buys, and

such advertisements may include direct response. All advertisements and promotions shall be in accordance with the prior approval of the Licensor. A detailed statement of outlining such advertisements shall be furnished to Licensor simultaneously with the Royalty Report due for the calendar quarter.

Sound-Track Albums

THE SOUND-TRACK ALBUM

Sound-track albums can be big business. The sound-track album related to the movie *Bodyguard*, featuring the vocal talent of Whitney Houston, among others, sold millions of units around the world and made a sizable sum of money for the producers of the movie—not to mention the record label that released the album, the owners of the compositions,[1] and the performers, including Whitney Houston, who acted in the movie and performed on the album. The sound track of *Titanic*, with Celine Dion's hit "My Heart Will Go On" is another example of a successful sound-track album. Even sound-track albums based on movies that don't sport a major hit song, even those that simply contain the score of the movie, can find a market. There are people out there who prefer movie sound-track albums to all other forms of recorded music. There are record labels (Varese Sarabande and Milan Records, for example) that specialize in this market. As a producer, you would do well not to ignore this possibility.

SOUND-TRACK ALBUM DEAL

One of the mysteries of Hollywood to me is that record labels owned by or affiliated with major studios don't always distribute the sound-track albums of movies released by that major studio—even where the major studio owns the copyright to the movie. Thus, for example, the sound-track album from a Universal Pictures release may not be released by Universal Music Group. Thus, if the affiliated label turns you down, approach other labels.

Rights clearance—the major issue.
The major issue with sound-track albums is easy to identify—clearing the rights—but not as easy to execute. If any part of the movie process needs the assistance of an experienced lawyer, this one does—as you will recall from our discussion above about music clearance.

The types of music employed. There are basically two types of music employed in a movie—music composed and recorded especially for the movie and music that is preexisting and prerecorded and used in the movie. Let's review some examples:

Music composed and recorded specifically for the movie. This is music that is written pursuant to the producer's contract with the composer. In a properly constructed contract, the work-made-for-hire doctrine dictates that the producer (not the composer or lyricist) is the author and owns the music; assuming that the producer obtained a signed waiver from each musician and other person who contributed to the session(s), the producer will also be the owner of any sound recording made of such music. Most score music falls under this category.

Preexisting music—original masters and rerecordings. Country singer, Trisha Yearwood, sings a song entitled "The Song Remembers When." Movie producers know the truth contained in this title and use it to good advantage. When a producer makes a movie based on a story that happens in the fifties, for example, you're bound to hear popular music from that era—here comes Elvis. These great old original recordings pack an emotional charge that adds a wonderful dimension to the impact of the movie. *Pretty Woman,* with Richard Gere and Julia Roberts, and countless other movies use this technique.[2] The original recordings are full of nostalgia, but so are the compositions themselves. Thus, a producer might want to use an old song, but update or change the arrangement or performance. What strikes me as the music clearance nightmare of all time, the movie *Moulin Rouge* features a literal smorgasbord of nostalgic tunes rerecorded especially for the movie sound track.[3]

Clearance issues related to preexisting music. It is the preexisting music that causes the problems here (I'm assuming that you were paying attention when we talked about putting a composer under contract). We have discussed these issues in the context of using pre-existing music in the movie itself; the issues exist in spades when contemplating the use of these masters on a sound-track album.

Clearance of the composition—mechanical license. We are talking about the musical composition (the musical notes that form the melody and the lyrics)—not about a specific recorded performance of the musical composition); there's only one "Your Song," but there are, at least, Elton John's version (the original) and Ewan McGregor's version (from *Moulin Rouge*). Clearing a composition for an audiovisual work (such as a movie), as you know, requires a synchronization license. The sound-track album is not an audiovisual work, so the correct term is not a synchronization license. However, you will need a legal basis for including the composition on the sound-track album— a so-called mechanical license. As a practical matter, since you have to obtain a synchronization license from the owner (or administrator) of the composition—usually a music publishing company—in order to use the composition in the movie; you and your lawyer should add the mechanical license (or, if you want to use plain English, the right to use the composition on the sound-track album to be released in connection with the movie) to the synchronization license agreement; the example below is taken from a standard synchronization license.

> Publisher hereby grants to Producer and Producer's successors, assigns and licensees an irrevocable license under copyright to reproduce any and all of the Compositions on sound-track albums and other records relating to the Picture and to distribute such records in the United States and Canada.

Unlike some European countries and Japan—which use a centralized clearance system[4]—in the United States, you must clear each and every composition with the appropriate party. In the case of a composition, the clearance is usually done through a music publishing company. ASCAP and BMI and the record label or sheet music publisher can be helpful in contacting the right party, but they may not necessarily be the correct party. It is important to remember that there may be more than one composer and/or more than one lyricist for each composition. Thus, there may be more than one contact to make in clearing the song.

If you are not using the song in the movie, but only on the album (a somewhat rare event, but it does happen), you can take advantage of the "compulsory license" system under the Copyright Act. This allows you to cover the song—get a band or artist to record the song and put it on your album by paying a statutory "mechanical license" to the publisher and writer. You should note, however, that it is possible to get a less-than-statutory-rate in a negotiated deal.

Clearance of the master—master use license. If you use the original recording of a composition on the sound track of the movie, you will have to have a "master use license."[5] You must make sure that the master use license also covers the use of the master on sound-track albums related to the movie, as in this example.

> May Jure Records, Inc. ("Record Company") hereby consents to Producer's use of the master recording ("Master") embodying the performances of Marv Dream Boat and Murphy Hunkamonk p/k/a The Flames (the "Group") of the musical composition entitled "Your Love Is My Talisman" as a featured vocal over the end titles (for up to three (3) minutes thirty (30) seconds in duration) in Producer's motion picture entitled "The Quest" and all in-context trailers, advertisements, featurettes and promotional material therefor, as well as excerpts therefrom (collectively referred to herein as the "Picture"). Record Company hereby grants Producer, and Producer's successors, assigns and licensees, the non-exclusive worldwide right, license and authority in perpetuity to reproduce and perform the Master in the sound track of or in timed-relation with the Picture for the purpose of exhibiting, distributing, exploiting and performing the Picture, and on sound-track albums and other records relating to the Picture, throughout the world in any and all media now known or hereafter devised and in any and all manners or formats now known or hereafter devised.

Clearance of the artist—name and likeness and credits. Be careful when clearing the master that the record label or other licensing entity grants the license inclusive of any obligations to the performer(s) and also grants you the right to use the name and likeness of the performer(s) on the sound-track album and in promoting the album. Usually, the record label has these rights and will grant them in the normal course of granting the master use license. If the label makes it your responsibility to get the artist's approval, then make the master use license agreement (and your obligations under it) conditioned on your ability to get that approval.

> Company hereby grants to Producer the right to use the Group's name and the name and likeness of the members of the Group in

connection with the promotion and advertising of the Picture and home video and sound-track recordings related to the Picture which include the Master. The Producer shall accord Record Company and the Group appropriate credit on all prints of the entire Picture which include the Master, together with similar credit for home video and sound-track albums which include the Master, as follows:

"Your Love Is My Talisman"
Performed by The Flames
Words and Lyrics by Terry Toonsmyth
Produced by Recardo Proughdooser
The Flames appear courtesy of May Jure Records

The record company will desire a credit, usually in a particular way in order to satisfy its major constituents—the artist, the writers of the song, and the producer of the master recording. The example used above (The Flames appear courtesy of May Jure Records) is a typical format.

By the way, suppose you want to have an established artist perform a composition that you own or control. Most recording artists have managers and agents and lawyers; you can use any of these to make your inquiry to the artist. Moreover, virtually all recording artists have record deals—meaning that they have signed a contract with a record company. This contract makes them exclusive to that company and, therefore, in order to perform/record your song and in order for that recording to make it on the sound-track album, you will have to get the record company's permission. This is not always an easy thing to do. Record companies pay a lot of money to have an artist's exclusivity and they don't give that right up easily. It will help a lot if the artist really wants to do the song and pushes the label (it also helps, in that regard, if the artist has a lot of clout with the label). And it might help if you agree to let the label distribute the sound-track album—assuming that the label is interested (and it may not be) and that you can work out a deal with the label. In any event, you will probably have to give the label the right (not the obligation) to put the track on the artist's next album and on "best of" and other compilation albums. There will also undoubtedly be restrictions on how you can promote the artist's performance. For example, let's suppose you get the hottest artist in the world (let's call her, Top Artist) to perform one song on your sound track; you probably won't be able to promote or package the sound-track album as "Top Artist-Sound Track from *The Quest*" and you may not even be able to place stickers on the package if Ms. Top Artist's song breaks out into a hit single—though you'll try to get that right if you can.

Payments. Because the clearance issues are complicated, the payments are also complex. Here's how it works.

Mechanical royalties. Mechanical royalties are paid to the owner(s) and/or administrators of the music composition—usually a music publishing company and the writer/composer. If you use the compulsory license scheme (where the permission of the owner isn't necessary—don't forget that a separate synchronization license and fee will be necessary if you use the song in the movie itself) and the rate is set by statute.[6] One of the reasons that producers may want to negotiate with the owner (or administrator), in any event, is that licensees have the ability under the statute to negotiate a mechanical royalty rate that is less than the statutory rate. Here the music publisher agrees to a three-quarter rate.

> Producer will pay to Publisher mechanical royalties at seventy-five percent (75%) of the minimum statutory rate under the United States Copyright Act (for records distributed in the United States) and seventy-five percent (75%) of the minimum rate used by CMRRA (for records distributed in Canada) in effect as of the date of initial release of the record concerned and will otherwise comply with the terms and conditions contained in the standard mechanical license issued by The Harry Fox Agency; provided, however, that no royalties shall be payable in respect of records for which no royalties are payable under the agreement between Producer and the record company distributor of such records.

The obligation to pay mechanical royalties is triggered by the sale of an album (on whatever format—vinyl, CDs, audiocassettes, etc.). The Harry Fox Agency, as agent for many music publishers, grants the mechanical license and collects mechanical royalties. Again, remember that there may be more than one person receiving a portion of the royalties—usually Harry Fox will help sort out the problem of multiple payees.

Master use fees. Master use fees are paid to the owner(s) of the copyright in the master recording. Usually, this is the record company, which in turn will often take care of any payments to the performer and record producer. The master use fee can be a one-time fee or a royalty based on sales or a combination (for example, an advance against a royalty). There is no set formula for the master use fee; it depends mainly on the popularity of the song.

Reuse fees. Reuse fees are not a clearance issue, technically, but it is potentially a payment obligation issue. If the master recording was made using union musicians (for example, musicians who are members of the American Federation of Musicians), the use in the movie and on the sound-track album may trigger the obligation to pay those musicians based on a new use. You will need a lawyer to help you assess whether or not this liability exists.

> Upon Producer's written request, Company shall provide Producer with all the necessary information to enable Producer to pay all reuse fees which may be required by any applicable unions, in accordance with such unions' contracts and regulations. Producer hereby agrees to pay all such reuse fees and any and all pension and/or welfare payments required with respect to Producer's use of the Master as provided herein. Producer hereby agrees to indemnify and hold harmless Company from and against any and all claims, demands or actions with respect to such fees and payments.

Calculation of revenues.

Now that the rights are in place, as soon as the sound-track album is produced, it can be distributed as another source of revenue. Often, the sound-track album is released even prior to the release of the movie.

Omnibus distribution deal. One approach, of course, is simply to grant the sound-track distribution rights to the same company that is theatrically distributing the movie. In this case, all or a negotiated portion of the revenues generated by the distributor from the exploitation of the sound-track album will be counted as part of the gross revenues for the purposes of calculating the amount flowing back to you. Alternatively, revenues from the exploitation of the sound track may be placed in a separate bucket with a different formula for calculating your share. In this case, "cross collateralization," discussed above, will be an issue and something that probably should be resisted by the producer.

An important thing to keep in mind, in any event, is the obligation to pay royalties to the artist, the record producer, the owner of the composition (including the publisher, composer, and lyricist) and other participants (including AFM members for reuse fees—those pesky payments due for the use of recorded performances separate and apart from the movie itself). Make sure, for example, either that the money coming in is enough to cover these payments and still leave a profit for you, or that the distributor agrees to take these obligations for you. Obviously, if there isn't enough money to cover these obligations, you would be better off not distributing a sound-track album.

Record label deal. Another logical approach is to go directly to a record label. Virtually all the major labels (including those that are affiliated with major movie studios) distribute sound-track albums from time to time. Remember also our discussion above about labels (Varese Sarabande and Milan Records are two) that specialize in movie sound-track albums. Thus, you have some choices.

In these deals, the advances run from very little (for albums comprised solely of score) to $500,000 or more (for albums with "hits" by major artists). The royalty rates also range from low (in the 14 percent range) to high (in the 18 percent range, with escalations based on sales thresholds to 19 and 20 percent). The sales levels range from fifteen thousand (for albums with score only) to several millions (for song albums with hits).[7]

The issue respecting payments to third parties (including reuse fees) is also relevant in this case—either the label must agree to pay these obligations directly or there must be enough money to cover them, plus a profit.

The deal in this case is similar to when the movie distributor controls the sound-track rights—except that the movie distributor doesn't deduct a fee for itself and a separate contract will have to be negotiated and signed. Running around putting all these deals together on an ad hoc basis creates a lot of work for the producer, who at this point may want to opt for sitting back and letting somebody else do the work.

Home Video

HOME VIDEO

Anywhere from about six months to a year after the theatrical release, the local video store will start carrying copies of your movie for rent or sale. Thanks to the invention of the videocassette player and its progeny (including the DVD player), we can now rent and own movies and watch them at home and in our cars or wherever and whenever we want. Like television, which was predicted at the time of its invention to be the death of the movie industry, home video has not visibly affected the theatrical market and, significantly, has offered a huge posttheatrical release market for movies. It has been a boon. And the change from VHS format to DVD will offer yet another boon as the populous at large rerents and repurchases favorite motion pictures.

THE HOME VIDEO DEAL

The structure of a home video deal is typically a license. The licensor has to deal with the usual licensing issues: Where can the videos be distributed (the territory)? For example, the license can be worldwide or limited to specific geographic territories. For how long a period will the licensee be allowed to distribute the videos (the term)? A typical term might be eight or twelve years. Are there timing restrictions (hold backs)? For example, the licensor will insist that the video not be released within six to twelve months after the theatrical release of the movie. What types of video product can the licensee distribute? For example, there are a variety of formats—videotape (VHS or Beta) and DVD. The issues related to territory, term, hold backs, and the like, are discussed in detail above. Here we will focus primarily on the issues that are unique to video distribution.

Definitions.

Above, we asked the question, "What types of video product can the licensee distribute?" In today's world, as you know, there are a wide variety of types and each type can be handled in its own unique way. It will help in our discussion to look at some examples of the various concepts included in the realm of home video.

Videogram. This is the catchall word that includes videocassette, videodisc, and compact disc. These terms are defined below.

"Videogram" means any type of Videocassette, Videodisc, or Compact Disc but only to the extent that the specific type of electronic storage device and its format is authorized in the agreement of the parties.

"Videocassette." This rather technical description of a videocassette refers to the standard plastic cassette that plays in a VHS or Beta (now relegated to specialized uses) cassette player. In this illustration, video-cassette and videodisc and compact disc are not the same media.

"Videocassette" means a VHS or Beta cassette or electronic storage device in any authorized format designed to be used in conjunction with a reproduction apparatus which causes a Motion Picture to be visible on the screen of a television receiver in a substantially linear form. A Videocassette does not include any type of Videodisc or Compact Disc.

"Videodisc." In this agreement, the term videodisc refers to a round, flat disc that contains a movie and plays on a laser disc or DVD player. Notice that a videodisc is not a videocassette or a compact disc.

"Videodisc" means any laser or capacitance disc or other form of mechanical storage device designed to be used in conjunction with a reproduction apparatus which causes a Motion Picture to be visible on the screen of a television receiver. A Videodisc shall include DVD. A Videodisc does not include any type of Videocassette or Compact Disc.

"Compact disc." A compact disc may be the same size as a standard five-inch DVD, but has a specialized meaning. It is a disc containing a movie that is played in a computer. Note the language "viewing in a substantially linear manner." When a producer and director create a movie, their intent is to play out the scenes in a specific order—much like a printed book. Until the dawn of the computer, there wasn't much thought about this, but the computer offers at least the theoretical capability to play the scenes in any order and to even manipulate the images in various ways. In a video distribution context, this interactive way of looking at a movie is generally not favored—thus, the "in a linear manner" and other language to clarify that this disc is not interactive.

"Compact Disc" means a combined optical and electronic storage device designed to be used in conjunction with a computer that causes a Motion Picture to be visible on the screen of a monitor or television receiver for viewing in a substantially linear manner. Compact Disc shall include CD-Rom, 3DO and LD-Rom, provided that in each case such Compact Discs contain only the complete linear version of the Picture as licensed herein in a format which is not capable of interactive use or manipulation to create an Interactive Multimedia Work or otherwise alter the Picture from the version licensed herein. A Compact Disc does not include any type of Videocassette or Videodisc.

"Digital video disc (DVD)." A DVD is an optical disc format that plays on a specialized player—a DVD player, naturally. Many computers have DVD drives and will play a movie in DVD format. Standard DVDs normally contain copy protection and encryption protection.

"DVD" means digital video discs (DVD) and is a type of Videodisc. DVD shall incorporate state of the art copy protection and regional encryption and shall contain only the complete linear version of the Picture as licensed herein and shall not be capable of use or manipulation as a Multimedia Interactive Work.

Compensation.

At the crux of every deal is money, of course. Let's take a look at how the licensor and licensee make money under home video arrangements.

Royalty—basic compensation. In a typical video distribution deal, the distributor (licensee) pays a royalty of 25 percent of the purchase price, after the distributor has recouped certain costs. In this example, the licensor is paid 25 percent of the actual distribution price (or the actual price of the videos sold by the distributor) less the initial distribution costs (the costs incurred by the licensee in connection with the listed items below—quality control costs, mastering costs, artwork [jacket design] and manufacturing costs). After the royalty is paid, the licensee keeps the residual.

> Licensee will pay Licensor a royalty with respect to the Picture at a rate of 25% of the Actual Distribution Price (defined below) after deduction for Initial Distribution Costs (defined below) for videocassette or DVD units ("Units") sold by Licensee. As used in this paragraph, "Actual Distribution Price" shall mean the price the Units are actually sold to a distributor of the Units or in the case of sales made directly by Licensee the retail price, net of sales tax. In any event, however, Actual Distribution Price shall be no less than $8.00 per Unit. "Initial Distribution Costs" will mean actual and verifiable costs incurred by Licensee in connection with (i) obtaining quality control reports on the elements of the Picture, (ii) transfer of the Picture to the proper digital format for mastering to DVD or VHS, (iii) jacket design; and (iv) manufacturing costs.

Advance. A video deal often includes an advance to the licensor against the royalty. The advance is exactly that—an amount paid in advance of the natural schedule of royalties. For example, licensee pays licensor $50,000. Then licensee starts selling DVDs and videocassettes and the licensor's royalties start mounting up. However, the licensee has the right to wait until the licensor's royalty pool has reached $50,000 before licensee starts paying overages to licensor— the licensee, in other words, starts paying the royalty from $50,001.

> An advance against Royalties of $50,000 (net of any tax such as withholding tax) will be paid upon the execution of this Agreement. Any and all advances against Royalties pursuant to this paragraph

shall be made by wire transfer (net of any wire transfer charges) to the account provided in writing by Licensor.

Home video rights.

The video licensing agreement, of course, will list the various rights and the parameters of such rights related to the distribution of videos. Here's the typical list.

Right to exploit videos. The licensee gets the right to manufacture the videos, put them in packages, promote and sell and in other ways exploit them. Note, however, that exploit does not include the right to do anything that impinges on any licensee who has the theatrical, television, or Internet rights, other than for promotional purposes.

The right to manufacture (during the Term only), package, distribute, advertise, market, promote, sell, sublicense or otherwise exploit Units; provided, however, that this grant of rights does not include the right to authorize the use of any Units for viewing in any public assembly, for broadcasting by television, cable, pay-per-view, video on demand, or Internet (except for theatrical trailers not in excess of one (1) minute on Licensee's web-site) or for theatrical exhibition.

Licensee credit. The licensee has the right to put the company name and trademark and presentation announcement (remember the "presented by" credit discussed above) on the videos and the packaging. The licensee may also put a notice on the video and its packaging as the exclusive distributor. The credit may not be placed on the video in such a way that interferes with the movie. In a case where the video rights are licensed separately, the licensor's lawyer is concerned, because the rights related to video are described in broad terms, that the licensee may abuse these rights by playing a video over the Internet, on television, or in a theater or doing anything else that might cross over into the rights of other licensees—licensees that hold the rights for theatrical exhibition, television, or the Internet.

The right to announce and include on the Units, the Unit jackets and packaging, any tapes or trailers of the Picture, and on all advertising and publicity relating to the Units, in such manner, position, size, form and substance as Licensee may elect except on the Picture itself where Licensee's credits may only precede or follow the Picture so as not to interfere with the content of the Picture or any of Licensor's credits or copyright notices contained therein), the following: (a) Licensee's name, trademark and presentation announcement; and, (b) the designation of Licensee as the exclusive distributor of the Units.

Names and likenesses. The licensee's lawyer, who knows the rules related to publicity (because the attorney has probably done production work a few times) wants to make sure that the licensee can safely use the names, likenesses, voices, and other identifying characteristics of cast members and all others associated with the promotion of the picture and other distribution activities. The licensor's lawyer, who drafted these agreements, knows that some cast members may have negotiated restrictions in the use of their names and likenesses.

The right (subject only to such limitations as may be contained in Licensor's contracts with such persons) to issue and authorize publicity and to use, broadcast and publicize, in connection with the distribution and exploitation of the Units, the names, photographs, likenesses, voices and other sound effects of all members of the cast and any other persons connected with the Picture.

Art work. The licensee's lawyer also wants to make sure that it can safely use the art work that the licensor made for the theatrical release of the movie. In some cases, the licensor's lawyer will insist that the licensor have the right to approve the use of the art, especially when the art is used in the packaging.

The right to produce or reproduce such art work and photographs pertaining to the Picture as Licensee will deem necessary for the advertising, promotion and exploitation of the Units.

Excerpts. The licensee will also ask for the right to show portions or excerpts from the movie on television or the radio in order to promote the movie in those two media. Note that the length of the excerpt will always be limited (here it is a minute).

The right to use and televise excerpts, not to exceed one (1) minute in length, from the Picture, and to use and transmit over the radio any dramatic, literary or musical material contained in the Picture, for promotional purposes only.

Synopsis. Finally, the licensee wants to be able to use a summary of the story of the movie (which as you know by now is a derivative work of the movie) for promotional purposes. Here the word "brief" is used, but remember our discussion about limits on the length of summaries above. The licensor's lawyer will want to make sure that the contract for the grant of rights is not more specific; for example, if the rights agreement limits the synopsis to 7,500 words, the term brief may give the licensee in this case the right to exceed the licensor's limit.

The right to prepare, publish and use brief synopses of the Picture for promotional purposes only.

Reserved rights. As is typical, the licensor clarifies that there are to be no implied licenses in the agreement—if the licensor doesn't specifically grant the right, the right is reserved to the licensor.

All Rights not granted herein are reserved to the Licensor.

Representations and warranties.
We have discussed and you have seen examples of standard representations and warranties that are part of every licensing agreement. We won't look at any examples here, but understand that licensees will always insist on the licensor's representations and warranties related to the rights being licensed. They want to avoid the caveat emptor axiom of the old common law.[1] The licensee wants to make sure, among other things, that the licensor has the rights being licensed and is authorized in a legal sense to license those rights to the licensee, that there are no encumbrances or restrictions on those rights, that the rights are still valid (are not in the public domain), and that no right of any third party is going to be infringed. The licensor also wants assurances in this area, largely because the licensee will be paying money in installments in the future. The licensor asks, therefore, for the licensee to represent and warrant that the licensee is legally authorized to enter into the agreement. Of course, the parties will insist that there be an obligation to indemnify for breaches of representations and warranties.

Delivery requirements.
You have also learned that the licensor, in any distribution contract, has an obligation to deliver certain materials, including a master print

of the movie, related to the distribution process. Since the video delivery requirements may differ from theatrical and television distribution agreements, let's take a quick look at an illustration.

General delivery requirements. Delivery of the materials, of course, are the lifeblood of the agreement from the perspective of the licensee. Without the materials, the licensee can't really distribute—which means the licensee can't make money. Thus, the licensee requires that the materials are to be delivered by a certain date. From the point of view of the licensor, the concern is getting paid. Shocking as it may seem, the history of the video business is checkered with examples of distributors not paying the licensor his or her advance. Therefore, the licensor will use the leverage of delivery of the materials to make sure the licensee pays the money. In this example, we know that the licensor must be powerful or the movie a good one or both, because the licensee has agreed to pay certain costs (in this case, up to $5,000) and also the cost of shipping.

> Licensor hereby agrees to deliver to Licensee the following materials for the Picture (collectively, the "Materials.") within 30 days of the Agreement Date, subject to Licensee's payment of Advance against Royalties (described above) and Material cost (not to exceed $5000) in full. Licensor may withhold delivery of Materials if Licensee fails to pay the Advance by its due date. The freight and shipping of the Materials will be borne by Licensee.

Delivery materials. Here is an illustration of a list of materials a licensee needs delivered in order to distribute the video. This list, obviously, is not generated by lawyers—it is supplied to the licensee's lawyer by the licensee (more particularly by the licensee's staff in charge of creating the video packages, referred to here as units that will be distributed). First, in order to create copies of the movie, the licensee needs a master of a certain type and quality (here, a digital Betacam NTSC) and screen size (here "Vista size") and a trailer; it was probably the ever-observant lawyer who thought about making sure that the master actually contains the movie. Second, the licensee/distributor wants a copy of the final shooting screenplay and a list of subtitles (the dialogue from the screenplay that corresponds to each segment in the movie) in order to make a removable subtitle track for the DVDs (it is possible with a DVD, because of the multiple tracks available, to make the subtitles removable; it is not possible, of course, with a videocassette). The licensee also wants color transparencies (color slides from the set or locations used in the creation of key art). Finally, the licensee wants a list of items related to the packaging—the licensor's lawyer inserted the words "if available"—of the video: cover key art (the art without the writing); the stylized version of the title; the photos on the back cover; a sample video box to use as a reference in making the box for this territory; mechanical boards with color call-outs (a predigital term referring to the process of using a board with color separations to make posters and other key art); the credit block (a list of credits in the industry-custom way as approved by the licensor's lawyer—remember that credits are negotiated contract points); a synopsis of the story (sometimes included on the box or in the liner notes); the copyright notice (again, so the licensee won't have to guess); posters and other art- and design-related stuff.

a. A complete and uncut broadcast quality Digital Betacam NTSC containing the Picture (Vista size) and one (1) trailer;

b. English script and list of English language subtitles for use in creating a removable subtitle track for DVD Units; detailed information regarding run time, aspect ratio and type of audio track;

c. Ten (10) color transparencies; and

d. If available, any original key art elements pertaining to the Picture, which may be supplied traditionally or digitally (on a format acceptable to Licensee) and which may include (i) front cover key art, (ii) title treatment, (iii) back cover photos, (iv) printed video box for use as a reference only (2 copies), (v) photo-static copies of mechanical boards with color call-outs, (vi) credit block (if applicable), (vii) story synopsis, (viii) Licensor's company logo (and notices, if any), (ix) current copyright notice for Program content, (x) posters and (xi) any other special elements or instructions needed to create the Unit jacket or replicate any artwork design (such as logos or copyright notices of third parties and logos for awards and other special designations).

Licensee complaints.

What happens if the licensor delivers the materials, but the materials are defective? Or, what happens if the licensor delivers some, but not all, of the items included in the materials list? The licensee will insist on having the right to complain, within a certain time period (here the period is ten days; if the licensee doesn't complain in that time period, the licensee is deemed to have given approval) and get satisfaction or terminate the agreement and get all money advanced back. The licensor's lawyer will say, "Wait a minute, the licensor deserves a chance to make it right" (the legal term is cure the defect) and the licensee's lawyer will agree, so long as the time for curing the problem doesn't drag out forever (here the cure period is one month). The licensee's lawyer gets the final say here (remember that the failure to properly deliver the materials will defeat the whole purpose of the agreement as far as the licensee is concerned). Usually, the licensee will have two remedies—either to terminate the agreement or to create or fix the materials itself in good faith. If the licensor—as is shown in this example—has a lot of power, the licensee will still have to get the licensor's approval over the creation of any material.

> Within ten (10) days after the tendered delivery of each item specified above, Licensee will advise Licensor if any Materials are unacceptable, unsuitable or incomplete and Licensor will promptly thereafter deliver suitable and complete materials. If Licensee fails to notify Licensor within said ten (10)-day period that the Materials are unacceptable, unsuitable or incomplete, the Materials will be deemed approved by Licensee. If Licensee finds any defects in the Materials and Licensor fails to cure such defects within one (1) month from Licensee's notice specifying the reasons for such defects, Licensee will have the right but not the obligation to (i) terminate this Agreement with respect to the Picture, in which event all of the obligations of Licensee hereunder with respect to such Picture will terminate and all Rights revert to Licensor; or (ii) subject to Licensor's prior written consent, create or cause to be created any and all Materials necessary to meet the Release Date.

Licensor's approval of art. As we discussed above, licensors of intellectual property (including the video rights to a movie) have a natural interest in protecting the property's good will. The packaging of the finished product makes an impression on the public and so the licensor's lawyer will usually insist on the right of the licensor to approve the packaging and everything related to it. Okay, but the licensee has an interest in getting the product out into the marketplace so the licensee can start recouping the advance and making a profit. So, the licensee's lawyer will counter by agreeing to the licensor's approval, but insisting that it be done in a certain time frame—and, if not, that approval is deemed given by the licensor. And further, the licensee's lawyer reasons, why should the licensee have to get approval for any artwork sent over by the licensor—"If you don't like it, don't send it over"—seems logical enough. Therefore, the licensee's lawyer may add a sentence (such as the one in the example below) to the effect that if the licensor sent it, it is approved. Finally, nothing could be worse for the licensee than to get a shipment of sparkling DVDs on a truck only to have the licensor's lawyer call and say, "The licensor changed his or her mind, we'll have to repackage the lot of them." So, the licensee's lawyer clarifies that the licensee can rely on licensor's approvals (that means, if the licensor changes his or her mind, the licensee can add the extra costs involved to the recoupable distribution costs).

A copy of the camera-ready art board for all jackets and labels created by Licensee for the Units will be sent to Licensor for Licensor's prior written approval. Approvals will be deemed given if Licensor does not disapprove of any materials in writing within ten (10) Days from the date such materials are received by Licensor (the "Artwork Approval Period"). Notwithstanding the foregoing, Licensor agrees that all materials provided by Licensor to Licensee hereunder will automatically be deemed approved. Licensor specifically acknowledges that Licensee has the right, for all purposes, to rely upon Licensor's approvals and hereby agrees that in the event Licensor requests any changes after approval is given or the Artwork Approval Period has expired, the cost of such change shall be considered Initial Distribution Cost.

Mandatory labels. The licensor in this case (where video distribution rights are divided up by territory) wants to control the pattern of sales. The licensor must police efforts by the various licensees to sell (or allow the sale of) videograms outside the licensed territory. Hence, the licensor demands that each video be labeled with the territory's code (here Japan) and that the packaging give notice that the video is not supposed to be sold outside of the applicable territory.

Licensee will include the phrase "Not for sale outside of Japan" on each Unit jacket. Each and every DVD Unit shall be encoded with the applicable Regional Code.

Licensee-created materials. You remember that under certain circumstances the licensee may create materials related to the movie in

THE MOVIE BUSINESS

order to effectively distribute and exploit videos of it. And you also remember all of the rules related to copyright and ownership. If the licensor gives permission to the licensee to create materials related to the movie or to create different versions of the movie itself, the courts might find that the licensee, as the creator, is also the owner of the copyright. That is certainly not a result that the licensor is willing to allow, because with ownership is the right to make derivative works and so on. The licensor takes this exercise, to the extent possible, out of the courts' hand by clarifying that the licensor, not the licensee, is the owner of licensee-created material. And if the courts in this territory are stubborn and find that the licensee owns the material as a matter of law, the licensor's lawyer clarifies that the licensee will license to the licensor an unrestricted and perpetual right to use the materials in any way the licensor wants.

Licensor will at all times have unrestricted free access to all alternate language tracks and dubbed versions, masters, advertising and promotional materials, artwork and other materials created by Licensee pursuant to this Agreement. Licensee will promptly give Licensor notice of each person or entity who prepares any dubbed or subtitled tracks for the Picture and of each laboratory or facility where the tracks are located. Promptly after completion of any dubbed or subtitled version of the Picture, Licensee will provide Licensor with immediate unrestricted free access to all dubbed and subtitled tracks. Licensor will immediately become the owner of the copyright in all dubbed and subtitled tracks, subject to a non-exclusive free license in favor of Licensee to use such tracks during the Term solely for the exploitation of the Licensed Rights. If such ownership is not allowed under a Law in the Territory, then Licensee will grant Licensor a non-exclusive free license to use such dubbed or subtitled tracks worldwide in perpetuity without restriction. In creating dubbed and subtitled versions, Licensee will comply with all dubbing, subtitling or editing requirements applicable to the Picture or its trailers supplied by Licensor in creating any authorized dubbed, subtitled or edited version of the Picture or its trailers. The Picture and its trailers must be exhibited at all times in their original continuity, without alteration, interpolation, cut or elimination.

Linear format. The licensor does not want the licensee to get any bright ideas about the way the film is edited or cut. The licensor says,

"Okay, go ahead and change the language or add subtitles to suit the audience, but not the sequence of the scenes."

Licensee's rights to the Picture shall be limited to its linear format only.

Sales matters.

The licensor wants to make sure that somewhere in the agreement the licensee has an affirmative obligation to go out there and try to sell videos. Like all licensing agreements, a lot of time is spent clarifying the rights the licensee has, but rights are not obligations. The licensee has sales-related issues too.

No warranty, obligation to sell. I can imagine a discussion like this: Licensor says, "So, now that you have the deal, how many videos do you think you can sell here?" The licensee thinks, "Mmm, if I give the licensor a number, his [or her] lawyer will ask me for a guarantee." So the licensee says, "Wait a minute; I can't make any guarantees on the number of units—it's all a crap shoot." The licensor is thinking, "Wow, this licensee isn't going to do anything." So the licensor says, "Wait a minute, I'm not looking for a guarantee, but I want to know that you're going to give it your best." The licensee's lawyer whispers to his or her client, "Best efforts really means something," so the licensee says, "Okay, I'll give it my best, but within the realm of reason." The results:

Licensee makes no warranty or representation as to the amount of Royalties which may be earned hereunder. Licensee will use reasonable best efforts to maximize revenues.

Free goods. All salespeople need samples. The licensee is no exception. The licensee will want to give copies of the movie away to vendors who, if they like it, will order many copies. The licensee, moreover, will want to clarify that no royalties are owed to licensor on these free copies. The licensor will probably say, "Okay, but we will want to limit the number of such units to a reasonable amount."

Licensee will have the right to give, at no charge, DVD Units and VHS Units (if VHS Units are manufactured) for promotional purposes, provided that (i) free copies of DVD Units and VHS Units will be limited to no more than 100 Units for every 10,000 Units sold and (ii) no Royalties are owed to Licensor with respect to such Units.

Licensor copies. Here is the other side of the coin. The licensor would like to get some copies. However, these copies cost money and the licensee will also want to limit the numbers. In this case, the licensee is limiting the units to promotional use and is again clarifying that these copies do not bear royalties.

Licensor will be entitled to receive 25 DVD Units and 25 VHS Units (only if VHS Units are manufactured), free of charge, provided that (i) such Units are used by Licensor for promotional purposes only, and (ii) no Royalties will be payable to Licensor with respect to such Units.

Accounting.

Someone has to keep track of the money. Virtually all licensing agreements will provide for some accounting standards and audit rights.

Earnings statements. The parties will decide on how often the earnings statements will be made available to the licensor. Here the time period is quarterly. Some contracts start out quarterly, but change to semiannual or even annual as time goes on. The earning statements, in this case, are required to contain separate wholesale price data for both DVDs and VHS videocassettes. The requirement is only for units sold and paid for and not returned. Note that payment of royalties must accompany the earnings statement.

Licensee will render to Licensor quarterly statements for the Picture, within one (1) month after the end of each quarter, indicating the number of Units sold, paid for and not returned, and the wholesale prices thereof, based on DVD and VHS Units sold respectively. Any Royalties due and payable to Licensor by Licensee pursuant to any such statement will be paid to Licensor simultaneously with the rendering of the statement.

Audit rights. The licensee will have control of the distribution process, including the tracking of sales and the payment of distribution costs and royalties. The licensor will demand to have access to that process by having the right to audit the licensee's records. First, the licensor requires the licensee to keep "full and complete" records of all video sales transactions. Second, the licensor has a right to audit those records, but (because an audit is disruptive) the licensee will demand that the number and frequency of audits be kept to a reasonable number. The cost of the audit is borne by the licensor. The audit must be done by people who know what they are doing. The licensor must give reasonable notice and the audit must be done during normal business hours.

> Licensee will keep full and complete records of all transactions relating to the Picture. No more frequently than once per each year of the Term, and upon five (5)-days' notice, Licensor may, at its own expense, audit Licensee's records in order to verify earnings statements rendered hereunder. Any such audit will be conducted by a qualified employee of Licensor or a certified public accountant upon reasonable notice to Licensee and during Licensee's normal business hours.

The right to question records. The purpose of the audit is to verify the accuracy of the earnings statements and the royalty payments. Thus, if the licensor's auditors find a discrepancy or something internally wrong with the records related to video sales, the licensor may question the records. Since the licensee would like to think that at some point the issues have all been put to bed, the licensor's auditors must raise their questions within a certain time period (here the period is three years). If the audit shows that the licensee has underpaid the licensor by more than 5 percent (the actual percent is negotiable) of the amount reported on the earnings statement, the licensor can shift the cost of the audit to the licensee. Of course, regardless of the percentage, if the audit shows underpayment, the licensee is obligated to make it up.

> Any statement not questioned by Licensor by notice within three (3) years from the date of such statement will be deemed final and conclusive. Licensor's right to examine Licensee's records will be limited to only those books, records and accounts applicable and relevant to the Picture. In the event that such audit reveals the underreported amount equaling more than five percent (5%) of the amount previously reported to Licensor, Licensee agrees to bear reasonable costs incurred for such audit and pay the underreported amount to Licensor without any delay.

Television

TELEVISION

The movie comes to the small screen toward the close of its initial life cycle, after home video and after pay-per-view. Television, however, may be a substantial source of revenue and so a television deal is important.

Again, it is common that a television deal will be part of an overall distribution agreement. Separate television deals are also possible. Here, we will break the television agreement down to its essential parts.

THE BASIC TELEVISION DEAL

The terms of the television license are similar to other distribution agreements.

Territory, exclusivity, term, and language.

The basic terms of the agreement describe the territory, tell whether the license is exclusive, define the duration of the obligations and rights, and further limit the license (for example, by language).

Territory. The agreement defines the territory (the geographical boundaries of the license) and the term (the time limits) of the license.

A territory can be as small as a certain channel in a certain city or as large as the universe.

Exclusivity. Like all licenses, it is important to designate whether the license is exclusive to the licensee or not. Obviously, exclusivity comes with a cost.

Term. A typical term is seven years, but longer licenses are also possible (including licenses in perpetuity—or forever). The term is often, but not always, renewable.

Language. Another basic term is the "authorized language(s)," which can be described simply as the official languages of the countries in the territory. Authorized languages can be tricky, because territories do not always match up with languages. North America, as a territory, includes French-speaking Quebec. The distributor in France, however, may worry that copies of the movie in French might find their way from Quebec to France.

Rights.
Television rights are divided into two categories: pay and free.

Pay television rights. The term pay, of course, comes from the fact that the viewer has to pay money (above and beyond the purchase price of the television set itself) to watch. The viewer either pays a monthly or other periodic subscription fee or a one-time fee to watch a specific program.

> Subject to all of the terms and conditions set forth in this Agreement, and provided that neither Licensee nor any of its permitted sublicensees or assigns is in breach or default of this Agreement, Licensor hereby licenses to Licensee the following Rights in and to the Licensed Program (including the use of any and all music contained in the Licensed Program as delivered to Licensee), throughout the Territory during the Term (the "Licensed Rights"): (i) Pay Television Rights, including, Pay-Per-View; Demand View; Terrestrial; Cable and Satellite; and (ii) Free Television Rights, including, Terrestrial, Cable and Satellite. All rights not listed are Reserved Rights of Licensor.

Terrestrial. Generally, terrestrial broadcasts (the transmission of wireless frequencies from strategically placed broadcast and repeater towers on the land to an antenna connected to the television set) are free (see below). However, there are terrestrial broadcast services that charge a fee, and so terrestrial rights are listed in this category. A terrestrial system features specific frequencies broadcast across a finite spectrum of frequencies or waves. The antenna on your roof catches these frequencies and your television turns them into sight and sound. Perhaps the important thing to remember is that the number of frequencies (referred to as channels by the viewer at home) is limited. Once the frequencies are divvied, there are no more. Hence the enviable position for many years of NBC, ABC, and CBS (the networks).

Cable. Because of the limited and finite number of channels for terrestrial broadcast and because reception in certain geographical areas is poor, another electronic delivery system emerged using cable or wires. There are various cable technologies, but the modern cable systems will carry much more programming data than a terrestrial system—another reason for people wanting to abandon their antenna-based terrestrial systems in favor of cable.

Satellite. The next step in the evolution of television systems was the satellite. Satellites can cover a wide area (or footprint) with excellent reception (the satellite transmission does not have to contend with the mountains and other problems encountered by the terrestrial system. Satellites are also capable of broadcasting many channels of programming at the same time, so satellite systems are competitive with cable.

Pay-per-view. Most modern cable and satellite systems offer individual programs (for example, movies or sports specials) for a one-time fee. Typical pay-per-view systems offer a menu of selections at predetermined times.

Demand. On-demand viewing is a form of pay-per-view. The major difference is that an on-demand system allows the viewer to pick both the program and the time. True video-on-demand systems are not commonplace (except in hotels and other closed systems), but are a promise of the not-too-distant home of the future.

Free television.
Free television is free to the viewer. How do free television broadcast companies make money? Unlike the pay systems described above

that charge a subscription fee or a per-view fee, free television sells time to advertisers or sponsors. This time is divided up into spots. I know you're thinking it, so I'll ask the question for you—if a person pays for cable or satellite or terrestrial service, for example, why is there advertising? Good question. Of course, some pay channels, such as Home Box Office (HBO) and Showtime don't show advertising and make money solely by subscriptions. The other channels are called basic channels and they come, more or less, with the monthly cable, satellite, or terrestrial fee. The companies that provide these services also take a monthly fee; individual channels, which don't share in the monthly fees, carry advertising as a way to make money.

Terrestrial. Television started out as a sponsor-based free-to-the-public system. The programs were broadcast over the airwaves and captured by antennas attached to homes across the globe. Advances in technology changed the face of television, but terrestrial systems remain strong. The major terrestrial networks are NBC, ABC, CBS, and now Fox and these networks remain a dominant force in the world of television.

Cable. There are cable systems that are offered at little or no charge to the viewer and hence cable is also part of this category.

Satellite. There are also free satellite systems.

Television release obligations.
The television licensing agreement sets forth the specific obligations of the licensee broadcaster (and the sublicensee broadcasters).

Holdbacks/start dates. As discussed before, a holdback with respect to the use of television rights is designed to prevent a television broadcaster from negatively affecting the theatrical release of the movie. If the movie is available on television, the thought goes, people won't pay to go to the theater. Likewise, the television broadcast of the movie should be held back until after the video release. Free television should come after pay-per-view and pay cable or satellite. Where all rights (including theatrical, video, and television) are licensed to a single distributor, there is less of a case to demand specific holdbacks for various uses, because the distributor will be motivated to handle the distribution in such a way as to maximize commerciality. Holdback provisions are much more compelling when the movie owner licenses the various rights individually.

In releasing the Picture on Television Distributor will: Not author-
ize any telecasting or other exploitation of the Picture on Pay TV or
Free TV before the end of the Holdback Period specified in the
Deal Terms with respect to the specified Licensed Right.

Discrimination and unfair usage. Television licensors don't
want the licensees to either discriminate against their movie or use it
to gain an advantage for other pictures in their line-up. Suppose that a
television distributor has five movies to distribute, including yours.
But suppose that the other four movies are from a hot-shot, up-and-
coming production company. The licensee gets a chance to place three
of the five movies with a German broadcasting company, but in order
to gain favor with the hot-shot producer, he places three of that producer's movies with the Germans. This is discrimination. Now let's
imagine that the German company comes back and says, "Wait a
minute, we really want that big movie *The Quest,* and the licensee says,
"Okay, you can have *The Quest* if you agree to pay the same terms for
the other producer's smaller movies. That's an unfair use of your
movie.

Distributor will not discriminate against the Picture or use the Picture to secure more advantageous terms for any other picture, product or service.

Notice of first broadcasts. The licensor wants to know when and
where the movie will first be broadcast on television. This date allows
the licensor's attorney to check the dates in other agreements related
to the movie.

Distributor will notify Licensor in advance of the time and place of
the expected first Pay TV telecast and the expected first Free TV
telecast of the Picture in the Territory.

Number of "runs" and "play dates." In the television world, a run
means a single showing (or telecast) of a movie, usually within a
twenty-four-hour period. The concept of a run usually includes the
concept of a single transmission as well. For example, if a broadcaster
is capable of simultaneously transmitting the movie over a network (an
interconnected group of local stations), this single integrated broadcast would be a run. Alternatively, if the stations are not interconnected, but the signals do not overlap each other, then the broadcast
of the movie on the same day would also be considered one run. A

play date is one or more broadcasts of the movie during a twenty-four-hour period over nonoverlapping signals so that the movie is only capable of being received within the applicable geographic area during that period. The reason the licensor cares about such matters is that licensors want to control the commercial viability of their movies. Too many airings can negatively affect the movie's popularity and value.

> Distributor will not authorize the Picture to be telecast by any form of Pay TV or Free TV from or within the Territory for more than the number of authorized Run(s) or Play date(s) as specified for each such Licensed Right in the Deal Terms.

Language versions. A subtitled movie is one where the dialogue of the actors is translated and written somewhere on the screen as the movie plays. A dubbed version of a movie is one where the original language dialogue is replaced by human voices speaking another language. Licensors have to know about dubbed and subtitled versions for a variety of issues, including the possibility that the licensor might have granted certain rights to another broadcaster. For example, imagine that a licensor grants the exclusive French language rights to a French broadcaster, but the broadcaster who has the rights for Canada creates a French version for Quebec without telling the licensor. There will be trouble of course. Another reason is related to the guild requirements. Some actors who are bilingual negotiate for (or by guild rules have) the right to do the overdubbing work in the other language. Yet another reason might be the ability to control a given footprint. Suppose that a Japanese satellite broadcasting company wants the right to simulcast the movie in Japanese and English (because many of its subscribers watch the English channel to learn English), but it is discovered during the negotiations that the channel's footprint reaches the American military bases in South Korea, where the English language rights are controlled by another company. That would also be trouble.

> Distributor will not authorize the Picture to be telecast by any form of Pay TV or Free TV from or within the Territory in a dubbed version, unless specifically authorized in the Deal Terms, or in a subtitled version, unless specifically authorized in the Deal Terms, and, if authorized, only in the Authorized Language(s).

Unauthorized means of broadcast. I'm sure you remember all of the discussions we have had about the licensor's ability to split up the rights in various ways, including the means of broadcast. It is not un-common to grant pay television rights to a broadcaster specializing in pay television and free television rights to a company specializing in free television. The same holds true for cable and satellite rights. What the licensor is saying below is, "Just because I say you can broadcast the movie, doesn't mean that you can broadcast it using every means available."

> Distributor will not authorize the Picture to be telecast by any form of Pay TV or Free TV from or within the Territory by any means not specified in the Deal Terms, that is, Licensee will not authorize any terrestrial telecast of the Picture unless either Terrestrial Pay TV or Terrestrial Free TV Rights are specified in the Deal Terms, will not authorize any cable transmission or retransmission of the Picture unless either Cable Pay TV or Cable Free TV Rights are specified in the Deal Terms, and will not authorize any satellite up-link or down-link transmission of the Picture unless either Satellite Pay TV or Satellite Free TV Rights are specified in the Deal Terms.

Encryption (antipiracy). "Piracy" is an industry term used to de-scribe the illegal copying and exploitation of intellectual property, in-cluding movies. The movie industry is concerned about all kinds of piracy, but television is particularly ripe for piracy because the signal is out there in the air for any one to catch. With digital signals, pi-rates can illegally capture and use pristine, master quality, copies of movies. The motion picture industry has fought back using a variety of techniques, including encryption and encoding. An encrypted and encoded signal can only be received by special equipment (hopefully unavailable to the pirates). This technique could be defeated by the broadcaster's failure to transmit the encoded or encrypted form.

> Distributor will not authorize the Picture to be transmitted by any form of Pay TV from or within the Territory in any form other than an encoded or encrypted form.

Territorial integrity. One of the cornerstones of television li-censing is territorial integrity. The world broadcasting map, so to speak, is complex and broken up into logical cultural and national areas. Advertising (the life blood of free television) and subscriptions (the life blood of pay television) are sold by geographical areas. Licenses are allocated in the same way. All television licensing programs adhere to strict territorial boundaries. Broadcasters are put under a contractual obligation to honor those boundaries.

> Distributor will not authorize the Picture to be telecast by any form of Free TV or Pay TV transmission, whether or not encoded, from within the Territory which is primarily intended for reception outside the Territory or which is capable of reception, whether or not by means of retransmission or decoding devices, by a more than insubstantial number of home television receivers outside the Territory.

"Blackout protection." Blackout protection is simply the act of not relaying the broadcast transmission. Major League Baseball may insist, for example, that games be blacked out in the hometown market (unless there is a sellout) in order to protect the local team owner. In Mexico and Canada, the broadcaster must contractually promise to black out programming being transmitted from across the border in order to protect American broadcasters.

> Solely with respect to Canada and Mexico, if applicable, Licensee must provide "blackout border protection" as that term is commonly used in the United States television industry.

Usage reports. Usage reports are an important tool for the licensor to manage the television stage of the movie's life cycle. The reports tell the licensor where the movie is being exploited, how to track down problems with any dubbed or subtitled versions, where to find the dubbed or subtitled elements, and information related to runs and play dates for the movie. In this case, the usage reports are rendered on demand (promptly at licensor's request); sometimes, the reports are rendered periodically (for example, quarterly). As these reports are comprehensive in nature, the licensee will resist the trouble and expense of doing them often.

> Upon Licensor's request, Distributor will promptly provide Licensor with the following information: (1) the title of the Picture in the Authorized Language used for each telecast of the Picture; (2) each person responsible for preparing any dubbed or subtitled versions of the Picture; (3) each laboratory holding any dubbed or subtitled tracks for the Picture; and (4) the time, place and telecaster of each

telecast of the Picture, including all Runs and Play dates, since the last notice to Licensor. Distributor will include in all of its agreements with its licensees a requirement for them to maintain such information and such agreements shall allow Licensor to obtain such information directly from such licensees.

Commercials. Remember that with free television the networks and individual cable channels make money selling advertising time to sponsors. The contract, therefore, must provide that the licensee has the right to insert (and to grant to others to insert) commercials at certain points during the telecast of the movie.

If Free TV Rights are licensed, then Licensee may insert and permit others to insert commercial announcements within the Picture at those points designated by Licensee for such purpose but solely with respect to such Free TV exploitation.

Credits. In the television world, because time is money (and because the credit roll motivates the viewer to change the channel), broadcasters would love to eliminate credits—especially the end credits. But remember that the producer has an obligation to give a credit to those persons who worked on the movie and who negotiated the right to receive a credit in their contract. The producer must pass this obligation along to the broadcasting company. The producer/licensor also wants to make sure that all notices and trademarks pertaining to the movie are given due consideration during the telecast.

Licensee will require each broadcaster to televise all credits, trademarks, copyright notices, trade names and other symbols of the Picture appearing on the Materials furnished by Licensor, including but not limited to Licensor's logo.

Approval obligations. In this agreement, the licensor clarifies that he or she has the right to approve the terms of any sublicense. The approval must be given in writing prior to the sublicensing deal. This further allows the licensor to manage the television exploitation of the movie and to make sure that the downstream broadcasters are compatible with the image of the movie. The licensee, therefore, has the obligation to notify the licensor of the material contract terms and to provide the licensor with copies of the completed contracts. Note that this obligation does not apply to rights that have been purchased outright. Obviously, if a right is sold (as opposed to licensed), the purchaser's use of that right is usually unrestricted.

Except for television rights purchased outright by Licensee, Licensee agrees that it shall not enter into any agreement for the Free, Pay and Cable Television Exhibition of the Picture without Licensor's prior written approval. Licensor will have the right of prior written approval of all material terms of each license or subdistribution agreement for exploitation of any Theatrical Licensed Right which Licensee desires to enter into. Licensor shall be advised by Licensee, except for television rights purchased outright, of the principal television contract terms, and upon Licensor's request Licensee shall in any event provide to Licensor complete copies of the television contracts.

Conclusion of run(s) or play date(s). Virtually all television licenses are for a specific term of years, as opposed to an unlimited time. However, since the broadcast rights, in terms of runs and play dates are also set in number, most license agreements contain a provision like the one below that limit the term to the conclusion of the last authorized run or play date. For example, if the licensor has authorized three runs for terrestrial free television, the term (regardless of how many years is stated in the contract), will expire at the end of the third run. Likewise, if the term of the contract is five years, the contract will terminate at the end of five years, even if the licensee has failed to take all the authorized runs or play dates.

The Term of this Agreement with respect to any Theatrical Licensed Rights will expire at the earlier of the end of the Term (defined above), or the conclusion of the last of the Authorized Run(s) or Play date(s) with respect to the specific Theatrical Licensed Right.

Reversion of television rights licensed. The licensor is concerned that all rights related to the movie are exploited—and in a timely manner. The theory is that the hoopla surrounding the theatrical release starts a chain reaction, so to speak. Home video and television follow the theatrical release in a logical order and in a time frame designed to keep the title of the project in the minds of consumers. If too much time passes before the home video and then the television release, the public might be less likely to remember—or so goes the theory. To manage this overall pattern, the licensor requires the licensee to hit a certain target window for television—within three years after the movie is released theatrically (if it is released theatrically) or two years after its home video release. If the licensee doesn't hit those windows, the rights revert back to the licensor, who presumably goes after another deal with another broadcaster.

> Licensor shall have the discretionary option of canceling the applicable television rights granted to Licensee, if the Licensee has not concluded a television license sub-distribution agreement approved by the Licensor within: (i) three (3) years after the Picture's First Theatrical Release in the Territory if the Theatrical rights are licensed; or (ii) two (2) years after each respective Picture's First Video Release.

Secondary broadcasts.

A secondary broadcast is the simultaneous retransmission of the initial transmission of a movie to the public. Suppose that *The Quest* is showing on one of the network channels and is broadcast by that terrestrial network over its towers to the public and, at the same time, it is also retransmitted by a local cable company to its local cable subscribers. The cable retransmission is a secondary broadcast. Other examples work as well. The initial transmission can be by wire or satellite and the retransmission can be by a microwave, telephone, or satellite system. Secondary broadcasts have been a subject of heated debate and are regulated by statute in most territories.

"Compulsory administration." The laws governing secondary broadcasts are sometimes referred to as "compulsory administration." The effect of this type of legal system is to make it possible for cable or satellite systems to make secondary broadcasts without authorization from the original broadcasters or rights holders. The license required to broadcast, in other words, is a compulsory license and is governed by statute—in much the same way as the compulsory licensing scheme in the field of music.[1] In some cases, as noted here, the rights holders can join together in the form of collective management societies by collective contracts and demand the authority to approve or withhold approval of secondary broadcasts.

> "Compulsory administration," for the purpose of this Agreement, means any Law under which: (i) Secondary Broadcasts are subject to compulsory license; (ii) cable systems or the Persons may

make Secondary Broadcasts without first obtaining authorization from rights holders or Persons making originating broadcasts; or (iii) rights holders may only grant or withhold authorization for Secondary Broadcasts through collective management societies or collective contractual agreements.

Licensor's authority for secondary broadcasts. The licensor has to worry about secondary broadcasts because, as you know, the licensor is giving the licensee an exclusive broadcast right in the territory, but the licensor usually has no control over these secondary broadcasts. Thus, one important point is to clarify that secondary broadcasts are not a breach by licensor of the contract. In addition, the licensor will want to clarify that any approvals or authorizations mandated under any compulsory licensing scheme or otherwise will belong to licensor; this is part of the licensor's need to manage the rights to the movie as far as possible and will be consistent with the governing statute, in any event. Of course, the licensor, in this case, will also want to receive the royalties prescribed under the statute (which are likely to be nominal).

Licensor reserves all rights to make, authorize and collect royalties for any Secondary Broadcast of the Picture whether the primary broadcast originates inside or outside the Territory. Licensor does not grant any exclusivity protection against Secondary Broadcasts and no Secondary Broadcast of the Picture anywhere in the Territory at any time will be a breach of this Agreement by Licensor regardless of where the primary broadcast originated.

Licensee's duties regarding secondary broadcasts. In some nations, the secondary broadcast laws allow the initial broadcasters to grant or withhold permission for secondary broadcasts. In this case, since the licensee will enter into a contractual relationship with the initial broadcasters, as a matter of contract law the licensee is in a position to require the initial broadcasters to support the licensor's management of the television rights. Thus, as is illustrated here, the licensor puts the licensee under an obligation to put the broadcaster under an obligation to abide by the licensor's decisions about secondary broadcasts and to give notice to licensor of broadcasts that are likely to give rise to the secondary broadcast issue.

If broadcasters may grant or withhold authorization for Secondary Broadcasts of their primary broadcasts in a country within the Territory then: (i) Licensee will require each broadcaster in such country licensing the Picture to abide by Licensor's reasonable directions regarding Secondary Broadcasts of the Picture (even when such directions may require the broadcaster to prohibit Second Broadcasts of the Picture until after a date designated by Licensor) and (ii) Licensee will timely give Notice to Licensor of primary broadcasts to which Licensee reasonably believes this provision will apply.

Financial matters related to television.

The television deal is similar in many respects to any licensing deal—the possible payments include an advance against a royalty, with a possible minimum guarantee.

Minimum guarantee. The licensor will always try to get the licensee to accept the concept of a minimum guarantee, which means exactly what it sounds like—the licensee must pay the licensor a minimum amount, regardless of the amount of revenues generated by the exploitation of the television rights. Here is where experience comes in handy, because if the licensee guesses incorrectly the amount to pay the licensor will have to come out of pocket. Some minimum guarantees are on a per year basis (for example, the licensee has to pay $500,000 each year during a five-year term); but here the guarantee is for the entire term. This minimum guarantee is nonrefundable and works like an advance. Here the minimum guarantee/advance is paid out in installments.

> Licensee shall pay to Licensor a non-refundable minimum guarantee against Adjusted Gross Receipts, as such term is defined below, (the "Minimum Guarantee") in the amount of One Million United States Dollars (US $1,000,000), due and payable as follows:
> One Hundred Fifty Thousand United States Dollars (US $150,000) on or before November 15, 2004;
> Four Hundred Fifty Thousand United States Dollars (US $450,000) within thirty (30) days from Licensor's delivery of the Materials to Licensee; and
> Four Hundred Thousand United States Dollars (US $400,000) on or before October 1, 2005.

Overages. The advance/minimum guarantee is applied against a percentage of a defined basket of revenues. Here that basket is called adjusted gross revenues (although it could be net or gross, depending on the negotiation of the parties). Once the revenues start coming in, the licensee starts to recoup or simply receive the amount of the minimum guarantee paid to licensor. Once the licensee has received that amount, if additional revenues come in, over and above the minimum guarantee, the licensor starts receiving a negotiated share of the revenues that come into the basket. In this example, in North America, the licensee receives $1 million as a minimum guarantee against 50 percent of the adjusted gross revenues. Suppose that in the third year, the formula, 50 percent of the adjusted gross revenues, when applied to the real performance of the movie, shows an actual amount of $1,250,000. In this case, the licensor should receive overages in the amount of $250,000.

> The parties acknowledge and agree that the Minimum Guarantee shall be allocated as follows:
> Fifty Percent (50%) for the exploitation of the Licensed Rights in North America;
> Twenty-Five Percent (25%) for the exploitation of the Licensed Rights in Europe; and
> Twenty-Five Percent (25%) for the exploitation of the Licensed Rights in South America.

Profit split. Here the parties agree to split the profits—35 percent to the licensor and 65 percent to the licensee. The licensee, however, has to pay for all subdistributors out of the licensee's share. Moreover, the licensor has negotiated a floor of 35 percent of the adjusted gross—which means that, if the licensee hires too many subdistributors and gives away all his or her profits, the licensee can't come crying to the licensor—even if the licensor approves the subdistribution deals.

> All Adjusted Gross Receipts (as such term is defined below) derived from the exploitation of the Licensed Rights by Licensee shall be shared between Licensor and Licensee as follows: Thirty-Five Percent (35%) to Licensor and Sixty-Five Percent (65%) to Licensee. Any and all profit participation due under subdistribution agreements entered into by Licensee shall be paid by Licensee out of Licensee's share of Adjusted Gross Receipts and, notwithstanding Licensor's approval of any subdistributor(s) and/or the terms of any subdistribution agreement(s), in no event shall Licensor receive less than Thirty-Five Percent (35%) of all Adjusted Gross Receipts hereunder.

Adjusted gross revenues. The term adjusted gross, as we have discussed, is the mid-level revenue pool from which to draw money (the big three are gross, adjusted gross, and net). In our example, the licensor has negotiated a percentage of the adjusted gross basket of revenues. The definition is gross receipts less only recoupable distribution costs, which is determined as "the direct, actual, reasonable and verifiable costs" incurred by licensee in connection with (1) obtaining masters and other materials for the movie; (2) shipping materials for the delivery of the movie to broadcasters of sublicensees; (3) translating the screenplay of the movie for dubbing and subtitling purposes; (4) dubbing; (5) marketing and promotion; and (6) registering copyrights and trademarks.

> For purposes of this Agreement, "Adjusted Gross Revenues" shall be defined as all gross receipts derived from all sources relating to the exploitation of the Licensed Rights (including, without limitation, any and all video and television exploitation throughout the Territory) actually received by, or credited to the account of, Licensee and/or the Affiliated Companies (defined in this Agreement) and its or their parent(s), subsidiaries, affiliates, successors and/or permitted licensees and assigns ("Gross Receipts"), less only Recoupable Distribution Costs (defined in this Agreement), if any, subject to the maximum limits for Recoupable Costs (defined in this Agreement).

Cap on recoupable distribution costs. As we have discussed before, it is to the licensor's advantage to limit the recoupable distribution costs. Here the limits are different for different situations, which seems logical and natural.

> Notwithstanding anything to the contrary contained herein, the parties acknowledge and agree that the amount of Recoupable Distribution Costs that may be deducted from Gross Receipts during the Term shall be capped as follows:
> If the Licensed Program is broadcast by the Fox or WB terrestrial free television networks in the United States, the maximum amount of Recoupable Distribution Costs that may be deducted from Gross Receipts during the Term hereof shall be Five Hundred Thousand United States Dollars (US $500,000) for costs incurred in connection with items (1) through (4) above, and Two Hundred Fifty Thousand United States Dollars (US $250,000) for costs incurred

in connection with [the items described in clauses (5) and (6) of the above paragraph]; and

If the Licensed Program is broadcast by any other terrestrial free television networks in the Territory, the maximum amount of Recoupable Distribution Costs that may be deducted from Gross Receipts during the Term hereof shall be Three Hundred Fifty Thousand United States Dollars (US $350,000) for costs incurred in connection with items (1) through (4), and One Hundred Fifty Thousand United States Dollars (US $150,000) for cost incurred in connection with [the items described in clauses (5) and (6) of the above paragraph].

No cost more than once. It seems like an obvious point, but this common provision is evidence that somewhere along the line some enterprising licensee tried to deduct the same expenditure more than one time.

In no event may any cost incurred by Licensee that is deducted from Gross Receipts as a Recoupable Distribution Cost for any reason be deducted more than once.

Licensee is responsible for costs above the cap and unrecouped costs. The agreement finally clarifies that if the licensee exceeds the specified limits or spends money on items that are not itemized, the licensee is solely responsible.

All costs and expenses incurred by Licensee that are not specifically listed herein as Recoupable Distribution Costs, including, without limitation, payment of any amounts to the Licensee Affiliates or any licensees, or that exceed the limits on Recoupable Distribution Costs set forth above, or the parameters of reasonable industry custom shall be the sole responsibility of Licensee and may not be deducted from Gross Receipts or characterized as a Recoupable Distribution Cost under any circumstances.

No cross collateralization. From the point of view of the licensee, it is important not to allow the licensor to cross collateralize his or her share of the adjusted gross revenues. Here is the problem that the licensee's attorney is trying to avoid—suppose that the adjusted gross revenues are as follows: $500,000 in North America, $250,000 in South America, and $250,000 from Europe. With cross collateralization, the licensor would be able to demand $1 million, by lumping all the revenues into one pot. This is bad for the licensee, because the licensee won't have any cash flow—all the money that comes in will have to go to the licensor in the form of a minimum guarantee. Remember, however, that in the agreement the licensee asked that the minimum guarantee be allocated 50 percent, 25 percent, 25 percent from North America, South America, and Europe, respectively, and the licensor agreed. So, in the example I just offered, without cross collateralization, the licensor will collect only $500,000 ($250,000 from North America, $125,000 from South America, and $125,000 from Europe).

> Each of the following regions within the Territory shall be treated as separate and independent accounting units and there shall be no cross-collateralization between the Adjusted Gross Revenues derived therefrom: North America, South America and Europe.

Payment of the minimum guarantee upon termination. The licensor agrees to the principle of no cross collateralization, to allow the licensee to have some cash flow, but—the licensor pushes back in the following scenario. Suppose in the first year the revenues are as set forth above ($500,000 in North America, $250,000 in South America, and $250,000 from Europe). Now suppose that the agreement is terminated. "Wait a minute," the licensor says, "the minimum guarantee was $1 million and I only got paid $500,000." To make the licensor happy, the licensee agrees that if the agreement is terminated prior to the minimum being paid, the licensor will be able to cross collateralize the revenues for the purpose of satisfying the minimum guarantee.

> Notwithstanding the foregoing, however, if this Agreement expires or is terminated prior to Licensor's receipt of the full amount of the Minimum Guarantee from Licensee pursuant to the payment schedule set forth above, Licensee shall promptly pay the unpaid balance of the Minimum Guarantee to Licensor and, if necessary, shall be entitled to cross-collateralize Adjusted Gross Revenues received from the respective countries within the Territory for such purpose.

Recoupment of the minimum guarantee.

Just in case the parties forget, this provision will remind them that the licensee has the right to recoup the minimum guarantee. This means, again, that the licensee can keep all of the adjusted gross revenues, including the percentage due licensor, until the licensee has recouped an amount equal to the minimum guarantee. After that, the licensee must start paying overages to the licensor.

> Licensee will retain Licensor's share of Adjusted Gross Revenues until Licensee has recouped therefrom the Minimum Guarantee paid to Licensor; provided, however, that at no time during the Term of this Agreement may Licensee retain any portion of Licensor's share of Adjusted Gross Receipts that is in excess of the amount of the Minimum Guarantee that has been paid and received by Licensor.

Music publishing proceeds.

Music is its own source of revenue in the context of television. The broadcast of the movie on television, depending on the laws and practices of the particular territory, can trigger the obligation on the part of the licensee to pay performance royalties and/or other type of compensation to the composer and/or publisher.

Publishing rights. Revenues generated by music used in or in connection with the movie are based on so-called publishing rights. The right to perform music over the airwaves (terrestrial or satellite or cable) gives the composer or the publishing company administering the publishing rights the right to demand a payment from the licensee for licensee's use.

> During the Term and throughout the applicable term of copyright protection (including any extensions, renewals, revivals and resuscitations thereof) in the country of exploitation, any and all proceeds derived from the exploitation of the music publishing rights to music created or produced for use in or in connection with the Licensed Program (the "Publishing Proceeds") . . .

In the United States, performance royalties are paid to the music publisher and composer by the broadcaster through the applicable performing rights society (for example, ASCAP, BMI, or SESAC) based on a "cue sheet" (a list of musical pieces contained in the program, including the name of the publisher, composer, and the performing rights society) submitted by the licensee.

Licensee production costs. The licensee may incur production and/ or administrative costs related to music. For example, the licensee may

THE MOVIE BUSINESS

produce television and or radio ads or trailers for the movie and in that connection use music owned or controlled by the licensor. The licensee gets to recoup those costs prior to the licensee and licensor splitting the proceeds on a fifty-fifty basis. It is important to note in this example that the licensee is not entitled to keep 100 percent of the revenues prior to the equal sharing of revenues. This is normal, because the licensor will have obligations to the composer(s) on the other side of the transaction. Thus, enough of the cash will have to flow to the licensor to resolve these obligations.

> Less only the direct, actual, reasonable and verifiable music production and administration costs incurred by Licensee that have not been deducted from Gross Receipts as set forth above (the "Unrecouped Production Costs"), shall be shared between Licensor and Licensee as follows:
>
> Licensee shall pay to Licensor Thirty-Five Percent (35%) of all Publishing Proceeds until such time as Licensee has recouped all of its Unrecouped Production Costs.
>
> Following Licensee's recoupment of its Unrecouped Production Costs, Licensee shall pay to Licensor Fifty Percent (50%) of all Publishing Proceeds.

Delivery.

As with all other media, television licensing agreements call for the delivery by the producer (licensor) of all items and materials needed by the licensee to broadcast the movie over its system.

Delivery date. On a date certain, the licensor has an obligation to make delivery. Note the addition of the words, "provided that licensee is not in default." Licensee's attorney is likely to balk at this addition, because it gives licensor significant leverage in the event of a dispute.

> Provided that Licensee is not in default of its obligations to pay the Minimum Guarantee to Licensor as set forth above, Licensor shall deliver the Delivery Items (as such term is defined herein) for the Licensed Program to Licensee, at Licensee's expense, no later than November 15, 2004 ("Delivery Date"). The reasonable shipping and/or delivery costs incurred by Licensee hereunder shall be deemed Recoupable Costs.

Delivery items. We have discussed the delivery items in the context of theatrical distribution. The concept of delivery is the same, but the actual items, of course, are tailored to television. Each television broadcaster will need a high-quality master (in this case it is an NTSC video master tape), music cue sheets (for the purpose of tracking the payment of performance royalties), an English-language version of the screenplay (to use in connection with the translation and overdubbing or subtitling, as the case may be, the movie sound track), and a separate tape with music and sound effects.

Licensor shall physically deliver the following materials ("Delivery Items") for the Licensed Program to Licensee on or before the applicable Delivery Date:

1. One NTSC video master tape;
2. Music cue sheets for the sound-track music;
3. English language script; and
4. Music and effects in DAT or DA-88 format.

In addition, Licensor agrees to timely provide Licensee with copies of any promotional materials for the Licensed Episodes that are owned and controlled by Licensor and available for use by Licensee ("Additional Materials"). Licensee agrees to reimburse Licensor for any and all expenses incurred by Licensor in connection with creating or producing the Delivery Items within thirty (30) days of receipt thereof by Licensee.

Print Publishing

NOVELIZATION

Print publishing rights related to a movie can include any number of projects, but primarily such rights include novelization of the screenplay and the printing of the screenplay itself. Comic books are also a possibility, but if the movie is based on a comic book series (*Spider Man, Batman, Superman, X-Men*, etc.,), it is not at all realistic to think that the right to publish a competing comic book will be allowed by the original rights holder.

Novelization is a specific form of print publication. As you know, many movies are based on novels (for example, *The Firm* by John Grisham and *Jurassic Park* by Michael Crichton); novelization is where the novel is based on the screenplay. The movies from the *Star Wars* series have all spawned novels based on the screenplays and the characters that appear in the screenplays. There are many other examples.

Publishing means exploitation of hard cover or soft cover printed publications of a novelization of a Motion Picture or artwork, logos or photographic stills created for use in the Motion Picture that are included in such novelization.

Novelizations and separated rights (revisited).

Novelizations, as you recall, are also covered in the separated rights provision of the WGA agreement. The production company can exploit novelization rights on its own, but if a WGA writer is qualified to receive separated rights under the WGA agreement, the company must follow certain procedures for obtaining the novelization rights from the writer. In essence, the writer will have the right to decide whether to write the novelization and negotiate with the publisher directly. If an agreement is reached with the publisher, the writer gets all the money from the publisher, except for certain amounts that will go to the company for the use of the title, artwork, and logo from the movie. If an agreement is not reached within a certain time, the company can make its own deal, conditioned only on payment to the writer of a \$3,500 advance against a royalty of 35 percent of the company's adjusted gross receipts (with deductions for artwork and payments to the writer) from the publication of the novel.[1]

If a writer is a WGA member, therefore, the novelization deal will be designed to follow the requirements mentioned above related to separation of rights. The production company or studio desiring to control the novelization rights will first have to get the writer to acknowledge that he or she has no intention to write the novelization.

> Pursuant to an agreement with Quest Productions LLC ("Company"), I (Robert Writealot) rendered services as writer in connection with the screenplay (the "Screenplay") for the theatrical motion picture entitled "The Quest" (the "Picture"). As writing credits for the Picture have not yet been determined, I do not know whether I will be entitled to all or any part of separated rights in the Screenplay pursuant to the WGA Agreement. I have been advised that Big Print Publishing Co. ("Big Print") wishes to proceed with preparation of a "paperback" type novelization ("Novelization"). I hereby acknowledge and agree to all parties concerned that, even if I ultimately am awarded separation of rights, I do not intend to write the Novelization and that Company may proceed with the arrangements with Big Print for the preparation and publication of the Novelization.

In addition, the writer must waive his or her right to negotiate with the publishing company directly, another of the possible separated rights that WGA writers might have.

> I hereby waive any right I might have under the WGA Agreement to negotiate directly with Big Print or any other publisher of the

Novelization (which right would otherwise attach if I were entitled to separation of rights with respect to the Screenplay).

Also, the writer's compensation must be set at or above the minimum rate of $3,500 against the royalty defined in the WGA basic agreement. Note in the illustration below that the writer gets the minimum only if it is ultimately determined that the writer is entitled to separation of rights. If the writer is not entitled to separation of rights under the WGA's scheme, the minimum compensation for separated rights will not be paid to this writer for a novelization. In essence, the writer and production company are using the WGA's standard as the basis of compensation here.

If I am determined to be entitled to separation of rights with respect to the Screenplay, I will accept the applicable minimum royalty provided for in the WGA Agreement, namely, an advance of $3,500 against an amount equal to thirty-five percent (35%) of "adjusted gross receipts" (as defined in the applicable provision of the WGA Agreement) with respect to the Novelization.

The writer and production company anticipate the need for the writer to request a waiver from the WGA itself and to decide the course of action if the WGA does not grant that waiver. Here the writer agrees to request the waiver, but the production company agrees that if the WGA does not grant it, the writer's waiver under this novelization acknowledgment letter will not be effective.

Since, under the WGA Agreement, I am not obligated to advise, waive and agree until writing credits (and separated rights) for the Picture have been determined, or until the WGA has designated a "negotiating writer," as provided in the WGA Agreement, I hereby request that, in this case, the WGA waive this provision of the WGA Agreement. If the WGA does not grant such waiver, my advice, waiver and agreement in this letter of advice shall be of no effect.

SCREENPLAY

Another form of exploitation in the medium of the printed word is the simple publication of the screenplay itself. The market certainly does not seem as open as novels, but there is a market for screenplays. The rights holder hands the screenplay to a company that specializes in this market and receives a royalty back (part of which will usually be paid to the original writer, of course).

Don't forget, in this regard, our discussion about a writer's separated rights under the WGA agreement. Under certain circumstances (discussed above), a WGA writer will have a nonexclusive right, with the production company that hired the writer, to publish less than a substantial portion or portions of a screenplay.[2]

Stage

FROM THE SCREEN TO THE STAGE

Stage plays and other types of live performances based on movies is a recent theme (the opposite—movies based on stage plays—is a classic phenomenon going back to the 1920s and reaching its zenith in 1965 with *The Sound of Music*). *Beauty and the Beast* and *Lion King*, both based on feature animation projects of the same name, are examples of successful transitions from the large screen to the stage. Live-action movies—*Sunset Boulevard*, *Footloose*, and *Strictly Ballroom*, for example—have also made the trek from large screen to stage. Stage play rights are, therefore, carefully considered by the original rights holder during the negotiation of the rights agreement and are often part of the bundle of reserved rights. Producers, however, are more and more inclined to aggressively negotiate for and even pay increased consideration for these rights.

THE DEFINITION OF LIVE PERFORMANCE

Let's first take a look at the scope of the rights in question. The example provision below defines the rights that the movie producer wants to capture in the rights deal. The bundle of rights are defined in essence as the "performance [of the movie] . . . by live players . . . before a live audience." The provision naturally excludes short promotional live performances (here, performances that are less than fifteen minutes), as these performances will not compete with a full-blown stage production. Included in this definition are lengthy readings, musicals, dramas, and even pantomime.

> Live Performance means performance of a Motion Picture or its Underlying Materials by live players, whether by reading, performance, musico-dramatic rendition or pantomime, where the performance occurs directly before a live audience or its broadcast live and without prerecorded material directly to the public, but excluding performances less than fifteen (15) minutes in length done for the purposes of advertising or publicizing the Motion Picture.

LIVE PERFORMANCE EXPLOITATION

Producers who hold live performance rights can exploit them in a number of ways: For example, the producer can produce the stage play directly, hire someone to produce the play, or license the rights to someone. To go into any of these options in detail will require me to write another book (no thanks), but I will give you a flavor of what is entailed.

I want to make a major point here, lest you think I am telling you this part is easy. As you know by now, no aspect of movie exploitation is easy—but stage plays are particularly challenging. Stage plays, believe it or not, are more risky than movies. It takes virtually the same amount of effort to mount a play on Broadway as it does to produce a movie (development, production, and distribution), but at the end of the day there are big differences: The end result of movie production is a completed film that can be exploited in various media and at various times. Movies made in the 1930s are still being exploited today. Stage plays, on the other hand, evaporate into memory when the last curtain is drawn. In sum, even if a movie flops in the box office, with video and television there is still a chance. If people don't show up for a play, and the play is canceled, there is nothing to exploit until the play is financed and mounted again sometime in the future—if ever.

Doing the live production directly will require the following steps: adapting the screenplay into a stage play; raising a significant amount of money to mount the play; hiring a director (who only stays around until the play opens), a music supervisor, a stage manager; sound, lighting, stage design personnel, musicians and actors (there are potential guild—Actors' Equity Association, or Equity, is the main theatrical guild—issues here too). Then there is rehearsing, showcasing, finding a theater, advertising, and praying that people will come. If the people don't come, all the money you raised (way back at the beginning of the process) will be lost—and quickly too, since it is very expensive to let a play continue to run in the red.

In my opinion, the better part of valor seems to be to license the rights to a professional stage producer or theater and take a royalty. Rights owners will have the same set of issues in this medium as in every medium—input on the creative process (adapting the movie to the stage will require a lot of cutting and reshaping and the movie producer will want to ensure that the adaptation process doesn't detract from the good will that the movie has built), chain of title–related issues (theaters and stage producers also want to avoid infringement claims) and financial terms (yes, everyone will want to make money on the deal).

With regard to financial terms, note that there is no set formula for determining the advance or royalty to the owner of the movie. A lot depends on the stature of the movie and the competition, if any, for the stage play rights. As a possible guideline, it is typical in standard stage play deals (not adaptations from movies, necessarily) for the copyright owner to take money from "gross box office" (6 percent is a number often quoted in these deals). Advances are also common, but there is no way to generalize.

If the movie producer has responsibilities to third parties with regard to the stage play—for example the screenwriter—these obligations must be taken into account when computing the compensation package from the licensee. Also, the movie producer will want to negotiate a piece of any merchandising (especially where there is new merchandise created for the stage play) and sound-track album sales, where applicable.

SEPARATED DRAMATIC RIGHTS UNDER THE WGA AGREEMENT

Dramatic rights under the WGA agreement are also separated rights and are controlled by writers who qualify for them.[1] The company owns the copyright in dramatic work, but must exercise the rights in accordance with the WGA agreement and must, in any event, pay the writer.

Under the WGA agreement, if the writer exercises the dramatic rights, he or she must submit a copy of the performance to the movie company, abide by any provisions respecting the title, and offer the company the opportunity to provide any needed financing.

Interactive Works

From Passive to Interactive

Up until the 1970s, the film experience was largely sitting in the dark (except for popcorn and the occasional snuggle). But the microchip has allowed movies to move in a decidedly different direction (at least for the younger set). It is possible now to have any number of heroes blasting away at the bad guys with cyber bullets (or vice versa, if you are into the antihero genre). Interactive multimedia has become big business. Certain movies (usually, the blockbuster variety) have been able to do business in this space. Harry Potter is an example of books turned into a movie series and also becoming computer games. The James Bond 007 movies have also been turned into successful interactive works.

Definition of "Interactive Multimedia"

In the example provision below, interactive multimedia is defined in technical terms. It is where a multimedia work is "perceived" and "manipulated" on a computer (or computer-like game machine like one of the many models available on the market from the likes of Sony, Sega, Nintendo, Konami, etc). The word manipulated takes this medium away from the realm of movies, which are merely viewed. In sum, the person enjoys these products by interacting with them, not by just looking at them.

Interactive Multimedia means exploitation of an Interactive Multimedia Work by means of a computing device that allows the Interactive Multimedia Work to be directly perceived and manipulated by
the user of the computing device and that either stores the Interactive Multimedia Work on the user's computing device or accesses
the Interactive Multimedia Work by electronic means from another
computing device interconnected with and located in the immediate
vicinity of the user's computing device.

As technology advances, the methods of enjoyment expand. It is
possible, of course, to enjoy playing interactive multimedia games
over the Internet with others—possibly many others at the same time.
"Interactive networked multimedia" is defined here as the exploitation of interactive multimedia work over a "communications system."

Interactive Networked Multimedia means exploitation of an Interactive Multimedia Work over the facilities of a communications system that allows the user of a computing device to engage in
two-way transmissions over the system to access the Interactive
Multimedia Work, irrespective of the operator of the system or the
means by which signals are carried, and that stores the Interactive
Multimedia Work for transmission over the system at a place distant
from the place where the user's computing device is located.

INTERACTIVE MULTIMEDIA EXPLOITATION

The most common way for a producer to exploit these rights is to
license them to a company (called in this world a developer) with experience in developing interactive multimedia games. The developer
then finds a publisher or distributor for the game. The terms of a
license agreement should be second nature to you now: What are
the rights being licensed (see above)? What are the financial terms
(advance and royalty rate)? Can the producer have creative input/
approval to protect the good will built up in the movie on which the
rights are based?

Internet

THE NET

And finally (do I hear a faint hooray?), we come to the brave new world of the Internet and its promised potential for the motion picture business. In addition to networked interactive multimedia (discussed before), the Internet offers a new distribution platform for movies. Broadband technology has made it possible for consumers to use a computer to access movies on the Internet.[1] This in turn has given rise to the beginnings of movies-when-you-want-them and other flights of imagination. Many have wondered, including myself, whether consumers will sit down and watch a movie on a computer screen. To date, the answer is not many. Nevertheless, it is possible to imagine how the Internet might be used in connection with an on-demand movie rental or purchase system. The Internet is already being used by consumers to transfer movies from their computers to their digital television sets and/or removable storage devices like hard drives and DVD drives. Nevertheless, let's look at how an Internet broadband movie deal might look today.

WEB SITES

The interesting recitation set forth below provides a definition for the basic elements of this new platform for movies. The "Internet" is defined as wired or wireless networks that use computer terminals and terminal servers. The focal point is the Web site, the address on the Internet where the movie is playing (or can be found)—in essence, the theater. Again, because of the peculiar nature of intellectual property, which can be separated into as many distribution means as exist, the distributor's lawyer in this context enumerates as many of the electronic means as possible, including means that come into existence after the execution of the agreement.

> Company has obtained the long-term use of an Internet/Broadband website identified as "moviesonline.com" (the "Site") on which it intends to offer the public access to motion pictures and other programming utilizing streaming video or similar technology. The Site operates on wired and wireless networks known as the Internet, Internet II, or any other online services network which utilizes computer terminals, terminal servers, modems, cable modems, HGC, coaxial cable, XDSL, routers, splitters, switches, and/or video, using digital algorithms, one and/or two digital services, or any other means now existing or hereafter created.

TERRITORY

We discussed the problems posed by the Internet related to territorial exclusivity when we talked about Internet rights in the context of an all rights, all media distribution deal.[1] We need to review the major concepts here because unless the movie is being distributed *only* over the Internet and *only* by one broadband network, the problems with territorial exclusivity will always have an impact on Internet exploitation of your movie. For a content owner (producer) who wishes to distribute the movie in the traditional way, starting with theatrical distribution, it will be very difficult to have a separate Internet release, unless the theatrical distributor also controls the Internet rights. If the owner (producer) splits the rights by territory, it will be almost impossible to have a separate broadband network release.

First, because it is currently impossible to effectively put a territorial boundary around the Internet, content owners who have granted exclusive theatrical rights in other jurisdictions either refuse to allow exhibition over the Internet or grant the license to the distributor in a given territory subject to a condition—for example, a content owner will require the distributor to refrain from Internet exploitation until technology is developed that will contain the signal in a given territory. This, of course, still precludes a worldwide Internet distribution by a separate Internet broadcaster.

Owners also use a "most favored nations" approach: The content owner holds back on the Internet rights in its territorial distribution agreements, but promises to license these rights to the various distributors if such rights are ever licensed to any other distributor. A provision like this in a distribution agreement for the Japan rights, for example, obviously also prevents an owner from licensing an exclusive, worldwide Internet distribution right to any broadband carrier.

Often, territorial distributors who don't win on the Internet point may insist that at least the owner refrain from granting such rights to other distributors or, if granted, indemnify the distributor for any injury caused by the broadcast of the movie by others over the Internet. This also has a chilling effect on an owner's ability to grant exclusive Internet rights.

In sum, at this point, a producer must chose between a traditional release and an Internet release, unless the producer is prepared to grant all distribution rights to a single distributor worldwide.

RIGHTS

The rights provision in an Internet broadband distribution agreement is similar in purpose but different in detail as the same provision in other distribution deals. The distributor obtains the right to modify the movie electronically for Internet use and then to display the movie on the Internet at the designated Web site. The distributor wants to have the right to store the movie in its electronic database for the purpose of delivering the movie on demand. In addition, the distributor wants the right to use the marks and promotional materials related to the movie.

> Owner hereby grants to Company, exclusively in the territory of North America, the right and license (a) to digitize, encode or otherwise prepare the Picture for viewing on the Site, (b) to publicly distribute, transmit, perform, display and market the Picture on the Site, (c) to prepare dubbed or subtitled versions of the Picture for foreign language viewing, (d) to maintain the Picture in its archives for on-demand access and related use on the Site during the term

of this Agreement, and (e) to use and distribute all trademarks, service marks, and promotional material associated with the Picture. The rights granted herein are exclusive.

DELIVERABLES

As we have seen before in distribution contracts, the producer/copyright owner has an obligation to deliver materials to the distributor. Ironically, in this case, the items to be delivered are rather simple when compared to the more traditional means of distribution. I suppose that the Internet geeks can do the technical stuff better than the movie producer anyway.

Owner shall deliver master materials in form of high quality half-inch videocassette, suitable for digitizing, at Owner's cost, and subject to Company's approval. In addition, if available and at no additional charge, Owner will provide Company promotional/sales materials and dialogue sheets, for use in connection with publicizing the Picture on the Internet and in other media and dubbing.

COMPANY OBLIGATIONS

The distributor takes on the obligation of making the movie technically ready for the Internet—including digitizing the movie and whatever else needs to be done to stream the movie into cyberspace. The distributor obtains applicable performance licenses for the music used in the movie. Remember that theatrical distribution in the United States at least does not require a performance license, whereas television does. The Internet is still being analyzed in many jurisdictions. The distributor agrees to maintain the necessary equipment and computer software to play the movie—which is natural, since the distributor is presumably the entity establishing and controlling the Web site. A question might arise, in this regard, whether the distributor should be held liable for technical interruptions. It will seem logical to the movie owner's lawyer that the distributor is in the best position to control technical matters related to the Webcast, but the distributor's lawyer will at least want to resist having his or her client liable for attenuated liability related to technical failures (for example, so-called consequential damages related to a technical failure).

Company shall be responsible for all costs associated with digitizing and transmitting on the Internet and broadband services. Company shall also obtain a public performance license, if any, applicable to Internet/Broadband transmission for music used in the Picture. Company shall maintain technical equipment and software necessary to distribute the Picture over the Site.

CONSIDERATION

This example reflects the newness of the Internet—in that the owner of the movie gets stock in the distributor and a percentage of the distributor's revenues. In the early days of broadband exhibition of movies, no one was quite sure how or whether the movies would make money. Moreover, many motion picture owners were reluctant to let the movies play over the Internet, for fear that they would be pirated—the Internet, of course, is a digital platform, so the copies being streamed to the customer's computer are pristine and perfect (this fear has less bearing now that DVDs—also a digital format have become the media of choice for home viewing). Start-up broadband Webcasters would often offer stock as an incentive. Here, the distributor is offering stock and a piece of the revenues generated. Eventually, when this form of distribution becomes widely accepted (if ever), the deal will be more like traditional distribution in other media—an advance against a royalty.

The License fee payable to Company for the rights to the pictures shall be comprised of the following: An initial non-returnable payment of 250,000 shares of Company's common stock valued by the parties at $0.25 per share payable upon Owner's delivery to Company of all masters and materials necessary to the execution of the rights granted Company hereunder, plus five percent (5%) of the actual net revenues collected by Company from the Site and any other sources relating to the Internet/Broadband exploitation of the Picture, payable no later than 30 days after the end of each calendar quarter commencing with July 1, 2005. For calendar quarters subsequent to July 1, 2005, the quarterly payments due hereunder may not be less than $15,000 per quarter.

OTHER TERMS

Like all other forms of distribution, the distributor will insist on receiving representations and warranties related to the movie. The modern Internet operator will have the same concerns about chain of title and possible third-party claims as any theatrical or video distributor or television broadcaster. Indemnity and hold-harmless agreements and all the other points that we have discussed will also be relevant in the Internet broadband agreement.

EPILOGUE

Let me tell you the story of our movie, *The Quest*. (First, let's get in the mood. You are sitting there at the premier. There is a pain in the pit of your stomach—caused by the fact that the main investor, with a face like stone, is sitting just four seats to your left. The theater lights go dim. There is a hush of anticipation.)

In the opening scene we see our hero, Prince Lumine, bending over the figure of his dying father, King Lumine. "Take this amulet, my son. It is all I have to give you now," the king gasps. "With it, seek the Treasure of Ximm and save our kingdom from the hands of the traitor, Xamdorr." With these words, King Lumine dies. ("So far, so good," you think.)

Realizing he is in danger and in need of advice, the prince makes his way to a tavern in the woods, Wolf's Lair Inn. There, in the corner, by prearrangement, sits the king's wise consigliere, Avocar. The counselor doesn't waste time. He tells the prince that the amulet is magic and, among other things, holds the key to an ancient map to the castle of Xamm de Knoor, home of the evil Lord Xamdorr. The prince leaves by a hidden trap door when guards of the evil lord enter the tavern. ("Hey, this is turning out okay," you say to yourself.)

Prince Lumine, of course, finds the map. And on his way, he gathers around him men and women of courage and skill (General Scrivener, the old king's loyal commander; Gildemork, the leader of the Centaurs; Drexx, the strategist and the holder of the Star Key; and, of course, the beautiful—and brave—Marianne.) They approach

Lumine's patron saint, St. Angeles—who gives them the Treasure of Ximm to finance their venture. Then, together, they gather the equipment and soldiers they need. Finally, they arrive at the ancient and evil castle of Xamm de Knorr. (You're excited now. You can feel the tension of the climax building in the theater. Your investor turns to you and winks, with a subtle thumbs up.)

Now comes the big assault scene. General Scrivener leads the charge on the castle walls as the prince leads a small band of his best warriors through secret tunnel ways and trap doors of the evil castle. (You're enthralled now. It's all hanging together. "Man, that final edit was amazing," you say to yourself.)

The battle outside the castle walls is not going well. And, to make matters worse, when the prince arrives in the throne room of the castle, the evil Lord Xamdorr is waiting with his guards. "Prepare to die, Xamdorr. I'm here to avenge the death of my father," the prince warns as he holds the now blazing amulet above his head. But Lord Xamdorr laughs. "You see, young prince, you have forgotten one thing. You have no legal right to the amulet, as its provenance is unproven in your hands. And without that right, your little quest will come to naught." Xamdorr pulls a large and mysterious parchment scroll from his jacket. "This document shows the true provenance of the amulet—it belongs to me as the heir of my father, Xeethra the Great!" Xamdorr reaches for the amulet. ("What drama," you whisper aloud.)

"Not so fast, Xamdorr," comes a voice from behind the prince. "Avocar?!" says the prince. The wise old counselor draws a small, burned, and bloodied parchment roll from his vest. "This document is a bill of sale. It bears the signature and seal of Xamdorr himself. Just before his death, King Lumine deeded to Xamdorr the parcel of land on which this castle stands in exchange for the amulet. The king saved the document from the fire; I found it clutched in his hand." Avocar looks at the prince. "The amulet is legally yours, my Prince."

Xammdorr turns to run, but Marianne, sword drawn, blocks his way. A battle ensues. The prince and his warriors win the day! (Tears of joy are streaming down your face now as cheers come up from the audience.)

As our movie comes to an end, the prince expresses his gratitude to Avocar, Attorney of the Realm, for saving the day. The prince and Marianne kiss. (Naturally.)

In our fictitious movie, *The Quest*, of course, the lawyer turns out to be the hero of the story in the end, but, hey, give lawyers some credit. The road to your quest is laden with traps and pitfalls that perhaps the lawyer will be able to move out of your way or help you avoid. Try to remember us, too, when you get your next big idea for a movie.

Good luck on your quest!

Kelly Charles Crabb

NOTES

BOOK ONE
I HAVE A GREAT IDEA FOR A MOVIE
YOUR QUEST AND HELP ALONG THE WAY

1. For an excellent treatise on how to structure a story, a topic that is beyond the scope of this book, see generally Christopher Vogler, *The Writer's Journey,* 2d ed. (Studio City, Cal.: Michael Wiese Productions, 1998).

2. See *Sony Corp. of America v. Universal City Studios, Inc.* 464 U.S. 417 (1984).

3. William Shakespeare, *Henry VI,* Part II, act IV, scene ii.

4. The issue related to the scope of a manager's services has a history of controversy. As the talent world changes, the freedoms that managers enjoy related to doing business with their clients have become a source of envy for agents—who are restricted by law from entering into business relations with their clients. See discussion in note 6.

5. California Labor Code §§ 1700–1700.47.

6. Ibid., § 1700.4, which defines a "talent agent" as "a person or corporation who engages in the occupation of procuring, offering, promising, or attempting to procure employment or engagements for an artist or artists, *except that the activities of procuring, offering, or promising to procure recording contracts for an artist or artists shall not of itself subject a person or corporation to regulation and licensing under this chapter.*" (Italics added.) The italicized portion has been cited by managers to show that managers can, without registration, procure work for a client.

FROM IDEA TO TREATMENT

1. The United States Constitution, Article 8, reads: "The Congress shall have power . . . [t]o promote the progress of science and *useful arts,* by securing for lim-

ited times to *authors* and inventors the exclusive right to their respective *writings* and discoveries." (Italics added.)

2. The U.S. Copyright Act, 17 U.S.C. §§ 101–810, is the federal legislation enacted by Congress under this constitutional grant of authority to protect the writings of authors.

3. Note the constitutional language, "for limited times." A common question asked of entertainment lawyers is how long copyright lasts. For example: "How long will protection last on my screenplay?" As a general rule of thumb, works created prior to 1900 are no longer protected. In the discussion of "Public Domain" later on, we will look at the complications related to calculating the exact time limit.

4. *Romeo and Juliet,* by William Shakespeare, is old enough to have fallen into the public domain (more on that later). Copyright protection does not last forever.

5. Convention for the Protection of Literary and Artistic Works, Berne, 1886, as amended in Paris in 1971 (the Berne Convention). There are actually two treaties that govern international copyright: the Berne Convention and the Universal Copyright Convention (UCC), which was originally written in 1952 and also revised in 1971. Most countries of the world are signatories of one of these or both. Since the UCC came after the Berne Convention, the UCC is more or less designed to work hand in hand with the Berne Convention rather than supersede it. A major point of these two conventions is that author's rights are respected in another country as though the author were a national (citizen) of that country. For example, this means that a U.S. author's work will be subject to Japanese copyright laws in Japan.

6. There are other reasons to register your work with the USCO. These will be discussed in greater detail in the context of a screenplay later in text.

7. 17 U.S.C. § 101.

8. By the way, the copyright notice and other technical procedures were required by previous versions of the Copyright Act, but these technical formalities were largely done away with when the Copyright Act of 1976 became law.

9. 46 Cal.2d 715, 299 P.2d 251 (1956).

10. See the discussion about "Public Domain." The Copyright Act says that "original works of authorship" are protected. As we discussed, ideas and concepts are not "works of authorship" and facts are not "original." See, for example, Paul Goldstein, *Copyright's Highway: From Gutenberg to the Celestial Jukebox* (Palo Alto, Cal.: Stanford University Press, 2003), p. 189.

11. The next major case to come along was *Blaustein v. Burton,* 9 Cal.App.3d 161, 183, 88 Cal.Rptr. 319, 334 (2d Dist. 1970), where Mr. Blaustein, a movie producer, approached the agent of Richard Burton and Elizabeth Taylor with the idea of producing a movie version of Shakespeare's play *The Taming of the Shrew,* starring the famous married couple. The agent liked the idea and, apparently, so did Mr. and Mrs. Burton, who made the movie with Franco Zefferelli and did not involve Mr. Blaustein. He promptly sued everyone, including the Burtons. Certainly, Blaustein's

idea was not protected, as the play was clearly in the public domain and Blaustein had not added anything to the play to raise a question of copyright infringement. Nevertheless, the court found that there was an implied contract between the Burtons and Blaustein, even though Blaustein and the agent never discussed the terms of an agreement. Still, because Blaustein was a professional producer, the court found the necessary implication—why else would a producer approach the Burtons' agent (obviously, the court took notice of the fact that in Hollywood there is no tradition of floating ideas to make others happy).

12. The submission agreement covers many other things as well. For example, the submitter will be required to represent and warrant that the story idea is original with that individual and does not infringe the rights of any third party. See "Receiving Submissions" later in text.

13. 53 F.3rd 549 (2d. Cir. 1995).

14. No. 02-7221, slip op. (2nd Cir. Nov. 7, 2002).

15. See, for example, California Labor Code § 3351.5: " 'Employee' includes . . . (c) any person while engaged by contract for the creation of a specially ordered or commissioned work of authorship in which the parties agree in a written instrument signed by them that the work shall be considered a work made for hire, as defined in Section 101 of Title 17 of the United States Code, and the ordering or commissioning party obtains ownership of all the rights comprised in the copyright in the work."

16. The Copyright Act defines derivative works as works "based upon" the copyrighted work, including "art reproduction[s], abridgement[s], condensation[s], or any other form[s] in which a work may be recast, transformed, or adapted." 17 U.S.C. § 101. The act further states that "[a] work consisting of editorial revisions, annotations, elaborations, or other modifications which, as a whole, represent an original work of authorship, is a 'derivative work.' "

17. Do not copy someone else's recently modified version—with annotations in footnotes or commentaries or artwork, etc. You had better be sure that the copies you are making are free from this type of issue. Note further that the fact that *Romeo and Juliet* was in the public domain when Robbins got his brainstorm does not mean that the play *West Side Story* is also in the public domain. Don't get confused about this—making a play based on a public domain work is something that anyone can do, but when Robbins and his collaborators created the book, music, and script for *West Side Story,* a brand-new copyrightable work was created. Someone else could come along and make a modern-day movie based on *Romeo and Juliet* without any problem, but if they tried to copy *West Side Story* they would be sued.

18. While it is true that works created in or prior to 1900 are clearly in the public domain, works created after 1900 may not be. In 1998, knowing that copyright protection for its signature properties—Mickey Mouse (in 2003) and Donald Duck, Goofy, and Pluto (a few years later)—was about to expire, The Walt Disney Company, the estate of George Gershwin, and some of their supporters came to Washington

to seek help from Congress. Congress enacted the so-called Sonny Bono law (the Copyright Term Extension Act, named after the late pop singer and congressional representative from California who had supported the measure), which extended copyright protection to works created after January 1, 1923 (Mickey first appeared in 1928), by twenty years. Thus, Mickey Mouse and his friends are safe for now. See, for example, C. Sprigman, "The Mouse That Ate the Public Domain: Disney, the Copyright Term Extension Act, and *Eldred v. Ashcroft*," available at writ.news .findlaw.com/commentary/20020305_sprigman.html.

USING SOMEONE ELSE'S STORY

1. "In perpetuity" can fairly be read to mean, whether the contract says so or not, the duration of the copyright and any extensions. When the copyright has run its course and the property falls into the public domain, as you know, the ability of the licensor to withhold permission from any party (including the licensee in this transaction) no longer exists. For this reason, to avoid the other obligations in the agreement, the licensee should limit all aspects of the agreement to the duration of the copyright protection. Why should this licensee have to continue making payments, for example, if everyone else in the world can use the material for free?

2. See discussion on page 274.

3. As a legal technicality, you may be interested to know that the protection the producer is seeking here is not copyright protection—titles are not protected by copyright law. Rather, the producer is seeking protection from a claim of trademark infringement or a claim, under the Lanham Act, 15 U.S.C. 22, of the unfair trade practice of "passing off"—where the owner of the book is saying, in essence, that "by using the title of my famous book, you are trading unfairly on its success."

4. The world of law can be divided basically into three camps or jurisdictions: Common law (the legal tradition of England—applicable to the United Kingdom, the United States of America, Australia, and many other English-speaking nations), civil law (the legal tradition of continental Europe—for example, France, Germany, Italy, Spain, and Japan—which fashioned its laws after the tradition of Europe after ending its feudal period in 1868) and all others (too many and too diverse to discuss here). The point of this little discourse is that the film business is a worldwide business.

5. Under civil law, there are several categories of rights: The right of integrity (the right to preserve the work in its original form), the right of attribution (the right to claim credit as author of a work and to prevent others from making false claims), the right of publication (the right to publish or not), the right to withdraw (the right to withdraw the work from circulation), and the right of criticism (the right to respond to critics and have the response published in the same publication as the critic's).

6. In the Visual Artists Rights Act of 1990, 17 U.S.C. 106A, Congress recognized the concept of moral rights for American artists. However, the rights under this act extend only to painters, sculptors, and photographic artists. In Europe and Japan, the concept extends to artists of all kinds.

7. See discussion on page 24.

8. See discussion under "Identifying the Elements," note 3, on page 481.

9. See discussion about "Errors and Omissions Insurance" on page 321.

10. Other examples of this type of credit based on source material include: "From a play by . . ." "From a novel by . . ." "Based on a story by . . ." and "From a series of articles by . . ."

11. J. Thomas McCarthy, *The Rights of Publicity and Privacy,* 2d ed. (St. Paul, Minn.: Thomson West, 2004), § 8:64.

12. It is beyond the scope of this book to go into an in-depth discussion of the law of defamation. The most important point about defamation is perhaps that it must involve a lie. The producer can defend himself absolutely by proving that the statement in question is the truth. However, frequently it is not easy to get at the truth and there is always the risk that someone could bring a lawsuit—something that the major distributors like to avoid, to put in mildly. A cause of action based on defamation does not survive the death of the person in question. See discussion on page 286.

13. Sometimes called false light privacy, this tort makes it actionable to make it appear that the person is guilty of bad character by putting that person in a situation that leads to that conclusion. This cause of action is also not available to a deceased person.

BOOK TWO
THE SCREENPLAY:
NOTHING HAPPENS UNTIL IT'S FINISHED
HIRING A WRITER

1. William Goldman, *Adventures in the Screen Trade: A Personal View of Hollywood and Screenwriting* (New York: Warner Books, 1984), 39.

2. For this reason, producers should never become a signatory in their own names. The practice is for the production company doing the movie to become a signatory. This leaves the producer free to hire or do business with nonmembers for other projects.

3. The WGA Screen Credits Manual (see www.wga.org) provides some guidance for the determination of the "Screenplay by . . ." credit. For example, there are certain percentage requirements: "Any writer whose work represents a contribution of more than 33% of a screenplay shall be entitled to screenplay credit, except where the screenplay is an original screenplay. In the case of an original screenplay, any subsequent writer or writing team must contribute 50% to the final screenplay." For this purpose, an "original screenplay" is a screenplay that is "not based on source material and on which the first writer writes a screenplay without there being any other intervening literary material by another writer pertaining to the project." (Also, if a writer is furnished or uses research material, the screenplay is still considered an original screenplay.) A "non-original screenplay" is one that is based upon source material and all other screenplays not covered by the definition of screenplay. A sequel is an exam-

ple of nonoriginal screenplay. The percentage requirements do not end the inquiry. Moreover, the WGA Screen Credits Manual warns that "the percentage contribution made by writers to a screenplay obviously cannot be determined by counting lines or even the number of pages to which a writer has contributed." The arbiters determining who gets credit are instructed to read "any source material and all literary material provided to them in connection with the development of the final screenplay" and consider the following specific elements: "dramatic construction; original and different scenes; characterization or character relationships; and dialogue." The WGA Screen Credits Manual adds: "A writer may receive credit for a contribution to any or all of the above-listed elements. It is because of the need to understand contributions to the screenplay as a whole that professional expertise is required on the part of the arbiters. For example, there have been instances in which every line of dialogue has been changed and still the arbiters have found no significant change in the screenplay as a whole. On the other hand, there have been instances where far fewer changes in dialogue have made a significant contribution to the screenplay as a whole. In addition, a change in one portion of the script may be so significant that the entire screenplay is affected by it."

4. There is a way to draft this provision to take care of this issue. If the writer gets a shared credit, he or she gets a "fraction of the bonus, where the numerator is one and the denominator is the number of writers who get credit"—or something to this effect.

5. See discussion regarding the various permutations of this right (i.e., right of first negotiation, right of first negotiation/last right of refusal, etc.) on page 62.

6. There are other related credits that deserve mention here: (i) *"Story by . . ."* The term "story" means the dramatic events and characters underlying the screenplay. The WGA defines "story" as writing "distinct from screenplay and consisting of basic narrative, idea, theme or outline indicating character development and action." (ii) *"Screen Story by . . ."* is an appropriate credit when the screenplay is based upon source material (such as a book), but the story is new or different from the source material. (iii) *"Narration Written by . . ."* This credit is appropriate where the narration (explanatory material that is spoken off camera) is the major writing task of the writer. (iv) *"Based on Character Created by . . ."* This credit is given on a sequel to a writer or writers on the original movie (the writer or writers who developed the original characters). (v) *"Adaptation by . . ."* This is an unusual credit that is awarded by the WGA in cases where a writer shapes the structure of the screenplay without qualifying for the "Screenplay by . . ." credit. This credit is awarded only upon WGA arbitration.

7. At this writing, a print costs between $2,000 and $3,000, depending on the quantity.

8. See discussion on page 56.

9. See discussion on page 37.

OBTAINING AN EXISTING SCREENPLAY

1. The result could be different under the 1988 WGA agreement, but we will assume that the 2001 WGA agreement is the applicable one for you.

2. See Thomas Schatz, *The Genius of the System: Hollywood Filmmaking in the Studio Era* (New York: Metropolitan Books, 1989), for a general description of the studio system in the 1920s and '30s.

BOOK THREE
PACKAGING THE ELEMENTS
IDENTIFYING THE ELEMENTS

1. William Shakespeare, *Hamlet,* Act II, scene ii.

2. Which is not only a musical, but one with a religious theme to boot.

3. See California Family Code §§ 6750–6753 (1999, effective January 1, 2000). This California statute, originally enacted in 1939, is known as the Coogan Law. Jackie Coogan was a famous child actor of his era and pulled in over $4 million during his child acting career (and that was a boatload of money in the 1930s). But when poor Jackie grew up he "noticed" that his parents had spent all of his money. So what's a good American boy supposed to do? He sued them, naturally. His parents' defense was that the law gave them the right to spend it all and, as it turns out, they were correct. To right this wrong, the California legislature enacted the Coogan Law. Because the law had no real teeth, it was amended in 1999. See Screen Actors Guild, Government Relations Department, *California's New Coogan Law, Senate Bill 1162 Implementation, available at* www.sag.org/cooganletters/educlong1.html (last visited February 23, 2003), for an analysis of the new Coogan Law. New York and other jurisdictions have child actor laws. See, e.g., New York Arts and Cultural Affairs Law § 35.03.

4. See Buck Houghton, *What a Producer Does: The Art of Moviemaking (Not the Business)* (Los Angeles: Silman-James Press, 1992). Mr. Buck's book is the alter ego of this book; it talks only about the creative aspects of producing a movie and stays away from the legal and business side. About creative producers, Mr. Buck states: "There is only *one* function, and to subdivide it [into creative producer and line producer, for example] is to weaken it. For that vitally necessary person is basically a storyteller who is uniquely armed with a creative understanding of how motion pictures are made in the overview—not a promoter, nor a banker, nor a mechanic, nor a credit hungry writer, and he should be left to do his job without interference from . . . to point out a few more . . . the leading lady's agent, a super production manager, some guy who had a hold on the story property, nor the money man." Ibid., vi.

5. In 2002, there were believed to be about 35,000 screens in the United States (including drive-ins) out of about 150,000 screens worldwide.

BOOK FOUR
GETTING THE MONEY TO MAKE IT HAPPEN
PRODUCTION MONEY RULES

1. The two statutes are the Securities Act of 1933 and Securities and Exchange Act of 1934.

2. The term "accredited investor" as defined in Rule 15 of the General Rules and Regulations promulgated pursuant to Regulation D under the Securities Act of 1933, means, among other things, that an Investor, *together with an investor's spouse,* must have either:

(i) a net worth of at least One Million Dollars ($1,000,000); or

(ii) annual income of at least Three Hundred Thousand Dollars ($300,000) in each of the last two years and a reasonable expectation of making at least Three Hundred Thousand Dollars ($300,000) income this year. In the event that a spouse's income is not included, then the Three Hundred Thousand Dollar ($300,000) annual income amount is decreased to Two Hundred Thousand Dollars ($200,000).

An investor subscribing to purchase shares through a trust, partnership, corporation or other entity, in order to qualify as an "accredited investor," must generally have total assets in excess of Five Million Dollars ($5,000,000).

In the case of husband and wife purchasing securities, the net worth and income requirements set forth above will be applied to their combined net worth and income. In the case of a prospective Investor that is a partnership, the net worth and income requirements are applicable to each partner. Further, if the partnership has been formed for this investment, each partner is counted as an Investor. If an Investor is purchasing securities in a fiduciary capacity, the suitability standards may be satisfied by the Investor, the fiduciary account, or the donor who is directly or indirectly supplying the funds to purchase the securities.

Such representations by investors will be reviewed to determine suitability, and the Company will have the right to refuse an offer to purchase securities if the prospective purchaser does not meet the applicable suitability requirements, or the securities are otherwise an unsuitable investment for the prospective purchaser.

3. The following is taken from a typical investment offering:

"The Investor suitability standards adopted by the Company require each accredited investor to make representations in writing as follows: (a) The Investor is a resident of California or other state where the securities have been qualified for sale, or are exempt from qualification; (b) The Investor is purchasing the securities for such person's own account and not with a view to, or for sale in connection with, any distribution of the securities; (c) The Investor (either alone or with such investor's purchaser representative) has such knowledge and experience in financial and business matters that the Investor is capable of protecting such person's own interests in connection with the investment; and (d) The Investor is able to bear the economic risk of the investment in the securities. (e) The Investor meets the following conditions:

"The Investor is an 'excluded purchaser,' as that term is defined in Rules of the California Commissioner of Corporations under the Corporate Securities Act of 1968, and similar provisions in other states, and must be an 'accredited investor,' as such term is defined in the Securities Act of 1933, as amended."

4. In fact, one of the things your lawyer will do is make the investor promise that the investment will not be resold to some third parties—as this sale might violate the securities laws.

5. See discussion on page 175.

6. "Off the top" has another, similar, usage in the entertainment industry. When defining gross proceeds for the purpose of calculating net proceeds and other similar concepts, certain off-the-top expenses (for example, residuals, taxes, trade dues, etc.) are generally not included.

BRINGING THE MONEY HOME

1. Compare this arrangement to the one where the sales agent simply takes a flat fee plus a percentage of the producer's revenues. See "Sales Agent Agreements for a Flat Fee" on page 190.

2. For a detailed discussion of how banks use movies as collateral, see "No Liens" on page 385.

3. The slightly broader legal term joint venture can also be used to describe a co-production deal. A joint venture is also a deal (or venture) between two or more parties for a stated purpose.

4. There are potential tax issues, especially when one or more of the parties are foreign, that must be examined. See discussion on page 72.

THE STUDIO AS FINANCIER

1. *Identifying the Elements,* for a discussion of the possible credits for producers. We discuss producer credits again in greater detail in *Assembling the Main Players.*

2. The Producers Guild of America is not a guild in the same way as WGA, DGA, or SAG. The PGA provides seminars, counseling services, and materials that support producers and gives out awards, but, for example, does not impose a collective bargaining agreement on the major studios. See the PGA's Web site at www.producersguild.org.

BOOK FIVE
PRODUCING THE MOVIE
SOME LEGAL PRELIMINARY MATTERS

1. See the International Alliance of Theatrical Stage Employees, Moving Picture Technicians, Artists and Allied Crafts of the United States, Its Territories and Canada, AFL-CIO, official Web site, available at www.jatse.lm.com/ (last visited February 23, 2003). In IATSE's own words, this union is "the labor union representing technicians, artisans and craftspersons in the entertainment industry, including live theatre, film and television production, and trade shows."

2. See discussion on page 262.

3. These steps are outlined on page 258.

ASSEMBLING THE MAIN PLAYERS

1. Stevens Bach, *Final Cut: Dreams and Disaster in the Making of Heaven's Gate* (New York: Onyx, 1987).

2. According to the "mini biography" of Alan Smithee on www.IMDb.com, "The Directors Guild contract generally does not permit a director to remove her/his name from films. The Directors Guild has been striving for decades to establish the director as the 'author' of a film, and part of getting the credit for the successes is taking the blame for the failures. The only exceptions they make are cases in which a film was clearly taken away from a director and recut heavily against her/his wishes in ways that completely altered the film. Directors are required to appeal to the Guild in such cases. If the appeal is successful, their name is replaced by Alan Smithee. That is the only permissible pseudonym for a director. So if you notice a film directed by Alan Smithee, it is certain it is not what its director intended, and likely that it is not any good."

3. Go to www.IMDb.com and search under Alan Smithee.

4. In computing gross, it is customary for motion picture studios to deduct certain expenses off the top. These off the tops include such things as trade dues (for example, fees paid by the studio to the Motion Picture Association of America), residuals paid to SAG and other guild members, the costs of converting foreign money to dollars and other costs of doing business internationally, taxes paid, costs incurred by the studio to collect theatrical rentals, theater audits, and the cost of collecting rentals from the theater owners.

5. See discussion on pages 214–16.

6. According to SAG, the actual calculation is as follows: First, the producer calculates the actor budget (all actors, including stunt performers). Second, the producer adds the stand-ins ($125 per stand-in) and SAG extras ($110 per SAG extra). Third, the producer adds 13.8 percent (at this writing) for health, welfare and pension benefits. Fourth, the producer takes 40 percent of the aggregate amount of

all these items as the bond deposit. Discussion with SAG, Motion Picture Contracts, March 5, 2003.

7. See discussion on page 216.

FINISHING ALL PRODUCTION DETAILS

1. Screen Actors Guild Codified Basic Agreement of 1989 for Independent Producers, Rule 24 ("Screen Credits"), pages 37–38.

THE LEGAL DETAILS

1. See Motion Picture Association of America, Rules for Registration of and Disputes Relating to United States Theatrical Motion Picture Titles (2001).

2. Actual damages need not be proved if the false statement falls into a slander per se category. See "Damages" on page 288.

3. The four categories are accusing the person of sexual misconduct, criminal activity, having a loathsome disease, or making false and derogatory statements about the person's business.

4. Courts sometimes limit liability for fictionalization even if the characters in the work are based on real people. See *Polydoros v. Twentieth Century Fox Film Corp.,* 965 P. 2nd 724 (Cal. 1998). But be careful.

5. See Motion Picture Association of America, Jack Valenti, Movie Ratings, How It Works, available at www.mpaa.org/movieratings/about/index.htm (last visited February 16, 2003).

6. See National Music Publishers' Association, Inc., News & Views, New Statutory Mechanical Royalty Rate, January 1, 2000, available at www.nmpa.org/nmpa/nv-fw9900/newrate.html (last visited August 23, 2004).

7. The following discussion of clearance procedures is based on the instructions and questions listed on the Motion Picture and Television Producers Liability Insurance application of Truman Van Dyke Company, which is used with permission.

BOOK SIX
MAKING MONEY WITH THE MOVIE
THEATRICAL DISTRIBUTION

1. It is no accident that the motion picture industry is located in Los Angeles. The early pioneers moved away from the eastern coast of the United States to escape the so-called trust, the Motion Picture Patents Company owned by Thomas Edison. Edison's heavy-handed policies in licensing the newly developed motion picture technology made California—located far from the East Coast—the movie capital of the world. See Schatz, *The Genius of the System,* 16–17.

2. Clark Gable was under contract to MGM, as well as Jimmy Stewart, Frank Sinatra, Fred Astaire and Ginger Rogers, Gene Kelly, Elizabeth Taylor, Lucille Ball, Jean

Harlow, Laurel and Hardy, Esther Williams, Buster Keaton, Greta Garbo, Red Skelton, Bette Davis, Jimmy Durante, Margaret O'Brien, Donna Reed, Robert Young, Lana Turner, Jane Powell, Wallace Beery and Marjorie Main, Peter Lawford, Joan Crawford, Lionel Barrymore, Paul Newman, Kathryn Grayson, Hedy Lamarr, Mario Lanza, Greer Garson, Angela Lansbury, Rosalind Russell, Robert Taylor, and Jackie Cooper. Two of MGM's stars, Spencer Tracy and Katharine Hepburn, hold the records for the most Oscars won by an actor and actress, respectively. See Schatz at note 7, below. See also Seeing-Stars: The Ultimate Guide to Celebrities & Hollywood, The Movie Studios, available at www.seeing-stars.com/studios/mgm.shtml (last visited November 11, 2002).

3. In other years, MGM produced such classics as *Boys Town* (in 1938), *The Philadelphia Story* (in 1940), *Mrs. Miniver* (in 1942). But it was the lavish musical genre that set MGM apart. In addition to *The Wizard of Oz*, MGM produced *Meet Me in St. Louis* (in 1944), *Anchors Away* (in 1945), *The Harvey Girls* (in 1946), *Easter Parade* (in 1948), *The Pirate* (in 1948), *Show Boat* (in 1951), *An American in Paris* (in 1951), *Singing in the Rain* (in 1952), *Seven Brides for Seven Brothers* (in 1954), *Guys and Dolls* (in 1955), and *Gigi* (in 1958). Ibid.

4. From that point, 20th Century Fox Studios produced many successful films, such as: *The Grapes of Wrath* (in 1940), *Rebecca* (in 1940), *Song of Bernadette* (in 1943), *Laura* (in 1944), *State Fair* (in 1945), and *Miracle on 34th Street* (in 1947). Many legends of the industry got their start working under contract at Fox: Child star Shirley Temple (who made most of her classic musicals there), Elizabeth Taylor, Henry Fonda, Marilyn Monroe, Jane Russell, Richard Burton, Natalie Wood, Betty Grable, Gene Hackman, Julie Andrews, Charlton Heston, Tyrone Power, Jean Harlow, Sonja Henie, Gregory Peck, Michael Douglas, Kathleen Turner, Will Rogers, Susan Hayward, Carmen Miranda, Milton Berle, Roddy McDowall, Jeanne Crain, Bruce Willis, and Barbra Streisand (to name just a few). See Seeing-Stars: The Ultimate Guide to Celebrities & Hollywood, The Movie Studios, The Historical M-G-M Studios, available at www.seeing-stars.com/studios/foxstudios.shtml (last visited October 30, 2002).

5. Fox had other successes, such as *Hello, Dolly!* (in 1969), *Patton* (in 1970), *M*A*S*H* (in 1970), *The French Connection* (in 1971), and *The Poseidon Adventure* (in 1972). Ibid.

6. In fact, 20th Century Fox has always had good luck with movie sequels. Fox produced the fourteen Sherlock Holmes mysteries starring Basil Rathbone, as well as the five *Planet of the Apes* adventures (1968–73), the three thrillers based on 1976's *The Omen*, and the several *Alien* films starring Sigourney Weaver. Ibid.

7. See Schatz, *The Genius of the System*, 34–43. See also, Seeing-Stars: The Ultimate Guide to Celebrities & Hollywood, The Movie Studios, Universal Studios, available at www.seeing-stars.com/studios/universalstudios.shtml (last visited September 21, 2002).

8. The early stars at Warner Bros. included Humphrey Bogart, Ingrid Bergman, James Cagney, Errol Flynn, John Barrymore, Edward G. Robinson, Bette Davis, Barbara Stanwyck, Dick Powell, George Raft, Loretta Young, Douglas Fairbanks, Jr., Joan Crawford, Burt Lancaster, Paul Muni, Carole Lombard, Gary Cooper, Dennis Morgan, Peter Lorre, Cary Grant, Henry Fonda, Doris Day, and Rin Tin Tin. Ronald Reagan made his screen debut at Warners, in 1937's *Love in the Air,* and he married another Warner's star, actress Jane Wyman. See Seeing-Stars: The Ultimate Guide to Celebrities & Hollywood, The Movie Studios, Warner Bros. Studios, available at www.seeing-stars.com/studios/warnerhollywoodstudios.shtml (last visited November 11, 2002).

9. Walt Disney still holds the record for the most individual Academy Awards at thirty-one. See Seeing-Stars: The Ultimate Guide to Celebrities & Hollywood, The Movie Studios, Walt Disney Studios, available at www.seeing-stars.com/studios/disneystudios.shtml (last visited November 13, 2002).

10. Disney's impressive list of classic animation features includes, along with *Snow White, Pinocchio* (in 1940), *Fantasia* (in 1940), *Dumbo* (in 1941), *Bambi* (in 1942), *Song of the South* (in 1946), *Cinderella* (in 1950), *Alice in Wonderland* (in 1951), *Peter Pan* (in 1953), *Lady and the Tramp* (in 1955), *Sleeping Beauty* (in 1959), and others. Ibid.

11. Ibid.

12. See Seeing-Stars: The Ultimate Guide to Celebrities & Hollywood, The Movie Studios, Sony Pictures (Columbia Pictures and TriStar), available at www.seeing-stars.com/studios/sony.shtml (last visited November 12, 2002).

13. The late Sun International, for example, reportedly made money distributing a series of truth-is-stranger-than-fiction movies—*In Search of Noah's Ark,* etc.—using a "four-wall" strategy.

14. 222 N.Y. 88 (1917).

15. Of course, the producer and the investors still don't make out very well, but $100,000 is $100,000.

16. Here is a stripped-down version of a lab access letter:

This letter will serve as the Lab's irrevocable authority to use the negative and master material delivered by Owner to process orders instituted by Distributor, including, but not limited to, orders for duplicate preprint material, positive prints, trailers, textless main and end titles, video tapes, videocassettes and other services and materials as submitted. This letter will also serve as the Lab's irrevocable authority, in perpetuity, to release the negative material solely and exclusively to Distributor or its nominee at Distributor's request.

All materials or services which the Lab may supply to or on order of Distributor are to be paid for solely by Distributor, and Owner will not be responsible for any financing arrangements which the Lab may make with Distributor.

Moreover, the Lab may not look to Owner nor assert any claim or lien against it or its property by reason of any work, labor, materials or services which the Lab may perform for or furnish to Distributor hereunder.

The Lab also agrees not to permit the removal of the original negatives, master materials and sound tracks and other pre-print materials from the Lab's facilities without the written authorization of an officer of Distributor *and* Owner during the Term.

17. See MPAA Ratings, page 292.

MERCHANDISING LICENSING

1. Pat Upton, *Make Millions in the Licensing Business*, (New York: Monarch Press, 1985), chap. 11 § 8. Ms. Upton has created a chart, beginning in 1904, showing a historical outline of character-based merchandising: (1904) *Buster Brown* comic strip characters were licensed for products; (1913) President "Teddy" Roosevelt permitted his name to be used in association with the marketing of the Teddy Bear in exchange for a royalty; (1929) *Buck Rogers* toys sold strongly; (1932) Herman Kamen, the father of modern licensing, established a marketing program at Disney centered around Mickey Mouse (introduced as a character in 1928); (1930) Shirley Temple, the child star, licensed her name on dolls; (1940s) Hopalong Cassidy and Tom Mix, motion picture cowboys, licensed their names for toys and other items; (1950s) licensing programs were developed for television programs (*Zorro, Annie Oakley,* and *Howdy Doody,* for example); (1955) Disney launched the first complete family of licenses around a television/movie character, Davy Crocket; (1960s) Batman and Robin raised the stakes; (1970s) *Star Wars* moved merchandising into the modern era.

2. Peter Pan does work as a trademark when it comes to peanut butter—but that is a different story altogether.

3. Under some circumstances in the United States, where a mark is used openly and prominently, protection limited to the territory where it is used may be available without registration—but that is a subject for another day.

SOUND-TRACK ALBUMS

1. Including Dolly Parton, who wrote the song, "I Will Always Love You." I recall Miss Parton being interviewed by Johnny Carson on the *Tonight Show;* when asked if it bothered her that her version of the song didn't have the success that Miss Houston's version achieved, Dolly replied, "Yes, I cry all the way to the bank."

2. Even the title seems to rely on a Golden Oldie—the late Roy Orbison's "Oh, Pretty Woman."

3. The "Elephant Love Medley" alone contains portions of about a dozen great songs about love—as clever and enjoyable as the track is, I can't listen to it without imagining the headaches suffered by the lawyer(s) responsible for clearing the rights to all those pieces of music.

4. In Japan, for example, music is cleared through JASRAC (Japanese Society for Rights of Authors, Composers and Publishers).

5. Note that the compulsory license applicable to covers does not work for masters. You must contact the owner of the master—usually a record company—and obtain a master use license.

6. See note 6, page 485, "The Legal Details."

7. See also Donald S. Passman, *All You Need to Know About the Music Business* (New York: Free Press, 2003), 337–41.

HOME VIDEO
1. See discussion on page 24.

TELEVISION
1. See Library of Congress, Copyright Office, Circular 73, explaining Section 115 under the Copyright Act. "Section 115 provides that once phonorecords of a musical work have been distributed in the United States with the copyright owner's consent, anyone else may, under certain circumstances and subject to certain conditions, obtain a "compulsory license" to make and distribute phonorecords of the work without express permission of the copyright owner." The procedures for obtaining a compulsory license are explained. The rate of the royalty fees owed are fixed by Copyright Arbitration Royalty Panels.

PRINT PUBLISHING
1. See generally "Separated Rights" on page 114.
2. See "Separated Rights" on page 114.

STAGE
1. Ibid.

INTERACTIVE WORKS
1. While it is possible to use narrowband technology to view a movie on a computer, it is not a serious contender.

INTERNET
1. See "Internet (broadband) and digital cinema—the concept of exclusivity" at pages 350–51.

INDEX

About the Author

Kelly Charles Crabb has a bachelor's and a master's degree from Brigham Young University and a Juris Doctor degree from Columbia Law School, where he was a member of the *Columbia Law Review*. He is a member of the bar of the states of New York and California and currently lives and practices entertainment law in Los Angeles, where he teaches and lectures frequently. In 1998, he produced a sixty-minute television special based on his musical play *All My Friends Are Cowboys*. He is married and the father of five children.